LONDON:

THE DEFINITIVE WALKING GUIDE

ABOUT THE AUTHOR

Colin Saunders was born in Barnet in 1942 and has lived in Greater London for most of his life. He started walking for pleasure in 1967 with the Vanguards Rambling Club, and for some years led walks for the weekly excursions organised by the Ramblers' Association. Colin is an enthusiastic participant in long distance challenge walks. He was one of the first members of the Long Distance Walkers Association, founded in 1972, and has been chairman of their London Group. He is also a member of the British Walking Federation, Open Spaces Society, Living Streets and Ramblers' Association, and was one of the founder members of the London Walking Forum in 1990.

For many years, Colin was a consultant on matters connected with walking for pleasure and fundraising. He played a major role in the Strollerthon, one of Britain's largest charity walks, which during his twelve-year association raised nearly £4 million for Save the Children and other children's charities.

Other books by Colin Saunders:

Walking in the High Tatras (with Renáta Nárožná, ISBN 1-85284-150-8)

The Vanguard Way (Vanguards Rambling Club, ISBN 0- 9530076-0-X)

Manual on Navigation and Leadership (Ramblers' Association, ISBN 0-900613-83-1)

In preparation: *Capital Ring Guidebook* (Aurum Press)

Contributor to: *The Wandle Guide* (Sutton Leisure Services, ISBN 0-907335-33-0)

LONDON:

THE DEFINITIVE WALKING GUIDE

by
Colin Saunders

2 POLICE SQUARE, MILNTHORPE, CUMBRIA, LA7 7PY
www.cicerone.co.uk

ISBN 1-85284-339-X

A catalogue record for this book is available from the British Library

ACKNOWLEDGEMENTS AND SOURCES

All photographs are by the author. Maps are designed by Colin Saunders and digitalised by Alex Burrow. The author is grateful to the following for their help and encouragement in writing this book: British Walking Federation (IVV), Countryside Agency, Department for Education and Employment, Greater London Authority, London Walking Forum (especially its Orbitals Working Party), Long Distance Walkers Association, Living Streets, Radar (Royal Association for Disability and Rehabilitation), Ramblers' Association, Royal Parks Agency, Woodland Trust, Stuart McLeod, Ann Sayer, Jim Walker, officers of the 33 London Cities and Boroughs and of adjacent county and district councils, members of the Vanguards Rambling Club, and members of the public and local societies who responded to appeals for information.

DISCLAIMER

The purpose of this book is to draw attention to the many opportunities for recreational walking that exist in Greater London, and to indicate where further information can be obtained. All information shown is subject to change. The inclusion of any information does not constitute a recommendation. The author and publisher will accept no responsibility for the consequences of participating in any walk. You are advised to obtain any literature available before setting out, to satisfy yourself that the walk is suitable.

Front cover: *Tower Bridge and Pool of London (Thames Path National Trail)*

CONTENTS

The Right Honourable The Lord Mayor

Alderman Michael Oliver

THE MANSION HOUSE LONDON EC4N 8BH

TELEPHONE 020-7626 2500
FACSIMILE 020-7623 9524

With the advent of the 21st century, London is a city poised to undergo dramatic changes. Among a whole series of ambitious plans, the Capital's current administration has vowed to tackle the gridlock on the streets A transport revolution is promised with walking right at its heart.

It therefore gives me great pleasure to introduce you to the first ever *London - the definitive walking guide*. This book provides a wealth of information about one of London's most overlooked treasures - its network of leisure walking routes. Although London may not be the first choice for many as a walking destination, even the City of London is crossed by two major recreational routes (Thames Path National Trail and Jubilee Walkway), and several shorter routes explore the intriguing minutiae of the Square Mile's heritage. Further out, ever greener routes such as the Capital Ring and London Loop take advantage of the glorious countryside that amazes by being within or just outside Greater London.

Pleasurable walks abound throughout Greater London, and this book lists nearly 300 routes extending over 2,300 kilometres (1,450 miles). The London Walking Forum's work in encouraging the development of the Capital's network of walking routes is to be commended.

So, if you're planning a day out on foot in London, I strongly recommend this book as your first point of reference. Whether you wish to explore London's greenery and waterways, or wander between its historic and contemporary attractions, this guide is your instant reference to London's comprehensive and varied network of walking routes. I hope it provides you with many enjoyable days out. Happy walking!

INTRODUCTION

The range of opportunities for leisure walking in London is vast – just take a glance at the maps in this book. It became clear during my research that the original title for this book, The Complete Guide to Walking in London, would have to be changed, as more walks were coming to light all the time, right up to the publisher's deadline and beyond. It was just not going to be possible to include everything.

People sometimes say to me that, as an experienced walker, it must be terrible to live in London. But in my opinion we are spoilt for choice, with a wealth of interesting walking and lovely scenery on our doorstep. Anyone who thinks there is no good walking in London is in for a very pleasant surprise. Every one of the 33 London boroughs and cities has some good walking, and I hope to convince any sceptics that opportunities for enjoyable walks in 'The Smoke' vastly exceed their expectations. I will show just how easy it is for people living or staying in London to venture out and walk – not just to the shops, station or bus stop but for the sheer fun of it – on mostly green routes that take you well away from roads and traffic.

The benefits of walking for health have been well documented. I started walking regularly for pleasure over 30 years ago, not for the effect it might have on my health, but for the good companionship of the many friends I have made. I have since walked and scrambled in all kinds of terrain, including many of the highest mountains in Europe, and I frequently take part in 'tough' challenge walks. Yet even after such bold enterprises, I still take great pleasure in walking in London, whether along one of the routes in this book, or just strolling through a park. There is surely a moral to be drawn from the fact that, even in London, when walking for pleasure on footpaths or in parks, you are likely to be greeted with a smile and a 'good morning', instead of the grim faces you see on the streets.

I have set out in as much detail as possible how and where you can walk for pleasure in and around London. I do not give detailed step-by-step descriptions of individual routes, but all the named routes I have been able to identify within London are listed, including, where possible, their main attractions, how to get there and how to get further information. Many are waymarked and can in theory be followed without a map or guide, but I strongly recommend you get hold of any available literature. I have also included details of the wide choice of guided walks on offer.

Do please use public transport if you can. It is a pity to travel by polluting car for an environmentally friendly walk, in a society that is being encouraged to minimise car use. Widespread public transport is available in London, and unlimited travel at very low cost is possible using the excellent travelcards, bus passes and other comprehensive tickets. By leaving your car at home you can enjoy your walk with no worries about parking, how to get back to it and who might be trying to break into it. You can imbibe without guilt, and you will reduce, however slightly, your contribution to other people's breathing difficulties.

By Merton Abbey Mills (Wandle Trail, Merton's Heritage Trails)

You cannot talk about walking in London nowadays without mentioning the London Walking Forum (qv). As a founder member myself, I would like to acknowledge the part they have played, both in developing walking routes and in helping me with this book.

I have taken great care to be accurate, but can accept no responsibility for the consequences of any errors or changes that may have crept in. I hope to update the book from time to time, so please notify me of any changes, comments or suggestions care of Cicerone Press or email me at colinsaund@aol.com. Thank you very much for reading this book.

Colin Saunders, 2002

USING THIS BOOK

The main purpose of this book is to serve as a directory of the many possibilities for recreational walking in London, whether guided or self-guided, and to help you choose where to walk. There is no intention to provide a step-by-step guide to any route, and you should not rely on this book to guide you round – most routes have their own literature, which you should try to obtain before setting out. Every effort has been made to provide accurate information about the routes in this book, but details may change and you should not rely on them. Before setting out, do check any information that may significantly affect your enjoyment of the walk, such as availability of transport, refreshments or toilets.

The book is divided into three sections:

1. General information. Chapters on the London Walking Forum, safety on walks, suggestions for people with wheelchairs or buggies, and for those who are new to walking, travelling to walks, buying equipment and maps, health walks, and the governing bodies of walking.

2. Self-guided walks. The vast majority of opportunities for walking in Greater London are self-guided, and this is reflected in the size of this section. It includes details of the principal recreational routes (the Strategic Network), other named routes, walking in parks, and walks described in other media.

3. Other walking opportunities. Guided walks (walks with a leader) – some are free, some involve a charge. Includes information about walking clubs and groups, walks for the general public, and walking festivals, charity walks and challenge walking.

Eight appendices provide an index of routes in order of borough and distance, plus supporting lists of proposed and discontinued routes, parks and open spaces, books of self-guided walks, guided walks, equipment and map shops, and contact details.

Abbreviations and symbols

BC	Borough Council	**ml**	miles
Bus	Bus services	**NR**	National Rail (surface trains)
CC	County Council	**p&p**	Postage and packing
CTL	Croydon Tramlink	**qv**	Quod vide (which see, qqv in plural)
DC	District Council		
DLR	Docklands Light Railway	**RB**	Royal Borough
GR	Grid reference	**&**	Information for people using a wheelchair or buggy
km	kilometres		
LB	London Borough	**sae**	Stamped addressed envelope – a reminder to enclose one when ordering literature by post where no separate p&p charge is specified
LU	London Underground		

Suttons Parkway, Hornchurch (London Loop Section 23)

1: GENERAL INFORMATION

LONDON WALKING FORUM

 The London Walking Forum (see Appendix H for contact details) was established in 1990 as a partnership between the Corporation of London, the Countryside Commission (now Countryside Agency), the Sports Council, local authorities, and other bodies and individuals with an interest in walking in the London area. The Forum also enjoys a close working relationship with Transport for London, the Ramblers' Association and the Living Streets (formerly the Pedestrians Association.

Although initially concerned mainly with recreational walking, the Forum today operates as a professional membership body, providing a mechanism for information exchange and offering good-practice guidance to all organisations with an interest in walking in the disciplines of transport, health, leisure, tourism and the environment.

In the early 1990s, the London Planning Advisory Committee (now superseded by the Greater London Authority) approved the idea of a strategic network of walking routes for the capital. London boroughs are still encouraged to incorporate details of specific routes in their Unitary Development Plans (UDPs): this means that many of the walks in this book now have a planning status to ensure that the routes and their surrounding environment are protected.

The Forum continues to co-ordinate local authorities and other groups working on many of London's leisure walking routes – particularly those that cross one or more borough boundaries – as well as promoting walks on a London-wide basis. It operates in four regional sectors covering the west, northeast, southeast and southwest parts of Greater London, and there is an overall executive committee.

The Forum's administrative headquarters is currently located in the offices of the Corporation of London.

Validation and Seal of Approval The Forum has established a system of validation for all routes in the Strategic Network (see Section 2), and awards a Seal of Approval, which guarantees a walk of high standard. A panel of inspectors, consisting of both borough officers and users from such bodies as the Ramblers' Association, assesses each route that has been put forward for recognition in this way. Routes that have been validated and awarded the Seal of Approval to date are indicated under the 'LWF status' for each route.

Updates In partnership with the Greater London Authority, the Forum will update progress on the existing and proposed routes in this book, as well as report on other matters of interest to walkers in London, through www.londonwalking.com.

SAFETY FIRST

As in all situations there is a possibility of accidents or discomfort while walking. All walkers should be aware of this and take commonsense steps to minimise the risks.

Barbed wire Take special care on paths with barbed-wire fences. This is usually only encountered in farmland to prevent livestock straying. In some places the path may be narrow and rough, so that you are forced to walk close to the wire, and if you slip you may damage your clothing or cut yourself.

Cumberland Basin (Regent's Canal Towpath)

Canal towpaths These are sometimes quite narrow, especially where the path passes under a bridge. There may be a handrail, but vertigo sufferers may feel uncomfortable. See also Routes Shared with Cyclists below.

Dogs must be on a lead when in the presence of livestock. Other people's dogs can sometimes be aggressive – their owners should have them under control. If this concerns you, there are gadgets that are supposed to (but may not) deter dogs by emitting ultrasonic sounds that dogs can hear but humans cannot.

Getting lost Although it is possible to follow some well-signposted routes without a guidebook or leaflet, you are strongly advised to obtain one beforehand to minimise the chances of getting lost. Some routes described in this book are either totally or partially unsigned, when you need to concentrate on the route description. Also try to take a street map or atlas that covers the area.

Golf courses Greater London and its surrounding counties are awash with golf courses, and many routes cross or skirt them. Public rights of way across golf courses should be (but are not always) clearly marked. Take care as you cross fairways and especially when near a tee. Always allow golfers to finish their stroke before proceeding.

Livestock Generally there is nothing to fear from livestock grazing on land crossed by routes in Greater London. Horses and cattle may approach out of curiosity, but if this concerns you they should stop if you shout or clap your hands loudly. In the London area you are most unlikely to encounter bulls on land that is accessible to the public, though certain 'safe' breeds are permitted in fields with public rights of way.

Railway crossings Occasionally a route may cross an unprotected railway line, where you should of course take great care while crossing. Remember that apparently distant trains can approach in seconds.

Roads Route designers should try to minimise walking beside or crossing roads, but it is sometimes unavoidable and you should exercise normal care. Occasionally you may find yourself on a road that has no pavement on either side, when you should generally keep right to face oncoming traffic – see the Highway Code below for more detail.

Routes shared with cyclists (including canal towpaths). Shared routes are being developed for walkers and cyclists. This is not a satisfactory solution, either for walkers or cyclists, but it is the option that local authority planners are currently pursuing to promote both activities economically. This book draws attention to this situation where relevant. Cyclists may come up without warning from behind, or from ahead round a bend, so bear this in mind. (If only they would use bells!) Some shared routes have separate lanes for walkers and cyclists, though people often ignore these, and children and dogs are liable to run into the wrong lane without warning. Canal towpaths do not have separate lanes, but cyclists who use them are supposed to have a licence from British Waterways. Take special care where the towpath is narrow.

Surfaces Most of the walks are on pavements, footpaths or tracks, which may have a surface that is hard and smooth (paved, concrete, tarmac, bonded gravel), soft (grass, sand, mud) or rough (earth, rocks, stones, loose gravel). Extended walking on a hard surface can come as something of a shock to those used to the softer surfaces of country walking, so additional protection such as an extra pair of socks may be helpful. On hard surfaces look out for loose paving stones or potholes, while on rough surfaces there may be loose stones or concealed holes, so keep one eye on the ground and the other on the

Coal tax post, Epsom Common (Chessington Countryside Walk)

13

view. Take special care when descending steep slopes with loose stones or wet grass as it is easy to slip. And then there is dog mess...

Walking alone If possible, walk with companions. This not only gives greater confidence in lonely areas but means that someone can go for help in case of an accident. Take your mobile phone if you have one.

Wet weather Some surfaces, including hard ones, are likely to become slippery and possibly muddy after rain. Take care especially when descending slopes. Routes that go close to rivers, streams and canals may get flooded after heavy rainfall, when you may have to divert. Gumboots may be useful, though not always comfortable over long distances, and gaiters are worth considering as they give protection and confidence when walking through mud or water.

Winter walking You are likely to encounter mud, or water on flooded paths, either of which may be deep in places. In cold weather the ground may be rock hard. Use suitable footwear – boots and gaiters can be especially helpful. Walking in fresh snow can be delightful, but be prepared for slippery conditions and hidden obstructions, especially on downhill sections. If you are walking in the afternoon always carry a torch in case it takes longer than you expect. Take spare clothing, including a hat, for when you stop and cool down.

HIGHWAY AND COUNTRY CODES

The routes in this book take you into urban and rural locations, where both the Highway and Country Codes may be relevant.

The Country Code is shown here in full. At time of writing a revised code is due to be published, though it is likely that its general advice will remain much the same.

- Enjoy the countryside and respect its life and work
- Guard against all risk of fire
- Fasten all gates
- Keep your dogs under close control
- Keep to public footpaths across farmland
- Use gates and stiles to cross fences, hedges and walls
- Leave livestock, crops and machinery alone
- Take your litter home
- Help to keep all water clean
- Protect wildlife, plants and trees
- Take special care on country roads
- Make no unnecessary noise

THE HIGHWAY CODE

The following extracts are Crown copyright material reproduced under Class Licence number C01W0000308 with the permission of the Controller of HMSO.

- Where there is a pavement or footpath, use it.

- Where there is no pavement or footpath, walk on the right-hand side of the road so that you can see oncoming traffic; keep close to the side of the road.

- Take care at sharp right-hand bends – it may be safer to cross the road well before you reach one so that oncoming traffic has a better chance of seeing you, then after the bend cross back to the right-hand side.

- Walk in single file if possible.

- Wear or carry something that will help you to be seen (especially at night or in poor visibility), such as light-coloured, bright, fluorescent or reflective items.

- When crossing roads, take great care and remember the Green Cross Code: think first, find a safe place to cross then stop; stand on the pavement near the kerb; use your eyes and ears; look all around for traffic and listen; wait till it's safe to cross; if traffic is coming let it pass; when there's no traffic near walk straight across the road; keep looking and listening for traffic while you cross.

Jacob sheep, Kenley Common (Kenley Common & Dollypers Hill Circular Walk)

WALKING WITH WHEELCHAIRS AND BUGGIES

Some walking routes in London are now suitable for wheelchairs and buggies, while many authorities are in the process of creating accessible routes and making existing ones accessible. Whilst the author has tried to be both positive and objective about accessibility and provide enough information for you to decide whether a particular route is suitable, it has to be recognised that some routes are just not suitable for wheeled vehicles of any kind. Please bear in mind that so far no formal assessment of routes in London has taken place and you should therefore approach all routes with caution.

We have tried to distinguish between accessibility for 'manual wheelchairs' (nonpowered wheelchairs for adults and older children), 'powered wheelchairs' and 'buggies' (pushchairs for infants). This takes account of obstructions (such as single steps) that can be negotiated by some people, such as those with companions, but may be impossible for others, such as people on their own using heavy powered wheelchairs. Buggies can be carried up or down flights of steps (at your own risk), but these will usually be out of the question for manual and powered wheelchairs, except where ramps or lifts are available.

Some stretches of routes have cobbled streets, especially in tourist areas of Central London – attractive but uncomfortable riding for wheelchair users. Paved 'runners' through cobbles are being installed or planned in some areas. All local authorities in London have a policy of installing dropped kerbs at road crossings, though in some areas this project is incomplete, and they may be blocked by inconsiderate parking. Some routes include slopes of varying steepness, or sections with uneven surfaces – this is mentioned in the route descriptions where applicable, so you can decide whether the route is suitable. In some places a Radar key is required to open barriers or toilets.

Routes that the author considers may be suitable could become inaccessible at any time – for example surfaces may deteriorate, work may be taking place on ramps, or lifts may be out of order. Therefore the description of any route in this book as 'accessible' does not imply that it will be when you go. You are advised to check in advance with the highways department of the local authorities concerned (indicated in the route descriptions).

Corporation of London Information Board, Ashtead Common (Chessington Countryside Walk)

Strategic Network

Most of the strategic routes are unfortunately unlikely to be completely accessible, due to the obstructions they present. These include uneven and hilly terrain, stiles, and narrow, overgrown and muddy footpaths. However, many routes may be wholly or partially suitable, depending on your circumstances, and additional information is provided where relevant at the ♿ symbol, which may be helpful when read in conjunction with the rest of the route description. Literature published for the route may provide further details. Here is a list of strategic routes (together with their borough location) for which the author has considered it worthwhile to provide additional information at the ♿ symbol:

Barnet Millennium Walk	Barnet
Barnet Totteridge Loop	Barnet
Brent River Park Walk	Ealing, Hounslow
Capital Ring Section 5	Lambeth, Wandsworth, Merton
Capital Ring Section 6	Merton, Wandsworth
Capital Ring Section 7	Richmond, Hounslow, Ealing
Capital Ring Section 11	Barnet, Haringey
Capital Ring Section 12	Haringey, Hackney
Capital Ring Section 13	Hackney, Waltham Forest
Capital Ring Section 14	Tower Hamlets, Newham
Capital Ring Section 15	Newham
Cray Riverway	Bromley
Diana Princess of Wales Memorial Walk	Kensington & Chelsea, Westminster
Dollis Valley Greenwalk	Barnet
Grand Union Canal Walk	Various
Grand Union Canal (Slough Arm)	Hillingdon
Green Chain Walk Section 1	Bexley
Green Chain Walk Section 4	Greenwich
Green Chain Walk Section 5	Greenwich
Green Chain Walk Section 10	Bromley
Greenway, The	Tower Hamlets, Newham
Havering Riverside Path	Havering
Heron and Kingfisher Walks	Newham
Hogsmill Walk	Kingston
Jubilee Walkway	Westminster, Lambeth, Southwark, Tower Hamlets, City of London, Camden
Lea Valley Walk	Tower Hamlets, Newham, Hackney, Haringey, Waltham Forest, Enfield
Leaves Green Circular Walk	Bromley
London Loop Section 8	Kingston
Parkland Walk	Haringey, Islington
Pymmes Brook Trail	Barnet, Enfield
Regent's Canal Towpath	Various
Ridgeway Walk	Bexley, Greenwich
River Crane Walk	Hounslow, Richmond
Tamsin Trail	Richmond
Thames Path National Trail	Various
Thames Path Southeast Extension	Greenwich, Bexley
Time Travellers	Tower Hamlets
Walk Back in Time	Waltham Forest, Hackney

Wandle Trail	Croydon, Sutton, Merton, Wandsworth
Waterlink Way	Greenwich, Lewisham, Bromley, Croydon

Other named self-guided walks

It has not been possible for the author to walk all of the Other Named Self-guided Walks listed in Section 2. However here is a summary of routes from that list that are indicated in their literature or elsewhere as being accessible. They are marked ♿ in the list.

Accessible Thames	Richmond
Hainault Forest Wild About Woods Trail	Redbridge
Havering Country Park Easy Access Trail	Havering
Lee Valley Park Walks and Nature Trails	Various
Merton's Heritage Trails	Merton
Nature Conservation Walk in Merton #5	Merton
Nature Conservation Walk in Tower Hamlets #1	Tower Hamlets
Waddon Community Trail	Croydon

Parks and open spaces

Most parks and open spaces have opportunities for walking with wheelchairs and buggies. Many are completely level, with tarmac paths. See Parks and Open Spaces in Section 2, and Appendix D.

GETTING STARTED

This is particularly for people who are new to walking for pleasure. You only need to make two decisions:

1. Put on your shoes. If you have never before thought seriously of walking as a leisure activity, don't panic – it's as easy as putting on your shoes. For help with what to wear, take a look at Equipment below.

2. Where to go, which is where this book comes in. There are three options:

    (a) *Doing your own thing* (self-guided walks). You have to take responsibility for finding your way. In London this is not difficult because there are so many options. If you are any good at map-reading you may prefer to devise your own route. For this you may find some useful guidance in *Navigation and Leadership – a manual for walkers* by the same author, published by the Ramblers' Association (see Appendix H for contact details) (£6.00 plus £1.50 p&p, ISBN 0-900613-83-1).

    (b) *Guided walks.* Walking with a leader in a group is probably the easiest way to start, but for some people the thought of teaming up with complete strangers is anathema. For others, this is an excellent way to make new friends – see Section 3.

    (c) *Walking events and challenges.* If you'd like to try something that will test your capabilities, a walking event or challenge may be what you need – see Section 3.

A word of warning

Do not aim too highly for your first walk. Even very fit people may find that their shoes are uncomfortable, so start gently and work up. If you have a medical condition, consult your doctor beforehand.

Crown & Horseshoes from River view, Enfield (New River Path)

GETTING THERE

In London, the best way to get to your walk is usually by public transport. For some people the car may be essential, but if you can please leave it at home. This will enable you more easily to do linear routes (starting and finishing at different points, as many do), to break off along the route if necessary, to minimise environmental damage, to avoid parking problems, and to have a drink during or at the end of your walk. Information on parking is usually available in the suggested literature for each route – please avoid parking in residential roads.

Travelcards and similar tickets are excellent value, offering unlimited travel after 9.30am Mondays to Fridays and all day Saturdays, Sundays and bank holidays. They enable you to hop at will from train to tube to bus to tram, and entitle you to discounts on riverbuses. A weekend travelcard offers discounted, unlimited travel for Saturday and Sunday. Family discounts are available. Details from London Transport Information (see below and Appendix H for contact details).

Camden Lock (Regent's Canal Towpath)

Travelcards can be used for all the routes shown in this book except the London Countryway and North Downs Way, but in some cases you may have to pay a supplement where the route goes outside Greater London. Always state your destination when buying your ticket, otherwise you may have to pay a penalty.

The route details show points along the route where public transport is available by train, tube, tram, light railway, bus or riverbus. For more details you can call either London Transport Information (020 7222 1234) for tube, buses, trams, light railway and riverbuses or National Rail Enquiries (08457 484950) for surface trains.

EQUIPMENT AND MAPS

One of the joys of recreational walking is that you do not need any special gear. What you do need is a little bit of common sense – listen to the weather forecast and wear appropriate clothing. In cold weather, wear several layers which you can remove and put back on, as you will soon warm up while walking but then cool rapidly when you stop. Young children and older people may need additional layers.

Most regular walkers carry their extra gear (such as rainwear, camera, food) in a rucksack, to leave both hands free, but a light bag with handles or shoulder-strap will do if you prefer not to carry things on your back.

Footwear

Experienced walkers know that the most important thing about walking is to have comfortable footwear, otherwise your walk will be spoiled, whatever the weather. For your first walks, any comfortable shoes you already have with low heels and patterned soles (such as trainers or well-built town shoes) should be suitable. See how they perform – your original shoes may turn out ideal for all your walking. If not, go to a specialist outdoor equipment shop and ask for advice.

In most cases, traditional walking boots will be too heavy in London; however, some routes (especially the London Loop) go into countryside and farmland, using rough or muddy paths, or in long wet grass, where boots may give an advantage, especially in winter. Gaiters can also be helpful in these conditions – with these you can stride through mud and quite deep water and hardly notice it. Rubber footwear (gumboots, wellingtons) may become uncomfortable on longer walks.

Duck Island Cottage, St James's Park (Diana, Princess of Wales Memorial Walk)

Before setting out on long walks in new shoes, try them out on short local walks to make sure they are comfortable. If you feel 'hot spots' developing on your feet, they are probably infant blisters, and you should stop and attend to them immediately by applying suitable protection (available in outdoor equipment shops).

Socks too should be chosen with care, as rough ones can also cause blisters. Many walkers find that two pairs are more comfortable than one, perhaps a thick pair over a thin pair. This varies among walkers and is a matter of experimentation.

Footwear is available using special 'breathable' materials designed to keep rain and water out, let perspiration out and air in. However, such gear is usually expensive.

Wet weather

An umbrella may not be much use while walking as rain is often accompanied by strong wind, turning your brolly into a windsail, and you may come close to doing a creditable impression of Mary Poppins. For walking it is usually better to wear a waterproof jacket, leaving both hands free. If you wear glasses, a brimmed hat or a peaked cap will help keep the rain off. See also Safety First in Section 1.

Maps

Most of the literature available for the self-guided routes listed in this book includes some sort of map. However, the standard and detail varies considerably and you are advised to carry at least a street map or atlas covering the area concerned. This will also be invaluable if you stray off route.

The Ordnance Survey Explorer series (orange cover) at 1:25,000 scale (4cm = 1km or 2.5in = 1ml) marks some of the strategic network routes with green lozenges (diamonds): nine sheets (146, 147, 160, 161, 162, 172, 173, 174 and 175) are needed to cover the whole of Greater London.

Equipment and map shops

Appendix G has a list of shops specialising in outdoor equipment and maps in Greater London. Some libraries have maps, though they may only be available for reference rather than loan.

HEALTH WALKS

A growing number of guided and self-guided walks are being developed to help people with health problems, encouraged by an initiative called Walking the Way to Health. The aim is to provide walks that are initially not too taxing, enabling, say, those with heart problems to gain confidence and perhaps move gradually on to more strenuous routes. The scheme is sponsored by Kia Cars, funded by the New Opportunities Fund, co-ordinated by the Countryside Agency and backed by the British Heart Foundation. See below for a summary of health walks in Greater London. More information can be obtained from the WHI Case Officer at the Countryside Agency in London (see Appendix H for contact details).

Walking the Way to Health sprang from a pioneering programme established by Dr William Bird at his surgery in Sonning, Oxfordshire, during the 1990s. Walking for health is nothing new, though it may have taken place at a subconscious level. People have always taken a brisk walk to think over a problem: this may be construed as a health walk – one that both stimulates and soothes the mind. Taking the sea air as you stroll along the promenade, or climbing the local hill before breakfast, or working up an appetite for lunch, or walking off the Christmas turkey – all are health walks. Fitness walking has long been the rage in North America: magazines devoted to the subject picture tanned and athletic-looking people striding out in fashionable gear, often to music with headphones clamped to their ears, or preceded by baby in a speed buggy.

Here is a summary of walks in Greater London, available at the time of writing, which have been designed principally as health walks.

St Govor's Well, Kensington Gardens (Diana, Princess of Wales Memorial Walk)

SELF-GUIDED WALKS

(see Other Named Self-guided Walks in Section 2 for more details):

Dollis Valley Health Walks (Barnet)

Folly Brook Circular Walk (Barnet)

Friary Park Circular Walk (Barnet)

Selsdon Wood Nature Reserve Self-guided Trails (Just Walk) (Croydon)

Woodlands Farm Health Walks (Bromley)

GUIDED WALKS WITH A LEADER OR INSTRUCTOR

Active Ealing – walking the way to health (Ealing)

Camden health walks (Camden)

Croydon YMCA health walks (Croydon)

Fitness for Life (Barnet)

Golden Walks (Islington)

Lewisham health walks (Lewisham)

Newham Striders (Newham)

Walking for health (Croydon)

Other programmes were being developed at the time of writing. For further details and updates see www.whi.org.uk.

GOVERNING BODIES

Walking is regarded by Sport England (formerly the Sports Council) as a sport, for which there should be at least one governing body. In fact it recognises three such bodies for walking including the Long Distance Walkers Association and the Ramblers' Association. The third is the Race Walking Association – if race walking interests you, find details in Appendix H.

Ingrebourne River at Hornchurch Country Park (London Loop Section 23)

At least four other organisations can claim to have nationwide involvement with various aspects of walking: British Walking Federation, Countryside Agency, Open Spaces Society and Living Streets. Brief outlines are shown here.

British Walking Federation (see Appendix H for contact details). Established 1983, this is the British arm of the IVV (Internationaler Volksport Verband – International Federation of Popular Sports), established in Germany in 1968. By encouraging the organisation of regular walking events, the IVV aims to encourage international friendship founded on participation in sport, the promotion of good health by regular exercise, and the ability of the whole family to take part. Anyone can take part in the awards scheme, for which you obtain cards to record your distances and participation in specified challenge events and on 'permanent trails' (see Section 3). On reaching certain targets you send in the cards and receive an award. You can join the BWF directly as an individual member, or join a club that is affiliated to IVV. Individual membership includes the BWF quarterly magazine *Footprint*, newsletters, the annual calendar containing details of events and permanent trails, and other benefits.

Countryside Agency (see Appendix H for contact details). Formerly the Countryside Commission, established in 1968. Its literature states that it is the statutory body working 'to conserve and enhance England's countryside; to spread social and economic opportunity for the people who live there; to help everyone, wherever they live and whatever their background, to enjoy the countryside and share in this priceless national asset'. The agency is responsible for co-ordinating policies and work connected with the national trails, of which two (Thames Path and North Downs Way) come through or past Greater London. It also co-ordinates the Walking the Way to Health initiative (see Health Walks, Section 1).

Living Streets (formerly Pedestrians Association) (see Appendix H for contact details). Established in 1929, this is a campaigning body whose current campaigns include: highlighting the appalling state of pavements, promoting safe walking routes to school, improving conditions for pedestrians, removing obstructions from footways, preventing parking and cycling on pavements, providing dropped kerbs at crossings, and reducing traffic speed. These proposals are described in the free guide *2020 Vision: 21 priorities for pedestrians in London*, produced jointly by Living Streets and London Walking Forum. Living Streets does not generally organise walking events, but everyone is welcome to support its aims by joining as an individual. Members receive the quarterly magazine *Walk*, containing news of the association's campaigns and other developments.

Long Distance Walkers Association (see Appendix H for contact details). Established in 1972 and describes itself as 'an association of people with the common interest of walking long distances in rural, mountainous or moorland areas'. This may mean anything from 32 to 160km (20 to 100ml). However, its local groups (including one in London – see Section 3) organise regular weekend walks for members, which rarely exceed 32km (20ml). It promotes organised 'challenge walks' (see Section 3) and maintains a national database of long distance trails (details published in its *Long Distance Walkers' Handbook*). Members receive the excellent magazine *Strider*, published three times a year, which contains news and much useful information.

Open Spaces Society (see Appendix H for contact details). The oldest of these organisations was originally founded in 1865 to fight for the preservation of Hampstead Heath and other London commons. It has since widened its scope considerably to cover the whole of England and Wales, fighting to maintain access to public open spaces and paths in town and country. Members receive free legal and campaigning advice, and the lively magazine *Open Space* three times a year.

Ramblers' Association (see Appendix H for contact details). Established in 1935, this is the largest and probably best known of the governing bodies, mainly through its high profile campaigns, for example 'the freedom to roam' and fighting transgressions of footpath law by landowners. It also played a leading role in the creation of national parks and national trails, and in getting rights of way shown on Ordnance Survey maps. The RA's aims are to encourage walking, protect footpaths, campaign for freedom to roam and protect the beauty of the countryside. It provides a free walking information service to the public and members. This includes the annual *Ramblers' Yearbook*, which is packed with useful information. Members receive the quarterly magazine *The Rambler*, and are entitled to join a local group, of which 20 cover Greater London (see Section 3), all organising regular walks for members.

MAP 1 – STRATEGIC NETWORK Orbital and radial routes

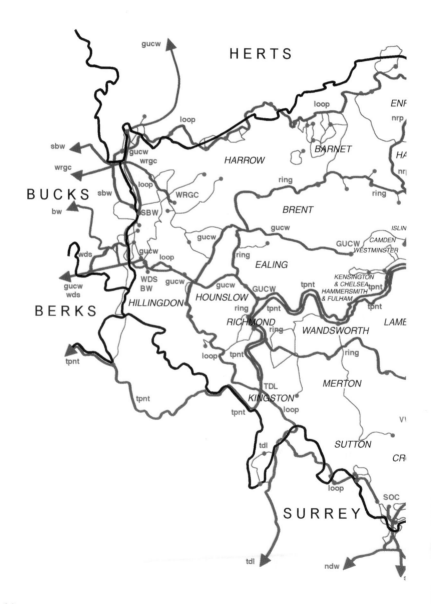

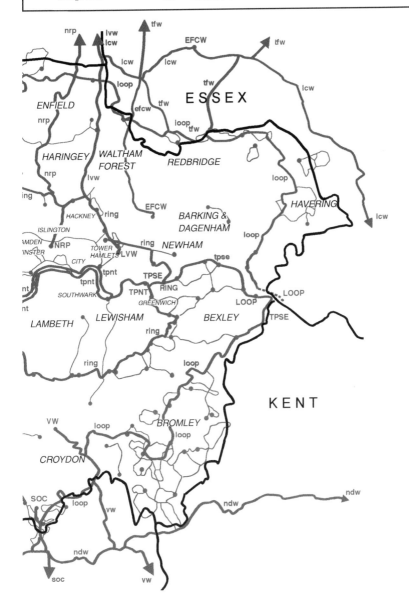

KEY

CAPITALS = start/finish points
NT = National Trail
RR = Ramble and Ride

bw	Beeches Way
efcw	Epping Forest Centenary Walk
gucs	Grand Union Canal (Slough Arm)
gucw	Grand Union Canal Walk
jub	Jubilee Walkway
loop	London Loop
lcw	London Countryway
lvw	Lea Valley Walk
ndw	North Downs Way NT
nrp	New River Path
ring	Capital Ring
sbw	South Bucks Way
soc	Socratic Trail
tdl	Thames Down Link
tfw	Three Forests Way
tpnt	Thames Path NT
tpse	Thames Path Southeast Extension
vw	Vanguard Way
wds	West Drayton-Slough RR
wrgc	West Drayton-Gerrards Cross RR

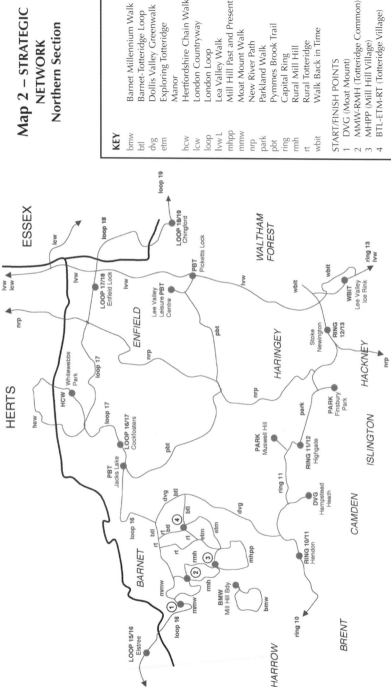

Map 2 – STRATEGIC NETWORK Northern Section

KEY

bmw	Barnet Millennium Walk
btl	Barnet-Totteridge Loop
dvg	Dollis Valley Greenwalk
etm	Exploring Totteridge Manor
hcw	Hertfordshire Chain Walk
lcw	London Countryway
loop	London Loop
lvw L	Lea Valley Walk
mhpp	Mill Hill Past and Present
mmw	Moat Mount Walk
nrp	New River Path
park	Parkland Walk
pbt	Pymmes Brook Trail
ring	Capital Ring
rmh	Rural Mill Hill
rt	Rural Totteridge
wbit	Walk Back in Time

START/FINISH POINTS

1 DVG (Moat Mount)
2 MMW-RMH (Totteridge Common)
3 MHPP (Mill Hill Village)
4 BTL-ETM-RT (Totteridge Village)

28

Map 3 – STRATEGIC NETWORK North West Section

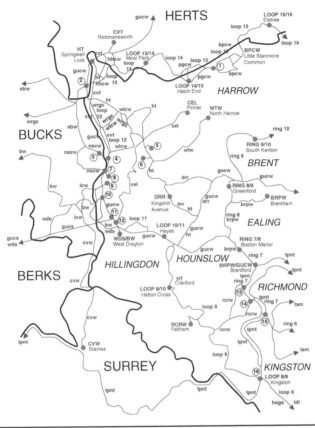

KEY	
bpcw	Bentley Priory Circular Walk
brpw	Brent River Park Walk
bw	Beeches Way
cvt	Colne Valley Trail
cvw	Colne Valley Way
cel	Celandine Route
drr	Dog Rose Ramble
gucs	Grand Union Canal (Slough Arm)
gucw	Grand Union Canal Walk
hare	Harefield Heights Circular Walk
hill	Hillingdon Trail
hogs	Hogsmill Walk
icw	Iver Circular Walk
loop	London Loop
nscw	Nine Stiles Circular Walk
pgcw	Pinner-Grimsdyke Circular Walk
rcrw	River Crane Walk
ring	Capital Ring
sbw	South Bucks Way
tam	Tamsin Trail
tdl	Thames Down Link
tpnt	Thames Path National Trail

wds	West Drayton-Slough Ramble and Ride
wide	Widewater Lock Circular Walk
wtw	Willow Tree Wander
wrgc	West Ruislip-Gerrards Cross Ramble and Ride

START/FINISH POINTS

1. BPCW - PGCW (Old Reddings)
2. LOOP 12/13 - HHCW (Harefield West)
3. CVW (Colne Valley Park Centre)
4. SBW (Denham Lock)
5. WRGC (West Ruislip)
6. WTW (Ickenham)
7. LOOP 11/12 - NSCW (Uxbridge Oxford Road)
8. CVT (Uxbridge Station)
9. ICW (Uxbridge Rockingham Road)
10. CVW (Cowley Lock)
11. GUCS (Cowley Peachey)
12. CEL (Yiewsley)
13. RCRW (Isleworth)
14. RCRW (Richmond Lock)
15. RING 6/7 (Richmond)
16. LOOP 8/9 – HOG - TDL (Kingston)

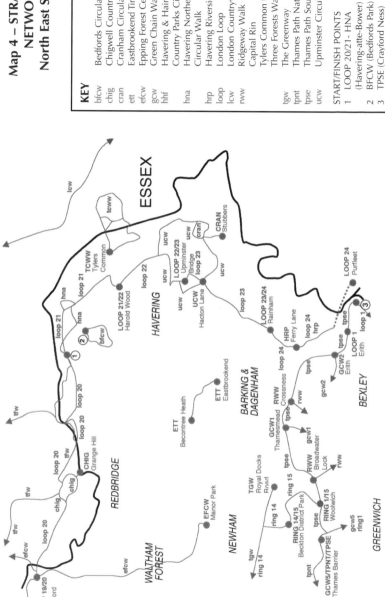

Map 4 – STRATEGIC NETWORK
North East Section

KEY

bfcw	Bedfords Circular Walk
chig	Chigwell Country Walk
cran	Cranham Circular Walk
ett	Eastbrookend Timberland Trail
efcw	Epping Forest Centenary Walk
gcw	Green Chain Walk
hhf	Havering & Hainault Forest
	Country Parks Circular Walk
hna	Havering Northern Area
	Circular Walk
hrp	Havering Riverside Path
loop	London Loop
lcw	London Countryway
rvw	Ridgeway Walk
	Capital Rin
	Tylers Common to Warley Walk
	Three Forests Way
tgw	The Greenway
tpnt	Thames Path National Trail
tpse	Thames Path Southeast Extension
ucw	Upminster Circular Walk

START/FINISH POINTS
1   LOOP 20/21- HNA
    (Havering-atte-Bower)
2   BFCW (Bedfords Park)
3   TPSE (Crayford Ness)

Map 5 – STRATEGIC NETWORK
Central Section

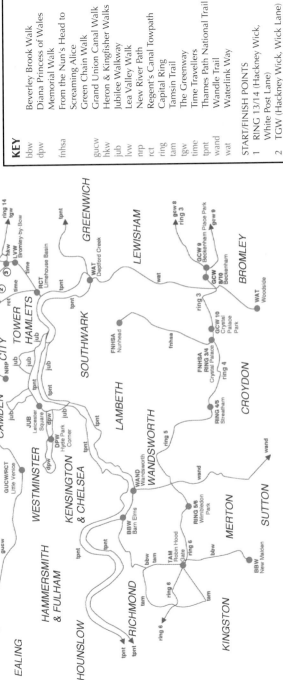

KEY

bbw	Beverley Brook Walk
dpw	Diana Princess of Wales Memorial Walk
fnhsa	From the Nun's Head to Screaming Alice
	Green Chain Walk
gucw	Grand Union Canal Walk
hkw	Heron & Kingfisher Walks
jub	Jubilee Walkway
lvw	Lea Valley Walk
nrp	New River Path
rct	Regent's Canal Towpath
ring	Capital Ring
tam	Tamsin Trail
tgw	The Greenway
time	Time Travellers
tpnt	Thames Path National Trail
wand	Wandle Trail
wat	Waterlink Way

START/FINISH POINTS
1. RING 13/14 (Hackney Wick, White Post Lane)
2. TGW (Hackney Wick, Wick Lane)
3. HKW / TIME (Three Mills Island)

Map 6 – STRATEGIC NETWORK
South East Section

KEY

bccw	Bromley Common Circular Walk
crw	Cray Riverway
fnhsa	From the Nun's Head to Screaming Alice
gcw	Green Chain Walk
loop	London Loop
pwcw	Petts Wood Circular Walk
rct	Regent's Canal Towpath
rww	Ridgeway Walk
ring	Capital Ring
srw	Shuttle Riverway
smc	St Mary Cray Circular Walk
spc	St Paul's Cray Circular Walk
time	Time Travellers
tpnt	Thames Path National Trail
tpse	Thames Path Southeast Extension
wat	Waterlink Way

START/FINISH POINTS
1. GCW 3/4/5 (Oxleas Meadows)
2. GCW 6 (Oxleas Wood)
3. GCW 7 (Shepherdleas Wood)
4. RING 1/2 (Falconwood)
5. SRW (Avery Hill Park)
6. CRW (Erith, Manor Road)
7. TPSE (Crayford Ness)
8. GCW 8/10 (Beckenham)

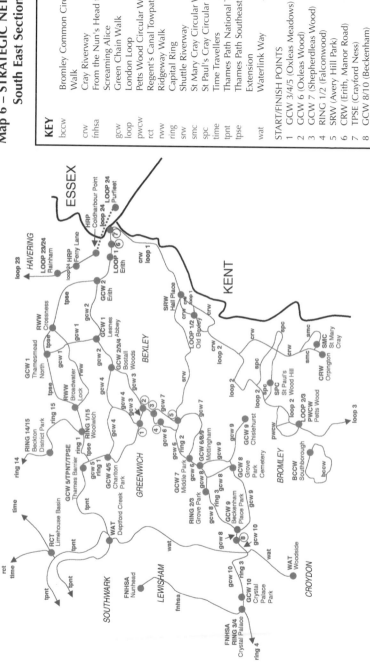

Map 7 – STRATEGIC NETWORK
Southern Section

KEY

bbw	Beverley Brook Walk
cchv	Coulsdon Common & Happy Valley Circular Walk
ches	Chessington Countryside Walk
dna	Discover New Addington
dcw	Downlands Circular Walk
fddw	Farthing Downs & Devilsden Wood Circular Walk
fnhsa	From the Nun's Head to Screaming Alice
gcw	Green Chain Walk
hogs	Hogsmill Walk
kcdh	Kenley Common & Dollypers Hill Circular Walk
loop	London Loop
ndw	North Downs Way National Trail
rcw	Riddlesdown Circular Walk
ring	Capital Ring
soc	Socratic Trail
sutt	Sutton Countryside Walk
tdl	Thames Down Link
tpnt	Thames Path National Trail
vw	Vanguard Way
wand	Wandle Trail
wat	Waterlink Way

START/FINISH POINTS
1 SOC (Old Coulsdon)
2 DCW (Farthing Downs)
3 DCW / CCHV (Coulsdon Common)

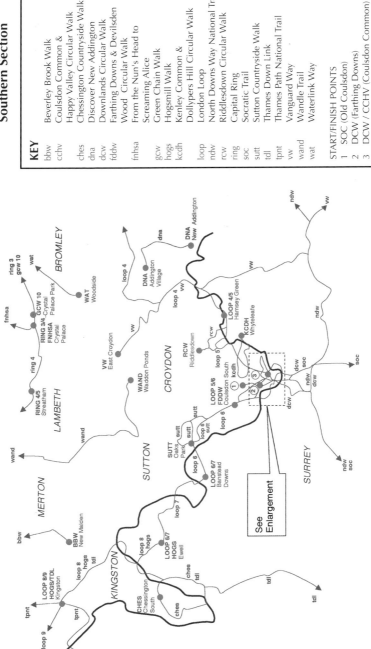

33

Map 7A – STRATEGIC NETWORK
Southern Section Enlargement

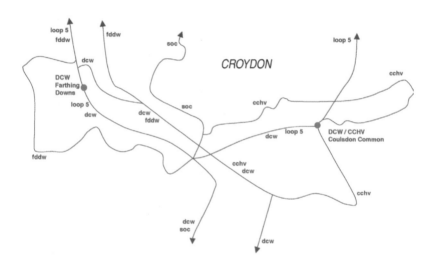

CROYDON

loop 5
fddw
soc
loop 5
cchv
dcw
DCW
Farthing
Downs
loop 5
dcw
dcw
fddw
soc
cchv
loop 5
DCW / CCHV
Coulsdon Common
dcw
fddw
cchv
dcw
cchv
dcw
soc
dcw

KEY	
cchv	Coulsdon Common &
	Happy Valley Circular Walk
dcw	Downlands Circular Walk
fddw	Farthing Downs & Devilsden
	Wood Circular Walk
loop	London Loop
soc	Socratic Trail

Map 8 – STRATEGIC NETWORK Bromley Area

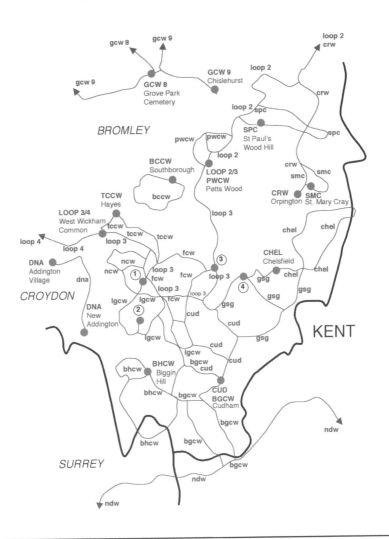

KEY

bccw	Bromley Common Circular Walk
bgcw	Berry's Green Circular Walk
bhcw	Biggin Hill Circular Walk
chel	Chelsfield Circular Walk
crw	Cray Riverway
cud	Cudham Circular Walk
dna	Discover New Addington
fcw	Farnborough Circular Walk
gcw	Green Chain Walk
gsg	Green Street Green Circular Walk
loop	London Loop
lgcw	Leaves Green Circular Walk
ncw	Nash Circular Walk
ndw	North Downs Way National Trail
pwcw	Petts Wood Circular Walk
smc	St Mary Cray Circular Walk
spc	St Paul's Cray Circular Walk
tccw	Three Commons Circular Walk

START/FINISH POINTS

1 NCW (Keston Common)
2 LGCW (Leaves Green)
3 FCW (Farnborough)
4 GSG (Green Street Green)

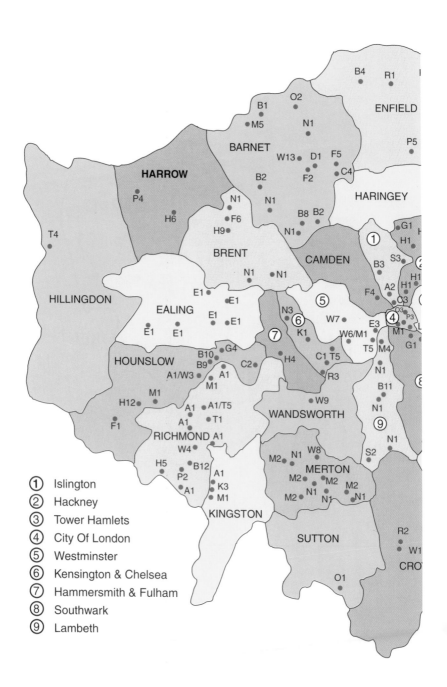

1. Islington
2. Hackney
3. Tower Hamlets
4. City Of London
5. Westminster
6. Kensington & Chelsea
7. Hammersmith & Fulham
8. Southwark
9. Lambeth

Map 9 – OTHER NAMED SELF-GUIDED ROUTES

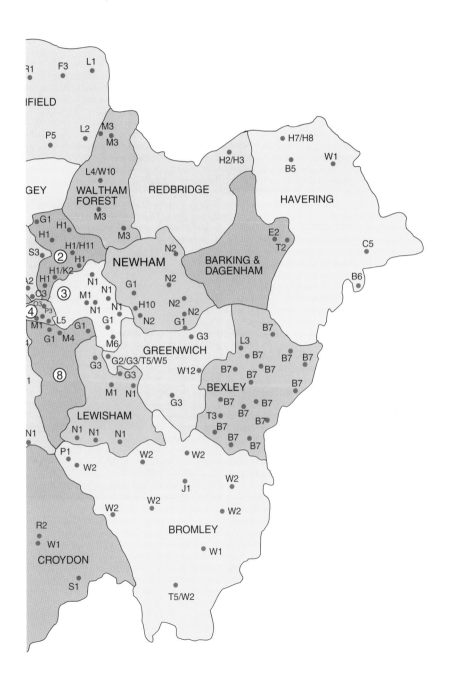

*Eltham from
Severndroog
Castle (Capital Ring
Section 1, Green
Chain Section 5)*

*Abbey Mills
Pumping Station
(Capital Ring
Section 14,
The Greenway)*

*Pumping equipment near
Abbey Mills Pumping
Station (Capital Ring
Section 14,
The Greenway)*

Observing deer in Richmond Park (Capital Ring Section 6)

Harrow School (Capital Ring Section 9, Harrow-on-the-Hill Walk)

2: SELF-GUIDED WALKS

INTRODUCTION

This section contains around 300 suggestions for walks to do on your own, with family or friends. Most involve obtaining a guidebook or leaflet, but a few that as yet have no associated literature can still be enjoyed without such help, as indicated in the individual descriptions.

To be included in this book, all or part of a route must either lie within Greater London or touch the boundary at some point. The only exception to this rule is the London Countryway, which lies entirely outside Greater London, but because of its name readers may expect to find it here. Routes must have a name and, ideally, should be described in a publication of some sort.

Self-guided walks in this book are divided into the following groups:

Strategic Network of recreational walking routes (referred to in this book as the Strategic Network), routes usually of at least 5km (3ml) that have been designed by local authorities and other organisations mainly to provide a good walk in pleasant surroundings. They are shown on Map 1 and its enlarged sections.

Other named self-guided routes promoted by local authorities and other bodies, such as heritage trails, town trails and nature trails. They aim for more than just a good walk, and are usually shorter than 5km (3ml) to allow time to enjoy points of interest along the way. Their approximate locations are shown on Map 9.

Parks and open spaces. Some have written guides, but these areas are ideal for just strolling around and exploring.

Other publications describing self-guided walks (such as books, audioguides, websites) are generally devised by individuals. They have no formal recognition but add to the variety of opportunities available in London.

There may be other self-guided walks that you have heard of but cannot find here. They may no longer exist (see Appendix C: Discontinued and dormant routes) or they may not yet have got off the ground (see Appendix B: Proposed routes). Or just possibly the author may not have identified them, in which case please write to him c/o Cicerone Press or email: colinsaund@aol.com.

STRATEGIC NETWORK WALKS

This covers major recreational routes, devised and promoted by local authorities and other organisations, that have been identified by the London Walking Forum as forming a Strategic Network. They include linear routes (starting and finishing in different places) and circular ones, and mostly link with each other to form a continuous web.

The network also includes some routes that do not currently link in, but are considered strategic from the point of view that they provide good recreational walking, and it is hoped that they will eventually be linked to the network through the creation of new routes where possible.

Key routes designated by the Mayor of London

The London Walking Forum has set standards for signage and information associated with routes in the Strategic Network. Most routes have not yet achieved these standards in all respects, but it is expected that in due course they will do so, earning the Forum's Seal of Approval. A select number of these routes will be designated by the Mayor of London as the core of the Strategic Network, to be maintained and managed, in partnership with local authorities, to defined standards which all routes in the network should eventually aspire to. It is anticipated that this scheme will initially cover the following six routes: *Capital Ring, Green Chain Walk, Lea Valley Walk, Jubilee Walkway* and *London Loop*, plus the *Thames Path National Trail* within Greater London.

Grid information

A grid for each route shows the following information:

Distance in kilometres and miles. This is the author's best estimate and may not correspond with that shown in the official literature, which is not always accurate. A time guide is not provided as walking speeds vary so much, but you can work this out. Allowing for stops of various kinds, most people manage around 3–4km per hour (2–2.5miles per hour) overall. If your party includes young children or less able-bodied walkers, or if you wish to stop and investigate all the points of interest, the overall speed may be slower. Few people walk at the legendary '4 miles an hour' (6.5km per hour) except in short bursts.

Location. This shows the London boroughs and cities through which the route runs. In some cases it continues outside Greater London, in which case the relevant county is also shown.

Start and finish points together with six-figure **grid references** (GR). These are commonly used to indicate locations on maps published by the Ordnance Survey (see Maps below). The grid reference is formally preceded by two code letters, which in the Greater London area are always TQ. In this book these code letters have generally been omitted for simplicity. Routes that go some distance into the surrounding counties have a different code which is shown here. The numeric reference consists of six figures, which are normally grouped together. In this book, for clarity, they are shown in two groups of three separated by a hyphen. The first three are 'eastings', because they lie east (to the right) of the grid line; the second three are 'northings', because they lie north of (above) the grid line. The first two figures in each group of three indicate the number that appears at the map edge for each grid line. The third figure in each group of three indicates the distance beyond the grid line, which you measure from the scale that appears at the map edge.

Green and blue factors expressed as the author's estimated percentages of the main route, excluding short cuts, alternatives or extensions. The 'green factor' is an indication of how much of the main route lies in parks, woods or other areas that can be broadly described as 'green', and an allowance is made for other areas that are well provided with trees, bushes or grass. The 'blue factor' is an indication of how much of the main route lies beside water features such as rivers, canals or lakes.

Recommended direction This is usually based on the way the principal route description is written. Of course, you can walk in the opposite direction if this is more convenient, but you will then have to reverse the route instructions, which can lead to confusion. If the route can easily be followed in either direction this is stated.

Terrain and surface including number of stiles if any – note that stiles may be removed, bypassed or replaced by gates. An approximate indication of how much of the route lies beside roads is included here.

Points of interest along the route. Some are further commented on in the route description that follows.

Signage Whether the route has signs and a brief description of them.

Refreshments and toilets Note that park cafés in particular may be closed during winter months or midweek, and that toilets may be closed either temporarily for maintenance or permanently as a result of persistent vandalism.

Public transport and break points A list of places along the route served by trains and buses is shown. See Getting There in Section 1.

Links with other routes in the Strategic Network. Most routes cross or share stretches with others, offering opportunities to link two or more together to make longer walks, or to adapt them to suit your requirements. The Strategic Network map (Map 1) and its sectional enlargements provide ideas for this.

Maps covering the route. Although some routes can in theory be followed without maps or guides from signage along the way, this is risky as signage may not be complete and existing signs may have been vandalised. Most route literature contains a map of some sort, and you are strongly advised to obtain this before setting out. It is a good idea to carry in addition a street map or atlas, or an Ordnance Survey Explorer map (see Equipment and Maps, Section 1) as this should help if you go astray. The grid shows the relevant Explorer sheet number(s). Some routes are marked on Explorer maps by means of green lozenges (diamonds), some are named on Geographers' AZ street maps and atlases – this is indicated where relevant.

LWF (London Walking Forum) status This shows either 'Validated with Seal of Approval' (see London Walking Forum, Section 1), or 'Pending validation', which means that at the time of writing either an application had still to be considered or no application had yet been received from the promoters. There is no requirement for promoters to make such an application, and some may not wish to do so at this stage.

Principal promoter The main organisation(s) that designed, developed, manages or promotes the route. In some cases many other organisations have been involved, usually by providing funding – this should be indicated in the route literature.

Further information which you can obtain before walking the route, from the contact indicated (see Appendix H for contact details). In the case of books, the information provided should enable you to obtain or order the book from a good bookseller. Prices shown are those current at time of writing and are subject to change. Standards vary considerably, and literature for routes that do not yet have the London Walking Forum's Seal of Approval may fall short of the required standards. Website addresses are shown where known.

A general description of the route follows. (Remember: this is **not** a step-by-step guide, so please do not rely on it to find your way.)

Route closures

Parts of some routes may be closed at certain times. An obvious but hopefully rare example is the situation during the 2001 outbreak of foot-and-mouth disease, which affected many routes in Greater London using paths that local authorities decided they should close.

A less well-known situation on some routes concerns **permissive paths**, to which the landowner allows public access, but there is no public right of way. To retain this status they must be closed on one day a year (usually in winter so unlikely to affect most walkers) – where this is known it is shown in the text.

Note too that paths may be closed for repairs or maintenance, and parks and other open spaces through which some routes pass may be closed at certain times, such as Christmas Day or for management purposes. You should be able to check this by contacting the highways or parks department of the local authority.

WALK DETAILS

BARNET LEISURE COUNTRYSIDE WALKS

A set of ten routes, of which six are included in the Strategic Network and described in more detail under their separate entries: *Barnet-Totteridge Loop, Exploring Totteridge Manor, Mill Hill Past and Present, Moat Mount Walk, Rural Mill Hill and Rural Totteridge* (all Map 2). Their distances range from 4.0 to 6.4km (2.5 to 4.0miles). The remaining four (two Dollis Valley Health Walks, Folly Brook Circular Walk and Friary Park Circular Walk), described as health walks, are shorter (see Other Named Self-guided Walks below).

Most of the routes occupy the great wedge of countryside between Barnet and Edgware that contains the prim hilltop villages of Totteridge and Mill Hill, where the towering grey façade and steep green roof of the National Medical Research Centre dominates the view from all around. This is lovely, rolling countryside, occupying the farmed valleys of Dollis Brook and Folly Brook (also known as Totteridge Valley).

Route descriptions and maps are shown on laminated cards in a plastic wallet costing 50p plus p&p and obtainable from LB Barnet (see Appendix H for contact details) Parks and Countryside Section, also some libraries and council offices. The six strategic routes all link up and can be combined into longer ones – for ideas see Map 2.

BARNET MILLENNIUM WALK (MAP 2)

Distance:	6.5km (4.1miles)
Location:	Barnet
Start/finish:	Mill Hill Broadway station (GR 214-919) – see text
Green factor:	49%
Blue factor:	18%
Recommended direction:	Anticlockwise
Terrain and surface:	Almost completely level, mostly on tarmac paths or pavements. One stretch across grass. No stiles. 3.0km (1.9 miles) beside roads
Points of interest:	Lyndhurst Park, Burnt Oak Brook, Watling Park, Silk Stream, Silk Stream Park, Montrose Recreation Ground, Grahame Park, Woodcroft Park
Signage:	Both ways on fingerposts: black 'Barnet Millennium Walk' and yellow sunburst above black '2000' on white background
Refreshments and toilets:	Pubs and cafés at Mill Hill Broadway and Burnt Oak. Public toilets at Burnt Oak (Watling Street)
Public transport and break points:	NR: Mill Hill Broadway. LU: Burnt Oak, Colindale. Buses at these points plus Lanacre Avenue
Links:	None
Map:	Explorer 173
LWF status:	Pending validation
Principal promoter:	LB Barnet
Further information:	Barnet Parks and Countryside Section, also some libraries and council offices

Pleasant and easy walking through little-known parks and open spaces in northwest London. The official starting point is Mill Hill Broadway station, or you can start from Burnt Oak station, which is on the route – this also enables you to omit some roadwalking. You pass through several small parks and walk beside Burnt Oak Brook and the Silk Stream, which feed the Brent Reservoir at Welsh Harp. Grahame Park has a large pond with a viewing platform.

 The route is entirely on level tarmac and pavements, except in Lyndhurst Park where you cross grass for 250m – this can be avoided on a signposted road alternative.

BARNET-TOTTERIDGE LOOP (MAP 2)

Distance:	5.4km (3.4 miles)
Location:	Barnet
Start/finish:	St Andrew's Church, Totteridge Village (GR 247-941); alternatively Totteridge & Whetstone Station (GR 261-940)
Green factor:	56%
Blue factor:	40%
Recommended direction:	Clockwise
Terrain and surface:	Mostly level, but with a long climb up Totteridge Lane. All but 200m on tarmac paths or pavements. No stiles. 2.0km (1.2 miles) beside roads
Points of interest:	Totteridge Village, St Andrew's Church, Totteridge Cattle Pound, Dollis Brook
Signage:	Almost complete both ways. Logo: '5' in white circle on blue arrow on white background, plus 'Barnet Countryside Leisure Walks'
Refreshments and toilets:	Pubs at Totteridge Village and near Totteridge & Whetstone station. No public toilets nearby
Public transport and break points:	LU: Totteridge & Whetstone. Buses: Totteridge Village, Whetstone
Links:	Rural Totteridge, Exploring Totteridge Manor, London Loop, Dollis Valley Greenwalk
Map:	Explorer 173
LWF status:	Pending validation
Principal promoter:	LB Barnet
Further information:	Included in *Barnet Countryside Leisure Walks* pack, 50p (+ sae) from LB Barnet Parks and Countryside Section, also some libraries

Number 5 in the **Barnet Countryside Leisure Walks** series. The official start is in Totteridge Village, or by starting from Totteridge & Whetstone station you get all the climbing out of the way first (a long but steady climb on a path beside a fairly busy road), then it is all downhill or level.

At high-lying Totteridge Village you pass a broad green, where the picturesque Orange Tree pub lies beside a duckpond, while next to pretty St Andrew's Church is the site of a historic cattle pound. The route links here with **Rural Totteridge** and **Exploring Totteridge Manor** in the same series. You descend into the valley of Dollis Brook and follow it back to Totteridge & Whetstone station, sharing with the **Dollis Valley Greenwalk** and Section 16 of the **London Loop**, which provides a link to High Barnet station.

The route has a hard surface all the way, except for 200m on grass at Totteridge Village. This can be avoided by following a residential lane called Lime Grove, turning left to rejoin the route along a footpath.

BEDFORDS CIRCULAR WALK (MAP 4)

Distance:	5.5km (3.4miles)
Location:	Havering
Start/finish:	Bedfords Park car park (GR 520-924)
Green factor:	91%
Blue factor:	5%
Recommended direction:	Anticlockwise
Terrain and surface:	Hilly countryside on a mixture of hard and rough surfaced paths and tracks. One stile. 0.3km (0.2miles) beside roads
Points of interest:	Bedfords Park and lake, Rise Park, historic tracks
Signage:	Partial both ways
Refreshments and toilets:	Cafés at Bedfords Park and Rise Park. Public toilets in Bedfords Park
Public transport and break points:	Buses at Chase Cross and Havering-atte-Bower
Links:	None
Map:	Explorer 175
LWF status:	Pending validation
Principal promoter:	LB Havering
Further information:	Free leaflet from LB Havering Countryside Service, also some libraries and council offices

Also described in some literature as 'Bedfords Area Circular Walk', or plain 'Bedfords Walk', this is a very pleasant green walk on the outskirts of Romford. The start lies at the highest point of Bedfords Park, but using public transport it makes sense to take a bus to Chase Cross, from which it is 350m along Lower Bedfords Road to join the route just after Point 3 on the leaflet. The route first descends quite steeply among meadows to the little lake. It climbs Foxes Hill then drops again to skirt the landscaped Rise Park and a golf course. Ancient green lanes are followed to climb back to the car park in Bedfords Park.

BEECHES WAY (MAP 3)

Distance:	26.0km (16.3miles)
Location:	Hillingdon, mostly in Buckinghamshire
Start:	West Drayton station (GR TQ 061-801)
Finish:	Cookham Bridge (GR SU 898-856)
Green factor:	Not known
Blue factor:	Not known
Recommended direction:	East to west
Terrain and surface:	Undulating countryside, mostly on rough paths and tracks. Stiles: not known. Distance beside roads: not known
Points of interest:	Grand Union Canal, Iver village, Langley Park, Black Park, Fulmer village, Burnham Beeches, River Thames
Signage:	Partial both ways – 'Beeches Way' on fingerposts and waymark discs
Refreshments and toilets:	Pubs at Iver, Iver Heath, Fulmer, Farnham Common, Littleworth Common, Cookham
Public transport and break points:	NR: West Drayton, Cookham. Buses at these points plus Iver, Iver Heath, Fulmer, Stoke Poges and Farnham Common
Links:	West Drayton to Slough Ramble and Ride, Grand Union Canal Walk, Colne Valley Trail, Colne Valley Way, Grand Union Canal (Slough Arm), London Loop, Iver Circular Walk, Thames Path National Trail
Map:	Explorer 172
LWF status:	Pending validation
Principal promoter:	Buckinghamshire CC
Further information:	Free leaflet (+ sae) from Buckinghamshire CC. Also included in *Chilterns and South Bucks* pack (£3.00) from Buckinghamshire CC

A lovely, undulating route connecting Greater London with the magical woodlands of Burnham Beeches (hence the name) as well as the extensive country parks of Langley Park and Black Park, passing through some pretty villages. Strong walkers should be able to complete the whole route in a day, or you can take two or three days. The first break point at Iver Heath is 8.0km (5.0miles) from the start. The route was the brainchild of Lorna Atkinson of Iver & District Countryside Association, and has been brought about with support from other members and Buckinghamshire County Council.

The first part of the route is shared with several others, as shown in the grid. From Langley Park the Beeches Way is pretty much on its own, through what could be considered the best part of the route, including Black Park and Burnham Beeches, until it joins the **Thames Path National Trail** at the finish in Cookham. Cookham station is a further 1.3km (0.8miles), or you can follow the Thames Path upstream to Bourne End station (2.1km/1.3miles).

BENTLEY PRIORY CIRCULAR WALK (MAP 3)

Distance:	7.2km (4.5miles), shorter options 2.7km (1.7miles) or 5.1km (3.2miles), plus link with Stanmore station 3.0km (1.9miles)
Location:	Harrow
Start/finish:	Stanmore Common car park (GR 160-936) or Old Reddings car park (GR 144-926)
Green factor:	60%
Blue factor:	11%
Recommended direction:	Clockwise
Terrain and surface:	Undulating with some fairly steep slopes. Mostly rough or tarmac paths, tracks and grass. No stiles. 1.2km (0.8miles) beside roads
Points of interest:	Stanmore Common and Little Common, Heriots Wood and Deer Park, Bentley Priory Open Space and Local Nature Reserve, farmland, Harrow Weald Common
Signage:	Partial both ways, consisting of yellow arrows on wooden posts, also some green fingerposts. A logo is due to be added at time of writing
Refreshments and toilets:	Pubs at Stanmore Little Common and The City. Public toilets at Stanmore Common
Public transport and break points:	LU: Stanmore. Buses: Stanmore, Stanmore Hill, Brookshill
Links:	London Loop Section 15, Pinner-Grimsdyke Circular Walk
Map:	Explorer 173
LWF status:	Pending validation
Principal promoter:	LB Harrow
Further information:	Further information: Free leaflet (+ sae) from LB Harrow libraries

A fairly strenuous circular walk on high ground through woods and open spaces. There are two alternative starting points at car parks, with bus routes nearby. Or you can take the underground to Stanmore and walk along the attractive London Loop Link up through Stanmore Country Park, a local nature reserve, to join this route at high-lying Stanmore Little Common. This is a pretty spot with ponds and cottages on unmade roads, dominated by the grey turrets of Stanmore Hall.

From there. you descend through a scented pinewood into the valley of Edgware Brook, passing Heriots Deer Park, where you may spot the appealing little muntjac deer. Now in Bentley Priory Open Space, you steadily climb beside a stream and fields back up to higher ground at The City, the local nickname for a hamlet that contains a pub with the strange name of The Case is Altered. It is also the location of the Old Reddings start/finish point, shared with the **Pinner-Grimsdyke Circular Walk.**

You stay on high ground for the rest of the route, for a while with Section 15 of the **London Loop,** passing through the wooded Harrow Weald Common then returning through Bentley Priory Open Space on open ground with fine views towards London. The Priory itself was an RAF headquarters during the Second World War, and is still used by them, consequently the grounds lie behind a double security fence. You pass through the Stanmore Common start/finish point then skirt a small lake on your way back to Stanmore Little Common.

BERRY'S GREEN CIRCULAR WALK (MAP 8)

Distance:	13.4km (8.4miles). Shorter option 6.5km (4.0miles)
Location:	Bromley, partly in Surrey
Start/finish:	Start/finish: Cudham Recreation Ground, Cudham Lane South (GR 446-597)
Green factor:	88%
Blue factor:	n/a
Recommended direction:	Anticlockwise
Terrain and surface:	Terrain and surface: Undulating country with some steep hills. Mostly on rough paths, tracks and grass. 38 stiles. 1.4km (0.9miles) beside roads
Points of interest:	Points of interest: Cudham church, birthplace of Little Tich, farmland, woodland, North Downs, North Downs Way
Signage:	Signage: Almost complete both ways. Logo: 'Berry's Circular Walk' in yellow on dark green background, surrounding yellow arrow
Refreshments and toilets:	Pubs at Cudham and Westerham Hill. Public toilets at Cudham
Public transport and break points:	Buses: Cudham, Westerham Hill

Links:	Cudham and Biggin Hill Circular Walks, North Downs Way
Map:	Explorer 147
LWF status:	Validated with Seal of Approval
Principal promoter:	LB Bromley
Further information:	Included in Pack One of *Bromley Circular Walks and Trails* (£2.50 plus 50p p+p) from LB Bromley Leisure & Community Services and libraries

An outstanding but strenuous walk in the **Bromley Circular Walks and Trails** series, with magnificent views. It leads to one of the highest points in Greater London near Westerham Hill on the ridge of the North Downs, at altitude 240m (788ft). Indeed, you only briefly drop below altitude 125m (410ft). There are those 38 stiles to consider – an average of one every 350m. The shorter option omits the North Downs section, but still includes 20 stiles.

Like the **Cudham Circular Walk**, with which the route is shared for a while, the route starts and finishes at the village of Cudham. You pass the church and the pretty Blacksmiths Arms pub, birthplace of Little Tich, an early 20th century music-hall artiste, then descend into farmland at the foot of a long, deep valley that stretches from Orpington right up to the North Downs ridge. You rise again through the hamlet of Luxted to pass Downe Scout Camp, then it is level walking for a while. Another climb leads to the North Downs ridge, where you briefly follow the **North Downs Way National Trail,** with an outstanding view southwards across The Weald towards the Ashdown Forest (though backed by the distant roar of M25 traffic).

You descend steadily along quiet lanes and the side of a serene valley to Cudham Place, an attractively renovated Victorian country house, and New Barn Farm with its clocktower. Another climb brings you to the hamlet after which this walk is named, Berry's Green, and one more crossing of the valley leads back to Cudham, passing Cudham Hall, now the impressive headquarters of the Amalgamated Electrical and Engineering Union. Save some energy for a final push up two long flights of steps!

BEVERLEY BROOK WALK (MAP 5)

Distance:	11.5km (7.2miles)
Location:	Kingston, Merton, Richmond, Wandsworth
Start:	New Malden station (GR 214-687)
Finish:	Putney (Embankment, GR 235-762)
Green factor:	64%
Blue factor:	49%
Recommended direction:	South to north

Terrain and surface:	Generally level, with one stepped footbridge. Mixture of tarmac, firm and rough paths, some grass. No stiles. 3.4km (2.1miles) beside roads
Points of interest:	Beverley Brook, Wimbledon Common, Richmond Park, Palewell Common, Barnes Common, Barnes Green, Barn Elms, River Thames
Signage:	Almost complete both ways. Fingerposts with white 'Beverley Brook Walk' on dark green background, or cerise and yellow discs with deer and arrow
Refreshments and toilets:	Pubs at New Malden, Kingston Vale, Barnes and Putney. Cafés at New Malden, Coombe Lane, Richmond Park, Barnes and Putney. Public toilets in Richmond Park
Public transport and break points:	NR: New Malden, Barnes, Barnes Bridge, Putney. LU: Putney Bridge. Buses: all these points plus Coombe Lane, Kingston Vale, Roehampton and Upper Richmond Road
Links:	Capital Ring, Tamsin Trail, Thames Path National Trail
Map:	Explorer 161
LWF status:	Validated with Seal of Approval
Principal promoter:	RB Kingston, LB Merton, LB Richmond, LB Wandsworth
Further information:	Free leaflet (+ sae) from local libraries and council offices

An attractive and easy walk mostly beside Beverley Brook, a tributary of the Thames, with long stretches through woodland on Wimbledon Common and beautiful Richmond Park. The route is signed from the current starting point at New Malden station, at first along roads then a track past a golf course, to pass under the A3 Beverley Way and join Beverley Brook beside Westcombe Avenue. (An extension is planned further south from here towards Worcester Park.)

A short stretch of roadwalking leads to Wimbledon Common, whose western perimeter you now follow beside Beverley Brook. Briefly joining Section 6 of the *Capital Ring* to cross the busy Robin Hood Way (A3) on a stepped footbridge, you continue beside the brook through Richmond Park, together with the *Tamsin Trail,* to Roehampton Gate then across Palewell Common.

Beverley Brook is inaccessible through most of Barnes, but there are brief glimpses at Priests Bridge and pretty Barnes Green. After crossing Barnes Common you rejoin the brook at Barn Elms for the final stage of its journey, meeting the Thames at the little dammed creek that forms its mouth, where the Beverley Brook Walk ends. You can follow the *Thames Path National Trail* downstream for 800m beside the sloping Embankment to Putney Bridge.

♿ Though fairly level, the route goes across grass in places and uses uneven paths that may be muddy in wet weather. There is a very narrow footbridge at the start of Wimbledon Common, and the footbridge over the A3 has shallow steps.

BIGGIN HILL CIRCULAR WALK (MAP 8)

Distance:	11.5km (7.2miles). Shorter options 4.5km (2.8miles) or 9.2km (5.7miles)
Location:	Bromley, plus some in Surrey
Start/finish:	Main Road, Biggin Hill (GR 418-595)
Green factor:	62%
Blue factor:	n/a
Recommended direction:	Clockwise
Terrain and surface:	Much is on level ground but some very steep ascents and descents. Mostly on rough paths, tracks and grass. 18 stiles (17 on 9.2km route, 1 on 4.5km route). 2.1km (1.3miles) beside roads
Points of interest:	Biggin Hill Airport, Pimlico Wood, farmland, Tatsfield village, Jugg Hill Wood
Signage:	Almost complete both ways. Logo: 'Biggin Hill Circular Walk' in yellow on dark green background, surrounding yellow arrow with pale blue flash
Refreshments and toilets:	Pubs at Biggin Hill and Tatsfield. Café at Biggin Hill. No public toilets nearby
Public transport and break points:	Buses: Biggin Hill, Tatsfield
Links:	Berry's Green Circular Walk
Map:	Explorer 147
LWF status:	Validated with Seal of Approval
Principal promoter:	LB Bromley
Further information:	Included in Pack One of *Bromley Circular Walks and Trails* (£2.50 plus 50p p+p) from LB Bromley Leisure & Community Services and libraries

A veritable switchback, and one of the longest walks in the **Bromley Circular Walks and Trails** series, occupying an area of high ground cloven by steep-sided valleys in the foothills of the North Downs. It passes through some of the best and hilliest countryside around London, and should prove a rewarding test of fitness for strong walkers.

The route starts at altitude 180m (590ft) on the broad plateau at Biggin Hill that proved so suitable for the famous wartime airfield (now a leading centre for private flying). The first stretch is gentle enough, passing through open spaces where you briefly link with the **Berry's Green Circular Walk.** Then you dive into the first valley and soon climb to an even higher level at Tatsfield in Surrey, which proclaims itself as 'London's Alps' at 229m (751ft). Its peaceful green, with duckpond, pub, store and post office, is all that one would expect of a typical English village, right on London's doorstep.

You descend into, and climb out of, two more valleys and through woodland to reach Norheads Lane, a glorious level stretch in open farmland. A gradual descent takes you across Oaklands Lane, part of a Roman road from London to the Sussex coast, then a final climb leads through more woodland back to Biggin Hill. But beware, there is a sting in the tail as you have three flights of what the route card euphemistically describes as 'some steps' to climb. These consist in short order of 66, 24 and 94 steps – save some energy for the end!

BRENT RIVER PARK WALK (MAP 3)

Distance:	11.5km (7.2miles)
Location:	Ealing, Hounslow
Start:	Brentham Open Space (GR 176-827)
Finish:	Brentford High Street (GR 173-773)
Green factor:	62%
Blue factor:	77%
Recommended direction:	North to south
Terrain and surface:	Almost completely level, with some very short slopes. Rough paths, tracks and grass to Uxbridge Road, then hard surface. Some steps, no stiles. Only 0.9km (0.6miles) beside roads
Points of interest:	River Brent, Pitshanger Park, Hanwell church, Brent Lodge Park, Wharncliffe Viaduct, Grand Union Canal and locks, Boston Manor Park, Brentford Canal Basin
Signage:	Almost complete both ways. Logo: 'BRP' on yellow arrow, 'Brent River Path Footpath' surrounding green background
Refreshments and toilets:	Pubs and cafés at Hanwell, and Brentford. Café and toilets at Brent Lodge Park. Public toilets at Boston Manor Park
Public transport and break points:	LU: Hanger Lane, Boston Manor. NR: South Greenford, Castlebar Park, Hanwell, Brentford. Buses at all these points plus Western Avenue, Pitshanger Lane, Argyle Road and Ruislip Road East
Links:	Capital Ring, Grand Union Canal Walk, Thames Path National Trail
Map:	Explorers 161 and 173 (route marked)
LWF status:	Validated with Seal of Approval

Principal promoter:	LB Ealing, LB Hounslow
Further information:	Free leaflet from libraries in LB Ealing and LB Hounslow Tourist Information Centre. Details shown on www.ealing.gov.uk/parks

One of the 'bluest' routes in this book, with easy walking mostly beside the River Brent, which in its lower stretches forms part of the Grand Union Canal. It is very green too, passing through riverside shrubbery, several parks and open spaces. Much of the route is used by Sections 7 and 8 of the **Capital Ring.**

Starting from a rather undistinguished spot beside the A40 (Western Avenue), not far from Hanger Lane station, you set off through Brentham Open Space and Pitshanger Park. There is some roadwalking at this end, but after Ruislip Road East there is hardly any, though you pass underneath two very busy main roads and the M4 motorway. The walk through Brent Lodge Park is very pretty, with the spire of Hanwell church rising between the trees. You pass under the impressive Wharncliffe Viaduct, where express trains cross high above en route to Wales, and testing your echoes is a popular pastime.

River Brent at Perivale Park

You join the **Grand Union Canal** towpath at the foot of Hanwell Locks, and pass Osterley Lock on the way to Brentford. This is a fairly busy section of the canal and there is a good chance of seeing some waterborne action. A large concrete plaque beside the towpath near Osterley Lock proudly records that a British Waterways team won a pile-driving competition in 1959.

Brentford Canal Basin is quite deserted nowadays. The towpath passes through a covered quay, then crosses a miniature 'wobbly bridge' over the dock entrance to finish at Brentford High Street. It connects here with the **Thames Path National Trail**, which continues along the Brent on a diversion from the big river.

St Mary's Church, Hanwerll,
From Brent Lodge Park

BROMLEY CIRCULAR WALKS AND TRAILS

The London Borough of Bromley includes a vast amount of fine walking country, including woods, commons, parks and farmland. The borough's Ranger Service and Active Lifestyles team have designed 13 circular walks, taking full advantage of these opportunities, ranging in distance from 3.5 to 12.0km (2.2 to 7.5miles) and in grade from easy to very strenuous. Most have earned the London Walking Forum's Seal of Approval. Some lead into comparatively remote open country, which, though now within Greater London, remains for many a corner of Kent – the Garden of England. Many of the routes interlink, and can easily be combined to form longer walks – see Map 6.

The Council has produced two very attractive packs of route descriptions on waterproof card, currently costing £2.50 each plus 50p p+p. Pack One includes **Berry's Green, Biggin Hill, Cudham, Farnborough, Green Street Green, Leaves Green** and **Nash** Circular Walks. Pack Two includes **Bromley Common, Chelsfield, Petts Wood, St Mary Cray, St Paul's Cray and Three Commons** (Hayes, Keston and West Wickham) Circular Walks, plus Bromley's bit of the linear **Cray Riverway.** For further details see the individual route entries. Pack Two also includes the short Jubilee Nature Trail (see Other Named Self-guided Walks below). A third pack is planned.

The walks are distinguished by their very high quality signage, though there are some gaps. An ingenious standard design shows the route name in yellow on a dark green background, surrounding a yellow arrow with a flash of a different colour for each route.

BROMLEY COMMON CIRCULAR WALK (MAP 6)

Distance:	6.5km (4.1miles)
Location:	Bromley
Start/finish:	Parkfield Recreation Ground, off Magpie Hall Lane, Southborough (GR 428-673)
Green factor:	62%
Blue factor:	3%
Recommended direction:	Clockwise
Terrain and surface:	Almost completely level, just one gentle ascent. Mostly on rough paths, tracks and grass. One stile. 2.3km (1.4miles) beside roads
Points of interest:	Parkfield Recreation Ground, Holy Trinity Church, River Ravensbourne, Bromley Common Cricket Club, Barnet Wood, Hayes Fruit Farm, Hayes Trout Fishery, Elmfield Wood, Bromley College
Signage:	Almost complete both ways. Logo: 'Bromley Common Circular Walk' in yellow on dark green background, surrounding yellow arrow with red flash
Refreshments and toilets:	Pubs at Southborough, Hayes and Bromley Common. No public toilets nearby
Public transport and break points:	Buses: Southborough, Hastings Road, Hayes, Bromley Common
Links:	None
Map:	Explorer 162
LWF status:	Validated with Seal of Approval
Principal promoter:	LB Bromley
Further information:	Included in Pack One of Bromley Circular Walks and rails (£2.50 plus 50p p+p) from LB Bromley Leisure & Community Services and libraries

One of the shorter and easier routes in the **Bromley Circular Walks and Trails** series. It starts and finishes at Parkfield Recreation Ground, just a short walk from bus routes at Southborough. You follow footpaths through Princes Plain to Holy Trinity Church, then a short road walk leads to a long stretch of open country through woods and across fields. You cross the River Ravensbourne twice and pass Hayes Trout Fishery, which boasts a wide variety of waterbirds. More woodland and fields lead to the modern buildings of Bromley College, then a final stretch beside roads and past two historic pubs (the Crown and the Chequers) takes you back to Parkfield Recreation Ground.

CAPITAL RING

Introduction. The Capital Ring, one of the Mayor of London's key routes (see Strategic Network introduction), is a surprisingly green route that encircles London within a radius of 6–16km (4–10miles) of Charing Cross. If the London Loop is sometimes known as the 'walkers' M25', then the Capital Ring is their North and South Circular Roads. For 120m (75 miles) it threads together parks and open spaces, mostly following pleasant residential roads in between. The route is an initiative of the London Walking Forum, which co-ordinates work among the boroughs to provide uniform signage and leaflets. The Forum was not alone with this idea, as Bob Gilbert's *Green London Way* (see Appendix E) published in 1991 follows the same principle, and the two routes frequently overlap.

The official start and finish of the circuit is on the south side of the Woolwich Foot Tunnel, but of course you can join and leave at any point. Much of it is shared with other major routes, including the **Thames Path Southeast Extension, Green Chain Walk, Thames Path National Trail, Grand Union Canal Walk, Brent River Park Walk, Dollis Valley Greenwalk, Parkland Walk, Lea Valley Walk** and **The Greenway**. The 15 sections summarised below have an average distance of 8.8km (5.5 miles) and are described more fully on the following pages.

Section		km	miles
1	Woolwich to Falconwood	11.4	7.1
2	Falconwood to Grove Park	6.6	4.1
3	Grove Park to Crystal Palace	13.9	8.6
4	Crystal Palace to Streatham	6.5	4.0
5	Streatham to Wimbledon Park	8.9	5.5
6	Wimbledon Park to Richmond	12.0	7.5
7	Richmond to Osterley Lock	7.7	4.8
8	Osterley Lock to Greenford	8.9	5.5
9	Greenford to South Kenton	8.8	5.5
10	South Kenton to Hendon	10.3	6.4
11	Hendon to Highgate	9.0	5.6
12	Highgate to Stoke Newington	7.3	4.6
13	Stoke Newington to Hackney Wick	6.5	4.0
14	Hackney Wick to Beckton District Park	8.3	5.1
15	Beckton District Park to Woolwich	6.6	4.1

Note: the distances shown in the table include station links.

Signs and further information. The route is indicated on the ground by a variety of signs and waymarks, which are very similar to those of the **London Loop**. In open spaces they consist mostly of a simple white disc, mounted on wooden posts and containing a directional arrow with the Big Ben logo in blue and text in green (but note that in Richmond black replaces green due to local conservation area considerations). A word of warning: the arrow's direction may not be clear until you are close up. It is easy to assume that it points ahead, but it may turn – look closely before continuing.

On streets the posts are replaced by larger aluminium signs strapped to lampposts and other street furniture, and additionally carry a walking man symbol. On link routes to stations the word 'link' is incorporated into the logo. At major focal points you will also meet tall green and white signposts that give distances to three points in either direction. Some of these locations may also have the big, round-topped information boards.

A guidebook to the Capital Ring by Colin Saunders is in preparation, to be published by Aurum Press in Spring 2003. Meanwhile individual leaflets are being published as each section of the Ring becomes ready. At the time of writing Sections 4, 6, 7, 10, 11 and 13 have signs and leaflets, with 5, 8 and 9 due to follow shortly. Sections 1–3 are scheduled to be validated (full signage and literature) by the London Walking Forum in the near future – on these sections there will be joint signage with the **Green Chain Walk**. Sections 12, 14 and 15 are expected to have complete signage and a route description in the course of 2003, and you may not be able to walk them until then. It is anticipated that the Capital Ring should be fully open by the end of 2003. The latest position can be checked on **www.londonwalking.com**.

CAPITAL RING: SECTION 1 (MAP 6)
Woolwich to Falconwood

Distance:	11.4km (7.1miles) including links with Woolwich Arsenal and Falconwood stations
Location:	Greenwich
Start:	Woolwich Foot Tunnel (GR 432-793)
Finish:	Falconwood (Eltham Park North, GR 441-753)
Green factor:	72%
Blue factor:	5%
Recommended direction:	North to south
Terrain and surface:	Mainly level but some steep slopes and two long flights of steps (with avoiding alternatives). Mixture of tarmac paths, pavements and rough paths, tracks and grass. No stiles. 2.4km (1.5miles) beside roads

Points of interest:	River Thames, Thames Barrier, Maryon Park, Maryon Wilson Park, Charlton Park, Charlton House, Hornfair Park, Woolwich Common, Eltham Common, Severndroog Castle, Oxleas Meadows, Oxleas Wood, Eltham Park North
Signage:	Partial Capital Ring signage both ways, otherwise follow Green Chain Walk signs
Refreshments and toilets:	Pubs at Woolwich, Charlton village, Shooters Hill and Falconwood. Cafés at Woolwich, Charlton village and Oxleas Meadows. Public toilets at Woolwich, Maryon Park, Charlton House and Oxleas Meadows
Public transport and break points:	Free ferry from North Woolwich (trains). NR: Woolwich Arsenal, Woolwich Dockyard, Falconwood. Buses at these points and at Thorntree Road, Charlton Village and Shooters Hill
Links:	Thames Path Southeast Extension, Thames Path National Trail, Green Chain Walk
Map:	Explorer 162
LWF status:	Validated with Seal of Approval (Mayor of London's key route)
Principal promoter:	London Walking Forum, LB Greenwich
Further information:	See Capital Ring introduction

This section shares its route with two others. From the start on the south side of the Woolwich Foot Tunnel it follows the **Thames Path Southeast Extension,** mostly beside the river with some grand views including the Thames Flood Barrier (popularly known simply as Thames Barrier), where the **Thames Path National Trail** starts. Just before this you join Section 5 of the **Green Chain Walk** and continue with it all the way to Falconwood and beyond, in fact as far as Crystal Palace Park in the Capital Ring's Section 3. In Maryon Park you face a stiff climb up 106 steps, but there is an avoiding route in less steep parallel streets. After that the walking is fairly easy, though with some short climbs, through a succession of parks and woods. At Oxleas Meadows you move briefly on to the Green Chain Walk's Section 3, and its Section 6 at Oxleas Wood.

Severndroog Castle

CAPITAL RING: SECTION 2 (MAP 6)
Falconwood to Grove Park

Distance:	6.6km (4.1miles) including links with Falconwood and Grove Park stations
Location:	Greenwich, Lewisham
Start:	Falconwood (Eltham Park North, GR 441-753)
Finish:	Grove Park (Baring Road GR 405-727)
Green factor:	35%
Blue factor:	n/a
Recommended direction:	Northeast to southwest
Terrain and surface:	Generally level or downhill with some short gentle climbs. Mainly on tarmac paths and pavements with some short stretches of rough ground and tracks. No stiles. 3.2km (2.0miles) beside roads
Points of interest:	Eltham Park South, Eltham Palace, King John's Walk
Signage:	No Capital Ring signage at time of writing (follow Green Chain Walk signs
Refreshments and toilets:	Pubs at Falconwood, Eltham and Grove Park. Cafés at Eltham and Grove Park. Public toilets at Grove Park
Public transport and break points:	NR/buses: Falconwood, Eltham, Mottingham, Grove Park
Links:	Green Chain Walk
Map:	Explorer 162
LWF status:	Validated with Seal of Approval (Mayor of London's key route)
Principal promoter:	London Walking Forum, LB Greenwich, LB Lewisham
Further information:	See Capital Ring introduction

Easy walking on mainly firm ground, with a fair amount of roadwalking but passing one of the jewels of the Capital Ring: Eltham Palace. For further description refer to Green Chain Walk Sections 6 and 8.

CAPITAL RING: SECTION 3 (MAP 6)
Grove Park to Crystal Palace

Distance:	13.9km (8.6miles) including link with Grove Park station
Location:	Lewisham, Bromley
Start:	Grove Park (Baring Road GR 405-727)
Finish:	Crystal Palace station (GR 341-705)
Green factor:	50%
Blue factor:	3%
Recommended direction:	East to west
Terrain and surface:	Mainly on roads and tarmac paths but with a long stretch on rough paths and tracks in Beckenham Place Park. Generally level but with some long and quite steep slopes. Steep steps at two railway bridges. No stiles. 5.3km (3.3miles) beside roads
Points of interest:	Downham Woodland Walk, Beckenham Place Park and mansion, Cator Park, Crystal Palace Park
Signage:	No Capital Ring signage at time of writing (follow Green Walk signs
Refreshments and toilets:	Pubs at Grove Park, Beckenham Place, Penge and Crystal Palace station. Cafés at Grove Park, Downham, Beckenham Place, Penge and Crystal Palace Park. Public toilets at Grove Park, Downham, Beckenham Place and Crystal Palace Park
Public transport and break points:	NR: Grove Park, Beckenham Hill, Beckenham Junction, New Beckenham, Kent House, Penge East, Penge West, Crystal Palace. CTL: Beckenham Junction. Buses at all these points, plus Downham
Links:	Green Chain Walk
Map:	Explorers 161 and 162
LWF status:	Validated with Seal of Approval (Mayor of London's key route)
Principal promoter:	London Walking Forum, LB Lewisham, LB Bromley
Further information:	See Capital Ring introduction

Generally fairly easy walking but the section through Beckenham Place Park is on rough ground, which may be difficult in wet conditions. For further details see Green Chain Walk Sections 8 and 10. This section of the Capital Ring overshoots the end of the Green Chain Walk to finish at Crystal Palace station.

CAPITAL RING: SECTION 4 (MAP 7)
Crystal Palace to Streatham

Distance:	6.5km (4.0miles) including link with Streatham Common station
Location:	Bromley, Croydon, Lambeth
Start:	Crystal Palace station (GR 341-705)
Finish:	Estreham Road (GR 297-707)
Green factor:	57%
Blue factor:	n/a
Recommended direction:	East to west
Terrain and surface:	Almost entirely on tarmac paths or pavements; one short stretch on rough path. Undulating with some fairly steep ascents and descents. No stiles. 3.0km (1.9miles) beside roads
Points of interest:	Westow Park, Upper Norwood Recreation Ground, Biggin Wood, Norwood Grove and mansion, Rookery Gardens, Streatham Common
Signage:	Complete both ways – see Capital Ring introduction
Refreshments and toilets:	Pubs at Crystal Palace and Streatham. Café at Rookery Gardens. Public toilets at Rookery Gardens and Streatham Common
Public transport and break points:	NR: Crystal Palace, Streatham, Streatham Common. Buses at these points and at Beulah Hill
Links:	Green Chain Walk
Map:	Explorer 161
LWF status:	Validated with Seal of Approval (Mayor of London's key route)
Principal promoter:	London Walking Forum, LB Bromley, LB Croydon, LB Lambeth
Further information:	See Capital Ring introduction

A rollercoaster of a walk among the ridges and valleys of the former Great North Wood. It is very steep in places, but you are rewarded with some fine views and pleasant scenery. From Crystal Palace station (close to Section 10 of the **Green Chain Walk**) you climb over a ridge then drop down through Westow Park and Upper Norwood Recreation Ground. A second ridge (Beulah Hill) is crossed, then comes a level stretch through Biggin Wood, one of the few remnants of the Great North Wood. A final climb in Norwood Grove leads through beautiful gardens and past the former mansion that now serves as an education centre. (Dog walkers must make a short diversion here over grass.) A welcome café serves refreshments at Rookery Gardens, then you descend Streatham Common to the section end near Streatham Common Station.

Cafeteria ('the mountain hut') at Oxleas Meadows

CAPITAL RING: SECTION 5 (MAP 5)
Streatham to Wimbledon Park

Distance:	8.9km (5.5miles) including link with Streatham Common station
Location:	Lambeth, Wandsworth, Merton
Start:	Estreham Road (GR 297-707)
Finish:	Wimbledon Park station (GR 253-721)
Green factor:	26%
Blue factor:	2%
Recommended direction:	Southeast to northwest
Terrain and surface:	Entirely level on tarmac paths or pavements but one footbridge with steep steps. No stiles. 7.0km (4.4miles) beside roads
Points of interest:	Streatham Pumping Station, Tooting Bec Common and ponds, Wandsworth Common, Wandsworth Prison, Wandsworth Cemetery, Wimbledon Mosque
Signage:	Partial both ways – see Capital Ring introduction
Refreshments and toilets:	Pubs at Streatham, Balham, Wandsworth Common, Earlsfield and Wimbledon Park. Cafés at Streatham, Tooting Bec Common, Balham, Earlsfield and Wimbledon Park. Public toilets at Balham and Earlsfield
Public transport and break points:	NR: Streatham, Streatham Common, Balham, Wandsworth Common, Earlsfield. LU: Wimbledon Park. Buses at these points and at Tooting Bec Road, Bedford Hill and Trinity Road
Links:	Wandle Trail
Map:	Explorer 161
LWF status:	Pending validation
Principal promoter:	London Walking Forum, LB Lambeth, LB Wandsworth, LB Merton
Further information:	See Capital Ring introduction

Easy walking across commons and through pleasant residential parts of south London, with much of interest. Soon after the start you go through a mysterious no-man's-land between railway lines, then a green dome ahead turns out to be Streatham Pumping Station. Tarmac paths lead across Tooting Bec Common, passing the Lido and ponds. At Wandsworth Common the route goes cheekily through the station ticket office, and boardwalks allow close inspection of pondlife. After hurrying past the brooding brown hulk of Wandsworth Prison, you follow a long straight road beside Wandsworth Cemetery. The **Wandle Trail** is crossed at Earlsfield station, then after Durnsford Road Recreation Ground comes Wimbledon Mosque with its green cupolas.

    The entire section uses level pavements or tarmac paths, apart from a footbridge with steps soon after the start off Estreham Road. This can be avoided by using a subway 200m north of the footbridge to rejoin the route in Conyers Road by Streatham Pumping Station.

Capital Ring: Section 6 (Maps 5, 3)
Wimbledon Park to Richmond

Distance:	12.0km (7.5miles) including link with Richmond station
Location:	Merton, Wandsworth, Richmond, Kingston
Start:	Wimbledon Park station (GR 253-721)
Finish:	Richmond Riverside (GR 176-747)
Green factor:	74%
Blue factor:	12%
Recommended direction:	Southeast to northwest
Terrain and surface:	Some quite long and fairly steep ascents and descents, mainly on rough tracks or paths and grass. Steps on footbridge over A3. No stiles. 1.8km (1.1miles) beside roads
Points of interest:	Wimbledon Park and lake, Putney Heath, Wimbledon Common and windmill, Beverley Brook, Richmond Park, Pen Ponds, Pembroke Lodge, King Henry VIII Mound, Petersham Park, Petersham Meadows, River Thames, Richmond
Signage:	Partially signed both ways – see Capital Ring introduction
Refreshments and toilets:	Pubs at Wimbledon Park, Kingston Vale, Petersham and Richmond. Cafés at Wimbledon Park, Wimbledon Common, Richmond Park and Richmond. Toilets: Wimbledon Park, Wimbledon Common, Richmond Park, Richmond
Public transport and break points:	LU: Wimbledon Park, Richmond. NR: Richmond. Buses at these points plus Wimbledon Park Side, Kingston Vale and Petersham
Links:	Beverley Brook Walk, Tamsin Trail, Thames Path National Trail
Map:	Explorer 161

LWF status:	Validated with Seal of Approval (Mayor of London's key route)
Principal promoter:	London Walking Forum, LB Merton, LB Wandsworth, LB Richmond
Further information:	See Capital Ring introduction

Possibly one of the finest walks in the whole book, with glorious scenery almost wall to wall. Wimbledon Park is less well known than the Common but very pretty, with an impressive chalet-style café and a large lake where quiet watersports take place. A longish uphill stretch along pleasant residential roads leads on to Putney Heath, then it is rough ground most of the way to Richmond.

A fascinating windmill beckons you on to Wimbledon Common – it rises above a café, and has a museum attached. You drop steeply down past tranquil Queen's Mere, then cross a golf course fairway to join the **Beverley Brook Walk** for a while. After crossing the busy A3 on a stepped footbridge you pass through Robin Hood Gate into Richmond Park, where you cross the **Tamsin Trail** and can expect to see several groups of red and fallow deer (do not approach them).

After climbing steadily to the Pen Ponds, positively heaving with waterbirds, you pass Pembroke Lodge café and King Henry VIII Mound, of prehistoric origin, into Petersham Park, then descend to the meadows with a fine view of Petersham church, village and River Thames. You now accompany the **Thames Path National Trail** downstream along the south bank beneath the grand buildings on Richmond Hill for the final stretch into Richmond, which surely has one of the finest riverside frontages along the Thames.

 The first 3.2km (2.0miles) from Wimbledon Park to the windmill on Wimbledon Common is mostly on tarmac paths or pavements, though with a long climb – quite steep in places. On Putney Heath the route follows a rough track, but you can follow a parallel road as far as the windmill car park. Beyond the windmill the route is mostly on rough paths, there are some steep slopes, and steps on the footbridge over the A3.

CAPITAL RING: SECTION 7 (MAP 3)
Richmond to Osterley Lock

Distance:	7.7km (4.8miles) including links with Richmond and Boston Manor stations
Location:	Richmond, Hounslow, Ealing
Start:	Richmond Riverside (GR 176-747)
Finish:	Osterley Lock (GR 159-789)
Green factor:	40%
Blue factor:	63%
Recommended direction:	Southeast to northwest

Terrain and surface:	Entirely level throughout except for steps at Richmond Lock footbridge (avoidable on an alternative route) and some short slopes. Mainly firm towpaths and tracks, sometimes on grass. No stiles. 1.3km (0.8miles) beside roads
Points of interest:	Richmond riverfront, Old Deer Park and observatory, Richmond Lock, River Thames, Old Isleworth, Syon Park, mansion and garden centre, Brentford Dock, Grand Union Canal and locks
Signage:	Complete both ways – see Capital Ring introduction
Refreshments and toilets:	Pubs at Richmond, Old Isleworth, Brentford and Boston Manor. Cafés at Richmond, Old Isleworth, Syon Park and Brentford. Public toilets at Richmond and Syon Park
Public transport and break points:	LU: Richmond, Boston Manor. NR: Richmond, Brentford. Buses at these points plus Old Isleworth
Links:	Thames Path National Trail, River Crane Walk, Grand Union Canal Walk, Brent River Park Walk
Map:	Explorer 161
LWF status:	Validated with Seal of Approval (Mayor of London's key route)
Principal promoter:	London Walking Forum, LB Richmond, LB Hounslow, LB Ealing
Further information:	See Capital Ring introduction

One of the 'bluest' and easiest sections of the Capital Ring, following the River Thames and the Grand Union Canal most of the way. Together with the **Thames Path National Trail** the section sets off from Richmond Riverside along the south bank to cross the Thames at Richmond Lock, using the venerable old footbridge. At times of heavy rain or high tides there may be flooding in this area. Now on the north bank, the route twists through the attractive village of Old Isleworth, sometimes away from the river, and passing the two eastern ends of the **River Crane Walk**. You walk through Syon Park, passing the great mansion of the Dukes of Northumberland, now a busy tourist attraction with a garden centre, miniature railway, butterfly house and children's playground.

At Brentford you leave the Thames to join the **Grand Union Canal Walk** and **Brent River Park Walk** along the canal towpath. This section finishes at Osterley Lock, with a signed link to Boston Manor station.

The route is fairly level, but there is uneven ground in some places beside the river and canal. Two long flights of steps on the footbridge at Richmond Lock can be avoided by using a signed alternative via Richmond Bridge and the north bank. In Syon Park the route crosses grass, but there is a parallel tarmac drive. At Brentford the towpath is reached across a small and rather wobbly swingbridge.

CAPITAL RING: SECTION 8 (MAP 3)
Osterley Lock to Greenford

Distance:	8.9km (5.5miles) including links with Boston Manor station and Greenford stations
Location:	Ealing
Start:	Osterley Lock (GR 159-789)
Finish:	Rockware Avenue, Greenford (GR 150-839)
Green factor:	67%
Blue factor:	70%
Recommended direction:	South to north
Terrain and surface:	Almost entirely level on tarmac or rough paths and tracks, grass and pavements. Some short gentle slopes. No stiles. 1.1km (0.7miles) beside roads
Points of interest:	Grand Union Canal, Hanwell Locks, Wharncliffe Viaduct, Brent Lodge Park, Perivale Park
Signage:	Not signed at time of writing – see Capital Ring introduction
Refreshments and toilets:	Pubs at Boston Manor, Hanwell and Greenford. Cafés at BrentLodge Park and Greenford. Public toilets at BrentLodge Park
Public transport and break points:	LU: Boston Manor, Greenford. NR: Hanwell, South Greenford, Greenford. Buses at these points plus Ruislip Road East
Links:	Grand Union Canal Walk, Brent River Park Walk
Map:	Explorer 173
LWF status:	Pending validation
Principal promoter:	London Walking Forum, LB Ealing
Further information:	See Capital Ring introduction

An easy walk, mostly following the River Brent. The route is partly shared with the *Grand Union Canal Walk*, starting on its towpath at Osterley Lock (with signed link from Boston Manor station), and the *Brent River Park Walk,* whose path is rough in places and may be muddy in wet weather. Highlights include the impressive Wharncliffe Viaduct and Brent Lodge Park, where the spire of Hanwell church rises majestically above the trees. At Ruislip Road the river is left behind to pass through Perivale Park, close to South Greenford station, and on through Cayton Road Sports Ground to Greenford.

CAPITAL RING: SECTION 9 (MAP 3)
Greenford to South Kenton

Distance:	8.8km (5.5miles) including link with Greenford station
Location:	Ealing, Harrow, Brent
Start:	Rockware Avenue, Greenford (GR 150-839)
Finish:	South Kenton station (GR 173-870)
Green factor:	60%
Blue factor:	13%
Recommended direction:	Southwest to northeast
Terrain and surface:	Mostly level but with some fairly steep ascents and descents. On tarmac and rough paths or tracks, grass and pavements. One stile. 3.2km (2.0miles) beside roads
Points of interest:	Paradise Fields Wetlands, Grand Union Canal, Horsenden Hill, Horsenden Wood, Harrow-on-the-Hill, Harrow School, Northwick Park
Signage:	Not signed at time of writing – see Capital Ring introduction
Refreshments and toilets:	Pubs at Greenford, Horsenden Hill, Sudbury Hill, Harrow-on-the-Hill and South Kenton. Cafés at Greenford, Horsenden Hill and Harrow-on-the-Hill. Public toilets at Horsenden Hill
Public transport and break points:	LU/NR: Greenford, Harrow-on-the-Hill, South Kenton. LU only: Sudbury Hill. Buses at all these points plus Whitton Avenue and Watford Road
Links:	Grand Union Canal Walk
Map:	Explorer 173
LWF status:	Pending validation
Principal promoter:	London Walking Forum, LB Ealing, LB Harrow, LB Brent
Further information:	See Capital Ring introduction

A very interesting section with some climbing and fine views. It starts beside the Westway Cross Shopping Park near Greenford station, and you soon enter Paradise Fields Wetlands, cleverly converted from the former Greenford Golf Course, where there is a pondlife viewing platform. You join the **Grand Union Canal Walk** to share its towpath as far as Horsenden Hill.

Horsenden Hill summit

The route crosses Horsenden Hill with good views via the summit at altitude 85m (279ft). You descend through Horsenden Wood then follow roads through Sudbury Hill before starting the long and sometimes steep climb to the old village of Harrow-on-the-Hill. Here, in term-time, straw-hatted boys from Harrow School mingle with tourists and visiting parents in the tearooms and antique shops. You pass the scattered buildings of the venerable old school, then descend on grass across its playing fields to cross busy Watford Road, where great care is needed. Finally you follow tracks past the straggling buildings of Northwick Park and St Mark's Hospitals, then cross Northwick Park itself to South Kenton station.

CAPITAL RING: SECTION 10 (MAPS 3, 2)
South Kenton to Hendon Park

Distance:	10.3km (6.4miles) including link with Hendon Central station
Location:	Brent, Barnet
Start:	South Kenton station (GR 173-870)
Finish:	Hendon Park (GR 235-883)
Green factor:	41%
Blue factor:	16%
Recommended direction:	West to east
Terrain and surface:	Mainly level on firm or tarmac paths or tracks and pavements, with some rough ground and steep climbs. No stiles. 5.5km (3.4miles) beside roads

Points of interest:	Preston Park, Fryent Country Park, Barn Hill, Gotfords Hill, St Andrew's Churches, Welsh Harp Open Space, Brent Reservoir, Hendon Park
Signage:	Partial both ways – see Capital Ring introduction
Refreshments and toilets:	Pubs and cafés at South Kenton, Preston Road, West Hendon Broadway and Hendon Central. No public toilets
Public transport and break points:	LU: South Kenton, Preston Road, Hendon Central. NR: Hendon. Buses at all these points plus Church Lane and West Hendon Broadway
Links:	None
Map:	Explorer 173
LWF status:	Validated with Seal of Approval (Mayor of London's key route)
Principal promoter:	London Walking Forum, LB Brent, LB Barnet
Further information:	See Capital Ring introduction

Despite being mainly beside roads, this section includes some of the most rural parts along the whole Capital Ring, some fine hilltop views and a long lakeside stretch. From South Kenton station it crosses Preston Park to pass Preston Road station, then climbs steadily into Fryent Country Park, divided into two halves by the A4140 Fryent Way. From the wooded, pond-capped summit of Barn Hill you can see the rebuilding of Wembley Stadium and Central London. At a second and more exposed summit, Gotfords Hill, you are among fields with a fine view towards Harrow-on-the-Hill.

Following residential roads through Kingsbury you pass two neighbouring churches, little (old) and large (new), both dedicated to St Andrew. The green-spired little church, surrounded by dense greenery, is a haven for wildlife. Soon you reach Welsh Harp Open Space, which includes the huge Brent Reservoir, and follow a firm track along its north shore with a grandstand view of the sailing.

Brent Reservoir (Welsh Harp) at Cool Oak Lane

At the far end, the reservoir continuation beyond Cool Oak Lane has the appearance of a yacht harbour in a seaside creek.

A long roadside stretch leads across West Hendon Broadway (signed link to Hendon station), across the M1 motorway and under Hendon Way to the end of this section in Hendon Park, where a signed link takes you along a grassy avenue to Hendon Central station.

CAPITAL RING: SECTION 11 (MAP 2)
Hendon Park to Highgate

Distance:	9.0km (5.6miles) including links with Hendon Central and Highgate stations
Location:	Barnet, Haringey
Start:	Hendon Park (GR 235-883)
Finish:	Priory Gardens, Highgate (GR 287-882)
Green factor:	56%
Blue factor:	17%
Recommended direction:	West to east
Terrain and surface:	Mainly level on firm paths and pavements, but with some steep ascents and descents on rough ground especially towards the end. No stiles. 2.8km (1.8miles) beside roads
Points of interest:	Hendon Park, River Brent, Mutton Brook, Cherry Tree Wood, Highgate Wood, Queen's Wood
Signage:	Complete both ways – see Capital Ring introduction
Refreshments and toilets:	Pubs at Hendon Central, East Finchley and Highgate. Cafés at Hendon Central, Hampstead Garden Suburb, East Finchley, Highgate Wood and Queen's Wood. Kiosk in Cherry Tree Wood. Public toilets at Lyttelton Playing Fields, Cherry Tree Wood and Highgate Wood
Public transport and break points:	LU: Hendon Central, East Finchley, Highgate. Buses at all these points plus North Circular Road and Hampstead Garden Suburb
Links:	Dollis Valley Greenwalk
Map:	Explorer 173 (route marked)
LWF status:	Validated with Seal of Approval (Mayor of London's key route)
Principal promoter:	London Walking Forum, LB Barnet, LB Haringey
Further information:	See Capital Ring introduction

Most of the walking in this section is easy, but gets tougher towards the end with some steep slopes and rough ground. The surroundings are pleasant, at first following firm paths through a string of narrow parks and recreation grounds beside the River Brent and Mutton Brook. You pass the point where Mutton and Dollis Brooks combine to form the River Brent, and join the **Dollis Valley Greenwalk** for a while.

The route passes through East Finchley station, then comes a trio of woods, all remnants of the ancient Forest of Middlesex, starting with the small Cherry Tree Wood. Highgate Wood occupies fairly level ground on a hilltop at altitude 101m (331ft), while Queen's Wood straddles a deep valley with a steep climb to the section end near Highgate station.

 The route is fairly level most of the way, but the stretch in Queen's Wood may be too rough and steep, even for buggies – it can be avoided on parallel roads. Beside Mutton Brook the path is narrow with some steep slopes.

Capital Ring: Section 12 (Map 2)
Highgate to Stoke Newington

Distance:	7.3km (4.6miles) including link with Highgate station
Location:	Haringey, Islington, Hackney
Start:	Priory Gardens, Highgate (GR 287-882)
Finish:	Stamford Hill (GR 337-868)
Green factor:	61%
Blue factor:	9%
Recommended direction:	West to east
Terrain and surface:	Almost entirely level on firm paths and pavements, except for an avoidable steep climb on rough ground at the start. No stiles. 2.9km (1.8miles) beside roads
Points of interest:	Parkland Walk, Finsbury Park, Stoke Newington Reservoirs, Clissold Park, Abney Park Cemetery
Signage:	Not signed at time of writing – see Capital Ring introduction
Refreshments and toilets:	Pubs at Highgate, Manor House, Woodberry Down and Stoke Newington. Cafés at Highgate, Crouch End Hill, Finsbury Park, Manor House, Woodberry Down, Clissold Park and Stoke Newington. Public toilets at Finsbury Park and Clissold Park
Public transport and break points:	LU: Highgate, Finsbury Park, Manor House. NR: Crouch Hill, Finsbury Park, Harringay Green Lanes, Stoke Newington. Buses at all these points plus Crouch End Hill and Lordship Grove
Links:	Parkland Walk, New River Path
Map:	Explorer 173
LWF status:	Pending validation
Principal promoter:	London Walking Forum, LB Haringey, LB Hackney
Further information:	See Capital Ring introduction

CHECK OPENING DATE – see Capital Ring introduction

Easy walking in surroundings that are surprisingly green in such a densely populated part of London. This is largely achieved by following most of the **Parkland Walk** (London's longest nature reserve) along a former railway line among trees and shrubs. You come to this very soon after the start near Highgate station – by using its Archway Road exit you avoid the steep climb mentioned in grid, which is only necessary for those continuing from Section 11 to Section 12.

After crossing the main East Coast railway line into Finsbury Park, you leave the Parkland Walk and skirt a small lake. A long stretch of road leads between the Stoke Newington Reservoirs, where you cross the **New River Path**, and into Clissold Park. Fittingly you pass two historic churches into Stoke Newington Church Street, whose cosmopolitan atmosphere is fed by a range of ethnic cuisines. Finally comes the wonderfully eerie Abney Park Cemetery, now a nature reserve, with drunkenly leaning tombstones surrounded by a wealth of greenery.

 The surface of the Parkland Walk is uneven and may be muddy. The entrance used by the Capital Ring into Abney Park Cemetery has seven steps, which can be avoided by continuing outside to the finish of the section at Stoke Newington station, with a level entrance nearby.

CAPITAL RING: SECTION 13 (MAPS 2, 5)
Stoke Newington to Hackney Wick

Distance:	6.5km (4.0miles) including link with Hackney Wick station
Location:	Hackney, Waltham Forest
Start:	Stamford Hill (GR 337-868)
Finish:	White Post Lane, Hackney Wick (GR 373-845)
Green factor:	77%
Blue factor:	77%
Recommended direction:	Northwest to southeast
Terrain and surface:	Almost entirely level with some short slopes. Mainly on towpath, narrow and rough surface in places. No stiles. 1.1km (0.7miles) beside roads
Points of interest:	Springfield Park, Lee Navigation, Walthamstow Marshes and nature reserve, Hackney Marsh
Signage:	Complete both ways – see Capital Ring introduction
Refreshments and toilets:	Pubs at Stoke Newington, Lea Bridge Road and Hackney Wick. Cafés at Stoke Newington and Hackney Wick. Toilets at Springfield Park
Public transport and break points:	NR: Stoke Newington, Clapton, Hackney Wick. Buses at all these points plus Clapton Common, Lea Bridge Road and Homerton Road

Links:	Lea Valley Walk, Walk Back in Time
Map:	Explorer 173
LWF status:	Validated with Seal of Approval (Mayor of London's key route)
Principal promoter:	London Walking Forum, LB Hackney, LB Waltham Forest
Further information:	See Capital Ring introduction

Easy walking along a section dominated by the Lee Navigation waterway, using its towpath, and with mainly green surroundings. From Stoke Newington the route follows residential roads into the very pleasant Springfield Park, which slopes down to the Lee Navigation. Along its towpath, shared with the **Lea Valley Walk** and **Walk Back in Time**, you may see an occasional narrowboat, and you pass Walthamstow Marshes, whose nature reserve merits a small diversion, and Hackney Marsh, crammed with football pitches.

 Mostly hard surface, but some stretches are on uneven ground. There is a short downward flight of steps in Springfield Park, with a steep and uneven earth ramp alongside (avoidable with a diversion), and some canal footbridges have steep slopes, sometimes ribbed.

CAPITAL RING: SECTION 14 (MAP 5, then 4 or 6)
Hackney Wick to Beckton District Park

Distance:	8.3km (5.1miles) including links with Hackney Wick and Royal Albert stations
Location:	Tower Hamlets, Newham
Start:	White Post Lane, Hackney Wick (GR 373-845)
Finish:	Beckton District Park (Stansfeld Road, GR 422-811)
Green factor:	51%
Blue factor:	9%
Recommended direction:	Northwest to southeast
Terrain and surface:	Almost entirely level on firm ground, with some short gentle slopes and one flight of steps. No stiles. 0.8km (0.5miles) beside roads
Points of interest:	Lee Navigation, Old Ford Lock, The Greenway, Bow Back Rivers, Abbey Mills Pumping Station, East London Cemetery, Beckton District Park
Signage:	Not signed at time of writing – see Capital Ring introduction

Refreshments and toilets:	Pubs at Hackney Wick and Plaistow. Cafés at Hackney Wick and Beckton District Park. Public toilets at Plaistow and Beckton District Park
Public transport and break points:	NR: Hackney Wick, West Ham. LU: West Ham, Plaistow. DLR: Pudding Mill Lane, Royal Albert. Buses at all these points (not Pudding Mill Lane) plus High Street Stratford, several points in Plaistow, Lonsdale Avenue and Tollgate Road (Beckton District Park)
Links:	Lea Valley Walk, Time Travellers, The Greenway, Heron Walk, Kingfisher Walk
Map:	Explorer 162
LWF status:	Pending validation
Principal promoter:	London Walking Forum, LB Tower Hamlets, LB Newham
Further information:	See Capital Ring introduction

CHECK OPENING DATE – see Capital Ring introduction

Incredibly, this easy section through a densely populated part of London manages to find a route that is almost completely without traffic. This is mainly achieved by following for 4.6km (2.9miles) *The Greenway*, an almost straight broad track running high between houses along the top of the Northern Outfall Sewer with a bonded gravel surface throughout. Note that The Greenway is a permissive path (see Route Closures, Strategic Network, Section 2), shared with cyclists and closed at night.

First, though, you follow the Lee Navigation towpath for a while, together with the *Lea Valley Walk* and *Time Travellers*. You join The Greenway at Old Ford Lock. At a railway line you must divert briefly from The Greenway through an industrial area, then you cross the intricate network of the Bow Back Rivers, used by the *Heron and Kingfisher Walks*. The palatial former Abbey Mills Pumping Station stars on the way to West Ham, then you have an aerial view over the East London Cemetery as you approach Plaistow. You leave The Greenway to cross Newham Way on a long footbridge, then enter Beckton District Park, where tree species are marked out for your information, and a small diversion can take you past its lake.

 The first 700m along the towpath are level but uneven – this can be avoided by starting at the west end of The Greenway in Wick Lane. Access points to The Greenway are ramped, as is the footbridge over Newham Way

On The Greenway near Pudding Mill Lane

CAPITAL RING: SECTION 15 (MAPS 4 or 6)
Beckton District Park to Woolwich Foot Tunnel

Distance:	6.6km (4.1miles) including links with Royal Albert and Woolwich Arsenal stations
Location:	Newham, Greenwich
Start:	Beckton District Park (Stansfeld Road, GR 422-811)
Finish:	Woolwich Foot Tunnel (south side, GR 432-793)
Green factor:	35%
Blue factor:	29%
Recommended direction:	Northwest to southeast
Terrain and surface:	Almost entirely level on tarmac paths or pavements. No stiles. 1.6km (1.0miles) beside roads
Points of interest:	Beckton District Park, New Beckton Park, UEL London Docklands Campus, Royal Albert and King George V Docks, London City Airport, Royal Victoria Gardens, River Thames, Woolwich Foot Tunnel
Signage:	Not signed at time of writing – see Capital Ring introduction
Refreshments and toilets:	Pubs and cafés at Cyprus, North Woolwich and Woolwich. Public toilets at New Beckton Park and Woolwich
Public transport and break points:	DLR: Royal Albert, Beckton Park, Cyprus, Gallions Reach. NR: North Woolwich, Woolwich Arsenal. Woolwich Free Ferry. Buses at all these points
Links:	Thames Path Southeast Extension
Map:	Explorer 162
LWF status:	Pending validation
Principal promoter:	London Walking Forum, LB Newham, LB Greenwich
Further information:	See Capital Ring introduction

CHECK OPENING DATE – see Capital Ring introduction

The easiest section of the Capital Ring, but full of surprises at every turn, and a complete contrast to everything that has gone before. Beckton District Park leads on through New Beckton Park to the Dockland Light Railway's ultramodern station at Cyprus. Ideally, the route would then continue through the remarkable London Docklands Campus of the University of East London. That is not yet possible, but it is well worth making a diversion to see the vast expanse of the Royal Albert Dock (now devoid of shipping but a well used watersports centre) and a row of colourful circular student apartments with butterfly wing roofs. There are also cafés here. Opposite is London City Airport, whose flight path you will soon pass under – but do not fear noise as all aircraft that use it must have engines that are relatively quiet.

Apartments at the University of East London (Docklands Campus)
beside Royal Albert Dock

After retracing your steps to Cyprus station, you cross the Gallions Roundabout to rejoin the Thames, where you walk on the river wall beside Gallions Reach. You pass the King George V Dock (also no longer in commercial use) and its entrance lock. You continue along the river wall bsdie Royal Victoria Gardens and past North Woolwich station to the Woolwich Foot Tunnel, which takes you under the Thames back to Capital Ring Section 1 at Woolwich. There are lifts (for operating times phone 020 8921 5493 or visit www.greenwich.gov.uk/council/ strategicplanning/foottun2.htm), but purists may prefer to use the spiral staircases, consisting of 126 steps on the north side and 101 on the south side. The footsore can use the Woolwich Free Ferry, but they will not then be able to claim to have completed the Capital Ring on foot!

 Most of the section is level with a hard surface, but some short stretches of the river wall have a rough surface and steps. This can be avoided by walking along the Woolwich Manor Way.

CELANDINE ROUTE (MAP 3)

Distance:	15.8km (9.9miles)
Location:	Harrow, Hillingdon
Start:	Pinner station (GR122-895)
Finish:	Grand Union Canal, Yiewsley (GR 057-809)
Green factor:	62%
Blue factor:	65%
Recommended direction:	Northeast to southwest
Terrain and surface:	Almost completely level, with some short slopes. Mostly rough riverside paths, tracks or grass, which may be muddy or flooded in wet weather. 4.9km (3.1miles) of roadwalking. Two stiles, one barrier to duck under
Points of interest:	Pinner village, River Pinn, Eastcote House grounds, Pynchester Moat, Swakeleys, Hillingdon Hill, Brunel University, St Lawrence Church at Cowley, Grand Union Canal
Signage:	Intermittent. Logo: blue celandine plant on yellow arrow with blue background
Refreshments and toilets:	Pubs and cafés at Pinner, Eastcote, Ruislip and Hillingdon Hill. Public toilets at Pinner, Ruislip, Hillingdon Hill and Yiewsley
Public transport and break points:	LU: Pinner, Hillingdon. NR: West Drayton (via London Loop). Buses at these points, also Eastcote Village, Ruislip, Swakeleys Road, Hillingdon Hill, Pield Heath Road and Yiewsley
Links:	Hillingdon Trail, West Ruislip to Gerrards Cross Ramble and Ride, London Loop, Grand Union Canal Walk
Map:	Explorers 172, 173
LWF status:	Pending validation
Principal promoter:	LB Harrow, LB Hillingdon
Further information:	Free leaflet (+ sae) from LB Harrow and LB Hillingdon libraries

This route, named after the lesser celandine plant that grows in woodlands in this area, provides easy walking, generally through woods and meadows beside the River Pinn. Pinner village is a pleasant place to start, and you are soon in Pinner Memorial Park with its lake. At Ruislip you cross the **Hillingdon Trail** and **West**

Ruislip to Gerrards Cross Ramble and Ride, and short diversions can be made to the grounds of the former Eastcote House, the remains of Pynchester Moat, and the Jacobean house, Swakeleys.

'The Case is Altered' pub at Eastcote

From Hillingdon southwards the river is less accessible, and lengthy diversions along roads are necessary. However, you get to see the attractive old buildings and church of Hillingdon Hill Conservation Area and the riverside campus of Brunel University. The route finishes on the **Grand Union Canal** at Yiewsley, where you also join Section 11 of the **London Loop**.

Chelsfield Circular Walk (Map 8)

Distance:	11.0km (6.9miles) including link with Chelsfield Green (station and car park)
Location:	Bromley, plus some in Kent
Start/finish:	Chelsfield Green (GR 469-641)
Green factor:	71%
Blue factor:	n/a
Recommended direction:	Clockwise
Terrain and surface:	Undulating with some gentle climbs. Mainly on rough paths, tracks and grass. 15 stiles. 1.8km (1.1miles) beside roads or on lanes
Points of interest:	Chelsfield Green, St Martin of Tours Church, Goddington House, farmland, woodland, Chelsfield village

Signage:	Almost complete both ways. Logo: 'Chelsfield Circular Walk' in yellow on dark green background, surrounding yellow arrow with white flash
Refreshments and toilets:	Pubs at Chelsham station, Chelsham village and Crockenhill. No public toilets nearby
Public transport and break points:	NR: Chelsfield. Buses: Chelsfield station, Chelsfield village, Crockenhill
Links:	Green Street Green Circular Walk
Map:	Explorers 147 and 162
LWF status:	Validated with Seal of Approval
Principal promoter:	LB Bromley
Further information:	Included in Pack Two of Bromley Circular Walks and Trails (£2.50 plus 50p p+p) from LB Bromley Leisure & Community Services and libraries

One of the *Bromley Circular Walks and Trails* series, this walk takes you into quite remote countryside, just crossing into Kent. The circuit starts and finishes at Chelsfield village, with a signed link to Chelsfield Green car park, close to the station, along a long and narrow green that is also part of the *Green Street Green Circular Walk.* You head for the spire of the little church of St Martin of Tours, then drop down across farmland into Goddington Park, with a distant view of its black and white mock Elizabethan manor.

Feeling ever more remote, you climb very gradually through flinty farmland, with fine vistas northwards across the Thames, to reach the furthest point of the circuit at the edge of Crockenhill village in Kent. The circuit is completed through more farmland and woods back to pretty Chelsfield village, which clusters around the brilliant white weatherboard Cross Hall, an old inn and some attractive cottages.

CHESSINGTON COUNTRYSIDE WALK (MAP 7)

Distance:	8.0km (5.0miles)
Location:	Kingston, plus some in Surrey
Start/finish:	Chessington South station (GR 179-633)
Green factor:	79%
Blue factor:	3%
Recommended direction:	Either way
Terrain and surface:	Mostly level on rough paths, tracks and grass. Some fairly steep ascents and descents. Seven stiles. 1.2km (0.8miles) beside roads

Points of interest:	Bonesgate Stream, Horton Country Park, Equestrian Centre, Epsom Common, Ashtead Common, Stew Pond, farmland, Chessington World of Adventures, Barwell Court Lake, Winey Hill viewpoint
Signage:	Complete both ways. Logo: 'Chessington Countryside Walk' and yellow lesser celandine flower on green and white background
Refreshments and toilets:	Pubs and cafés at Chessington. Public admitted to refreshment and toilet facilities at Horton Park Equestrian Centre and Chessington Golf Centre
Public transport and break points:	NR: Chessington South. Buses: Chessington, West Park Hospital, Leatherhead Road
Links:	Thames Down Link
Map:	Explorer 161
LWF status:	Validated with Seal of Approval
Principal promoter:	Lower Mole Project, RB Kingston
Further information:	Free leaflet (+ sae) from Lower Mole Project and RB Kingston libraries

Totem pole, Horton Country Park

A very green route through magnificent open countryside on the southern fringe of Greater London, dipping into Surrey. The leaflet is designed so that you can follow the route in either direction. Some paths and tracks are actually bridleways, shared with horseriders and cyclists – take care.

Going clockwise from Chessington South, you pass through Horton Country Park, where colourful green wood-peckers and jays may be seen. On Epsom Common you pass the tranquil Stew Pond, popular with anglers, then continue on to Ashtead Common and descend the fields of Rushett Farm. You may hear the shrieks of excited children as you pass through the car park of Chessington World of Adventures, then climb above Barwell Court Lake to Winey Hill. On a clear day the magnificent 360-degree panorama extends across Surrey and to the Telecom Tower and Canary Wharf in London.

CHIGWELL COUNTRY WALK (MAP 4)

Distance:	4.5km (2.8miles)
Location:	Entirely in Epping Forest District (Essex) but touches Redbridge boundary
Start/finish:	Grange Hill station (GR450-926)
Green factor:	78%
Blue factor:	n/a
Recommended direction:	Clockwise
Terrain and surface:	Undulating country, mostly on rough paths and tracks. Stiles: not known. 1.1km (0.7miles) beside roads
Points of interest:	Chigwell village, St Mary's Church, farmland, views
Signage:	Complete both ways. Logo
Refreshments and toilets:	Pubs at Grange Hill and Chigwell. No public toilets nearby
Public transport and break points:	LU: Grange Hill. Buses: Grange Hill, Chigwell
Links:	London Loop
Map:	Explorer 174
LWF status:	Pending validation
Principal promoter:	Epping Forest DC
Further information:	Included in pack Country Walks and Rides in Epping Forest District (£2.00 + sae) from Epping Forest DC Planning Services

This comparatively short and easy circular walk lies completely outside Greater London but just squeezes into this book as its start/finish point at Grange Hill station is right on the boundary with the London Borough of Redbridge. It also provides a link with Grange Hill station for the **London Loop**, with whose Section 20 the route is briefly shared.

The route follows footpaths and green lanes through undulating farmland and orchards on either side of Chigwell, with some fine views along the way. Chigwell is a pleasant village with a fine old church and the startlingly half-timbered King's Head Inn, featured (as the Maypole) in Charles Dickens's *Barnaby Rudge*.

This route is one of the series *Country Walks and Rides in Epping Forest District* promoted by Epping Forest District Council. The pack includes 10 other self-guided walks in various parts of the district, plus several cycle and horse rides.

COLNE VALLEY CIRCULAR WALKS

A pack of eight circular walks produced by Groundwork Thames Valley on behalf of a number of authorities funding the Colne Valley Park, which straddles the River Colne from Rickmansworth to Staines. Ranging in distance from 5 to 13km (3 to 8miles), four of the routes touch Greater London and are included in this book – see **Harefield Heights, Iver, Nine Stiles** and **Widewater Lock Circular Walks (Map 3)**. The other four, all outside Greater London, are the Chalfont Park, Old Shire Lane, Staines Moor and Wraysbury Circular Walks. Improvements on the ground are planned for all these routes, and the pack and leaflets are being updated. The price of the new pack was not available at time of writing – contact Groundwork Thames Valley for details.

COLNE VALEY RAMBLE AND RIDE SERIES

A series of walks devised by Groundwork Thames Valley to link stations, enabling you to walk one way and return by train. They are aimed at encouraging people to use public transport to reach the Colne Valley Regional Park. Two of the routes (**West Drayton to Slough** and **West Ruislip to Gerrards Cross**) start in Greater London and go out into Buckinghamshire. The others (both outside Greater London) are: Staines to Sunnymeads and Chorleywood or Rickmansworth to Gerrards Cross. Free leaflets (+ sae) for each route can be obtained from the Colne Valley Park Centre.

COLNE VALLEY TRAIL (MAP 3)

Distance:	12.5km (7.8miles)
Location:	Hillingdon, plus some in Buckinghamshire and Hertfordshire
Start:	Uxbridge station (GR 056-841)
Finish:	Rickmansworth (Riverside Drive, GR 056-942)
Green factor:	71%
Blue factor:	63%
Recommended direction:	South to north
Terrain and surface:	Mostly level but with some steep climbs away from the valley. Mixture of hard towpaths and rough footpaths and tracks. No stiles. 1.2km (0.8miles) beside roads
Points of interest:	Grand Union Canal, River Colne, Denham Country Park, canal locks and marinas, lakes (flooded gravel pits), Frays Valley Local Nature Reserve, Rickmansworth Aquadrome

Signage:	Complete both ways
Refreshments and toilets:	Pubs at Uxbridge, Widewater Lock, Coppermill Lock and Rickmansworth. Cafés at Uxbridge, Denham Lock and Rickmansworth. Public toilets at Uxbridge and Rickmansworth
Public transport and break points:	LU: Uxbridge, Rickmansworth. NR: Denham, Rickmansworth. Buses at all these points plus South Harefield and Harefield
Links:	Colne Valley Way, London Loop, Grand Union Canal Walk, Nine Stiles Circular Walk, Widewater Lock Circular Walk, West Ruislip to Gerrards Cross Ramble and Ride, Hillingdon Trail, Harefield Heights Circular Walk
Map:	Explorer 172 (route marked)
LWF status:	Pending validation
Principal promoter:	Groundwork Thames Valley
Further information:	Free leaflet (+ sae) from Colne Valley Park Centre

Mostly easy waterside walking, but with some steep climbs where the route leaves the canalside. About a third of the route follows the towpath of the *Grand Union Canal Walk*, also used here by Sections 12 and 13 of the *London Loop* and several other routes (see Links above). You are in the valley of the River Colne all the way, but only see the river briefly where it comes close to the canal.

You should see plenty of waterborne activity, in the form of birds, narrowboats and anglers, and boats using locks are always a focus of interest, but beware of cyclists and joggers coming up fairly fast from behind. Elsewhere, you walk beside or close to disused gravel pits and water-filled former quarries that make excellent nature reserves. Between Coppermill and Springwell Locks you climb out of the valley for a while to follow a bridleway through woods, providing good views and a different perspective of the valley. The route finishes by going through the park known as Rickmansworth Aquadrome, where watersports of various kinds may be seen.

Note that at time of writing it is planned to combine this route with the *Colne Valley Way* further south to form one route of about 30km (19miles) from Rickmansworth to Staines. Some route changes may take place at that time.

COLNE VALLEY WAY (MAP 3)

Distance:	16.5km (10.3miles)
Location:	Hillingdon, but mostly in Surrey, Berkshire and Buckinghamshire
Start:	Staines (Ashby Lammas Recreation Ground, GR 030-718)
Finish:	Cowley Lock (GR 052-822)
Green factor:	Not known
Blue factor:	Not known
Recommended direction:	South to north
Terrain and surface:	Fairly level but some slopes, mostly on rough paths and tracks. One stile. Distance beside roads: not known
Points of interest:	River Thames, Staines Moor, River Colne, King George VI and Wraysbury Reservoirs, Arthur Jacob Nature Reserve, Colnbrook village, Old Slade Nature Reserve and lake, Colne Brook, Grand Union Canal, Cowley Lock
Signage:	Complete both ways
Refreshments and toilets:	Pubs at Staines, Colnbrook, Little Britain, Cowley. Cafés and public toilets at Staines
Public transport and break points:	NR: Staines, Iver. Buses at Staines, Colnbrook, Iver, Cowley
Links:	Thames Path National Trail, Colne Valley Trail, Grand Union Canal (Slough Arm), Iver Circular Walk, London Loop, West Drayton to Slough Ramble and Ride, Beeches Way
Map:	Explorers 160, 172 (route marked)
LWF status:	Pending validation
Principal promoter:	Groundwork Thames Valley
Further information:	Free leaflet (+ sae) from Colne Valley Park Centre

Fairly gentle walking along the Colne Valley Regional Park. At time of writing this route is due to be absorbed into the extended **Colne Valley Trail**, when some route changes may take place. From the River Thames near Staines (a short walk from the town centre and **Thames Path National Trail**) you cross Staines Moor, an ancient pasture that has remained unploughed for at least a thousand years. You then pass the embankments of two enormous reservoirs (King George VI and Wraysbury) and visit the Arthur Jacob Nature Reserve and Colnbrook village.

There follows a stretch where you pass under the Heathrow Airport flight path, then some major roads, but despite this there are some very green stretches where wildlife has made a home, particularly between the Colnbrook Bypass and the M4 at Thorney Park. From there (in company with several other routes – see above) you follow the **Grand Union Canal (Slough Arm)**, then the River Colne, passing the charming Little Britain Lake to finish at Cowley Lock, where you meet the **Grand Union Canal Walk**.

COULSDON COMMON & HAPPY VALLEY CIRCULAR WALK (MAP 7A)

Distance:	5.3km (3.3miles)
Location:	Croydon, plus some in Surrey
Start/finish:	Coulsdon Common (Fox Lane, GR 319-569)
Green factor:	98%
Blue factor:	2%
Recommended direction:	Clockwise
Terrain and surface:	Generally level but several steep ascents and descents. Mostly on rough paths, tracks or grass. No stiles. 0.7km (0.4miles) beside roads
Points of interest:	Coulsdon Common, Happy Valley Park, farmland
Signage:	None
Refreshments and toilets:	Pub at Fox Lane. No public toilets nearby
Public transport and break points:	Buses: Fox Lane
Links:	London Loop, Farthing Downs & Devilsden Wood Circular Walk, Downlands Circular Walk, Socratic Trail
Map:	Explorer 146
LWF status:	Pending validation
Principal promoter:	Corporation of London
Further information:	Included in free pack (+ sae) *Coulsdon Commons Circular Walks* from Corporation of London West Wickham and Coulsdon Commons and Downlands Project

This route in the Corporation of London's **Coulsdon Commons Circular Walks** series is one of the greenest and most attractive in the network, but you will need plenty of energy for some steep climbs along the way.

The circuit (almost a figure-of-eight) starts and finishes at the highest point of the walk, altitude 175m (575ft) on Coulsdon Common, south of Old Coulsdon, which is also crossed by Section 5 of the **London Loop**. After a gentle start you descend into Happy Valley, an idyllic setting of woods and grassland where rare plants can be found, and you would scarcely believe you are in the London Borough of Croydon. Several other routes in the Strategic Network come together here (see above). You climb very steeply back up to Coulsdon Common and more level walking for a while, but keep some strength in reserve, as the sting is in the tail. Towards the end, as you cross dry valleys on the east side of the common, there are three steep descents in succession, followed of course by three steep ascents. Finally you pass the Corporation of London depot at Merlewood and a pond before returning to Fox Lane.

COULSDON COMMONS CIRCULAR WALKS (MAP 7)

A set of four circular walks devised by the Corporation of London in very attractive countryside in the southern part of Croydon borough, extending into Surrey. See the individual entries for the **Coulsdon Common & Happy Valley, Farthing Downs & Devilsden Wood, Kenley Common & Dollypers Hill** and **Riddlesdown Circular Walks**. The four route descriptions are available in a free pack (plus sae) available from Corporation of London West Wickham and Coulsdon Commons and the Downlands Project. Although they do not touch, the Coulsdon Common and Farthing Downs routes come close enough to enable you to combine them into a satisfying (though energetic) full day's walk.

The background to these areas is interesting. In the late 19th century, when much of the countryside around London was threatened with large scale development, the Corporation of London acquired several large tracts of land to preserve them for public recreation. They included six open spaces on or near the London/Surrey border: Coulsdon Common, Farthing Downs, Kenley Common, Riddlesdown, Spring Park and West Wickham Common. Others included Epping Forest and Burnham Beeches, and more recently Hampstead Heath.

CRANE VALLEY – see River Crane Walk

CRANHAM CIRCULAR WALK (MAP 4)

Distance:	7.3km (4.6miles)
Location:	Havering
Start/finish:	Stubbers Outdoor Pursuits Centre, Ockenden Road, near Corbets Tey (GR 574-847)
Green factor:	90%
Blue factor:	n/a
Recommended direction:	Clockwise
Terrain and surface:	Almost completely level, with one short gentle slope and a short flight of steps. Mostly on rough paths, tracks and grass. 1 stile. 0.7km (0.4miles) beside roads

Points of interest:	Russell's Lake, Cranham Marsh Nature Reserve, Cranham Hall, All Saints Church, Spring Wood
Signage:	Almost complete, clockwise only. Logo: green 'Circular Walk' on white background
Refreshments and toilets:	None
Public transport and break points:	Buses: Ockenden Road
Links:	Upminster Circular Walk
Map:	Explorer 175
LWF status:	Pending validation
Principal promoter:	LB Havering
Further information:	Free leaflet *Cranham Area* from LB Havering libraries

Cranham Hall and All Saints' Church

A fairly short, easy and very pleasant walk in the **Countryside Footpaths in Havering** series. It starts and finishes beside Russell's Lake at the car park of Stubbers Outdoor Pursuits Centre, served by bus from Romford and Upminster. A link path leads between Stubbers and Cranham Marsh Nature Reserve where the circuit proper starts – actually a lopsided figure-of-eight, partly shared with the **Upminster Circular Walk**.

First you follow the smaller loop around South Marsh and through Spring Wood, both rich in wildlife. Spring Wood contains some of the tallest ash trees in Essex. The larger loop passes idyllic Cranham Hall, and goes through the churchyard of All Saints to fields and duckponds beyond. You pass under the Upminster–Grays railway line then follow a straight lane for a while – it has no pavement so you must take care. A new woodland, Great Barn Wood, is to be created here. You skirt more fields with a different perspective of Cranham Hall and church, then return along the link path to Stubbers.

CRAY RIVERWAY (MAP 6)

Distance:	22.0km (13.7miles)
Location:	Bromley, Bexley
Start:	Orpington Library (Aynscombe Angle, GR 466-666)
Finish:	Erith (Manor Road, GR 525-776)
Green factor:	55%
Blue factor:	41%
Recommended direction:	South to north
Terrain and surface:	Almost entirely level, just a few short gentle slopes. Mostly on pavements and tarmac paths, but some on rough paths or grass. Two stiles. 6.4km (4.0miles) beside roads
Points of interest:	River Cray, Orpington Library and Museum, Priory Gardens, Riverside Gardens, St Mary Cray village and church, St Paul's Cray water meadows, village and church, Foots Cray Meadows, Five Arch Bridge, Old Bexley village, Hall Place, Churchfield Wood, Crayford Marshes, Darent raised dam, River Thames
Signage:	Bromley: Partial, both ways. Logo: 'Cray Riverway' in yellow on dark green background, surrounding yellow arrow with pale blue flash. Bexley: Almost complete both ways. Fingerposts: Blue or yellow text on grey background
Refreshments and toilets:	Pubs and cafés at Orpington, St Mary Cray, St Paul's Cray, Foots Cray, Sidcup Place Park, Old Bexley, Hall Place, Crayford and Erith. Public toilets at Orpington, St Mary Cray, Sidcup Place Park, Old Bexley, Hall Place, and Crayford
Public transport and break points:	NR/buses: Orpington, St Mary Cray, Bexley, Crayford, Slade Green, Erith
Links:	St Mary Cray and St Paul's Cray Circular Walks, London Loop, Shuttle Riverway, Thames Path Southeast Extension
Map:	Explorer 162
LWF status:	Pending validation
Principal promoter:	LB Bromley, LB Bexley
Further information:	Bromley section: Included in Pack Two of Bromley Circular Walks and Trails (£2.50 plus 50p p+p) from LB Bromley Leisure & Community Services and libraries. Bexley section: Free leaflet from LB Bexley libraries and council offices

Most of this route is pleasant and easy walking along a narrow green strip in urban surroundings, beside or close to the River Cray, with a bonus at the end in quite remote countryside beside two more rivers, the Darent and Thames. However, there is one long road section north of St Paul's Cray, which includes a stretch without pavement where you must take great care. The route is effectively divided in two sections administered by Bromley and Bexley – hopefully they will be able to produce co-ordinated signage and route description in due course.

From the start beside Orpington Library and Museum the route immediately enters pretty Priory Gardens, passing several large ponds filled with waterbirds. At Riverside Gardens, where the Cray emerges from a culvert, you skirt another pond to enter the ancient village of St Mary Cray. From here to the end of Bromley's section, the route is all beside roads at present, but St Paul's Cray is an attractive village with lovely water meadows, church, village green and weatherboarded pub. The route is shared in places with the *St Mary Cray* and *St Paul's Cray Circular Walks.*

St Paul's Cray Water Meadows

At Foots Cray, and for the rest of the route through Bexley borough to Erith, you are in company with Section 2 of the **London Loop**, starting with idyllic Foots Cray Meadows, where you pass the ancient Five Arch Bridge. The river is currently inaccessible through Old Bexley, so there are two alternative routes away from the river, either via Old Bexley village, passing Bexley station, or using paths and tracks through farmland and woodland. The alternatives reunite at historic Hall Place, close to the **Shuttle Riverway**. Two more diversions from the riverside are necessary, at Crayford and Barnes Cray, then the route stays beside the Cray all the way to its confluence with the River Darent at Crayford Marshes, rich in wildlife.

The Cray Riverway continues through remote countryside beside the Darent, past an impressive raised dam, then along the south bank of the Thames, here a kilometre (half a mile) wide, with a good view of the Queen Elizabeth II Bridge. The route finishes at Manor Road in Erith, and you can continue with the London Loop and **Thames Path Southeast Extension** to Erith town centre and station.

♿ As far as St Paul's Cray the route is almost entirely level with a hard surface and dropped kerbs, but a 100m stretch in Riverside Gardens is on earth or grass. North of St Paul's Cray much of the route is on narrow or rough paths and grass, or road without pavement, so may not be suitable.

CROSSNESS PATHWAY – see Thames Path Southeast Extension

CUDHAM CIRCULAR WALK (MAP 8)

Distance:	12.9km (8.1miles), or shorter option of 9.1km (5.7miles)
Location:	Bromley
Start/finish:	Cudham Recreation Ground, Cudham Lane South (GR 446-597)
Green factor:	94%
Blue factor:	n/a
Recommended direction:	Clockwise
Terrain and surface:	Undulating country with some steep hills. Mostly on rough paths, tracks and grass. 14 stiles (16 on shorter route). 0.8km (0.5miles) beside roads
Points of interest:	Cudham church, birthplace of Little Tich, farmland, woodland, Biggin Hill Airport, Downe village, High Elms Country Park
Signage:	Almost complete both ways. Logo: 'Cudham Circular Walk' in yellow on dark green background, surrounding yellow arrow with pale green flash. Some older signs still in place bearing stylised green 'CCW' on white background
Refreshments and toilets:	Pubs at Cudham and Downe. Public toilets at Cudham
Public transport and break points:	Buses at Cudham and Downe
Links:	Berry's Green, Leaves Green, Farnborough and Green Street Green Circular Walks, London Loop
Map:	Explorer 147
LWF status:	Validated with Seal of Approval
Principal promoter:	LB Bromley
Further information:	Included in Pack One of *Bromley Circular Walks and Trails* (£2.50 plus 50p p+p) from LB Bromley Leisure & Community Services and libraries

One of the **Bromley Circular Walks and Trails** series, this fine walk in rolling countryside south of Bromley is almost entirely green, with just a couple of short stretches along quiet country lanes. It straddles the long, deep and narrow valley that pokes into the foothills of the North Downs southwest of Orpington, which you cross twice. There are some smaller valleys to cross too, but most of the walking is along contour lines or on gentle slopes.

The route starts, together with the **Berry's Green Circular Walk**, high up at altitude 185m (607ft) in Cudham Recreation Ground. It soon passes the attractive church and the pretty Blacksmiths Arms pub, birthplace of Little Tich, a great music-hall artist of the early 20th century. After crossing farmland in the main valley, you contour above West Kent Golf Course, with Biggin Hill Airport opposite, where you are likely to see several light aircraft movements. The route skirts Downe village, home of Charles Darwin, and passes through High Elms Country Park, where you join Section 3 of the **London Loop** for a while. This area is a meeting point of several other routes in the *Bromley Circular Walks and Trails* series (see grid), so there are many opportunities to combine routes. Finally you cross the main valley again, then climb steadily back to Cudham through more farmland.

The shorter option passes through Downe Bank Nature Reserve and has two long flights of steps (one down, one up).

DIANA, PRINCESS OF WALES MEMORIAL WALK (MAP 5)

A truly astonishing exploration of some of London's most famous sights, as listed below, with many stunning views. There are plenty of less well known fascinations to discover too, such as St Govor's Well in Kensington Gardens, whose message can only be read if you walk round it six times! The route has a hard surface throughout, providing easy walking with just a few gentle slopes in mostly green surroundings and often beside water. It is a lopsided figure-of-eight, with its hub at Hyde Park Corner – the obvious place to start and finish, but any point along the route serves just as well. The route is even more enjoyable on Sundays, when The Mall and Constitution Hill are closed to traffic.

One of the impressive signs marking the Diana, Princess of Wales Memorial Walk

Distance:	11.8km (7.4miles)
Location:	Westminster, Kensington & Chelsea
Start/finish:	Hyde Park Corner (GR 284-798) – see text
Green factor:	85%
Blue factor:	25%
Recommended direction:	Either way
Terrain and surface:	Almost completely level, some gentle slopes, on hard surface throughout. No stiles. 1.5km (0.9miles) beside roads
Points of interest:	Green Park, The Mall, St James's Park and lake, Horse Guards, Birdcage Walk, Buckingham Palace, Constitution Hill, Wellington Arch, Hyde Park Corner, Hyde Park, The Serpentine, Kensington Gardens, the Italian Gardens, Peter Pan statue, The Round Pond, Kensington Palace, Albert Memorial, Royal Albert Hall, Serpentine Gallery, Rotten Row
Signage:	Complete both ways (see text)
Refreshments and toilets:	Cafés, kiosks and public toilets at frequent intervals in the parks. Pubs at various points outside the parks
Public transport and break points:	LU: Green Park, St James's Park, Hyde Park Corner, Lancaster Gate, Queensway. Buses at or near all these points, also at Palace Gate and Royal Albert Hall
Links:	Jubilee Walkway
Map:	Explorer 173
LWF status:	Pending validation
Principal promoter:	Royal Parks Agency
Further information:	Free leaflet available from Royal Parks Agency and park administration offices. Souvenir guidebook *A Walk for Diana* (Royal Parks Agency £9.95 plus £1.50 p&p, ISBN 0-9531426-6-3)

You follow what must surely be the most impressive signage of any route in London. It consists of a slightly raised steel and brass disc set in the ground, some 50cm (20in) diameter, moulded in the shape of a heraldic rose. Footprinted arrows attached to most discs point the way, and at some places an additional outer disc names the location. Fingerposts are used at Hyde Park Corner. The only other signed route permitted in these Royal Parks is the **Jubilee Walkway**, which you approach in St James's Park and at Buckingham Palace.

The route is completely accessible throughout, as are most of the public toilets in the parks. The slope at The Dell in Hyde Park is steep but short.

DISCOVER NEW ADDINGTON (MAP 7)

Distance:	4.7km (2.9miles)
Location:	Croydon
Start:	Homestead Way, New Addington(GR 391-615)
Finish:	Lodge Lane, New Addington (GR 375-636)
Green factor:	94%
Blue factor:	n/a
Recommended direction:	South to north
Terrain and surface:	Downhill or level most of the way. Mostly on grass; otherwise rough paths or tracks. No stiles. 0.3km (0.2miles) beside roads
Points of interest:	Woodland and parkland
Signage:	Complete both ways. White arrows on wooden posts bearing vertical text 'Discover New Addington'
Refreshments and toilets:	Pub, fast food outlets and public toilet in central New Addington. Pub at Addington village
Public transport and break points:	Buses: Homestead Way and Lodge Lane. CTL: Addington Village Interchange (Lodge Lane)
Links:	None
Map:	Explorer 161
LWF status:	Pending validation
Principal promoter:	LB Croydon
Further information:	No leaflet available at time of writing

A surprisingly green route through New Addington, a high-lying town to the southeast of central Croydon. Developed mainly during the 1950s in the foothills of the North Downs, and at first stark and forbidding, the town has matured with time and growth of greenery into a pleasant hilltop community.

The route can be walked in either direction; however, with a substantial end-to-end drop of around 70m (230ft), it is better to go south–north, then it is almost all level or downhill. Although there is at present no printed route description, the arrowposts are easily spotted and followed. The first half of the route follows an almost continuous belt of open spaces, and the only main road you encounter is crossed through a subway. This leads to a succession of woodlands along the town's eastern border, and the route finishes with a level walk through another playing field leading to Addington Village Interchange, recently developed as a focal point for buses and trams in the area.

DOG ROSE RAMBLE (MAP 3)

Distance:	12.5km (7.8miles)
Location:	Hillingdon, Ealing
Start/finish:	Kingshill Avenue, Hayes (GR 103-829), or Northolt station (GR 132-845)
Green factor:	64%
Blue factor:	27%
Recommended direction:	Anticlockwise
Terrain and surface:	Generally flat with one longish gentle climb and a couple of short steep slopes. Mainly on rough paths, tracks and grass which may get very wet and muddy after rain. No stiles. 1.9km (1.2miles) beside roads
Points of interest:	Yeading Brook, Grand Union Canal, Willowtree Marina, Northolt & Greenford Countryside Park, West London Mosque, St Mary's Church, Northolt Green, Islip Manor Park
Signage:	Almost complete both ways. Logo: deep pink dog rose on yellow arrow on deep pink background
Refreshments and toilets:	Pubs at Yeading and Northolt. Restaurant and toilets at Willowtree Marina
Public transport and break points:	LU: Northolt. Buses: Kingshill Avenue, Yeading Lane, Ruislip Road, Northolt
Links:	Hillingdon Trail, Grand Union Canal Walk
Map:	Explorers 172 and 173 (route marked)
LWF status:	Validated with Seal of Approval
Principal promoter:	LB Ealing, LB Hillingdon
Further information:	Free leaflet (+ sae) from LB Ealing and LB Hillingdon libraries

The circular Dog Rose Ramble takes its name from the plant that can be seen along this surprisingly green route in such an apparently unpromising part of London. Much of it follows the line of Yeading Brook (shared with the **Hillingdon Trail**), but you do not see much of that well known West London watercourse as it lies behind bushes most of the way. However, water enthusiasts will not be disappointed as you join the **Grand Union Canal Walk** for nearly a third of the route. The official leaflet claims the route distance as 16km (10miles), which seems to be an overestimate.

St Mary's Church, Northolt

Although the official start/finish point is at Kingshill Avenue in a remote corner of Hayes, the route can easily be joined just over halfway round from Northolt station along Mandeville Road to Point 13 on the official route description. Then you will finish at Northolt Green, a lovely grassy spot beside a tinkling stream with two pubs nearby.

Starting from Northolt, a pleasant walk through Islip Manor Park leads via a footbridge over the busy A40 Western Avenue to a golf course and rural Sharvel Lane, pervaded by farmyard fragrances. Do not be perturbed by the sound of gunfire – this comes from the West London Shooting Ground and is well under control behind high earth banks!

You join Yeading Brook at the remote 'Golden Bridge', actually a modern concrete structure on the site of a historic crossing point. A long stretch on rough and grassy paths follows, through brookside playing fields, crossing several roads including Kingshill Avenue. Then comes the canal towpath, or you can divert along the opposite bank to take in the colourful Willowtree Marina. You pass the headquarters of construction giants Taylor Woodrow – not without interest as their yard contains intriguing sections of structures awaiting transport, and the company has made the area look quite attractive.

You leave the canal beside the West London Mosque, then a climb through Belvue Park is rewarded with a glimpse of picturesque St Mary's Church and the delights of Northolt Green.

DOLLIS VALLEY GREENWALK (MAP 2)

Distance:	16.5km (10.3miles)
Location:	Barnet
Start:	Moat Mount car park (Barnet Way, Edgware, GR 210-941)
Finish:	Hampstead Heath extension (Meadway Close, Hampstead Garden Suburb, GR 259-882)
Green factor:	78%
Blue factor:	65%
Recommended direction:	North to south
Terrain and surface:	Generally level on mixed rough and tarmac paths, some grass. Some steepish climbs at north and south ends. One stile. 2.0km (1.3miles) beside roads
Points of interest:	Dollis Brook, Mutton Brook, River Brent, Moat Mount Local Nature Reserve, Totteridge Fields, Brook Farm Open Space, Whetstone Stray, Windsor Open Space, Little Wood, Big Wood, Hampstead Heath extension
Signage:	Almost complete, both ways. Discs: white arrow and 'Dollis Valley Greenwalk' on dark green background. Some fingerposts
Refreshments and toilets:	The only facilities close to the route are cafés at Temple Fortune. Several minutes' walk off route there are pubs or cafés at Barnet, Whetstone, Finchley, Hampstead Garden Suburb and Hampstead. No public toilets nearby
Public transport and break points:	Buses: Barnet Way, Hampstead Garden Suburb and at frequent intervals along the route. LU: High Barnet, Totteridge & Whetstone, Woodside Park, West Finchley, Finchley Central, Golders Green
Links:	London Loop, Moat Mount Walk, Barnet Totteridge Loop, Capital Ring
Map:	Explorer 173 (route marked)
LWF status:	Validated with Seal of Approval
Principal promoter:	LB Barnet
Further information:	Free leaflets (+ sae), in two sections: *Moat Mount to Woodside Park* and *Woodside Park to Hampstead Heath*, from LB Barnet libraries and council offices

A generally easy and very green walk reaching from open country right up to Hampstead Heath, with little roadwalking, and mostly beside Dollis Brook or Mutton Brook, tributaries of the River Brent. There are a few steepish climbs at either end, elsewhere the path undulates and meanders gently through brookside open spaces and woodland strips that separate residential districts of North London.

The start lies close to a bus route. The first third is shared with Section 16 of the **London Loop,** and for short distances with the **Moat Mount Walk** and **Barnet-Totteridge Loop.** Note that a permissive path (see Route Closures section in the Introduction) west of Hendon Wood Lane is closed each year on 28 February, but can be avoided on alternative paths nearby. Dollis Brook is not encountered until Totteridge Fields, some 2.5km (1.5miles) from the start, but is then a fairly constant companion. Occasionally you must follow short diversions along roads where the brook is inaccessible.

Beyond Finchley the route passes under several busy main roads, where the River Brent is formed by the confluence of Dollis Brook and Mutton Brook. You now follow the latter eastwards past Temple Fortune, together with Section 11 of the **Capital Ring.** The final section climbs away from the brook through Little Wood and Big Wood to the pleasant avenues of Hampstead Garden Suburb. The finish is on Hampstead Heath near a bus route, but you can continue further south across the heath for a further 2km (1.25 miles) into cosmopolitan Hampstead village, with its huge choice of pubs, bistros and cafés.

Totteridge Park, with
London Loop main signpost

From Moat Mount to Leeside in Barnet the route is uneven and steep in places, with several kissing gates. It is then mostly on undulating tarmac, however there are several fairly short stretches where the surface is uneven and the path is narrow: north of Woodside Park, south of Dollis Road and at Temple Fortune. The final stretch past the North Circular Road includes some steep slopes

Downlands Circular Walk (Map 7)

Distance:	10.7km (6.7miles). Shorter option 4.8km (3.0miles)
Location:	Croydon, partly in Surrey
Start/finish:	Farthing Downs (top car park, GR 302-572) or Coulsdon Common (Fox Lane, GR 318-568)
Green factor:	92%
Blue factor:	n/a
Recommended direction:	Anticlockwise
Terrain and surface:	Mainly level but with some steep slopes, on rough paths, tracks and grass. 9 stiles. 0.7km (0.4miles) beside roads
Points of interest:	Farthing Downs, Devilsden Wood, Coulsdon Common, Happy Valley, farmland, Chaldon church, Alderstead Heath, North Downs, Pilgrims Way, Piles Wood
Signage:	Complete both ways. Logo: green flower on white background plus text 'Downlands Circular Walk'
Refreshments and toilets:	Pubs at Coulsdon Common and Stanstead Road. Occasional kiosk at Farthing Downs. Public toilets at Farthing Downs
Public transport and break points:	Buses: Coulsdon Common, Chaldon
Links:	London Loop, Farthing Downs and Devilsden Wood Circular Walk, Coulsdon Common and Happy Valley Circular Walk, Socratic Trail, North Downs Way
Map:	Explorer 146
LWF status:	Validated with Seal of Approval
Principal promoter:	Downlands Project
Further information:	Free leaflet (+ sae) from Downlands Project. Some details are included on the Downlands Project page on www.countryside-management.org.uk

One of the greenest routes in the network, covering really lovely countryside in the North Downs on the fringes of Greater London and into Surrey. There are two alternative starting points, on Farthing Downs or Coulsdon Common, both with car parks and on Section 5 of the **London Loop**. With public transport you may prefer Coulsdon Common as Farthing Downs is 2.0km (1.3miles) from the nearest transport (Coulsdon South station).

From either start you proceed downhill through woods into the aptly named Happy Valley, a glorious swathe of grassland, rising steeply on either side into the surrounding woodland. In spring and summer the whole area is ablaze with flowers, including orchids and the rare greater yellow rattle. It is the meeting point of several routes, as indicated in the grid. You climb steadily into the North Downs, at first through farmland, then past historic Chaldon church with its fine wall painting. Wooded Alderstead Heath was a secret food store during the Second World War, and Tollsworth Manor was for a time Chaldon Youth Hostel. You join the **North Downs Way** for a ridge walk that reaches altitude 220m (722ft), and an optional spur of the Downlands Circular Walk continues with it for a kilometre (half a mile) to the Harrow pub.

Descending gently at first from the ridge you walk through the widely spread Chaldon village, on a lane with no pavement where care is needed. The descent steepens beside Piles Wood back to Happy Valley and your chosen finish point.

DUKE OF NORTHUMBERLAND'S RIVER – see River Crane Walk

EASTBROOKEND TIMBERLAND TRAIL (MAP 4)

Distance:	5.2km (3.3miles)
Location:	Barking & Dagenham
Start/finish:	Becontree Heath (Dagenham Civic Centre, Rainham Road, GR 495-868)
Green factor:	97%
Blue factor:	7%
Recommended direction:	Northwest to southeast
Terrain and surface:	Mostly level, some gentle slopes. No stiles. No walking beside roads (one road to cross)
Points of interest:	Dagenham Civic Centre, Central Park, Eastbrookend Country Park, Millennium Centre, lake, viewing mound, The Chase Nature Reserve
Signage:	Complete both ways. Discs have stylised tree and 'Eastbrookend Timberland Trail'
Refreshments and toilets:	Cafés and toilets at the Civic Centre, Central Park Pavilion and Millennium Centre
Public transport and break points:	Buses: Becontree Heath, Dagenham Road, Dagenham East. LU: Dagenham East
Links:	None
Map:	Explorers 174 and 175
LWF status:	Pending validation

Principal promoter:	LB Barking & Dagenham
Further information:	Free leaflet (+ sae) from Eastbrookend Country Park, also LB Barking & Dagenham libraries and council offices

A short and easy circular route along a green corridor between Dagenham and Romford, very walker friendly with just one road to cross. Created with support from Timberland, the shoe and outdoor clothing manufacturers, it is one of only 12 such trails in the country, one in each of the community forests – in this case Thames Chase.

From Dagenham Civic Centre the route goes through Central Park, Eastbrookend Country Park and The Chase Nature Reserve, passing a viewing mound and a lake. At the south end of the country park, a link leads in 1.2km (0.8miles) to Dagenham East station. However, the borough council is planning a separate route (Dagenham Village Trail) which will extend across the railway line, beside the River Beam and round to Allard Road – this would provide a continuous linear route of nearly 6km (3.8miles).

EPPING FOREST CENTENARY WALK (MAP 4)

Distance:	24.7km (15.4miles)
Location:	Newham, Redbridge, Waltham Forest, plus some in Essex
Start:	Manor Park station (GR 419-857)
Finish:	Epping station (GR 462-015)
Green factor:	80%
Blue factor:	10%
Recommended direction:	South to north
Terrain and surface:	Undulating with some steep slopes, mostly on rough paths and tracks. No stiles. 1.7km (1.1miles) beside roads
Points of interest:	Wanstead Flats, Alexandra Lake, Epping Forest, Bullrush Pond, Highams Park and lake, River Ching, Queen Elizabeth's Hunting Lodge, Connaught Water, Epping Forest Conservation Centre, Ambresbury Banks, Epping town
Signage:	None
Refreshments and toilets:	Pubs at Manor Park, Leytonstone, Chingford, High Beach and Epping. Cafés at Manor Park, Leytonstone, Chingford, Bell Common and Epping. Public toilets at Wanstead Flats, Leytonstone, High Beach and Epping

Public transport and break points:	LU: Leytonstone, Wanstead, Snaresbrook and Epping. NR: Manor Park, Wanstead Park, Leytonstone High Road, Wood Street Walthamstow, Highams Park and Chingford. Buses at all these points plus Lake House Road, Snaresbrook Road, Waterworks Corner, Chingford Hatch, Whitehall Road, Goldings Hill and Bell Common
Links:	London Loop, London Countryway, Three Forests Way
Map:	Explorer 174 (route marked)
LWF status:	Pending validation
Principal promoter:	Ramblers' Association
Further information:	Booklet (£1.00 plus 30p p+p, Fred Matthews and Harry Bitten, ISBN 0-85203-021-5) from Epping Forest Information Centre (Corporation of London)

A very green route that starts easily on Wanstead Flats but becomes more strenuous in places as it progresses northwards. It was created to celebrate the centenary in 1978 of the Epping Forest Act of 1878, whereby the Corporation of London acquired the forest for the enjoyment of Londoners. The route was designed by Fred Matthews and Harry Bitten of the Ramblers' Association's West Essex Group, with support from the Corporation of London. It forms the handle of a trident of long distance routes leading from London across East Anglia, to Cambridge, Harwich and Bradwell-on-Sea, together with the Three Forests Way, Essex Way and Harcamlow Way.

From the start at Manor Park station the route crosses Wanstead Flats, close to Alexandra Lake – the first of several lakes and ponds along the route. The greenery is of the open kind for the first few kilometres, interrupted by the busy Green Man Roundabout at Leytonstone, then you come to the first wooded part of Epping Forest by Snaresbrook, forming a long and narrow green lung between the suburbs. For most of the remainder of the walk you are among trees, crossing the occasional road and with frequent open areas including The Highams Park with its lake, and for a while you walk beside the River Ching.

At Chingford you cross Section 19 of the **London Loop** by the historic Queen Elizabeth's Hunting Lodge. Now you leave London's built-up area to skirt serene Connaught Water and enter a fairly remote section of the forest. At High Beach you pass the Epping Forest Conservation Centre, and cross the **Three Forests Way** (also the Forest Way, not covered in this book), then the rest of the route is shared with the **London Countryway**, passing the Iron Age fortress of Ambresbury Banks. At Bell Common you cross the M25 motorway, fortunately out of sight in a tunnel below, and leave the forest to descend into Epping.

ERITH RIVERSIDE WALK – see Thames Path Southeast Extension

EXPLORING TOTTERIDGE MANOR (MAP 2)

Distance:	6.4km (4.0miles)
Location:	Barnet
Start/finish:	Totteridge (St Andrew's Church, Totteridge Lane, GR 261-940)
Green factor:	70%
Blue factor:	6%
Recommended direction:	Clockwise
Terrain and surface:	Undulating with some steepish slopes. Mostly on rough paths, tracks and grass. 7 stiles. 1.2km (0.8miles) beside roads
Points of interest:	St Andrew's Church, Totteridge Valley, farmland, National Institute for Medical Research, Folly Brook
Signage:	Almost complete, clockwise only. Logo: '7' in white circle on blue arrow on white background, with text 'Barnet Countryside Leisure Walks'
Refreshments and toilets:	Pubs at Totteridge and Mill Hill. No cafés or public toilets
Public transport and break points:	Buses: Totteridge, Mill Hill
Links:	Barnet-Totteridge Loop, Rural Totteridge, Mill Hill Past and Present
Map:	Explorer 173
LWF status:	Pending validation
Principal promoter:	LB Barnet
Further information:	Included in *Barnet Countryside Leisure Walks* pack, 50p plus p&p from LB Barnet libraries and council offices

One of the **Barnet Leisure Countryside Walks** series, starting and finishing at St Andrew's Church in Totteridge village (together with **Barnet-Totteridge Loop** and **Rural Totteridge**). Starting on level ground you follow a footpath behind the Orange Tree pub, passing two duckponds. The route falls and rises a couple of times to cross Totteridge Valley and Folly Brook, eventually reaching the ridge along which Mill Hill village straggles. You return across the valley, this time walking beside Folly Brook for several hundred metres then finally climbing gently beside the Darlands estate back to Totteridge.

FARNBOROUGH CIRCULAR WALK (MAP 8)

Distance:	7.2km (4.5miles) or short route 1.7km (1.0miles)
Location:	Bromley
Start/finish:	Church Road, Farnborough (GR 443-642)
Green factor:	69%
Blue factor:	n/a
Recommended direction:	Clockwise (short route anticlockwise)
Terrain and surface:	Undulating countryside with some fairly steep slopes. Mostly on rough paths, tracks and grass. Three stiles. 0.9km (0.6miles) beside roads
Points of interest:	Farnborough village, farmland, woodland, Wilberforce Seat, Holwood Manor, Keston Common and Ponds, Caesar's Well, St Giles the Abbot Church, Gypsy Lee's grave
Signage:	Complete. Logo: 'Farnborough Circular Walk' in yellow on dark green background, surrounding yellow arrow with grey flash
Refreshments and toilets:	Pubs and café at Farnborough. Public toilets at Farnborough and Keston Ponds
Public transport and break points:	Buses: Farnborough, Keston Ponds
Links:	London Loop, Cudham Circular Walk, Leaves Green Circular Walk, Three Commons Circular Walk, Nash Circular Walk
Map:	Explorer 147
LWF status:	Validated with Seal of Approval
Principal promoter:	LB Bromley
Further information:	Included in Pack One of *Bromley Circular Walks and Trails* (£2.50 plus 50p p+p) from LB Bromley Leisure & Community Services and libraries

A delightful high-level walk in open country, only briefly dropping below the 100m contour. It is one of the ***Bromley Circular Walks and Trails*** series, from the attractive village of Farnborough. The shorter option follows a separate loop, which can be combined with the long one to make a lopsided figure-of-eight totalling 8.9km (5.5miles).

The long route sets out from Farnborough along an ancient track leading to open fields, which may be ploughed. You pass through a wood then cross a valley and more fields to Bogey Lane, another old track. The extensive view is of nothing but fields and trees, and you would hardly believe you are looking towards London.

Here you join Section 3 of the **London Loop** for a while, and make brief contact with the **Cudham** and **Leaves Green Circular Walks**.

The route skirts a field and smallholding, with a fine view of imposing Holwood Manor, home of the 18th century prime minister William Pitt the Younger. You climb quite steeply into woodland, passing a stone seat commemorating the spot where William Wilberforce is said to have discussed the abolition of slavery with Pitt. This lies at the highest point of the route, at about 170m (558ft), and from here it is all downhill or level. At Keston Common you brush the **Three Commons** and **Nash Circular Walks**, then pass Caesar's Well, source of the River Ravensbourne, and the three Keston Ponds. A short road stretch then a long fenced path take you back to Farnborough.

If you have the energy, it is now worth following the short route, which first passes the pretty church of St Giles the Abbot, in whose graveyard is buried the famous fortune-teller, the original Gypsy Lee. The route then goes out into adjacent countryside before returning to Farnborough.

Canada geese at Keston Ponds

Farthing Downs & Devilsden Wood Circular Walk (Map 7)

Distance:	6.5km (4.1miles)
Location:	Croydon
Start/finish:	Coulsdon South station (GR 299-590)
Green factor:	85%
Blue factor:	n/a
Recommended direction:	Anticlockwise
Terrain and surface:	Some steep ascents and descents. Mostly rough paths, tracks and grass. No stiles. 1.0km (0.6miles) beside roads

Points of interest:	Farthing Downs, grazing cattle, viewpoint, Devilsden Wood
Signage:	None
Refreshments and toilets:	Pub and café at Coulsdon. Occasional kiosk on Farthing Downs, also toilets (200m off route)
Public transport and break points:	NR/buses: Coulsdon South
Links:	London Loop, Downlands Circular Walk, Coulsdon Common & Happy Valley Circular Walk, Socratic Trail
Map:	Explorer 146
LWF status:	Pending validation
Principal promoter:	Corporation of London
Further information:	Further information: Included in free pack (+ sae) *Coulsdon Commons Circular Walks* from Corporation of London West Wickham and Coulsdon Commons or Downlands Project

Some of the finest countryside and best views in Greater London are covered by this route in the **Coulsdon Commons Circular Walks** series. There is a fair amount of climbing to do in the foothills of the North Downs, but the effort is well worthwhile. In spring and summer you should see a fine display of wild flowers (including orchids) and herbs.

From Coulsdon South station you climb steadily beside roads for several hundred metres, together with Section 5 of the **London Loop**, up to Farthing Downs, one of the Corporation of London's commons, where you are likely to see cows of the Sussex breed chomping the grass. A little more climbing brings you to the top of a long ridge, which you follow for a kilometre (half a mile), with fine views on either side. Just before the car park you descend into farmland in a dry valley, although in wet weather it can get very muddy. A contouring path leads through a small wood, then you climb back up to the ridge and enter the ancient Devilsden Wood. Nearby is Happy Valley, crossed by several other routes (see above). Just one more climb brings you back to a different part of Farthing Downs, which you follow below the ridge back to Coulsdon South.

Bracket Fungus in Devilsden Wood

109

FROM THE NUN'S HEAD TO SCREAMING ALICE (MAP 6)

Distance:	8.0km (5.0 miles)
Location:	Bromley, Lewisham, Southwark
Start:	Nunhead station (GR 354-760)
Finish:	Crystal Palace station (GR 341-705)
Green factor:	25%
Blue factor:	n/a
Recommended direction:	North to south
Terrain and surface:	Mostly level and firm, but with some steep slopes, flights of steps and rough paths in places. No stiles. 5.0km (3.1miles) beside roads
Points of interest:	Track of old railway, Brenchley Gardens, Horniman Gardens and Museum, Sydenham Hill Wood, site of Crystal Palace, Crystal Palace Museum
Signage:	None
Refreshments and toilets:	Pubs at Nunhead, Lordship Lane, Crescent Wood Road and Crystal Palace. Cafés at Horniman Museum and Crystal Palace. Public toilets at Horniman Gardens and Crystal Palace
Public transport and break points:	NR: Nunhead, Crystal Palace. Buses at these points, also Horniman Gardens, Forest Hill and Brenchley Gardens
Links:	Capital Ring, Green Chain Walk
Map:	Explorer 161
LWF status:	Pending validation
Principal promoter:	Friends of the Great North Wood
Further information:	Leaflet (£1.00 inc. p+p) from Friends of the Great North Wood

This charmingly named route closely follows the line of the former railway from Nunhead to Crystal Palace ('Screaming Alice' in Cockney rhyming slang). Although most of it follows pleasant residential roads, there are delightful green stretches including Horniman Gardens, Sydenham Hill Wood (a local nature reserve) and Brenchley Gardens, where the former railway track has been completely grassed over. The leaflet published by the Friends of Great North Wood is clear, interesting and well written, but you may need a street atlas to complement its map, which is not always sufficiently detailed for routefinding. At Crystal Palace station you encounter Sections 3 and 4 of the **Capital Ring**, while the west end of **Green Chain Walk** Section 10 lies nearby in the park.

GRAND UNION CANAL WALK (MAP 3)

Distance:	42km (26miles) from Little Venice to Rickmansworth – see text
Location:	Westminster, Kensington & Chelsea, Hammersmith & Fulham, Ealing, Brent, Hounslow, Hillingdon. Some in Buckinghamshire and Hertfordshire
Start:	Little Venice (Warwick Avenue, GR 262-819) or Brentford (High Street, GR 173-773)
Finish:	See text
Green factor:	30%
Blue factor:	98%
Recommended direction:	Southeast to northwest
Terrain and surface:	Almost entirely level but with some short steep slopes. Mostly on hard or firm surfaces but parts may be muddy or under water after heavy rainfall. No stiles. Minimal walking beside roads – just an occasional road crossing
Points of interest:	See text
Signage:	Mostly black fingerposts with white British Waterways logo and 'Grand Union Canal Walk'. Some discs with arrows
Refreshments and toilets:	Pubs at frequent intervals adjacent or close to the towpath. Cafés at Paddington, Ladbroke Grove, Acton Lane, Abbey Road, Alperton, Uxbridge, Rickmansworth. Public toilets at Paddington, Ladbroke Grove, Alperton, The Parkway, Uxbridge
Public transport and break points:	LU: Warwick Ave, Royal Oak, Westbourne Park, Kensal Green, Willesden Junction, Harlesden, Alperton, Perivale, Greenford, Boston Manor, Uxbridge and Rickmansworth. NR: Paddington, Kensal Green, Willesden Junction, Harlesden, Greenford, Brentford, Hayes and Harlington, West Drayton, Denham and Rickmansworth. Buses at all these points plus North Circular Rd, Ruislip Rd, Hayes Rd (Bull's Bridge), Stockley Park, Yiewsley, Cowley, South Harefield, Harefield and Batchworth
Links:	Regent's Canal Towpath, Thames Path National Trail, Capital Ring, Dog Rose Ramble, Brent River Park Walk, London Loop, Hillingdon Trail, West Drayton to Slough Ramble and Ride, Beeches Way, Grand Union Canal Slough Arm, Iver Circular Walk, Colne Valley Trail, Colne Valley Way, Nine Stiles Circular Walk, Widewater Lock Circular Walk, Harefield Heights Circular Walk

Map:	Explorer 161, 172, 173 (route marked, also on AZ street maps and atlases)
LWF status:	Validated with Seal of Approval
Principal promoter:	British Waterways
Further information:	Guidebook *The Grand Union Canal Walk* (Anthony Burton and Neil Curtis, Aurum Press, ISBN 1-85410-244-3, price £9.99). Free leaflet (+ sae) *Exploring London's Canals* from British Waterways

Very easy and interesting walking, almost entirely beside water. However, unless you are a canal fanatic, it is advisable to take it in bite-sized chunks or make an occasional diversion, as unbroken towpath walking can pall after a while. Be prepared for some short but very steep slopes where the towpath changes levels (usually at locks) or on access ramps from bridges, and there is a long, steady climb beside the Hanwell flight of locks between Brentford and Bull's Bridge. You only occasionally need to cross a road, but beware cyclists and joggers approaching quite fast from behind.

There are two alternative starting points, at Little Venice or Brentford. Both branches head westish to unite at Bull's Bridge near Southall, then the canal turns northwards past West Drayton, the **Grand Union Canal Slough Arm** and Uxbridge, dipping briefly into Buckinghamshire near Denham, and on into Hertfordshire. The route continues northwest through Northamptonshire and Warwickshire to finish at Gas Street Basin in Birmingham, a total distance of 234km (146miles), but a reasonable target for London walkers is Rickmansworth, 42km (26miles) from Little Venice.

Waterside Café, Little Venice

Many other London routes take advantage, sometimes for long stretches, of the ease of passage provided by the Grand Union towpaths (see Links above), which also link the **Thames Path National Trail**, the **Regent's Canal Towpath,** the **Capital Ring** (Sections 7, 8 and 9) and the **London Loop** (Sections 10, 11, 12 and 13).

Although much of the canal system in London passes through areas of light industry and warehouses, or residential districts, the waterside and towpaths have been colonised by plants, and grass verges have been planted, providing a moderately green experience in unexpected ways. There is usually something of interest on the water, in the form of waterbirds or colourful narrowboats. You occasionally pass locks, or a marina or mooring where families have chosen to live afloat. This may result, depending on lifestyle, in pretty and well-kept dwellings or delightfully decrepit jumbles of rags, old bikes and firewood. There are too many individual points of interest to detail here – for those, the guidebook (covering the whole route to Birmingham) is essential reading.

The sections from Little Venice to Sainsbury's in Alperton (9.5km/5.9miles), and from Brentford to Glade Lane in Southall (5.1km/3.2miles) have a hard surface throughout. There are some cobbled stretches and short steep slopes, and a long steady slope at Hanwell locks on the Brentford section. Elsewhere the towpath is uneven or narrow, with occasional steps and ribbed slopes, and may be muddy in places.

GRAND UNION CANAL (SLOUGH ARM) (MAP 3)

Distance:	8.0km (5.0miles)
Location:	Hillingdon, mostly in Buckinghamshire and Berkshire
Start:	Cowley Peachey (Turnaround Bridge, off High Road, GR TQ 056-809)
Finish:	Slough Basin (Stoke Road, GR SU 980-807)
Green factor:	52%
Blue factor:	100%
Recommended direction:	Either way
Terrain and surface:	Almost entirely level, with some short steep slopes at access points. Mostly hard surface with some uneven and narrow stretches . No stiles. Minimal walking beside roads
Points of interest:	Grand Union Canal, aqueducts, Slough Basin, marinas
Signage:	White text on black posts
Refreshments and toilets:	Pubs at Cowley, Yiewsley, Langley and Slough. Cafés at Slough. Public toilets at Slough
Public transport and break points:	NR: West Drayton, Iver, Langley and Slough. Buses at all these points plus Cowley Peachey and Yiewsley
Links:	Grand Union Canal Towpath, London Loop, Beeches Way, Iver Circular Walk, Colne Valley Trail, Colne Valley Way, West Drayton to Slough Ramble and Ride
Map:	Explorer 160 and 172 (route marked)

LWF status:	Pending validation
Principal promoter:	British Waterways, Groundwork Thames Valley
Further information:	Free leaflet (+ sae) *Exploring the Slough Arm* from Colne Valley Park Centre and British Waterways

Very easy walking, entirely beside water and with no road crossings, but be aware that cyclists and joggers may approach from behind. The surroundings are fairly evenly divided between urban and rural, and peace is abandoned as you pass under the M25. You cross three aqueducts, and there is plenty to see on the water in the form of waterbirds and the occasional narrowboat.

♿ The towpath is level, but the surface is uneven and narrow in places, and can be muddy in wet weather.

Green Chain Walk

This extensive and intricate network should provide many happy days of walking through the dozens of woodlands and open spaces that cover this part of London. They form the South East London Green Chain, and the network of routes that links them is known simply as the Green Chain Walk (sometimes abbreviated GCW in the following route descriptions).

The network takes the shape of a broad blade extending 29km (18miles) from its haft at various points beside the Thames in the northeast to its tip at Crystal Palace Park in the southwest. It connects with other key routes including the Capital Ring, London Loop and Thames Path. Branches from the Thames Barrier, Thamesmead and Erith come together at Oxleas Wood and Meadows, the fulcrum of the network, where a cafeteria sits atop a promontory looking for all the world like a welcoming mountain hut in the Alps! On a fine day this is a glorious place to rest awhile, admire the view and maybe meet other Green Chain Walkers.

Its 10 sections, together with numerous spurs and links, cover 65km (40miles) and are a delight to explore, with many possible combinations and opportunities for circular walks. The following pages describe each section individually. For convenience, here is a summary with approximate distances (including spurs and links):

		km	ml
1	Thamesmead to Lesnes Abbey	3.5	2.2
2	Erith to Bostall Woods	5.2	3.3
3	Bostall Woods to Oxleas Meadows	4.3	2.7
4	Charlton Park to Bostall Woods or Oxleas Meadows	8.8	5.6
5	Thames Barrier to Oxleas Meadows	6.7	4.2
6	Oxleas Woods to Mottingham	6.2	3.9
7	Shepherdleas Wood to Middle Park, Eltham	7.5	4.6

		km	ml
8	Mottingham to Beckenham Place Park	8.4	5.2
9	Mottingham or Chislehurst to Beckenham Place Park	9.0	6.1
10	Beckenham Place Park to Crystal Palace Park	5.8	3.6

Working out the various ways of linking the sections can be a challenge, especially as you may find yourself having to walk in the opposite direction from the route description (then you just reverse the directions and follow the arrows). Map 6, which includes the Green Chain Walk, may help you work out how to link the sections.

The network is one of the earliest and best examples of several London boroughs co-operating for the good of walking, being administered by a project officer funded jointly by the London Boroughs of Bexley, Bromley, Greenwich and Lewisham. It has been nominated as one of the Mayor of London's key routes (see Strategic Network introduction), and all its sections have received the London Walking Forum's Seal of Approval.

Signage. The routes are exceptionally well signed throughout. All its signs bear the network's linked 'G-C' logo and text 'Green Chain Walk'. In parks, woods and open spaces this is on solid wooden posts topped by a yellow arrow. Other signs are metal and have white logo and text on a green background. On streets a metal plate or fingers are attached to lampposts or other street furniture. At major junctions where a section starts, or where sections or links meet, fingerposts bearing the location name show distances to other key points, and there is often an accompanying information board for the whole network. It is planned that sections shared with the Capital Ring will have joint signs, and there will also be signed links with stations within 1.6km (1.0miles).

Principal promoters. The network is jointly promoted and funded by the London Boroughs of Bexley, Bromley, Greenwich and Lewisham. A project officer, who supervises co-ordination and administration, is based at the Green Chain Walk Project office.

Further information. A laminated pack (current price £3.50 (cheques payagle to Greenwich Council), containing an introduction to the network and route descriptions for each of the 10 sections, is available from the Green Chain Walk Project office. Also tourist information centres, some libraries and council offices of LB Bexley, LB Bromley, LB Greenwich and LB Lewisham. Website: www.greenchain.com contains information about the route and events taking place along it.

GREEN CHAIN WALK: SECTION 1 (MAP 6)
Thamesmead to Lesnes Abbey

Distance:	3.5km (2.2miles)
Location:	Bexley
Start:	Thamesmead (Thameside Walk, off Crossway, GR 472-814)
Finish:	Lesnes Abbey Woods (GR 480-787)
Green factor:	69%
Blue factor:	29%
Recommended direction:	North to south
Terrain and surface:	Almost completely level with some gentle slopes and a few steps. Entirely on tarmac paths or pavements. No stiles. 0.2km (0.1miles) beside roads
Points of interest:	River Thames, Royal Arsenal Tumps, Southern Outfall Sewer, Southmere Lake, Lesnes Abbey, Lesnes Abbey Woods
Signage:	See Green Chain Walk introduction
Refreshments and toilets:	Café/bar at Southmere Lake. Toilets at Southmere Lake and Lesnes Abbey
Public transport and break points:	NR: Abbey Wood. Buses: Thamesmead, Abbey Wood
Links:	Thames Path Southeast Extension, Ridgeway Walk, Green Chain Walk Section 2
Map:	Explorer 162 (route marked)
LWF status:	Validated with Seal of Approval (Mayor of London's key route)
Principal promoter and further information:	See Green Chain Walk introduction

Anyone who pictures Thamesmead as a bleak and windswept new town beside the Thames is in for a surprise, at least as far as the GCW route is concerned. And hardly any of this section follows roads. Starting on the Thames promenade (buses nearby), it immediately dives 'inland' to follow a narrow green band through pleasant residential areas, often accompanied by artificial water channels. Soon there is a choice of routes to pass under busy Eastern Way, both of which link with the *Ridgeway Walk*, crossing the grassy bank of the covered Southern Outfall Sewer.

Then comes Southmere, a large lake where on a fine day you can watch watersports and waterbirds as you refresh yourself in the Lakeside Centre. A further narrow green swathe leads to a level footbridge across Abbey Road (buses), from which you burst out into a broad park surrounding the well-kept ruins and gardens of Lesnes Abbey. Immediately beyond this, in woodland, you join GCW 2.

   Almost the whole of this section uses tarmac paths or pavements with dropped kerbs. However at time of writing a small stepped footbridge near the start requires a short diversion through residential roads – you will need a street atlas for this. A steep ramp to cross the Ridgeway Walk also involves a short stretch of uneven path. A short diversion is necessary to avoid steps at Southmere Lake.

GREEN CHAIN WALK: SECTION 2 (MAP 6)
Erith via Lesnes Abbey to Bostall Woods

Distance:	5.2km (3.3miles)
Location:	Bexley, Greenwich
Start:	Erith (Corinthian Manorway, GR 510-788)
Finish:	Bostall Woods (Longleigh Lane, GR 471-779)
Green factor:	41%
Blue factor:	2%
Recommended direction:	East to west
Terrain and surface:	Generally fairly level at first, but some quite steep slopes later on. Mostly on tarmac paths and pavements, but some rough paths and tracks. No stiles. 1.9km (1.2miles) beside roads
Points of interest:	River Thames, St John the Baptist Church, Frank's Park, Lesnes Abbey Woods, Lesnes Abbey, Bostall Heath
Signage:	See Green Chain Walk introduction
Refreshments and toilets:	Pubs and cafés at Erith and Belvedere. Toilets at Lesnes Abbey and Longleigh Lane
Public transport and break points:	NR: Erith, Belvedere, Abbey Wood. Buses: at these points plus Knee Hill, Longleigh Lane and Bostall Hill
Links:	Thames Path Southeast Extension, London Loop Section 1, Green Chain Walk Sections 1, 3 and 4
Map:	Explorer 162 (route marked)
LWF status:	Validated with Seal of Approval (Mayor of London's key route)
Principal promoter and further information:	See Green Chain Walk introduction

This section climbs steadily from sea level beside the Thames to over 55m (180ft). The start can be reached from Erith station with a pleasant stroll along Erith Riverside (*Thames Path Southeast Extension)* of about one kilometre (half a mile), passing the start of *London Loop Section 1.*

Crossing busy Bronze Age Way on a ramped footbridge gives a fine view of 12th century St John the Baptist Church below, then you pass through Frank's Park. A short stretch beside roads leads to Lesnes Abbey Woods, where the route climbs quite steeply then twists down a sunken track to meet GCW 1 beside the abbey ruins. More climbing in the woods takes you past a couple of small ponds to Bostall Heath, across Knee Hill and on to meet GCW 3 and 4 on Longleigh Lane beside Bostall Woods.

Green Chain Walk: Section 3 (Map 6)
Bostall Woods to Oxleas Meadows

Distance:	4.3km (2.7miles)
Location:	Greenwich, Bexley
Start:	Bostall Woods (Longleigh Lane, GR 471-779)
Finish:	Oxleas Meadows (GR 439-762)
Green factor:	77%
Blue factor:	9%
Recommended direction:	Northeast to southwest
Terrain and surface:	Undulating with some fairly steep climbs. Mostly on rough paths, tracks and grass. No stiles. 0.8km (0.5miles) beside roads
Points of interest:	Bostall Woods, Plumstead Cemetery, East Wickham Open Space, Woodlands Farm, Oxleas Wood and Meadows
Signage:	See introduction
Refreshments and toilets:	Pubs at Wickham Lane, Edison Grove, Shooters Hill. Café at Oxleas Meadows. Toilets at Longleigh Lane and Oxleas Meadows
Public transport and break points:	NR: Falconwood. Buses: Longleigh Lane, Bostall Hill, Wickham Lane, Edison Road, Shooters Hill, Falconwood
Links:	Green Chain Walk Sections 2, 4, 5 and 6
Map:	Explorer 162 (route marked)

LWF status:	Validated with Seal of Approval (Mayor of London's key route)
Principal promoter and further information:	See Green Chain Walk introduction

The greenest GCW section, with only short bursts across or along roads. Together with GCW 4 it leads on from GCW 2 at Longleigh Lane between Bostall Heath and Woods, then almost immediately splits from GCW 4 to follow a combe down through the woods, coming out beside Plumstead Cemetery to cross Wickham Lane.

You climb over the broad but sometimes rather bleak East Wickham Open Space, then a short stretch along residential roads leads to Woodlands Farm – one of the few stretches of farmland through which the GCW passes. Now run by a trust, its current projects include a network of health walks (see Other Named Self-guided Walks below). Here the route follows a stream for several hundred metres.

You cross busy Shooters Hill to enter Oxleas Wood, a local nature reserve. Here you pass the junction with GCW 6 then continue round to Oxleas Meadows to meet GCW 4 and 5.

GREEN CHAIN WALK: SECTION 4 (MAP 6)

Charlton Park via Plumstead Common to Bostall Woods or Oxleas Meadows

Distance:	5.8km (3.7miles) plus branch from Plumstead Common to Oxleas Meadows 3.0km (1.9miles)
Location:	Greenwich
Start:	Charlton Park (GR 421-778)
Finish:	Bostall Woods (GR 471-779) or Oxleas Meadows (GR 439-762)
Green factor:	52%
Blue factor:	n/a
Recommended direction:	Charlton Park to Bostall Woods: west to east. Plumstead Common to Oxleas Meadows: north to south
Terrain and surface:	Fairly level from Charlton Park to Plumstead Common with some short slopes. Undulating elsewhere with some fairly steep slopes. Mixture of tarmac paths, pavements, rough tracks or paths and grass. No stiles. 2.0km (1.3miles) beside roads

Points of interest:	Charlton Park, Royal Artillery Barracks and Museum, Plumstead Common, The Slade, Winns Common, Bleak Hill, Great Bartlett Wood, Bostall Woods, Shrewsbury Park, Eaglesfield Recreation Ground, Oxleas Meadows
Signage:	See Green Chain Walk introduction
Refreshments and toilets:	Pubs at Charlton Village, Plumstead Common and Shooters Hill. Cafés at Charlton Village and Plumstead Common. Public toilets at Charlton Park, Plumstead Common, Bostall Woods and Oxleas Meadows
Public transport and break points:	NR: Falconwood. Buses: Charlton Village, Ha-Ha Road, Plumstead Common, Wickham Lane, Longleigh Lane, Bostall Hill, Shooters Hill
Links:	Green Chain Walk Sections 2,3 and 5, Capital Ring Section 1
Map:	Explorer 162 (route marked)
LWF status:	Validated with Seal of Approval (Mayor of London's key route)
Principal promoter and further information:	See Green Chain Walk introduction

A 'short cut' from Charlton Park to Bostall Woods, avoiding Oxleas Wood but passing through one of the hidden gems of southeast London, namely Plumstead Common. From Charlton Park the section starts with a long stretch beside fairly busy roads. However, it is not without interest as you walk beside the ha-ha (sunken wall) of the military training ground of the Royal Artillery Barracks, whose impressive 100m long façade can be seen in the distance. Also visible is its Rotunda, which houses a Museum of Artillery.

Plumstead Common is delightful. First there are some small open spaces on undulating ground, then the main part stretching away to your right is dominated by the mock Tudor clocktower of the RACS Links Building. Further on is The Slade, one of several small ravines caused by landslips in this area, which are havens for wildlife. (If you follow the southward branch, The Slade requires a short diversion.)

GCW 4 divides at Plumstead Common. One branch continues eastward, passing through The Slade with 90 steps down and 99 steps up. You cross Winns Common and Bleak Hill, then descend steeply into Great Bartlett Wood and across Wickham Lane. The route climbs steeply into Bostall Woods, but levels out to meet GCW 2 and 3 at Longleigh Lane.

The other branch heads southward, climbing sharply with two long flights of steps up to Shrewsbury Park, where you have fine views across the Thames. At Eaglesfield Recreation Ground you reach the summit of Shooters Hill at altitude 130m (427ft) with extensive views to the east into Kent. Nearby rises a distinctive water tower, visible for miles around. After crossing Shooters Hill you follow a quiet lane down to Oxleas Meadows to meet GCW 3 and 5. There are short links to GCW 6 and 7 and to Falconwood station via Section 3 through Oxleas Wood.

The Old Mill, Plumstead Common

A 150m stretch across level grass in Charlton Park can be avoided by starting in Cemetery Lane. There are some short but steepish slopes in the early part of Plumstead Common. Long flights of steps may make a descent in The Slade impractical, but it can be seen to advantage from the top by Plumstead Common Road. Beyond Plumstead Common there are some long and very steep slopes, flights of steps and mostly uneven ground.

GREEN CHAIN WALK: SECTION 5 (MAP 6)
Thames Barrier via Charlton Park to Oxleas Meadows

Distance:	6.7km (4.2miles)
Location:	Greenwich
Start:	Thames Barrier (GR 416-793)
Finish:	Oxleas Meadows (GR 439-762)
Green factor:	67%
Blue factor:	2%
Recommended direction:	Northwest to southeast
Terrain and surface:	Mainly level but hilly at first with some steep slopes and one very long flight of steps (with avoiding alternative). Mixture of tarmac paths, pavements, grass and rough paths and tracks. No stiles. 1.1km (0.7miles) beside roads

Points of interest:	River Thames, Thames Barrier, Maryon Park, Gilbert's Pit, Cox's Mount, Maryon Wilson Park, Charlton Park, Charlton House, Hornfair Park, Woolwich Common, Eltham Common, Severndroog Castle, Jack Wood, Oxleas Meadows
Signage:	See Green Chain Walk introduction
Refreshments and toilets:	Pubs at Woolwich Road, Charlton Village and Shooters Hill. Cafés at Thames Barrier, Charlton Village, Charlton House and Oxleas Meadows. Public toilets at Thames Barrier, Maryon Park, Charlton House and Oxleas Meadows
Public transport and break points:	NR: Charlton, Falconwood. Buses at these points plus Woolwich Road, Thorntree Road, Charlton Village and Shooters Hill. Riverbuses at Thames Barrier
Links:	Thames Path National Trail, Thames Path Southeast Extension, Capital Ring, Green Chain Walk Sections 3 and 4
Map:	Explorer 162 (route marked)
LWF status:	Validated with Seal of Approval (Mayor of London's key route)
Principal promoter and further information:	See Green Chain Walk introduction

One of the hilliest GCW sections, shared with Section 1 of the **Capital Ring**, but with outstanding views and surroundings. From the Thames Barrier (on the **Thames Path National Trail** and **Thames Path Southeast Extension**) a winding path leads through a narrow park to Woolwich Road. After this gentle start you have a choice of routes, both involving a long flight of steps. One climbs 73 steps part way up Cox's Mount into Gilbert's Pit, where sand used to be quarried for house floors before the days of carpets. A short diversion up the Mount involving 50 more steps gives a breathtaking view taking in the River Thames, Thames Barrier, Millennium Dome and The Valley (home of Charlton Athletic Football Club). The other route goes through Maryon Park and up a flight of 106 steps, which can be avoided on a short signed alternative along less steeply climbing streets.

An almost continuous succession of parks and open spaces follows. Maryon Wilson Park contains a deer park and animal farm. You skirt Charlton Park with an impressive view of Charlton House, said to be one of the finest examples of a Jacobean mansion in Britain – it is open to visitors if you feel so inclined.

The rather bland Hornfair Park leads on to wide open Woolwich Common, where you pass the old Royal Military Academy, training ground of some of the great generals of British history. After crossing busy Shooters Hill you climb into wooded Eltham Common and Castle Wood, passing the strangely named Severndroog Castle, actually the summerhouse of the former estate of Eltham Park.

Finally you pass through Jack Wood to Oxleas Meadows and the junction with

GCW 3 and 4. There are short links to GCW 6 and 7, and to Falconwood station via GCW 3 through Oxleas Wood.

 The first 4.0km (2.5miles), as far as Hornfair Park, has a hard surface, though there are some steep slopes, and a signed alternative route to avoid a long flight of steps. After Hornfair Park the route follows uneven, sometimes narrow and steep paths and tracks.

GREEN CHAIN WALK: SECTION 6 (MAP 6)
Oxleas Wood via Eltham to Mottingham

Distance:	6.2km (3.9miles)
Location:	Greenwich, Bromley
Start:	Oxleas Wood (GR 442-760)
Finish:	Mottingham Lane (GR 418-731)
Green factor:	48%
Blue factor:	2%
Recommended direction:	Northeast to southwest
Terrain and surface:	Mostly level with some short, gentle slopes and one stepped footbridge. Evenly split between tarmac paths or pavements and rough paths or tracks. No stiles. 1.9km (1.2miles) beside roads
Points of interest:	Oxleas Wood, Shepherdleas Wood, Eltham Park North and South, Conduit Head, Eltham Palace
Signage:	See Green Chain Walk introduction
Refreshments and toilets:	Pubs at Falconwood, Eltham and Mottingham. Cafés at Eltham. Public toilets at Eltham and Mottingham
Public transport and break points:	NR: Falconwood, Mottingham. Buses at these points plus Eltham and Middle Park Avenue
Links:	Capital Ring Sections 1 and 2, Green Chain Walk Sections 3, 7, 8 and 9
Map:	Explorer 162 (route marked)
LWF status:	Validated with Seal of Approval (Mayor of London's key route)
Principal promoter and further information:	See Green Chain Walk introduction

A relatively gentle GCW section, whose route is shared with Sections 1 and 2 of the **Capital Ring**. From Oxleas Wood (at the junction with GCW 3) it follows rough paths and tracks through Shepherdleas Wood (where GCW 7 provides an alternative route to Mottingham) and Eltham Park North. You pass the Long Pond, frequented by waterbirds, and a signed link with Falconwood station.

A broad, level footbridge over the A2 Rochester Road (where the Capital Ring's Section 1 hands over to Section 2) takes you into Eltham Park South, where a tarmac path leads to Eltham itself. A short, rough path through Conduit Meadow passes first a signed link to GCW 7 in Avery Hill Park then Conduit Head, a vaulted red-brick structure where the flow of water from springs was once controlled to feed the moat of Eltham Palace. Residential roads parallel to the High Street lead to the palace, which from the 14th to 16th centuries was the equivalent of Windsor Castle, being the royal out-of-town residence. The Great Hall and moat survive from those times, and the palace is open to the public.

An ancient track called King John's Walk leads down to Mottingham, passing the end of GCW 7 (link to Mottingham station). You cross a railway line by stepped footbridge, then the A20 Sidcup Road, to reach Mottingham Lane and the junction with GCW 8 and 9.

GREEN CHAIN WALK: SECTION 7 (MAP 6)
Shepherdleas Wood via Avery Hill Park to Middle Park, Eltham

Distance:	7.5km (4.6miles)
Location:	Greenwich, Bromley
Start:	Shepherdleas Wood (GR 441-756)
Finish:	Eltham (King John's Walk, GR 422-736)
Green factor:	44%
Blue factor:	4%
Recommended direction:	Northeast to southwest
Terrain and surface:	Mostly level with one short steepish slope and some short gentle ones. Evenly split between tarmac paths or pavements and rough paths or tracks. No stiles. 2.8km (1.7miles) beside roads
Points of interest:	Shepherdleas Wood, Pippenhall Meadows, Avery Hill Park, Southwood Park, Fairy Hill Park, The Tarn, Middle Park
Signage:	See Green Chain Walk introduction
Refreshments and toilets:	Pubs at Falconwood and Mottingham. Café at New Eltham. Public toilets at New Eltham and Mottingham
Public transport and break points:	NR: Falconwood, New Eltham, Mottingham. Buses at these points plus Bexley Road and Middle Park Avenue
Links:	Capital Ring Sections 1 and 2, Green Chain Walk Section 6, Shuttle Riverway
Map:	Explorer 162 (route marked)

LWF status:	Validated with Seal of Approval (Mayor of London's key route)
Principal promoter and further information:	See Green Chain Walk introduction

An alternative to GCW 8 from Oxleas Wood to Mottingham, through some less visited parks and open spaces. GCW 6 (together with Section 1 of the *Capital Ring*) leads from Oxleas Wood into Shepherdleas Wood, where GCW 7 starts. This passes Falconwood station, then goes along roads and an ancient track called Gravel Pit Lane. After crossing Bexley Road you pass through Pippenhall Meadows into Avery Hill Park, where a link leads back to GCW 6 in Conduit Meadow, and you pass the start of the *Shuttle Riverway*.

A narrow path between playing fields, including the training ground of Charlton Athletic Football Club, leads to New Eltham, where you pass the station, then skirt Southwood Park and walk through Fairy Hill Park. After Mottingham station you make a short but delightful detour around The Tarn, a park containing a small lake surrounded by woods and gardens. It contains a bird sanctuary and an 18th century icewell, where ice from the lake was stored in winter for use the following spring.

Finally you climb a steepish slope up through Middle Park, part of the Crown lands associated with Eltham Palace. It is a designated wildlife area, where the natural environment is enhanced to encourage plant and animal life. The end of this section is at King John's Walk, where you rejoin GCW 6 and Section 2 of the *Capital Ring*.

GREEN CHAIN WALK: SECTION 8 (MAPS 6, 8)
Mottingham to Beckenham Place Park

Distance:	7.1km (4.4miles) plus spur to Grove Park Cemetery 1.3km (0.8miles)
Location:	Bromley, Lewisham
Start:	Mottingham Lane (GR 418-731)
Finish:	Beckenham (Southend Road GR 375-707) or Grove Park Cemetery (GR 416-713)
Green factor:	62%
Blue factor:	5%
Recommended direction:	Northeast to southwest
Terrain and surface:	Mostly level but with some gentle and some steep slopes and a stepped footbridge. Evenly split between tarmac paths or pavements and rough paths or tracks. No stiles. 2.6km (1.6miles) beside roads

Points of interest:	Chinbrook Meadows, Hither Green Nature Reserve, Downham Woodland Walk, Beckenham Place Park and Mansion, River Ravensbourne
Signage:	See Green Chain Walk introduction
Refreshments and toilets:	Pubs at Mottingham, Grove Park and Beckenham Place Park. Cafés at Grove Park, Downham and Beckenham Place Park. Public toilets at Mottingham, Grove Park, Downham and Beckenham Place Park
Public transport and break points:	NR: Mottingham, Grove Park, Beckenham Hill. CTL: Beckenham Junction. Buses at all these points plus Downham and Southend Road
Links:	Capital Ring Sections 2 and 3, Green Chain Walk Sections 6, 9 and 10
Map:	Explorer 162 (route marked)
LWF status:	Validated with Seal of Approval (Mayor of London's key route)
Principal promoter and further information:	See Green Chain Walk introduction

Although there are few large open spaces along this section, it manages to follow a reasonably green route through the suburbs in partnership with Section 2 of the *Capital Ring*. Leaving the junction with GCW 6 and 9 at Mottingham Lane, it shortly passes the home of ace cricketer W G Grace, then follows a long path between former hospital grounds and playing fields. At Marvels Lane a spur of GCW 8 heads south beside the Chin Brook through Chinbrook Meadows, then with a steep climb meets GCW 9 again beside Grove Park Cemetery.

Meanwhile, the main line of GCW 8 turns west past Grove Park. A path leads across a footbridge over the busy railway line at Hither Green, passing a nature reserve, then you follow residential roads for a while to join the Downham Woodland Walk, which angles pleasantly through a narrow band of trees to Downham.

Soon you enter Beckenham Place Park, where the route crosses the River Ravensbourne then follows a long, bucking and snaking route through the park, passing the west end of GCW 9. Eventually you reach Beckenham Place Mansion, now used as a clubhouse for the popular golf course, and with a café, bar and toilets open to the public. The section finishes on the far side of the park on Southend Road, where GCW 10 starts.

GREEN CHAIN WALK: SECTION 9 (MAPS 6, 8)
Mottingham to Chislehurst via Sundridge to Beckenham Place Park

Distance:	6.8km (4.3miles) plus spur from Chislehurst 2.8km (1.8miles)
Location:	Bromley, Lewisham
Start:	Mottingham Lane (GR 418-731) or Chislehurst (Prickend Pond, GR 439-708)
Finish:	Beckenham Place Park (GR 383-706)
Green factor:	48%
Blue factor:	3%
Recommended direction:	Northeast to southwest
Terrain and surface:	Mainly level with some long gentle slopes and short steeper ones. Mixture of pavements and rough paths, tracks or grass. No stiles. 3.6km (2.2miles) beside roads
Points of interest:	Eltham College, Lower Marvels Wood, Marvels Wood, Prickend Pond, Whyte's Woodland, Elmstead Woods, Beckenham Place Park
Signage:	See Green Chain Walk introduction
Refreshments and toilets:	Pubs at Mottingham, Chislehurst, Sundridge Park and Beckenham Place Park. Cafés at Chislehurst and Beckenham Place Park. Public toilets at Mottingham, Chislehurst and Beckenham Place Park
Public transport and break points:	NR: Mottingham, Chislehurst, Elmstead Woods, Sundridge Park, Ravensbourne. CTL: Beckenham Junction. Buses at all these points plus Bromley Hill
Links:	Green Chain Walk Sections 6 and 8, Capital Ring Sections 2 and 3
Map:	Explorer 162 (route marked)
LWF status:	Validated with Seal of Approval (Mayor of London's key route)
Principal promoter and further information:	See Green Chain Walk introduction

An alternative to GCW 8 between Mottingham and Beckenham Place Park, also providing a link with Chislehurst. From Mottingham Lane (GCW 6 and 8, also Section 2 of the *Capital Ring*) the route follows roads passing the extensive Eltham College. It then crosses playing fields on grass to enter Lower Marvels Wood, climbing steadily, and on up to Marvels Wood and Elmstead Woods.

Meanwhile, the spur from Chislehurst, having started high up beside pretty Prickend Pond, follows a more level route along the High Street then through Whyte's Woodland into Elmstead Woods to join the main route. This continues beside Grove Park Cemetery, where a spur of GCW 8 comes in from Marvels Lane, then crosses a railway line on a level footbridge to descend New Street Hill.

A long footpath climbs gently among trees beside Sundridge Park Golf Course. This is followed by a fairly long stretch along residential roads, and you eventually descend past playing fields to cross the River Ravensbourne. A residential estate of unmade roads takes you past Ravensbourne station into Beckenham Place Park, where you rejoin GCW 8 and Section 3 of the *Capital Ring*.

GREEN CHAIN WALK: SECTION 10 (MAP 6)
Beckenham Place Park to Crystal Palace Park

Distance:	5.8km (3.6miles)
Location:	Bromley
Start:	Beckenham (Southend Road, GR 375-707)
Finish:	Crystal Palace Park (GR 344-705)
Green factor:	26%
Blue factor:	3%
Recommended direction:	East to west
Terrain and surface:	Mainly level with some short steepish slopes and a stepped footbridge. Entirely on tarmac or pavements. No stiles. 3.5km (2.2miles) beside roads
Points of interest:	Cator Park, St Paul's Church, Alexandra Recreation Ground, Crystal Palace Park
Signage:	See Green Chain Walk introduction
Refreshments and toilets:	Pubs and cafés at Penge and Crystal Palace. Café and public toilets in Crystal Palace Park
Public transport and break points:	NR: Beckenham Junction, New Beckenham, Kent House, Penge East, Penge West, Crystal Palace. CTL: Beckenham Junction, Beckenham Road. Buses at all these points plus Southend Road
Links:	Capital Ring Sections 3 and 4, Green Chain Walk Section 8, Waterlink Way
Map:	Explorer 161 (route marked)
LWF status:	Validated with Seal of Approval (Mayor of London's key route)
Principal promoter and further information:	See Green Chain Walk introduction

The intricacies of the previous nine GCW sections lead to this final single thrust with no complications. It is the least green section, but offers much of interest. Together with Section 3 of the **Capital Ring,** it takes over from GCW 9 at Southend Road and descends into the valley of the Pool River, passing graceful St Paul's Church and, via a ramped subway, New Beckenham station. The route then describes a horseshoe around the attractive Cator Park, crossing the **Waterlink Way**. More roadwalking, broken by small open spaces, leads to Penge, where you pass both East and West stations, then enter Crystal Palace Park. This, the westernmost point of the Southeast London Green Chain, is one of the jewels in its crown, a very popular haunt for South Londoners, with its lakes and fantastically unreal dinosaurs – now enclosed in a separate area with limited access. You can continue with some steep ascents along Section 4 of the **Capital Ring** to Crystal Palace station.

This section is mostly level, on tarmac paths or pavements all the way. The first 200m descend Stumps Hill Lane quite steeply. A stepped footbridge at Penge East station can be avoided by diverting at Lennard Road for some 600m via Parish Lane, Penge Lane, Queen Adelaide Road and St John's Road.

GREEN STREET GREEN CIRCULAR WALK (MAP 8)

Distance:	11.9km (7.4miles). Shorter option 7.8km (4.9miles)
Location:	Bromley
Start/finish:	Green Street Green High Street (GR 456-635), or Chelsfield station (GR 469-641)
Green factor:	61%
Blue factor:	n/a
Recommended direction:	Clockwise
Terrain and surface:	Undulating countryside with some steep hills. Mostly on rough paths, tracks and grass. 1 stile. 3.1km (1.9miles) beside roads or on lanes
Points of interest:	Chelsfield Green, St Martin of Tours Church, Chelsfield Lakes Golf Course, Pratts Bottom village, Norsted Manor, farmland, Broom Wood, High Elms Country Park
Signage:	Almost complete both ways. Logo: 'Green Street Green Circular Walk' in yellow on dark green background, surrounding yellow arrow with orange flash
Refreshments and toilets:	Pubs at Green Street Green and Pratts Bottom. Public toilets at Green Street Green
Public transport and break points:	NR: Chelsfield. Buses: Green Street Green, Chelsfield, Pratts Bottom

Links:	Chelsfield Circular Walk, Cudham Circular Walk
Map:	Explorer 147
LWF status:	Pending validation
Principal promoter:	LB Bromley
Further information:	Included in Pack One of *Bromley Circular Walks and Trails* (£2.50 plus 50p p+p) from LB Bromley Leisure & Community Services and libraries

This stimulating route, one of the **Bromley Circular Walks and Trails** series, requires considerable energy expenditure, but takes you into fine countryside with woods, open farmland, a manor house and an old inn said to have been frequented by Dick Turpin. It starts and finishes in the strangely named village of Green Street Green, well served by buses from Orpington, or you can take the train to Chelsfield station.

From Green Street Green you climb through residential roads and a recreation ground to Chelsfield station, where you join the **Chelsfield Circular Walk** along the narrow green leading to Chelsfield village and its pretty church of St Martin of Tours. Here you must take great care along a busy lane with no pavement. There is a fine view as you cross Chelsfield Lakes Golf Course high up overlooking a valley, then more descents and ascents bring you to the charming village of Pratts Bottom, whose green is surrounded by old cottages and Turpin's 17th century Bulls Head pub.

The short route returns directly from here to Green Street Green, and includes a long stretch beside a busy main road. The long route continues in up and down fashion, through woods and farmland, passing through a high and remote community surrounding Norsted Manor. At Broom Wood you reach altitude 155m (508ft) but soon descend into a deep and beautiful valley. Another steep climb leads into High Elms Country Park, where the route is briefly shared with the **Cudham Circular Walk**. You contour through the woods then descend back to Green Street Green, taking great care across the unprotected A20 Farnborough Way.

THE GREENWAY (MAPS 4 and 5)

Truly a phenomenon that goes unnoticed by most Londoners, The Greenway is a level, almost continuous and straight traffic-free route that carves through East London at high level, overlooking houses and gardens with some interesting views. A broad, bonded gravel track has been constructed on top of the Northern Outfall Sewer Embankment, which carries effluent from north of the Thames to the mammoth sewage disposal works at Beckton. Despite this unpromising factor the surroundings are very pleasant and a haven for wildlife, as the track is lined with grass and shrubs. (See **Ridgeway Walk** for a similar route in Southeast London.) **Note:** The Greenway is actually a permissive path (see Route Closures on page 41), closed at night, and may also be used by cyclists.

Distance:	7.1km (4.4miles)
Location:	Tower Hamlets, Newham
Start:	Wick Lane, Hackney Wick (GR 371-839)
Finish:	Royal Docks Road, Beckton (GR 439-820)
Green factor:	94%
Blue factor:	3%
Recommended direction:	Either way
Terrain and surface:	Almost entirely level. Some long flights of steps with alternative ramps. No stiles. 250m beside roads
Points of interest:	Lea Navigation, River Lea, Bow Back River, Abbey Mills Pumping Station, Channelsea River, East London Cemetery, Beckton Alps, Beckton
Signage:	Bright blue entrance gates with overhead 'Greenway' banner, and markers with cutout lettering
Refreshments and toilets:	Pubs and cafés at Plaistow and Beckton Alps. No public toilets nearby
Public transport and break points:	NR: Hackney Wick, West Ham. DLR: Pudding Mill Lane, Beckton. LU: West Ham, Plaistow. Buses: All these points (except Pudding Mill Lane) plus Wansbeck Road, High Street Stratford, Upper Road, Lonsdale Avenue, Newham Way and Eastern Gateway (Royal Docks Road)
Links:	Lea Valley Walk, Capital Ring, Heron and Kingfisher Walks
Map:	Explorer 162
LWF status:	Pending validation
Principal promoter:	Thames Water, Lea Valley Regional Park Authority, LB Tower Hamlets, LB Newham
Further information:	See text

Easily followed in either direction, the route is highly visible except at three points where you must make a short diversion. The distinctive, bright blue metal 'Greenway' banners at main access points can be seen for some distance, and frequent signs show names of roads where you can join or leave. There is no official publication, but most of the route is described in one of the Newham Walks (Three Mills and along the Greenway to St Mary's Churchyard), included in Other Named Self-guided Walks below. Section 14 of the *Capital Ring* follows part of The Greenway.

Walking west–east the route starts in Wick Lane, close to a bus route on Wansbeck Road and not far from Hackney Wick station. There are several points of interest. Early on you cross four waterways (River Lea, City Mill River, Waterworks River/Bow Back River and Channelsea River), where connections are made with the **Lea Valley Walk** and **Heron and Kingfisher Walks,** and pass the palatial former Abbey Mills Pumping Station. Later you have a grandstand view of flower-strewn gravestones in the East London Cemetery.

Dry skier at Beckton Alps

Near the east end is the 'Mountain Ski Village' known as Beckton Alps, whose summit is reached via a zigzag path from the Newham Way flyover junction. Though a mere pimple in comparison to the Swiss version, this volcano-like former refuse tip (now grassed over) is high enough to provide a superb 360-degree panorama over most of east and southeast London into Essex and Kent. The small diversion is well worth the effort, and you can watch brave souls tackling the dry-ski slope.

At the east end a bus goes along Eastern Gateway (Royal Docks Road), or you can follow the cycle-track south to the Docklands Light Railway stations at Beckton or Gallions Reach (1.0km/0.6miles).

  All of The Greenway is level, with ramps at most entry and exit points, and a bonded gravel surface, except where you have to divert.

HAREFIELD HEIGHTS CIRCULAR WALK (MAP 3)

A very pleasant walk in the **Colne Valley Circular Walks** series, set in the low hills between Uxbridge and Rickmansworth, with some fairly strenuous climbs tempered by level canalside walking. The route starts officially at the Coy Carp pub (formerly the Fisheries) beside Coppermill Lock at Harefield West. Alternative starting points are Batchworth (Point 5 in the route description) or Rickmansworth station, from where the leaflet provides a route description to Point 6, adding 1.4km (0.9miles) each way. From any starting point you can take a short cut between Hill End and Springwell Lock. Note that the route uses several sections of country roads with no pavement where you should take great care.

Distance:	10.2km (6.4miles). Shorter options 5.2km (3.3miles) or 6.5km (4.1miles)
Location:	Hillingdon, plus some in Hertfordshire
Start/finish:	Harefield West (Coy Carp pub, Coppermill Lane, GR 040-912)
Green factor:	70%
Blue factor:	25%
Recommended direction:	Anticlockwise
Terrain and surface:	Level on canal towpath, hilly elsewhere, some steep slopes. Mostly on rough paths and tracks. Six stiles. 2.2km (1.4miles) beside roads
Points of interest:	Park Wood, farmland, Juniper Hill, Grand Union Canal and locks, Rickmansworth Aquadrome, Copper Mill, viewpoints
Signage:	None
Refreshments and toilets:	Pubs at Coppermill Lock, Woodcock Hill and Rickmansworth. No cafés or public toilets nearby
Public transport and break points:	LU/NR: Rickmansworth. Buses: Mount Pleasant, Woodcock Hill, Batchworth
Links:	London Loop, Hillingdon Trail, Colne Valley Trail, Grand Union Canal Walk
Map:	Explorer 172
LWF status:	Pending validation
Principal promoter:	Groundwork Thames Valley
Further information:	Leaflet included in Colne Valley Circular Walks pack from Colne Valley Park Centre

From Harefield West you climb almost immediately through woodland into the hills towards Hill End, together with Section 13 of the **London Loop** and the **Hillingdon Trail**. You walk through farmland then descend into a deep valley, and climb again over Juniper Hill. After descending residential roads in Batchworth, you follow the **Grand Union Canal** towpath for a while, briefly encountering the **Colne Valley Trail**. Your enjoyment of the hills is not yet over, though, as you divert at Stockers Lock up to Cooks Wood and more farmland. Descending back to the canal you have fine views across the Colne Valley, then a final stretch of towpath takes you back to Coppermill Lock. There is a proposal to divert the route around the attractive Stockers and Springwell Lakes.

HAVERING NORTHERN AREA CIRCULAR WALKS (MAP 4)

Distance:	2.6km (1.6miles) or 8.4km (5.2miles)
Location:	Havering, plus some in Essex
Start/finish:	Havering-atte-Bower (North Road, GR 512-933)
Green factor:	79%
Blue factor:	n/a
Recommended direction:	See text
Terrain and surface:	Hilly country with steep slopes, mostly on rough paths and tracks. Number of stiles not known. 1.5km (0.9miles) beside roads
Points of interest:	Havering Country Park including alpine canopy of pine trees, Pyrgo Park, farmland, water towers
Signage:	Almost complete both ways
Refreshments and toilets:	Pubs at Havering-atte-Bower and Noak Hill. Public toilets at Havering-atte-Bower
Public transport and break points:	Buses: Havering-atte-Bower, Noak Hill
Links:	London Loop
Map:	Explorer 175
LWF status:	Pending validation
Principal promoter:	LB Havering
Further information:	Free leaflet (+ sae) from LB Havering libraries and council offices

Fairly strenuous walking in low hills along the boundary between Havering borough and Epping Forest District in Essex. This is virtually a miniature network, consisting of two small and one large interlocking loops, covered in the leaflet as one short walk (briefly entering Essex) and one separate long walk. The common starting point for both routes is the attractive village of Havering-atte-Bower, or you can start the long route at its east end in Noak Hill, taking in the short route along the way if you wish.

Most of the route lies in farmland and passes through the parkland of the former Pyrgo Park mansion, now demolished. There are some fine views of the surrounding countryside, featuring a prominent water tower, and from the short route you can see the splendid alpine canopy of pine trees in Havering Country Park. Much of the long route is shared with Section 21 of the *London Loop*.

The 'barge graveyard' near Rainham Marshes

HAVERING RIVERSIDE PATH (MAP 4)

Distance:	2.0km (1.3miles) each way
Location:	Havering
Start:	Ferry Lane, Rainham (GR 512-810)
Finish:	Coldharbour Point (GR 520-788)
Green factor:	85%
Blue factor:	90%
Recommended direction:	North to south and back
Terrain and surface:	Almost entirely level, with short flight of steps or ramp at the start. Some single high steps along the route
Points of interest:	River Thames, barge graveyard, heritage mural, Coldharbour Navigation Beacon
Signage:	Complete both ways
Refreshments and toilets:	Pubs and cafés at Rainham. No public toilets nearby
Public transport and break points:	NR/buses: Rainham
Links:	London Loop

Map:	Explorer 162
LWF status:	Validated with Seal of Approval
Principal promoter:	LB Havering
Further information:	Free leaflet available from LB Havering libraries

A fascinating walk beside the Thames, which forms part of Section 24 of the *London Loop* (qv for further details). The route is also expected to form part of the proposed Thames Path Northeast Extension (see Appendix B). The nearest public transport is about 1.5km (0.9miles) away at Rainham, and involves a rather tedious walk along a busy road through a commercial district.

Most of the route is completely level, with some gentle slopes. Some high steps at flood defences may require a substantial diversion. The final 400m beyond the waste transfer station is on grass or uneven ground.

Coldharbour Point

HERON AND KINGFISHER WALKS (MAP 5)

Distance:	Heron: 5.1km (3.2miles). Kingfisher: 2.4km (1.5miles)
Location:	Newham, Tower Hamlets
Start/finish:	Bromley-by-Bow (Three Mills Island, GR 384-828)
Green factor:	18%
Blue factor:	62%
Recommended direction:	Heron: anticlockwise. Kingfisher: clockwise
Terrain and surface:	Almost completely level but with some short slopes and steps, mostly on firm waterside paths. No stiles. Minimal walking beside roads
Points of interest:	Three Mills Island, Bow Backs Rivers, Lea Navigation and locks, Old Ford Nature Reserve, The Greenway, Abbey Mills Pumping Station
Signage:	None
Refreshments and toilets:	Pubs at Bromley-by-Bow. Café and public toilets at Three Mills Island
Public transport and break points:	LU: Bromley-by-Bow, West Ham. NR: Hackney Wick, West Ham. DLR: Pudding Mill Lane. Buses at all these points (not Pudding Mill Lane) plus Stratford High Street
Links:	Lea Valley Walk, Time Travellers, Capital Ring, The Greenway
Map:	Explorer 162
LWF status:	Pending validation
Principal promoter:	Lower Lea Project
Further information:	Free leaflet from Lower Lea Project

Fascinating, easy walking beside backwaters of the River Lea. These adjacent routes in the Lower Lea Project's *Waterway Discovery* series can be walked separately or together in the form of a figure-of-eight. Both start at Three Mills Island (as does *Time Travellers* in the same series), a heritage centre and home of a thriving film studio complex, which has been a setting for the *Big Brother* house. They explore a rather mysterious and easily overlooked part of East London, surrounded by (yet out of sight from) several busy roads. Here a spaghetti junction of waterways, collectively known as the Bow Backs, both feeds and plunders the River Lea and its Navigation, with intriguing names such as the Waterworks and Pudding Mill Rivers and the Prescott Channel. Vertigo sufferers should note that some of the paths go close to sheer drops into the water.

Both routes pass the little marina at Three Mills and use short stretches of **The Greenway**, carrying Section 14 of the **Capital Ring**. The shorter Kingfisher Walk follows Abbey Creek and passes the palatial former Abbey Mills Pumping Station, where you encounter a curious piece of pumping machinery shaped like a giant cast iron seashell. The longer Heron Walk follows the Three Mills and City Mill Rivers, returning beside the Old River Lea and Lee Navigation (together with the **Lea Valley Walk**), and sneaking a peek at Pudding Mill River.

Both routes are level with a firm surface of paving, bonded gravel or grit, but some short stretches are uneven, narrow or cobbled and may be overgrown or muddy, also close to a sheer drop into the water. The Heron Walk includes two flights of steps, which can be bypassed along nearby roads, and a short road stretch with undropped kerbs. There are a few steepish ramps, some ribbed. Barriers at some points may require a Radar key.

HERTFORDSHIRE UNION CANAL TOWPATH – see Time Travellers

HERTFORDSHIRE CHAIN WALK (MAP 2)

Distance:	11.6km (7.2miles) – see text
Location:	Enfield, continuing into Hertfordshire
Start/finish:	Whitewebbs Park (Whitewebbs Road, GR 329-998)
Green factor:	71%
Blue factor:	n/a
Recommended direction:	Clockwise
Terrain and surface:	Undulating with some fairly steep climbs, mostly on rough paths and tracks. Ten stiles. 2.6km (1.6miles) beside roads
Points of interest:	Whitewebbs Park, woodland, farmland
Signage:	None
Refreshments and toilets:	Pubs at Whitewebbs Road, Clay Hill, Crews Hill. No public toilets nearby
Public transport and break points:	NR: Crews Hill. Buses: Clay Hill, Crews Hill
Links:	London Loop
Map:	Explorer 174 (route marked, also on AZ street maps and atlases)
LWF status:	Pending validation
Principal promoter:	East Herts Footpath Society

Further information:	Booklet *Hertfordshire Chain Walk* (Castlemead Publications, ISBN 0-948555-36-X, price £4.50 plus 75p p+p), available from the publishers and bookshops in North London and Hertfordshire

The above details apply to Walk 1 only in the chain.

Pleasant walking in fairly hilly countryside north of Enfield. This walk is part of an imaginative scheme devised by the East Herts Footpath Society comprising a chain of fifteen interlinked circular walks extending 138km (86miles) through the east side of Hertfordshire from near Enfield to Ashwell in the far north of the county.

Walk 1 in the chain is the only one that touches Greater London. It starts on Whitewebbs Road north of Enfield, but using public transport Crews Hill station is more practical. Most of the route lies in open fields, but a fair chunk goes past or through woodland including Whitewebbs Park. The M25 motorway is crossed twice, and a short stretch at the south end is shared with Section 17 of the **London Loop**.

HILLINGDON NORTHERN/SOUTHERN LINKS – see Hillingdon Trail

HILLINGDON TRAIL (MAP 3)

Distance:	31.2km (19.5miles)
Location:	Hillingdon
Start:	Bath Road, Cranford (GR 100-770)
Finish:	Springwell Lock, (GR 043-929)
Green factor:	56%
Blue factor:	16%
Recommended direction:	South to north
Terrain and surface:	Level at first, rising into hilly country with some steep slopes. Mostly on rough paths, tracks and grass. 21 stiles (all in Sections 3–6). 5.2km (3.2miles) beside roads
Points of interest:	Cranford Park, Grand Union Canal, Yeading Brook, Ickenham Marsh Nature Reserve, River Pinn, Ruislip Lido, Ruislip Woods, Bayhurst Wood Country Park
Signage:	Complete both ways. Fingerposts: mainly white 'Hillingdon Trail' on brown background (some older plain wooden fingerposts remain in places). Arrowposts: white 'HT' between two white horizontal bands

Refreshments and toilets:	Pubs at North Hyde Road, Uxbridge Road, Yeading Lane, Ickenham, West Ruislip, Ruislip Lido, Harefield, Harefield West, Rickmansworth. Cafés at Cranford and Rickmansworth. Public toilets at Ruislip Lido and Bayhurst Wood
Public transport and break points:	Buses: Cranford, Hyde Road, Uxbridge Road, Yeading Lane, Kingshill Avenue, Ickenham, West Ruislip, Ruislip Lido, Harefield, Harefield West. NR: Hayes & Harlington, Southall. LU: Ickenham, West Ruislip
Links:	London Loop, River Crane Walk, Grand Union Canal Walk, Dog Rose Ramble, Willow Tree Wander, West Ruislip to Gerrards Cross Ramble and Ride, Celandine Route, Widewater Lock Circular Walk, Colne Valley Trail, Harefield Heights Circular Walk
Map:	Explorer sheets 161, 172, 173, plus short stretch on sheet 160 (route marked)
LWF status:	Validated with Seal of Approval
Principal promoter:	LB Hillingdon
Further information:	Pack of six sectional cards (£2.00 plus 50p p+p) from LB Hillingdon libraries

The designers of this route have, incredibly, managed to find a long and mostly green or waterside route through the western suburbs of London, of which very little follows roads – a considerable achievement. The route makes several links with others in the network (see above) and is divided into six sections as follows with approximate distances:

1. Cranford to Bulls Bridge, Southall (3km/2miles, no stiles)

2. Bulls Bridge to Yeading Lane (5km/3miles, no stiles)

3. Yeading Lane to A40, North Hillingdon (5km/3miles, 7 stiles)

4. A40 to Ruislip Lido (5km/3miles, 3 stiles)

5. Ruislip Lido to Harefield (6km/4miles, 7 stiles)

6. Harefield to Springwell Lock (8km/5miles, 4 stiles).

The route has not been planned with public transport in mind, and the pack provides little transport information, so you will need to do some research. However, the splendid walking makes up for this shortcoming. The official start (Cranford Park) and finish (Springwell Lock) are located at car parks, which are some distance from any public transport. A 'southern link' connects with buses at Cranford, while at the northern end you can walk a little further along the Grand Union Canal and Colne Valley Trail into Rickmansworth. A 'northern link' has now been absorbed by Section 13 of the London Loop.

Cranford Park, with its old church and ruined manor house, is a lovely place to start, and you briefly accompany Section 10 of the **London Loop** before joining the **Grand Union Canal** towpath for a long stretch past Southall. This leads to the broad green valley of Yeading Brook, shared with the **Dog Rose Ramble**. At

Ruislip you pass through a short but dark tunnel where a torch may be useful.

After crossing the River Pinn, the route follows footpaths beside housing estates leading to the famous Ruislip Lido. Once a noisy resort with power-boating and swimming, this is now a peaceful retreat surrounded by woods and nature reserves. Until now the route has been fairly level, but from here on you rise and fall, sometimes quite steeply, as you cross the hills that range north of London. You are rewarded with some splendid views, although much of this part is wooded – in quick succession you pass through Copse Wood, Mad Bess Wood and Bayhurst Wood (the latter is a country park). You brush the route of the **Widewater Lock Circular Walk** here, and visit the attractive hilltop village of Harefield.

There is a splendid view of Broadwater lake as you descend, then some respite from the climbing while you follow a second, shorter stretch of the Grand Union Canal, also used by Section 13 of the **London Loop** and several other routes. There is one more climb to go, up to the hamlet of Hill End, then you descend back to the canal where the route finishes beside the rather isolated Springwell Lock. However, you can fairly quickly reach the facilities and transport at Rickmansworth by following the **Colne Valley Trail** along the canal.

Ruislip Lido

HOGSMILL WALK (MAP 7)

Distance:	11.7km (7.3miles)
Location:	Kingston, continuing into Surrey
Start:	Kingston (Clattern Bridge, GR178-691)
Finish:	Ewell (Bourne Hall Park, GR 219-628)
Green factor:	48%

Blue factor:	58%
Recommended direction:	North to south
Terrain and surface:	Generally level but some climbing where the route leaves the riverside. Mostly on rough paths, but hard surface at the north end. No stiles. 4.7km (2.9miles) beside roads
Points of interest:	Kingston town centre, Hogsmill River, St John the Baptist Church, Bourne Hall Park
Signage:	Minimal
Refreshments and toilets:	Pubs and cafés at Kingston and Ewell. Pubs at Villiers Road, Berrylands and Old Malden Lane. Public toilets at Kingston town centre and Bourne Hall Park
Public transport and break points:	NR: Kingston, Berrylands, Malden Manor, Ewell East, Ewell West. Buses at all these points plus Malden Way, Kingston Road and Ruxley Lane
Links:	London Loop, Thames Path National Trail, Thames Down Link
Map:	Explorer 161
LWF status:	Pending validation
Principal promoter:	RB Kingston
Further information:	Free leaflet (+ sae) *The Hogsmill* from RB Kingston libraries and council offices

Although the whole of this route has been incorporated into the **London Loop** (Section 8), it provides an enjoyable walk in its own right, generally following the Hogsmill River. If you are following the London Loop anticlockwise (in the opposite direction to its route descriptions), the leaflet for the Hogsmill Walk may be helpful as it is written in that direction.

The route starts at the historic Clattern Bridge near Kingston's bustling Market Place and the **Thames Path National Trail.** It is some time before you leave the built-up area, but some riverside paths are included. After Berrylands you are beside the river or in green surroundings most of the time, but there are a couple of points where you must divert along roads. At Kingston Road you pass the confluence of the Hogsmill and the Bonesgate Stream. Finally a short boardwalk leads into Ewell, where the route finishes in the small but pretty Bourne Hall Park, beside the pond that is a source of the Hogsmill.

♿ The whole section is level, but lengthy stretches are on rough ground or grass, which may be difficult in wet weather.

Iver Circular Walk (Map 3)

Distance:	9.0km (5.6miles)
Location:	Hillingdon, but mostly in Buckinghamshire
Start/finish:	Uxbridge (Rockingham Road canal bridge, GR 049-838)
Green factor:	42%
Blue factor:	46%
Recommended direction:	Anticlockwise
Terrain and surface:	Mostly level but with two steady climbs, on a mixture of canal towpaths, rough paths and tracks and roads. No stiles. 4.1km (2.6miles) beside roads
Points of interest:	Colne Brook, farmland, Iver village, canal towpaths and lock, River Colne, Little Britain Lake, Fray's River
Signage:	None at present
Refreshments and toilets:	Pubs at Uxbridge, Iver and Cowley. Cafés and public toilets at Uxbridge
Public transport and break points:	LU: Uxbridge. NR: Iver. Buses: Uxbridge, Iver, Cowley
Links:	London Loop, Grand Union Canal Walk, West Drayton to Slough Ramble and Ride, Beeches Way, Colne Valley Way, Grand Union Canal Slough Arm
Map:	Explorer 172
LWF status:	Pending validation
Principal promoter:	Groundwork Thames Valley
Further information:	Included in *Colne Valley Circular Walks* pack from Colne Valley Park Centre

Interesting and fairly easy walking, one of the **Colne Valley Circular Walks** series. There is a high proportion of waterside walking, include Colne Brook and the charming Little Britain Lake, where contact is made with Section 11 of the **London Loop**. The route includes two stretches of the **Grand Union Canal** towpath, a magnet for trails in this area (see Links above), and where you should see much in the way of boats and birds. You pass through the ancient village of Iver on a low hill with good views across the Colne Valley. The route as it stands does include rather a lot of roadwalking, including some country lanes with no pavement where great care is needed, and you will be very aware of the proximity of the M25 motorway for much of the route. However, there is a proposal to improve this with a diversion taking in more of the Grand Union Canal Slough Arm.

Jubilee Walkway (Map 5)

Distance:	14.4km (9.0miles), plus loops through the City (adds 1.8km/1.1miles) and Bloomsbury (2.5km/1.6miles), and spur to Buckingham Palace (0.7km / 0.4miles)
Location:	Westminster, Lambeth, Southwark, Tower Hamlets, City of London, Camden
Start/finish:	Leicester Square (GR 298-808)
Green factor:	9%
Blue factor:	41%
Recommended direction:	Either direction
Terrain and surface:	Almost completely level, with one short gentle hill. Entirely on hard surfaces
Points of interest:	See text
Signage:	Silvery metal discs approximately 30cm (1ft) in diameter, set in ground, bearing crown surrounded by text 'Jubilee Walkway'. Some original 'Silver Jubilee Walkway 1977' may remain in places
Refreshments and toilets:	Many opportunities
Public transport and break points:	Many opportunities. The official start/finish point is close to both Leicester Square and Piccadilly Circus tube stations
Links:	Diana Princess of Wales Memorial Walk, Thames Path National Trail
Map:	Explorer 173
LWF status:	Validated with Seal of Approval (Mayor of London's key route)
Principal promoter:	Jubilee Walkway Trust
Further information:	Free leaflet available from tourist information centres in London, the Royal Festival Hall, outlets of participating local authorities, sponsors and Royal Parks Agency. Website: www.jubileewalkway.com

Relaunched on the occasion of Her Majesty the Queen's Golden Jubilee, this is one of the Mayor of London's key routes. It replaces the London Silver Jubilee Walkway, using the same route with some realignments and improvements.

This is a grand tour on foot of London's leading attractions, so good you walk it twice! It is really two routes in one, as it can easily be done at night, when most of the sights are lit up and present a glorious and completely different experience from the one you see in daylight. (Note that St James's Park, Victoria Tower Gardens and some other places through which the route passes are closed at night, but alternative parallel routes are obvious.) The Millennium Bridge forms part of the route, providing an opportunity for additional loops.

Nearly every household name in London's tourist circuit is there (and free, at least for the exterior views): Leicester Square, National Gallery, Trafalgar Square, Nelson's Column, The Mall, St James's Park, Parliament Square, Westminster Abbey, Big Ben, Houses of Parliament, 'Old Father Thames', former County Hall, British Airways' London Eye (the 'Millennium Wheel'), Royal Festival Hall, Royal National Theatre, Shakespeare's Globe, Tate Modern, Millennium Bridge, London Bridge, HMS Belfast, Tower Bridge, Tower of London, Bank of England, Mansion House, St Paul's Cathedral and Covent Garden (opera house and piazza). For a short distance in St James's Park the route runs very close to the **Diana Princess of Wales Memorial Walk**, and the whole route along the South Bank is shared with the **Thames Path National Trail**.

Then there are lots of places that are not particularly (or at all) famous, but are nonetheless well worth seeing, such as Victoria Tower Gardens, Lambeth Palace, Museum of Garden History, St Thomas' Hospital, National Film Theatre, Gabriel's Wharf, Oxo Tower, Clink Museum, Golden Hinde replica, Hay's Galleria, St Katharine Docks, Peter's Hill, City Art Gallery, Lincoln's Inn Fields, Soane Museum and some fascinating alleys off Fleet Street and in Covent Garden.

A City loop from the Mansion House partly follows the highwalks of the 1970s Barbican estate, with fascinating views of hidden churches, gardens and remains of the ancient London Wall. It goes through the Guildhall precinct and passes the Museum of London, returning to the main circuit at St Paul's Cathedral. A Bloomsbury/Euston loop from Chancery Lane goes through the district's historic streets and squares, passes the British Library and actually cuts through the British Museum. You pass Senate House (impressive headquarters of the University of London), and have good views of the Telecom Tower, returning to the main circuit at Kingsway. A spur from St James's Park takes you along Birdcage Walk right up to Buckingham Palace, where a panoramic panel is to be installed.

The route is completely level and hard surfaced, although some short cuts use steps. At time of writing a few kerbs are not dropped, but it is the intention that all will have been dropped in time for the Queen's Golden Jubilee. Cobbled surfaces are unavoidable along some parts of the South Bank, in St Katharine Docks, and at Covent Garden Piazza; however, local authorities plan to install paved runners through them where possible.

KENLEY COMMON AND DOLLYPERS HILL CIRCULAR WALK (MAP 7)

Distance:	7.2km (4.5 miles)
Location:	Croydon, plus some in Surrey
Start/finish:	Whyteleafe station (GR 338-585)
Green factor:	71%
Blue factor:	n/a

Recommended direction:	Clockwise
Terrain and surface:	Generally level but some steep or very steep ascents and descents. Mostly on rough tracks, paths or grass. No stiles. 2.1km (1.3miles) beside roads
Points of interest:	Kenley Common, Kenley Aerodrome, Dollypers Hill Nature Reserve
Signage:	None
Refreshments and toilets:	Pubs at Whyteleafe and Old Lodge Lane. Cafés at Whyteleafe. No public toilets nearby
Public transport and break points:	NR: Whyteleafe. Buses: Whyteleafe, Caterham Drive, Old Lodge Lane
Links:	London Loop
Map:	Explorer 146
LWF status:	Pending validation
Principal promoter:	Corporation of London
Further information:	Included in free pack (+ sae) *Coulsdon Commons Circular Walks* from Corporation of London West Wickham and Coulsdon Commons and Downlands Project

On this energetic walk you have the wind in your hair in the company of gliders at breezy Kenley Aerodrome. The ascent from Whyteleafe station is one of the steepest parts of the network, with more to come. The effort is worthwhile, though, as you can enjoy grand views from the meadows and woodlands of Kenley Common. In spring and summer there is a kaleidoscope of colours, when the fields are covered with wild flowers such as greater yellow rattle, sainfoin and various orchids. Halfway round you descend into a valley to go through Dollypers Hill Nature Reserve, managed by the Surrey Wildlife Trust, then climb back over Kenley Common. The route crosses Section 5 of the **London Loop** at two points.

Gliders at Kenley Common

KINGFISHER WALK – see Heron and Kingfisher Walks

LEA VALLEY WALK (MAPS 2, 5)

*Distance:	83km (52miles) – see text
*Location:	Enfield, Waltham Forest, Haringey, Hackney, Newham, Tower Hamlets (continuing from Bedfordshire, Hertfordshire and Essex)
*Start:	Luton, Bedfordshire (GR TL 061-249)
Finish:	Bromley-by-Bow (Gillender Street, GR TQ 382-822)
Green factor:	25%
Blue factor:	99%
Recommended direction:	North to south
Terrain and surface:	Almost entirely level and firm, with some gentle slopes at locks and bridges. In places the path is narrow and may be muddy. Minimal road walking
Points of interest:	River Lea, numerous locks and reservoirs, Waltham Abbey, Hazlemere Marina, Springfield Marina, Middlesex Filter Beds Nature Reserve, Walthamstow Marshes Nature Reserve, Hackney Marsh, Three Mill Visitor Centre
Signage:	Almost complete both ways. Links from most nearby stations by fingerposts and pavement discs
Refreshments and toilets:	Pubs and cafés at Waltham Cross, Waltham Abbey and Upper Clapton. Pubs Enfield Lock, Lea Valley Road, Northumberland Park, Tottenham Hale, Upper Clapton, Lea Bridge Road and Bromley-by-Bow. Basic toilets at Stonebridge and Tottenham Locks
Public transport and break points:	LU: Tottenham Hale, Bromley-by-Bow. DLR: Pudding Mill Lane, Devons Road. NR: Waltham Cross, Enfield Lock, Ponders End, Angel Road, Tottenham Hale, Clapton, Hackney Wick. Buses at all these points (except Pudding Mill Lane) plus Lea Valley Road, Lee Valley Leisure Complex, Angel Road and Lea Bridge Road
Links:	London Countryway, London Loop, Pymmes Brook Trail, Capital Ring, Walk Back in Time, The Greenway, Heron and Kingfisher Walks, Time Travellers
Map:	Explorers 162, 174 (route marked, also on AZ street maps and atlases)
LWF status:	Validated with Seal of Approval (Mayor of London's key route)

Principal promoter:	Lee Valley Park, British Waterways
Further information:	Guidebook *Lea Valley Walk* (£8.00, Leigh Hatts, Cicerone Press, ISBN 1-85284-313-6). (Replaces leaflets formerly published by the Lee Valley Park.)

*These details apply to the whole route.
Others are for Waltham Cross to Bromley-by-Bow only.

Easy but fascinating waterside walking, one of the Mayor of London's key routes (see Strategic Network introduction), and the first route in the network to receive the London Walking Forum's coveted Seal of Approval. The full distance may require up to a week to cover, but the Greater London section can provide one or two good full day walks, by starting just outside the boundary at Waltham Cross or Waltham Abbey and walking south to Bromley-by-Bow (20km/12.5miles), with many potential break points. The route uses the towpath of the Lee Navigation, once a busy commercial waterway and now much used by narrowboats and other recreational craft. The green factor shown above is a little misleading, as most of the route is green on one side or the other, but rarely on both sides together. Look out for cyclists, who are permitted to use the towpath with a licence.

Let us now consider a mystery: the correct title of this route is Lea Valley Walk, yet the authority that promotes it is the Lee Valley Park, and the navigable waterway is the Lee Navigation. The official explanation is that, generally, Lea is applied to natural manifestations of the river, while Lee is used for those created by humans. Back to the walking!

The Lea Valley Walk is a key route in the Strategic Network, crossed by some routes and giving others a piggy-back. The **London Countryway** makes its closest approach to Greater London along the Lea at Waltham Abbey, while Section 18 of the **London Loop** crosses at Enfield Lock. Picketts Lock is at one end of the **Pymmes Brook Trail.** Various sections of the towpath are used by **Walk Back in Time,** Section 13 of the **Capital Ring, Time Travellers** and the **Heron and Kingfisher Walks,** while **The Greenway** crosses it at Stratford Marsh. Time Travellers also provides a link with the Thames Path National Trail via the Limehouse Cut; at time of writing it is hoped eventually to extend the Lea Valley Walk further south beside Bow Creek directly to the Thames at Leamouth.

Springfield Marina, Clapton

The guidebook is written north to south, but the route is easily followed in either direction simply by following the towpath. However, just over 1km (0.6miles) north of Bow Locks the navigation is inaccessible, and you have to negotiate the very busy Bow Interchange (A11/A102), where at time of writing the crossing facilities and signage were inadequate. The north end of the Greater London section (actually just beyond the boundary at Waltham Abbey) has a signed link from Waltham Cross station. The current south end of the route is officially at Bow Locks, with pedestrian access from Gillender Road, off the Blackwall Tunnel Northern Approach near Bromley-by-Bow station. A proposed M25 link, the Northern Gateway Access Road, may affect the route at Rammey Marsh between Waltham Abbey and Enfield.

Riverside Café, High Bridge, Springfield, Clapton

Highlights of the route within Greater London include the Swan and Pike Pool near Enfield Lock, which provides a pleasant diversion, and two colourful marinas at Waltham Abbey and Springfield. Several large open spaces are passed, including Rammey Marsh, Springfield Park, and Walthamstow and Hackney Marshes (with their bird-rich nature reserves). For over 10km (6miles) south of Enfield Lock a series of immense reservoirs occupies the east bank, though only their grassy retaining embankments can be seen from the towpath. The photogenic House Mill is set behind a millpond at Three Mill Island. On the debit side, pylons and wires often occupy the sky, and a stretch near the Lea Valley Viaduct is frankly rather unpleasant.

 ♿ Much of the towpath has a hard level surface, but in places is narrow and uneven. Access at Bow Locks is restricted by a steeply curving and ribbed bridge. In the area around Hackney and Walthamstow Marshes the towpath has several squeeze-stiles (designed to exclude motorbikes) for which a Radar key may be needed.

Leaves Green Circular Walk (Map 8)

Distance:	11.0km (6.9miles). Short route 5.7km (3.6miles)
Location:	Bromley
Start/finish:	Leaves Green Common car park (GR 414-619)
Green factor:	85%
Blue factor:	n/a
Recommended direction:	Clockwise
Terrain and surface:	Undulating, with several long and quite steep ascents and descents. Mostly on rough paths, tracks and grass. Stiles: 13. 2.3km (1.4miles) beside roads
Points of interest:	Farmland, Keston and Downe churches, Downe village, Down House (Charles Darwin Museum), Biggin Hill Airfield, Buckston Browne House
Signage:	Complete both ways. Logo: yellow 'Leaves Green Circular Walk' on dark green background, plus yellow arrow with red flash
Refreshments and toilets:	Pubs at Leaves Green and Downe. Café at Downe. Tearoom at Down House. Toilets at Leaves Green Common car park and Down House
Public transport and break points:	Buses: Leaves Green, Keston, Downe
Links:	London Loop, Cudham Circular Walk, Nash Circular Walk
Map:	Explorer 147
LWF status:	Validated with Seal of Approval
Principal promoter:	LB Bromley
Further information:	Included in Pack One of *Bromley Circular Walks and Trails* (£2.50 plus 50p p+p) from LB Bromley Leisure & Community Services and libraries

An undulating route that has almost everything: glorious views, remote countryside, stately homes, farmland, a historic airfield and even a haunted house. One of the **Bromley Circular Walks and Trails** series, it starts from Leaves Green Common near the Kings Arms, a 17th century weatherboarded pub. You are soon in open country with an outstanding view across a dry green valley in the foothills of the North Downs. You descend to follow a long leafy track back up to the main road by Keston's cute little parish church, touching the **Nash Circular Walk**.

Ashmore Farm near Leaves Green

A pavement stretch follows, where the short route makes a beeline across a huge field back to Leaves Green, and where Section 3 of the **London Loop** scrapes past. The long route continues across more farmland, linking with the **Cudham Circular Walk**, to the attractive village of Downe, with two old inns, a teashop and another little church. Soon after that comes Down House (note the different spelling), where Charles Darwin wrote *Origin of the Species*. It is open to the public on certain days and has a tearoom and toilets. Nearby is Downe Court, which claims to be haunted by at least seven ghosts.

More farmland follows (including a horse stud), then a long stretch on a quiet metalled lane leads through West Kent Golf Course, passing the grandiose Buckston Browne House, now the base of an experimental farm. At the top of the hill lies Biggin Hill Airfield, a key base for the Second World War's Battle of Britain, now a busy civil airport. You will probably see several light aircraft movements at close range, but noise is not too great except when flying displays take place, and there is banger racing to the west of the route on some Sundays. Finally you make a detour around the airport's northern perimeter and cross a large field back to Leaves Green.

   A short level circuit of about one kilometre (half a mile) on a firm surface can be made at Leaves Green, linking some of the points described on the route card.

LIMEHOUSE CUT TOWPATH – see Time Travellers

LONDON COUNTRYWAY (MAPS 1, 2)

Distance:	328km (205miles)
Location:	See text
Start/finish:	Box Hill (River Mole stepping stones, GR 173-513)
Blue factor:	n/a
Recommended direction:	Clockwise
Terrain and surface:	Mostly in the hills surrounding London, with some quite steep slopes and some fairly level terrain. Mostly on rough paths and tracks. Stiles: not known. Approximately 32km (20miles) beside roads
Points of interest:	See text
Signage:	None
Refreshments and toilets:	Pubs at frequent intervals. Some cafés. Few public toilets
Public transport and break points:	Frequent opportunities – see text
Links:	North Downs Way, Thames Down Link, Thames Path National Trail, Beeches Way, South Bucks Way, Grand Union Canal Walk, Hertfordshire Chain Walk, New River Path, Lea Valley Walk, Epping Forest Centenary Walk, North Downs Way, Vanguard Way, Socratic Trail
Map:	Explorers 145, 146, 147, 160, 163, 172, 174, 175, 181 and 182
LWF status:	n/a
Principal promoter:	Long Distance Walkers Association
Further information:	Guidebook in preparation at time of writing. Meanwhile a reprint of the 1977 32-page booklet is available for £1.50 inc. p+p from Keith Chesterton

Although this route never enters or even touches Greater London, it is included for four reasons: London appears in the title; it offers a third level of circum-navigating the London area, beyond the Capital Ring and London Loop; it lies entirely within the London commuter belt; and last but not least it is an excellent walk passing through some of the best countryside around London. Many of London's strategic routes (see Links above) go out to meet the London Countryway. The route lies almost entirely outside the M25 motorway, making just two appearances of just a few kilometres each inside the circle. One is at Waltham Abbey, where it also comes closest (600m) to the Greater London boundary; the other near Caterham.

The creation of Keith Chesterton, a member of the Long Distance Walkers Association, which supported the idea from the outset, the London Countryway has become a favourite walk of LDWA members since the route description was first published in 1976. The official start and finish lies at the foot of Box Hill by the famous stepping stones across the River Mole (also on the North Downs Way), but of course you can start and finish at any other convenient point. The route is served by good train services at or near many points, such as Reigate, Dorking, Woking, Windsor, Maidenhead, Marlow, Great Missenden, Kings Langley, St Albans, Brookmans Park, Broxbourne, Cheshunt, Waltham Cross, Epping, Brentwood, Tilbury, Gravesend, Borough Green, Oxted and Merstham.

Approaching Richmond, by Petersham Meadows (Thames Path National Trail, Time Trails in London)

Richmond Bridge (Thames Path National Trail, Capital Ring, Time Trails in London)

Wandle Mouth, Wandsworth (Thames Path National Trail, Wandle Trail)

Fire Escape at Canary Wharf Riverside
(Thames Path National Trail,
Nature Conservation in Tower Hamlets)

Grant's Quay Walk and Tower Bridge,
City of London
(Thames Path National Trail)

Shadwell Basin (Thames Path National Trail, Nature Conservation in Tower Hamlets)

155

LONDON LOOP

Introduction. The London Loop, one of the Mayor of London's key routes, *almost* completely encircles Greater London, covering a total distance of around 240km (150 miles). It has been described as 'the M25 for walkers', although it rarely comes anywhere near the motorway. The route stays as much as possible within Greater London, to facilitate use of travelcards, but it has proved necessary to venture outside in places. The only gap in the circuit is between Sections 24 at Purfleet and 1 at Erith, where the River Thames provides a substantial barrier of almost a kilometre (half a mile) with no convenient crossing point (see Section 24 text if you wish to continue from there to Section 1).

The idea was put forward at a meeting of the London Walking Forum in the early 1990s. After a competition, the route was formally named the 'London Outer Orbital Path', and although you may sometimes see this version, or as initials LOOP, the route is popularly known and shown on Ordnance Survey maps as the London Loop.

The first of the 24 sections (Section 5) was opened on 3 May 1996, with a ceremony on Farthing Downs, and other sections have followed at the rate of two or three per year as signs are installed and leaflets for individual sections are published. The route became fully walkable in 2001 with the publication of the Aurum Press guidebook (see below), however at the time of writing some sections do not yet have signs or individual leaflets, and a few diversions are necessary where the preferred route is not yet available. The London Walking Forum estimates that the route should be fully signed and leafleted by 2003.

The following pages describe each section individually. For convenience, here is a complete list of the sections and approximate distances:

		km	ml
1	Erith to Old Bexley	13.5	8.4
2	Old Bexley to Petts Wood	11.5	7.2
3	Petts Wood to West Wickham Common	14.4	9.0
4	West Wickham Common to Hamsey Green	14.4	9.0
5	Hamsey Green to Coulsdon South	9.6	6.0
6	Coulsdon South to Banstead Downs	7.2	4.5
7	Banstead Downs to Ewell	6.4	4.0
8	Ewell to Kingston	11.7	7.3
9	Kingston to Hatton Cross	13.6	8.5
10	Hatton Cross to Hayes & Harlington	6.1	3.8
11	Hayes & Harlington to Uxbridge	11.7	7.3
12	Uxbridge to Harefield West	7.2	4.5
13	Harefield West to Moor Park	7.7	4.8
14	Moor Park to Hatch End	6.1	3.8

15	Hatch End to Elstree & Borehamwood	13.3	8.3
16	Elstree & Borehamwood to Cockfosters	16.8	10.5
17	Cockfosters to Enfield Lock	13.3	8.3
18	Enfield Lock to Chingford	10.4	6.5
19	Chingford to Chigwell	6.4	4.0
20	Chigwell to Havering-atte-Bower	9.6	6.0
21	Havering-atte-Bower to Harold Wood	6.9	4.3
22	Harold Wood to Upminster Bridge	6.9	4.3
23	Upminster Bridge to Rainham	6.4	4.0
24	Rainham to Purfleet	7.2	4.5

Signage. The route is indicated on the ground by a variety of signs and waymarks. In countryside locations they consist mostly of a simple white disc, mounted on wooden posts and containing a directional arrow with the flying kestrel logo in blue and text in green. (A word of warning: the arrow's direction may not be clear until you are close up. It is easy to assume that it points ahead, but it may turn – look closely before continuing.) In urban streets these are replaced by larger aluminium signs strapped to lampposts and other street furniture, and additionally carry a walking man symbol. On link routes to stations the word 'link' is incorporated into the logo. At major focal points you will also meet tall green and white signposts that give distances to three points in either direction. Some of these locations may also have the big, round-topped information boards.

Further information. An excellent guidebook to the whole route, written by David Sharp and with 1:25,000 scale Ordnance Survey maps, is published by Aurum Press (ISBN 1-85410-759-3, £12.99). Note that in this book the route is divided into 15 sections by combining some of those described here. The Ordnance Survey is marking the London Loop route on its Explorer maps as new editions are published.

In addition, individual leaflets for each section are available or planned, and can be obtained from relevant local authority outlets such as libraries or tourist information centres. The latest position regarding availability can be checked with the London Walking Forum (see Appendix H for contact details). Leaflets for Sections 1–8 (known as the Blue Sector) are currently only available in a boxed pack costing £6.00, available from the Downlands Project (see Appendix H for contact details). Similar packs for Sections 9–16 (Green Sector) and Sections 17–24 (Yellow Sector) are also being considered.

LONDON LOOP: SECTION 1 (MAP 6)
Erith to Old Bexley

Distance:	13.5km (8.4 miles) including links with Erith and Bexley stations
Location:	Bexley
Start:	Erith Riverside (GR 514-782)
Finish:	Old Bexley (High Street, close to Bexley station, GR 494-735)
Green factor:	55%
Blue factor:	58%
Recommended direction:	North to south
Terrain and surface:	Entirely level. Mixture of pavements, tarmac paths and rough surfaces. Two stiles. 3.3km (2.1miles) beside roads
Points of interest:	River Thames; Erith riverside; Queen Elizabeth 2 Bridge; Darent raised dam; Crayford Marshes; Crayford; Churchfield Wood; Hall Place; Old Bexley village
Signage:	No Loop signage at time of writing but meanwhile Cray Riverway signs can be followed
Refreshments and toilets:	Pubs and cafés at Erith, Crayford, Hall Place and Old Bexley. Public toilets at Crayford, Hall Place and Old Bexley
Public transport and break points:	NR: Erith, Slade Green, Crayford, Bexley. Buses at all these points plus Barnes Cray
Links:	Cray Riverway, Shuttle Riverway.
Map:	Explorer 162
LWF status:	Validated with Seal of Approval (Mayor of London's key route)
Principal promoter:	London Walking Forum, LB Bexley
Further information:	See London Loop introduction

Easy walking, mainly on pleasant paths beside three rivers (Thames, Darent and Cray) and through parks and woodland, although there are some rather unattractive urban parts. At time of writing London Loop signage has not been put up, but most of the route follows the *Cray Riverway*, whose signs are mostly in place. If you wish to walk this section from south to north you will find the Cray Riverway leaflet helpful as it is written in that direction.

From Erith station you make your way to the Thames, then follow it through most of Erith's riverside, except where industrial premises currently prevent riverside access. There is almost a seaside feeling along the pleasant promenade as the river is nearly a kilometre (half a mile) wide at this point. Beyond the town, you walk on a raised flood defence bank beside marshes, with good views of the Queen Elizabeth Bridge ahead. You turn inland to follow Dartford Creek (the River Darenth), passing its impressive flood protection barrier. There is a link here to Slade Green Station.

Now you follow a third river, the Cray, for the rest of this section, occasionally diverting where the riverside is not yet accessible. There is a link with the **Shuttle Riverway** at Hall Place. The section finishes close to Bexley station in the historic village of Old Bexley.

LONDON LOOP: SECTION 2 (MAP 6)
Old Bexley to Petts Wood

Distance:	11.5km (7.2miles) including links with Bexley and Petts Wood stations
Location:	Bexley, Bromley
Start:	Old Bexley (High Street, close to Bexley station, GR 494-735)
Finish:	Petts Wood (Jubilee Country Park, GR 440-680)
Green factor:	76%
Blue factor:	18%
Recommended direction:	Northeast to southwest
Terrain and surface:	Mostly level with some gentle slopes. Long flights of steps on three footbridges across railway lines near Petts Wood. One stile. 1.0km (0.6miles) beside roads
Points of interest:	Foots Cray Meadows, Five Arch Bridge, Cray Wanderers Football Ground, Sidcup Place Park, Scadbury Park, Petts Wood
Signage:	Almost complete (both ways)
Refreshments and toilets:	Pubs and cafés in Old Bexley, Foots Cray, Sidcup and Petts Wood. Public toilets at Old Bexley and Sidcup Place Park
Public transport and break points:	NR: Bexley, Albany Park, Petts Wood. Buses at all these points plus Sidcup and St Paul's Cray Road
Links:	Cray Riverway, St Paul's Cray and Petts Wood Circular Walks
Map:	Explorer 162

LWF status:	Validated with Seal of Approval (Mayor of London's key route)
Principal promoter:	London Walking Forum, LB Bexley, LB Bromley
Further information:	See London Loop introduction

This section manages to find a very green and mostly easy route through the suburbs of southeast London, with little roadwalking. It starts in Old Bexley High Street, close to Bexley station.

At first, it shares the route of the **Cray Riverway** through sports grounds and wasteland, then beside the River Cray in Foots Cray Meadows, possibly one of the most charming sections of the whole London Loop. Leaving the Cray Riverway at Foots Cray, the route winds through residential areas and more sports grounds (including Cray Wanderers, one of the oldest football clubs in Britain). After the formal gardens surrounding Sidcup Place (now a huge pub-restaurant) and Queen Mary's Hospital, you cross the busy Sidcup Bypass to reach Scadbury Park, a large nature reserve run by the London Borough of Bromley. Here the route is shared with **St. Paul's Cray Circular Walk**, passing the moated remains of Scadbury Manor, to emerge on to St. Paul's Cray Road.

The route descends gently on tracks among the trees and fields of Petts Wood (a National Trust property), linking with the **Petts Wood Circular Walk**. You cross three railway lines in quick succession to reach the section end in Jubilee Country Park, where there is a link to Petts Wood station.

LONDON LOOP: SECTION 3 (MAP 8)
Petts Wood to West Wickham Common

Distance:	15.5km (9.7miles) including links with Petts Wood and Hayes stations
Location:	Bromley
Start:	Petts Wood (Jubilee Country Park, GR 440-680)
Finish:	West Wickham Common (GR 396-654)
Green factor:	77%
Blue factor:	2%
Recommended direction:	Northeast to southwest
Terrain and surface:	Mostly level, but with some steps and quite steep slopes. Mostly on rough paths, tracks and grass. Three stiles. 2.7km (1.7miles) beside roads
Points of interest:	Jubilee Country Park, Crofton Wood, Darrick Wood, Farnborough village, Gypsy Lee's grave, farmland, High Elms Country Park, Wilberforce memorial, Caesar's Well, Keston Ponds, West Wickham Common

Signage:	Complete (both ways)
Refreshments and toilets:	Pubs and cafés at Petts Wood, Farnborough and Hayes. Pubs at Keston. Public toilets at Farnborough, High Elms Country Park and Keston Ponds
Public transport and break points:	NR: Petts Wood, Hayes. Buses at these points, also at Crofton, Farnborough, Keston Ponds and Keston village
Links:	Petts Wood, Farnborough, Cudham, Leaves Green, Nash and Three Commons Circular Walks
Map:	Explorer 162
LWF status:	Validated with Seal of Approval (Mayor of London's key route)
Principal promoter:	London Walking Forum, LB Bromley
Further information:	See London Loop introduction

This very pleasant section passes through attractive countryside linking several country parks and commons. Starting in the Jubilee Country Park, close to Petts Wood station, the first 4km (2.5 miles) are fairly level, alternating between paths through woods and commons and residential roads in Crofton. This leads to the charming village of Farnborough with its churchyard where Gypsy Lee is buried.

After that it is almost non-stop countryside with outstanding views. High Elms Country Park has magnificent trees, and fascinating remains of the old house, its gardens and outbuildings. The terrain now gets more undulating on footpaths through fields, with some quite steep slopes. In quick succession, the route is either shared with or brushes no fewer than six routes in the **Bromley Circular Walks and Trails** series (**Petts Wood, Farnborough, Cudham, Leaves Green, Nash and Three Commons**), so there are plenty of opportunities for making up longer routes and links at will.

At the top of one long climb is a memorial to the abolishment of slavery (because William Wilberforce discussed the subject with Prime Minister George Pitt here). You descend to the section's only water feature, Keston Ponds, passing a spring known as Caesar's Well, a source of the River Ravensbourne. Biggin Hill Airport lies a little to the south, and you are likely to see several movements by the small private aircraft that use it.

The route now becomes fairly level again through Keston village and along the well wooded West Wickham Common to the finishing point on Gates Green Road, where a link leads to Hayes station.

London Loop: Section 4 (Maps 8, 7)
West Wickham Common to Hamsey Green

Distance:	14.5km (9.1 miles) including link with Hayes station
Location:	Bromley, Croydon, plus some in Surrey
Start:	West Wickham Common (GR 396-654)
Finish:	Hamsey Green (GR 350-595)
Green factor:	74%
Blue factor:	n/a
Recommended direction:	Northeast to southwest
Terrain and surface:	Mostly level, but several steep slopes and flights of steps. Mostly rough ground on footpaths and tracks. Four stiles. 2.8km (1.8 miles) beside roads
Points of interest:	Greenwich Meridian Stone; St John the Baptist Church; Spring Park, Threehalfpenny Wood; Kennel Wood; Addington Hills and viewing platform; Heathfield Gardens; Bramley Bank Nature Reserve; Littleheath Wood; Selsdon Wood Local Nature Reserve; Puplet Wood; Kingswood
Signage:	Complete (both ways)
Refreshments and toilets:	Pubs at Hayes, Upper Shirley and Hamsey Green. Cafés or kiosks at Hayes, Coney Hall, Sparrow's Den and Hamsey Green. Public toilets at Coney Hall, Sparrow's Den, Addington Hills and Heathfield
Public transport and break points:	NR: Hayes. CTL: Coombe Lane. Buses at these points, also Upper Shirley, Selsdon, Forestdale and Hamsey Green
Links:	Three Commons Circular Walk, Vanguard Way
Map:	Explorers 162, 161, 146 (route marked)
LWF status:	Validated with Seal of Approval (Mayor of London's key route)
Principal promoter:	London Walking Forum, LB Bromley, LB Croydon, Tandridge DC
Further information:	See London Loop introduction

A well-wooded section with a fair amount of climbing, rewarded by some splendid views. The first stretch from West Wickham Common (also on the ***Three Commons Circular Walk***) leads through a residential area and recreation grounds, where you pass a stone marking the line of the Greenwich Meridian and the hilltop St. John the Baptist Church, over 700 years old. Then comes a long wooded stretch through Spring Park, Threehalfpenny Wood and Kennel Wood.

More residential roads lead to Upper Shirley, then another long, green section follows, with several points of interest. A steep climb brings you to the viewing platform at Addington Hills, with its magnificent panorama – on a clear day you can see Windsor Castle and hills to the north of London. The delightful gardens at Heathfield (with steeps flights of steps) are attached to Heathfield House, which is Croydon Council's training centre. Bramley Bank Nature Reserve is run by the London Wildlife Trust.

From Littleheath Wood, the route is shared for a while with the **Vanguard Way**. After Selsdon Wood Local Nature Reserve you pass out of Greater London into Surrey for the rest of this section. Beyond Farleigh, a wooded valley leads past the golf course of Selsdon Park Hotel, and the section finishes with a short road stretch into Hamsey Green, from where there are buses to Croydon.

LONDON LOOP: SECTION 5 (MAP 7)
Hamsey Green to Coulsdon South

Distance:	9.6km (6.0 miles)
Location:	Croydon, plus some in Surrey
Start:	Hamsey Green (GR 350-595)
Finish:	Coulsdon South station (GR 299-590)
Green factor:	72%
Blue factor:	n/a
Recommended direction:	East to west
Terrain and surface:	Mostly level, but three long climbs (two of them very steep with steps). Mostly rough tracks, footpaths and grassy fields. Two stiles. 1.6km (1.0miles) beside roads
Points of interest:	Riddlesdown, Kenley Common, Kenley Aerodrome, Kenley Observatory, Coulsdon Common, Happy Valley, Farthing Downs
Signage:	Complete (both ways)
Refreshments and toilets:	Pubs and cafes at Hamsey Green and Coulsdon South. Pubs at Godstone Road, Kenley Aerodrome and Coulsdon Common. Occasional kiosk at Farthing Downs. Public toilets at Farthing Downs
Public transport and break points:	NR: Coulsdon South. Buses: Hamsey Green, Godstone Road, Coulsdon Common, Coulsdon South

Links:	Riddlesdown Circular Walk, Kenley Common & Dollypers Hill Circular Walk, Coulsdon Common & Happy Valley Circular Walk, Farthing Downs & Devilsden Wood Circular Walk, Downlands Circular Walk, Socratic Trail
Map:	Explorer 146 (route marked). A tiny part covering about 300m is on sheet 161
LWF status:	Validated with Seal of Approval (Mayor of London's key route)
Principal promoter:	London Walking Forum, LB Bromley, LB Croydon, Tandridge DC
Further information:	See London Loop introduction

This very attractive section of quite strenuous walking features in quick succession four commons controlled by the Corporation of London: Riddlesdown, Kenley Common, Coulsdon Common and Farthing Downs – the latter providing a long ridge walk with fine views and grazing cattle. Each has its own walk with which this section can be combined – see **Coulsdon Commons Circular Walks.**

You pass Kenley Aerodrome, a renowned wartime air base, but you need not fear noise as it is only used for gliding nowadays. Two small observatories nearby are operated by the Croydon Astronomical Society. Between Coulsdon Common and Farthing Downs come Happy Valley and Devilsden Wood, owned by the London Borough of Croydon. The **Downlands Circular Walk** and **Socratic Trail** also pass through this idyllic area, where rare plants thrive, and you can scarcely believe you are in Greater London.

LONDON LOOP: SECTION 6 (MAP 7)
Coulsdon South to Banstead Downs

Distance:	7.2km (4.5 miles) including link with Banstead station
Location:	Croydon, Sutton, plus some in Surrey
Start:	Coulsdon South station (GR 299-590)
Finish:	Banstead Downs (near Brighton Road, GR 248-607)
Green factor:	69%
Blue factor:	n/a
Recommended direction:	East to west
Terrain and surface:	Generally fairly level but with a long gradual climb for the first 2km. Mostly on rough ground on footpaths and tracks. Five stiles. 1.7km (1.1miles) beside roads

Points of interest:	Little Woodcote Estate, The Oaks Park, Highdown Prison, Banstead Downs
Signage:	Complete (both ways)
Refreshments and toilets:	Pubs and cafés at Coulsdon and Banstead. Pub at Clockhouse. Café at The Oaks Park. Public toilets at Coulsdon and The Oaks Park
Public transport and break points:	NR: Coulsdon South, Banstead. Buses at these points, also Clockhouse and Sutton Lane
Links:	Sutton Countryside Walk
Map:	Explorers 146, 161 (route marked)
LWF status:	Validated with Seal of Approval (Mayor of London's key route)
Principal promoter:	London Walking Forum, LB Croydon, LB Sutton, Reigate & Banstead DC
Further information:	See London Loop introduction

Note that the first part of this section, immediately west of Coulsdon South station, may be affected by construction of the proposed Coulsdon Relief Road. The section starts with a long, steady climb through residential roads in Coulsdon and Clockhouse, but after that the route is almost entirely level in attractive countryside, with some fine views towards London. You pass the distinctive black weatherboard houses of the smallholdings on the Little Woodcote Estate, then open fields lead to The Oaks Park, with its café, toilets and nature trail. It was once the grounds of the mansion of the Earl of Derby, both providing names for the classic horse races at Epsom.

A long, straight track takes you into Surrey, passing the high walls of Highdown Prison. Once across busy Sutton Lane (close to Banstead village) you are on Banstead Downs, skirting a golf course. There is another very busy dual-carriageway road to negotiate before the end of the section, from where a signed Loop link leads to Banstead station (no Sunday service but buses from nearby Belmont).

LONDON LOOP: SECTION 7 (MAP 7)
Banstead Downs to Ewell

Although one of the shortest and, admittedly, least green sections of the London Loop, you pass much of interest. There is a signed link to the start on Banstead Downs from Banstead station (no Sunday service but buses at nearby Belmont). You follow pleasant residential roads for some distance through Belmont and East Ewell, where unfortunately it has not proved possible to negotiate formal access along a path beside a golf club. A pleasant green stretch follows, through the Woodland Trust's Warren Farm (signed link to Ewell East station) and Nonsuch Park, which contains the remains of a palace built by King Henry VIII. In Ewell you pass an ancient village lock-up (with a plaque telling a humorous tale about

165

a fire engine), and the section finishes in the small but pretty Bourne Hall Park with its pond, a source of the Hogsmill River. A signed link leads from here to Ewell West station.

Distance:	6.4km (4.0 miles) including links with Banstead and Ewell West stations
Location:	Sutton, but mostly in Surrey
Start:	Banstead Downs (near Brighton Road, GR 248-607)
Finish:	Ewell (Bourne Hall Park, GR 219-628)
Green factor:	40%
Blue factor:	2%
Recommended direction:	Southeast to northwest
Terrain and surface:	Level ground except for gentle descents on residential roads. Mostly pavements, with some firm paths and tracks. No stiles. 2.9km (1.8 miles) beside roads
Points of interest:	Banstead Downs, Warren Farm Woodland Trust Reserve, Nonsuch Park, remains of Nonsuch Palace, Bourne Hall Park, Hogsmill River
Signage:	Complete (both ways)
Refreshments and toilets:	Pubs and cafés in Banstead and Ewell. Café in Nonsuch Park. Public toilets in Nonsuch Park and Bourne Hall Park
Public transport and break points:	NR/buses: Banstead, Ewell East, Ewell West
Links:	None
Map:	Explorer 161 (route marked)
LWF status:	Validated with Seal of Approval (Mayor of London's key route)
Principal promoter:	London Walking Forum, LB Sutton, Reigate & Banstead DC, Epsom & Ewell DC
Further information:	See London Loop introduction

LONDON LOOP: SECTION 8 (MAP 7)
Ewell to Kingston

One of the 'bluest' sections of the Loop, shared with the **Hogsmill Walk**, whose leaflet is written north-south (useful if walking the Loop anticlockwise). It mostly follows the Hogsmill River, which rises at the ponds in Bourne Hall Park, where this section starts (signed link from Ewell West station). You may catch sight of all manner of river life, including with luck a water vole or a kingfisher.

Distance:	11.7km (7.3 miles) including links with Ewell West and Kingston stations
Location:	Kingston, plus some in Surrey
Start:	Ewell (Bourne Hall Park, GR 219-628)
Finish:	Kingston Bridge (GR 177-694)
Green factor:	48%
Blue factor:	58%
Recommended direction:	South to north
Terrain and surface:	Level (short ramps at subway under A3). Mostly hard surface with some short grassy stretches. No stiles. 4.7km (2.9 miles) beside roads
Points of interest:	Bourne Hall Park, Hogsmill River, St John the Baptist Church, historic Kingston, Chair of Majesty Coronation Stone, Clattern Bridge, River Thames
Signage:	Complete (both ways)
Refreshments and toilets:	Pubs and cafés at Ewell, Berrylands and Kingston. Pubs at Old Malden Lane and Villiers Road, Kingston. Public toilets at Ewell (Bourne Hall Park) and shopping centres in Kingston
Public transport and break points:	NR: Ewell (East and West), Malden Manor, Berrylands, Kingston. Buses at all these points plus Ruxley Lane, Kingston Road, Malden Way
Links:	Hogsmill Walk, Thames Down Link, Thames Path National Trail
Map:	Explorer 161 (route marked)
LWF status:	Validated with Seal of Approval (Mayor of London's key route)
Principal promoter:	London Walking Forum, Epsom & Ewell DC, RB Kingston
Further information:	See London Loop introduction

The first 3.5km (2.2 miles) run close beside the Hogsmill, with a short boardwalk where it passes under a railway bridge. At Tolworth Court Bridge the Bonesgate Stream comes in from the left, bringing with it the **Thames Down Link** to share the remainder of this section. At Old Malden and Berrylands the river is currently inaccessible and you must divert along residential roads. At the point where the river passes under the A3 dual carriageway, you must divert 200m to and from a subway. There is a signed link with Malden Manor station, and the route passes Berrylands station.

The road walk from Berrylands is rather tedious at present, until more of the river becomes accessible, but you are rewarded at Kingston with a fascinating array of historic buildings in the old market place. The River Thames marks the end of this section, and you briefly join the *Thames Path National Trail* to Kingston Bridge, where a signed link leads to Kingston station.

♿ The whole section is level, but lengthy stretches are on rough ground or grass, which may be difficult in wet weather.

London Loop: Section 9 (Map 3)
Kingston Bridge to Hatton Cross

Distance:	13.6km (8.5 miles) including links with Kingston and Hatton Cross stations
Location:	Richmond, Hounslow, Hillingdon
Start:	Kingston Bridge (GR 177-694)
Finish:	Hatton Cross (Great Southwest Road) (GR 105-757)
Green factor:	68%
Blue factor:	27%
Recommended direction:	Southeast to northwest
Terrain and surface:	Entirely level, mostly on grass and rough footpaths. Sections in Bushy Park subject to flooding. One stile. 4.5km (2.8 miles) beside roads
Points of interest:	River Thames, Bushy Park, Longford River, River Crane, Crane Park and shot tower, Hounslow Heath
Signage:	Not signed at time of writing
Refreshments and toilets:	Pubs and cafés at Kingston, Hanworth Road and Hatton Cross. Pubs at Hampton Road and Staines Road. Public toilets in Bushy Park
Public transport and break points:	NR: Kingston, Fulwell. LU: Hatton Cross. Buses: at these points, also Hampton Road, Staines Road, Great Chertsey Road, Hanworth Road, Staines Road, Great Southwest Road
Links:	Hogsmill Walk, Thames Down Link, River Crane Walk, Thames Path National Trail
Map:	Explorer 161 (route marked)
LWF status:	Pending validation
Principal promoter:	London Walking Forum, LB Richmond, LB Hounslow, LB Hillingdon
Further information:	See London Loop introduction

Easy walking, including some extensive green stretches. From Kingston Bridge you cross Bushy Park beside the Longford River, where you may see roe deer, and through the Woodland Gardens. Note that one particular area is subject to flooding in wet weather. After a stretch along residential roads and beside golf courses you join the *River Crane Walk* through Crane Park, passing a historic shot tower, remains of gunpowder mills that once endangered this area.

The Crane dives into a tunnel below the former railway marshalling yards at Feltham – eventually the route may continue through this area. For the moment, however, there is an opportunity to detour across Hounslow Heath, renowned for its past associations with highwaymen. You rejoin the Crane on a well wooded path, which may be muddy and overgrown, through to the Great Southwest Road and the link to Hatton Cross station. Section 10 continues ahead with the river, but to reach it you must make a diversion of one kilometre (half a mile) as there is no pedestrian crossing over the A30 here.

LONDON LOOP: SECTION 10 (MAP 3)
Hatton Cross to Hayes

Distance:	6.1km (3.8 miles) including links with Hatton Cross and to Hayes & Harlington stations
Location:	Hounslow, Hillingdon
Start:	Hatton Cross (Great Southwest Road, GR 105-757)
Finish:	Hayes (Station Road, GR 098-796)
Green factor:	35%
Blue factor:	49%
Recommended direction:	South to north
Terrain and surface:	Entirely level except for spiral ramp on to canal towpath. Narrow rough path (sometimes muddy) beside River Crane; firm on canal towpath. No stiles. 0.8km (0.5 miles) beside roads
Points of interest:	River Crane, Cranford Park, St Dunstan's Church, Grand Union Canal
Signage:	Not signed at time of writing
Refreshments and toilets:	Pubs and cafés at Hayes. Public toilets at Cranford Park Information Centre
Public transport and break points:	LU: Hatton Cross. NR: Hayes & Harlington. Buses at these points, also Bath Road, Hyde Road
Links:	Hillingdon Trail, Grand Union Canal Walk
Map:	Explorer 161 (route marked), plus 200m on 160

LWF status:	Pending validation
Principal promoter:	London Walking Forum, LB Hounslow, LB Hillingdon
Further information:	See London Loop introduction

Despite passing through one of the most traffic-ridden areas of London (A30, A4, M4), and below the approach to Heathrow Airport, this section includes much pleasant and easy walking. It lies mostly beside the River Crane, though access to the river is rather broken at present.

The first stretch follows the east bank of the Crane through Cranebank Water Meadow. You must divert along roads for a short distance to reach Berkeley Meads and the lush meadows of Cranford Park, spreading west of the Crane. The tower of St. Dunstan's Church guides you to a subway under the M4, and the route is now shared for a while with the **Hillingdon Trail**. Past the M4, the Crane is rejoined for a short distance through Dog Kennel Covert, then at North Hyde Road you divert on to the busy A312 dual carriageway (The Parkway), mercifully for just 200m. An intriguing spiral ramp takes you down to a canal towpath (part of the **Grand Union Canal Walk**), which you follow through a commercial area to Station Road, Hayes.

LONDON LOOP: SECTION 11 (MAP 3)
Hayes to Uxbridge

Distance:	12.5km (7.8 miles) including links with Hayes & Harlington and Uxbridge stations
Location:	Hillingdon, plus some in Bucks
Start:	Hayes (Station Road, GR 098-796)
Finish:	Uxbridge (Oxford Road, GR 052-846)
Green factor:	45%
Blue factor:	67%
Recommended direction:	Southeast to northwest
Terrain and surface:	Mostly level on canal- and riverside paths. Some gentle slopes in Stockley Park and on canal ramps. Canal towpaths are generally firm, but much of the route lies on rough and possibly muddy paths, or on grass. No stiles. 1.2km (0.8 miles) beside roads
Points of interest:	Grand Union Canal, Stockley Park, River Colne, Little Britain Lake
Signage:	Complete both ways

Refreshments and toilets:	Pubs and cafés at Hayes, West Drayton, Yiewsley and Uxbridge. Pubs at Little Britain and Cowley. Café and toilets at Stockley Park Golf Club
Public transport and break points:	NR: Hayes & Harlington, West Drayton. LU: Uxbridge. Buses at these points, also Stockley Park, Yiewsley and Cowley
Links:	Grand Union Canal Walk, Beeches Way, West Drayton to Slough Ramble and Ride, Celandine Route, Grand Union Canal (Slough Arm), Colne Valley Way, Iver Circular Walk, Colne Valley Trail, Nine Stiles Circular Walk
Map:	Explorers 160, 172
LWF status:	Validated with Seal of Approval (Mayor of London's key route)
Principal promoter:	London Walking Forum, LB Hillingdon
Further information:	See London Loop introduction

A good section for enthusiasts of waterside walking, as over two-thirds follows canal, river or lake. It might have followed the Grand Union Canal towpath all the way, but this could be tedious and the designers have sensibly made diversions into attractive green areas to the side. This leaves three separate sections where the route is shared with the *Grand Union Canal Walk*, at Hayes, West Drayton/Yiewsley and Uxbridge.

The first diversion skirts Stockley Park, north of the canal. This very green area has been created from an immense but exhausted gravel pit, which was filled with refuse and is now grassed over. Most of it is occupied by a golf course, but tarmac footpaths provide ample scope for walkers. Soaring towers on the skyline draw you towards a suspension footbridge across busy Stockley Road. Nearby is a splendid view across West London and the Colne Valley. You return to the canal towpath through West Drayton (starting points of the *Beeches Way* and *West Drayton to Slough Ramble and Ride*) and Yiewsley (end of the *Celandine Route*).

The Loop turns west along the *Grand Union Canal Slough Arm* for a short distance, then descends to follow the River Colne, sharing it with the *Colne Valley Way* and *Iver Circular Walk* past the delightful Little Britain Lake. A short road stretch leads back to the Grand Union Canal towpath and station link at Uxbridge, starting point of the *Colne Valley Trail* and *Nine Stiles Circular Walk*.

London Loop: Section 12 (Map 3)
Uxbridge to Harefield West

Another section dominated by water – the 'bluest' of the whole London Loop. Lakes formed from worked out gravel pits line the whole section, some feeding the canal with water. You pass four canal locks, a lockside tearoom and three canalside pubs, and there should be plenty of waterborne action, whether of wildlife or the human variety – boats and anglers.

Distance:	7.2km (4.5 miles) including links with Uxbridge station and bus stop at Harefield West
Location:	Hillingdon, plus some in Bucks
Start:	Uxbridge (Oxford Road, GR 052-846)
Finish:	Harefield West (Coppermill Lane, GR 040-912)
Green factor:	90%
Blue factor:	83%
Recommended direction:	South to north
Terrain and surface:	Mainly on firm and level canalside paths, but one short stretch on a rough track. No stiles. 200m beside roads
Points of interest:	Grand Union Canal and locks, Denham Country Park, Frays Valley Local Nature Reserve, Harefield Marina
Signage:	Not signed at time of writing
Refreshments and toilets:	Pubs at Uxbridge, Widewater Lock and Harefield West. Tearoom at Denham Lock. Public toilets at Colne Valley Park Visitor Centre (500m off route)
Public transport and break points:	LU: Uxbridge. Buses here and at Widewater Lock and Harefield West
Links:	Grand Union Canal Walk, South Bucks Way, Colne Valley Trail, Nine Stiles Circular Walk, Widewater Lock Circular Walk, Harefield Heights Circular Walk
Map:	Explorer 172 (route marked)
LWF status:	Pending validation
Principal promoter:	London Walking Forum, LB Hillingdon
Further information:	See London Loop introduction

From Oxford Road in Uxbridge the route generally follows paths beside the Grand Union Canal, but for variety makes a diversion around former gravel pits in the Frays Valley Local Nature Reserve, one of which is now a marina. At Denham Lock are gathered no fewer than six routes in the Strategic Network: *London Loop, Colne Valley Trail*, **Grand Union Canal Walk**, **Nine Stiles Circular Walk, South Bucks Way** and **Widewater Lock Circular Walk**. The section ends beside the Coy Carp pub near Coppermill Lock at Harefield West, start and finish of the **Harefield Heights Circular Walk**.

LONDON LOOP: SECTION 13 (MAP 3)
Harefield West to Moor Park

Distance:	7.7km (4.8 miles) including link with Moor Park station
Location:	Hillingdon, plus some in Hertfordshire
Start:	Harefield West (Coppermill Lane, GR 040-912)
Finish:	Moor Park (Westbury Road, GR 089-928)
Green factor:	62%
Blue factor:	n/a
Recommended direction:	West to east
Terrain and surface:	Steep hill soon after start, otherwise fairly level with some gentle slopes. Mostly on rough paths, tracks and grass. Seven stiles. 2.0km (1.3 miles) beside roads
Points of interest:	Old Park Wood, Bishops Wood, Batchworth Heath, farmland
Signage:	Not signed at time of writing
Refreshments and toilets:	Pubs at Harefield West, Woodcock Hill and Batchworth Heath. No public toilets
Public transport and break points:	Buses: Harefield West, Woodcock Hill, Batchworth Heath. LU: Moor Park
Links:	Colne Valley Trail, Grand Union Canal Walk, Harefield Heights Circular Walk, Hillingdon Trail, West Ruislip to Gerrards Cross Ramble and Ride
Map:	Explorer 172 (route marked)
LWF status:	Pending validation
Principal promoter:	London Walking Forum, LB Hillingdon, Three Rivers DC
Further information:	See London Loop introduction

A rather remote but very pleasant section, keeping fairly well away from settlements until the end at Moor Park. At Harefield West the route connects with the *Colne Valley Trail, Grand Union Canal Walk* and *West Ruislip to Gerrards Cross Ramble and Ride*. Soon after the start, together with the *Hillingdon Trail* and *Harefield Heights Circular Walk*, you face a stiff climb through Old Park Wood, but the rest is fairly level or gently undulating country, passing through several woods and crossing fields which may be ploughed.

LONDON LOOP: SECTION 14 (MAP 3)
Moor Park to Hatch End

Distance:	6.1km (3.8 miles) including links with from Moor Park and Hatch End stations
Location:	Harrow, but mostly in Hertfordshire
Start:	Moor Park (Westbury Road, GR 089-928)
Finish:	Hatch End (Grimsdyke Road, GR 122-914)
Green factor:	85%
Blue factor:	n/a
Recommended direction:	Northwest to southeast
Terrain and surface:	Some short steepish slopes but generally gently undulating. Mainly on rough paths, tracks and grass, which may be muddy at times. Two stiles. 700m beside roads
Points of interest:	Sandy Lodge Golf Course, Oxhey Woods, Nanscot Wood, farmland
Signage:	Not signed at time of writing
Refreshments and toilets:	Pubs and cafés at Moor Park and Hatch End. No public toilets nearby
Public transport and break points:	LU: Moor Park, NR: Hatch End. Buses at these points, also Hayling Road and Prestwick Road
Links:	Pinner-Grimsdyke Circular Walk
Map:	Explorers 172 and 173 (route marked)
LWF status:	Pending validation
Principal promoter:	London Walking Forum, LB Harrow, Three Rivers DC
Further information:	See London Loop introduction

A very green section, with little roadwalking. After crossing Sandy Lodge Golf Course, the route snakes through woodlands separating South Oxhey from Northwood and Pinner. It then crosses farmland around the little community of Pinnerwood, where you walk between charming cottages with well-kept ponds and lawns. Most of the section is in Hertfordshire, but comes back into Greater London towards the end. For a while the route is shared with the **Pinner-Grimsdyke Circular Walk** (also the South Oxhey Circular Walk, not covered in this book being completely outside Greater London).

LONDON LOOP: SECTION 15 (MAP 3)
Hatch End to Elstree

Distance:	13.3km (8.3 miles) including links with Hatch End and Elstree & Borehamwood stations. Additional link to Stanmore station 1.5km (1.0 miles) off route
Location:	Harrow, plus some in Hertfordshire
Start:	Hatch End (Grimsdyke Road, GR 122-914)
Finish:	Elstree (Allum Lane, GR 189-963)
Green factor:	60%
Blue factor:	n/a
Recommended direction:	Southwest to northeast
Terrain and surface:	Undulating. Mostly on rough paths, tracks and grass. Seven stiles. 3.6km (2.3 miles) beside roads
Points of interest:	Grimsdyke, Harrow Weald Common, Bentley Priory, Stanmore Little Common and ponds, Aldenham Country Park and Reservoir
Signage:	Not signed at time of writing
Refreshments and toilets:	Pubs and cafés or kiosks at Harrow Weald Common, Aldenham Country Park and Borehamwood. Public toilets at Aldenham Country Park (400m off route)
Public transport and break points:	NR: Hatch End, Elstree & Borehamwood. LU: Stanmore. Buses at these points, also Oxhey Lane and Harrow Weald Common
Links:	Pinner-Grimsdyke Circular Walk, Bentley Priory Circular Walk
Map:	Explorer 173 (route marked)
LWF status:	Pending validation
Principal promoter:	London Walking Forum, LB Harrow, Three Rivers DC, Hertsmere DC
Further information:	See London Loop introduction

This long section follows the green belt on the fringe of Greater London, crossing the Hertfordshire border several times. There are some longish stretches of roadwalking, but most of the time you are on tracks and footpaths through woods and fields. Together with the **Pinner-Grimsdyke Circular Walk** you walk beside Grim's Dyke, an ancient defensive earthwork. The heath and woodland of Bentley Priory, shared with the **Bentley Priory Circular Walk**, was once part of a large Royal Air Force station, now retreated to administrative offices behind high wire fences. From Stanmore Little Common, a signed London Loop link with Stanmore station passes through the attractive nature reserve of Stanmore Country Park.

After passing under the M1 motorway, great care is needed to cross a busy road into Aldenham Country Park – this needs improvement. You walk beside a reservoir where sailing dinghies may be racing, then cross farmland and skirt a golf course to reach the end of the section, very close to Elstree & Borehamwood station.

LONDON LOOP: SECTION 16 (MAP 2)
Elstree to Cockfosters

Distance:	16.8km (10.5 miles) including links with Elstree & Borehamwood
Location:	Barnet and Enfield, plus some in Hertfordshire
Start:	Elstree (Allum Lane, GR 189-693)
Finish:	Cockfosters (Cockfosters Station, GR 281-964)
Green factor:	51%
Blue factor:	8%
Recommended direction:	West to east
Terrain and surface:	Mainly level walking on rough paths, tracks and grass. One longish steep ascent, several fairly gentle ascents and descents. Two stiles. 7.0km (4.3 miles) beside roads
Points of interest:	Scratchwood and Moat Mount Open Spaces, Dollis Valley, Battle of Barnet, Monken Hadley Common, Jacks Lake
Signage:	Complete both ways
Refreshments and toilets:	Pubs at Borehamwood, Barnet, Hadley, and Cockfosters. Cafés at Borehamwood, Barnet, Trent Park and Cockfosters. Public toilets at Barnet and Trent Park
Public transport and break points:	NR: Elstree & Borehamwood. LU: High Barnet, Cockfosters. Buses at these points and at Barnet Way
Links:	Moat Mount Walk, Dollis Valley Greenwalk, Barnet-Totteridge Loop
Map:	Explorer 173 (route marked)
LWF status:	Validated with Seal of Approval (Mayor of London's key route)
Principal promoter:	London Walking Forum, LB Barnet, LB Enfield, Hertsmere DC
Further information:	See London Loop introduction

From Elstree, a long road walk leads to the ancient woodland of Scratchwood, then a long and frustrating diversion is necessary beside the hectic dual-carriageway of the A1 Barnet Way. One hopes that this situation will improve, but the annoyance is soon forgotten as you continue through lovely countryside all the way to Barnet. This consists of the woodland of Moat Mount and the valley of Dollis Brook, broken by one road stretch. Note that a permissive footpath here is required to close on 28 February each year (see 'Route Closures', in the Strategic Network introduction) but can be avoided on alternative paths.

The Church of St Mary the Vrgin, Monken Hadley

Skirting the east side of Barnet through hilly open spaces, you come to Hadley Green, site of the Battle of Barnet in 1471 during the Wars of the Roses. After passing the picturesque old Church of St. Mary the Virgin, through what was once a toll gate, you follow the edge of the well wooded Monken Hadley Common, run by a board of conservators. Soon after crossing the East Coast main railway line you can make a short diversion to view the serene Jacks Lake.

The official end of this section is at Cockfosters station, but if continuing on to Section 17 you can take a short cut. Soon after the Cock & Dragon pub keep ahead to the main road and cross into Trent Park, whose drive leads to the café and toilets mentioned at Point 1 in the Section 17 leaflet.

London Loop: Section 17 (Map 2)
Cockfosters to Enfield Lock

A long and very rural section. From Cockfosters station you are immediately in Trent Park, once the home of the Sassoon family, whose mansion across the lake is now part of Middlesex University. Then you follow Salmon's Brook through the farmland of Enfield Chase. A stiff climb leads to a busy road (The Ridgeway) and a descent into the valley of Turkey Brook. You follow this most of the way to the end of the section, passing through Hilly Fields Park and the Forty Hall Estate.

Distance:	14.7km (9.2 miles) including link with Enfield Lock station
Location:	Enfield
Start:	Cockfosters Station (GR 281-964)
Finish:	Enfield Lock (Bradley Road, GR 364-984)
Green factor:	62%
Blue factor:	28%
Recommended direction:	West to east
Terrain and surface:	Several gentle ascents and descents and two high stepped footbridges. Mostly rough paths, tracks and grassland. Five stiles. 2.0km (1.3 miles) beside roads
Points of interest:	Trent Park, Enfield Chase, farmland, Turkey Brook, Hilly Fields Park, Forty Hall Estate, Albany Park
Signage:	Complete both ways
Refreshments and toilets:	Pubs at Clay Hill, Turkey Street and Enfield Lock. Cafés at Trent Park, Forty Hall and Turkey Street. Public toilets at both ends of Trent Park and at Forty Hall
Public transport and break points:	LU: Cockfosters. NR: Gordon Hill, Turkey Street, Enfield Lock. Buses at all these points
Links:	Hertfordshire Chain Walk, New River Path
Map:	Explorer 173 (route marked)
LWF status:	Validated with Seal of Approval (Mayor of London's key route)
Principal promoter:	London Walking Forum, LB Enfield
Further information:	See London Loop introduction

At Clay Hill you briefly encounter the **Hertfordshire Chain Walk**. At Forty Hill you cross the **New River Path** and pass the spot where Sir Walter Raleigh is said to have famously laid down his cloak for Queen Elizabeth I to step on. The rural surroundings come to an end as you approach Turkey Street, passing its station. You cross two high stepped footbridges over the Great Cambridge Road and the railway line at Enfield Lock, with Albany Park in between.

LONDON LOOP: SECTION 18 (MAP 2)
Enfield Lock to Chingford

Distance:	6.5km (4.1 miles) including links with Enfield Lock and Chingford stations
Location:	Enfield and Waltham Forest, plus some in Essex
Start:	Enfield Lock (Bradley Road, GR 364-984)
Finish:	Chingford (Rangers Road, GR 393-947)
Green factor:	63%
Blue factor:	11%
Recommended direction:	Northwest to southeast
Terrain and surface:	Mostly level but with two long and fairly steep climbs. Mostly rough paths, tracks and grass. Nine stiles. 500m beside roads
Points of interest:	Turkey Brook, Lee & Stort Navigation, Swan & Pike Pool, Sewardstone Marsh Nature Reserve, Sewardstone Hills, Lea Valley reservoirs, Epping Forest, Gilwell Park
Signage:	Complete both ways
Refreshments and toilets:	Pubs at Enfield Lock, Sewardstone Road and Chingford. Cafés at Chingford. Public toilets at Chingford
Public transport and break points:	NR: Enfield Lock, Chingford. Buses at these points and at Sewardstone Road
Links:	Lea Valley Walk
Map:	Explorer 174 (route marked)
LWF status:	Validated with Seal of Approval (Mayor of London's key route)
Principal promoter:	London Walking Forum, LB Enfield, LB Waltham Forest, Epping Forest DC, Lee Valley Regional Park Authority
Further information:	See London Loop introduction

You are in green surroundings most of the way to Chingford, with very little roadwalking. There are three short waterside paths: beside Turkey Brook, the Lee Navigation (together with the **Lea Valley Walk**), and the River Lea diversion channel. A stiff climb into the Sewardstone Hills is rewarded with a magnificent view across north London and the massive Lea Valley reservoirs, then you pass Gilwell Park, former home of Lord Baden Powell and now headquarters of the Scout movement. In Epping Forest you encounter another steepish climb up to Hawk Wood, and a final roadside stretch leads into Chingford.

LONDON LOOP: SECTION 19 (MAPS 2, 4)
Chingford to Chigwell

Distance:	6.4km (4.0 miles) including links with Chingford and Chigwell stations
Location:	Waltham Forest, but mostly in Essex
Start:	Chingford (Rangers Road, GR 393-947)
Finish:	Chigwell High Road (GR 439-934) – see text
Green factor:	39%
Blue factor:	7%
Recommended direction:	West to east
Terrain and surface:	Fairly level all the way with one gentle climb soon after the start and a stepped footbridge at Buckhurst Hill. More than half is on a hard surface. One stile. 1.9km (1.2 miles) beside roads
Points of interest:	Queen Elizabeth's Hunting Lodge, Epping Forest, Roding Valley Recreation Ground and lake
Signage:	Partial both ways at time of writing
Refreshments and toilets:	Pubs at Chingford, Epping New Road, High Road Woodford Green, Loughton Way and Chigwell. Cafés at Chingford and Chigwell. Public toilets at Chingford
Public transport and break points:	NR: Chingford. LU: Buckhurst Hill, Chigwell. Buses at these points, also at Woodford Green High Road and Loughton Way
Links:	Epping Forest Centenary Walk
Map:	Explorer 174 (route marked)
LWF status:	Pending validation
Principal promoter:	London Walking Forum, Corporation of London, Epping Forest DC
Further information:	See London Loop introduction

Easy walking, though the early part may be muddy through Epping Forest, where you pass the historic Queen Elizabeth's Hunting Lodge and cross the *Epping Forest Centenary Walk*. Later, much of the route follows pavements and tarmac paths through recreation grounds, in one of which is a lake created from a former gravel pit. The section finishes with a long walk beside a busy road, but at time of writing a proposal is being considered to avoid it by diverting the end of this section to Debden.

LONDON LOOP: SECTION 20 (MAP 4)
Chigwell to Havering-atte-Bower

Distance:	9.6km (6.0 miles) including link with Chigwell station
Location:	Redbridge, Havering; plus some in Essex
Start:	Chigwell High Road (GR 439-934) – see text
Finish:	North Road, Havering-atte-Bower (GR 512-931)
Green factor:	91%
Blue factor:	2%
Recommended direction:	West to east
Terrain and surface:	Generally level, with some gentle slopes. Mostly on rough paths or tracks and on grass. Some fields may be ploughed. Six stiles. 800m beside roads
Points of interest:	Farmland, Hainault Forest Country Park, Havering Country Park
Signage:	Partial both ways at time of writing
Refreshments and toilets:	Pubs at Chigwell, Chigwell Row, Havering-atte-Bower. Cafés at Chigwell. Public toilets at Hainault Forest Country Park and Havering-atte-Bower
Public transport and break points:	LU: Chigwell, Grange Hill. Buses at these points, also at Chigwell Row and Havering-atte-Bower
Links:	Chigwell Country Walk, Three Forests Way
Map:	Explorers 174 and 175 (route marked)
LWF status:	Pending validation
Principal promoter:	London Walking Forum, Epping Forest DC, LB Redbridge, LB Havering
Further information:	See London Loop introduction

One of the most rural sections of the whole Loop, being almost entirely in open country or woodland, apart from an initial road walk at Chigwell (but see note in Section 19 regarding a possible diversion to Debden station). The route is shared for a while with the *Chigwell Country Walk*, which provides a link with Grange Hill station, and with the *Three Forests Way*. You continue to Chigwell Row across undulating farmland, where fields may be ploughed and cropped. Then comes Hainault Forest Country Park, with its lake, and you must take care as you cross Hainault Forest Golf Course. Amid more farmland you cross the infant River Rom, then another woodland stretch leads through Havering Country Park to the pleasant village of Havering-atte-Bower, from which the London borough takes its name.

LONDON LOOP: SECTION 21 (MAP 4)
Havering-atte-Bower to Harold Wood

Distance:	6.9km (4.3 miles)
Location:	Havering
Start:	North Road, Havering-atte-Bower (GR 512-931)
Finish:	Harold Wood Station (GR 548-906)
Green factor:	68%
Blue factor:	22%
Recommended direction:	Northwest to southeast
Terrain and surface:	Generally fairly level, some gentle slopes. Mostly on rough paths, tracks and grass. Five stiles. 2.3km (1.4 miles) beside roads
Points of interest:	Farmland, Carter's Brook, Paine's Brook
Signage:	Partial at time of writing
Refreshments and toilets:	Pubs at Havering-atte-Bower, Noak Hill and Harold Wood. Public toilets at Havering-atte-Bower
Public transport and break points:	Buses: Havering-atte-Bower, Noak Hill, Harold Hill, Harold Wood. NR: Harold Wood
Links:	Havering Northern Area Circular Walks
Map:	Explorer 175 (route marked)
LWF status:	Pending validation
Principal promoter:	London Walking Forum, LB Havering
Further information:	See London Loop introduction

From the attractive village of Havering-atte-Bower, the route first passes through high-lying, undulating farmland, sharing part of the *Havering Northern Area Circular Walks*, to reach Noak Hill. Then you follow a narrow green strip through the suburb of Harold Hill, part of the proposed Havering Greenway, which here lies beside Carter's and Paine's Brooks. These streams flow into the Ingrebourne River, which itself joins the Thames at Rainham Creek. The direct route across the busy A12 Colchester Road dual carriageway is not recommended at time of writing – to avoid this a 750-metre diversion to the controlled crossing at Gubbins Lane is necessary. A final stretch along residential roads brings you to Harold Wood station.

London Loop: Section 22 (Map 4)
Harold Wood to Upminster Bridge

Distance:	6.9km (4.3 miles)
Location:	Havering
Start:	Harold Wood station (GR 548-906)
Finish:	Upminster Bridge station (GR 551-868)
Green factor:	38%
Blue factor:	29%
Recommended direction:	North to south
Terrain and surface:	Almost completely level, one or two short gentle slopes. Mostly footpaths, tracks and grass, often with rough surface. Four stiles. 3.5km (2.2 miles) beside roads
Points of interest:	Ingrebourne River, farmland
Signage:	Complete both ways
Refreshments and toilets:	Pubs at Harold Wood and Upminster Bridge. Public toilets at Harold Wood
Public transport and break points:	NR: Harold Wood. LU: Upminster Bridge. Buses at these points, also at Southend Arterial Road, Hall Lane and Wingletye Lane
Links:	Upminster Circular Walk
Map:	Explorer 175 (route marked)
LWF status:	Pending validation
Principal promoter:	London Walking Forum, LB Havering
Further information:	See London Loop introduction

This section will, it is hoped, eventually follow the Ingrebourne River for nearly all its length, cutting the distance to 4.5km (2.8 miles) and raising both the green and blue factors to around 80%. At present much of the riverside is inaccessible and you must divert to some rather tedious roadside walking. However, the riverside that is now accessible provides enjoyable walking. Some of the route is shared with the *Upminster Circular Walk*, and when riverside access is complete this section will also form part of the proposed Ingrebourne Valley Greenway.

LONDON LOOP: SECTION 23 (MAP 4)
Upminster Bridge to Rainham

Distance:	6.4km (4.0 miles)
Location:	Havering
Start:	Upminster Bridge station (GR 551-868)
Finish:	Rainham station (GR 521-820)
Green factor:	49%
Blue factor:	28%
Recommended direction:	North to south
Terrain and surface:	Almost completely level with tarmac or firm gravel paths. No stiles. 3.3km (2.1 miles) beside roads
Points of interest:	Upminster Windmill, Ingrebourne River, Ingrebourne Marshes Nature Reserve, Hornchurch Country Park, airfield memorabilia, lakeside walk, Rainham village
Signage:	Complete both ways
Refreshments and toilets:	Pubs at Upminster Bridge, Hacton Lane, Rainham Road, Rainham village. Cafés and toilets at Rainham
Public transport and break points:	LU: Upminster Bridge. NR: Rainham. Buses at these points, also at Newmarket Way and South End Road
Links:	Upminster Circular Walk
Map:	Explorer 175 (route marked)
LWF status:	Pending validation
Principal promoter:	London Walking Forum, LB Havering
Further information:	See London Loop introduction

This section generally follows the Ingrebourne River, but at the south end this is currently inaccessible, requiring a diversion along roads. When this is improved, the distance will be cut to about 6km (3.8 miles), the green factor will rise to 78% and the blue to 50%. The current diversion, however, does provide a view of the delightful Albyns Farmhouse, now a private house.

Some of the route is shared with the **Upminster Circular Walk**, and when riverside access is complete this section will also, like Section 22, form part of the proposed Ingrebourne Valley Greenway, which here incorporates the Hacton and Sutton Parkways. You walk through Hornchurch Country Park, which has gone through several phases as a farm, military airfield, gravel quarry and rubbish tip, until its acquisition in 1980 by the local authority enabled the provision of a haven for wildlife and quiet outdoor activities.

The section ends at the unexpectedly attractive village of Rainham, now a fairly peaceful place following the opening of by-passes. In very wet weather, the subway under the very busy New Road may be flooded, then crossing it could be difficult.

Ingrebourne River at Hornchurch Country Park

LONDON LOOP: SECTION 24 (MAP 4)
Rainham to Purfleet

Distance:	7.2km (4.5 miles)
Location:	Havering, plus some in Essex
Start:	Rainham station (GR 521-820)
Finish:	Purfleet station (GR 554-781) – see text
Green factor:	55%
Blue factor:	61%
Recommended direction:	Northwest to southeast
Terrain and surface:	Almost entirely level, with one or two short gentle slopes. Mostly hard surface, some on grass. No stiles, some high steps. 2.6km (1.6 miles) beside roads
Points of interest:	River Thames, barge 'graveyard', heritage mural, Coldharbour Navigation Beacon, nature reserves
Signage:	No London Loop signs at time of writing. Partly signed as Havering Riverside Path

Refreshments and toilets:	Pubs and cafés at Rainham and Purfleet
Public transport and break points:	NR/buses: Rainham, Purfleet
Links:	Havering Riverside Path
Map:	Explorer 162 (route marked)
LWF status:	Pending validation
Principal promoter:	London Walking Forum, LB Havering, Thurrock DC
Further information:	See London Loop introduction

At the time of writing this section ends halfway at Coldharbour Point, while access through a nature reserve is negotiated, so you must return to Rainham. Apart from a long and horrendous road section from Rainham through an industrial area, the rest of the existing walk, shared with the **Havering Riverside Path**, is a fascinating contrast to the rest of the London Loop. It is hoped that the road walk can be significantly reduced or even eliminated if and when it becomes possible to create a path beside Rainham Creek.

The view to your right is dominated by the river, with its south bank diminutive in the distance, while shipping adds further interest. On the foreshore is a 'graveyard' of historic concrete barges used during the D-Day Landings of the Second World War, while a heritage mural painted by local students, a rice packaging plant and a waste transfer station occupy the adjacent land. To your left and ahead, Rainham and Wennington Marshes, including a former military firing range, were acquired in 2000 by the Royal Society for the Protection of Birds, who are creating a nature reserve for a rich variety of birds and other wildlife.

You are welcomed to Coldharbour Point by a navigation beacon serving river shipping. Opposite is the starting point of Section 1 of the London Loop at Erith, and it is frustrating that the ferry that used to cross here would have taken you directly to it. Anyone wishing to continue from Section 24 to Section 1 would need to travel by car, buses or taxi via the Dartford Crossing (13km / 8miles by road). A longer, but possibly more practical, alternative using public transport is by train from Rainham or Purfleet to Limehouse, Docklands Light Railway to Greenwich and train to Erith.

MILL HILL PAST AND PRESENT (MAP 2)

A very pleasant and interesting walk in the **Barnet Leisure Countryside Walks** series. The official start and finish point is in Mill Hill High Street, on a bus route, but you may find it more convenient to travel to Mill Hill East station. From there turn left then left again at the Railway Engineer pub to join the route along the former railway line.

Distance:	5.3km (3.3 miles)
Location:	Barnet
Start/finish:	Mill Hill High Street (GR228-925)
Green factor:	52%
Blue factor:	n/a
Recommended direction:	Clockwise
Terrain and surface:	Mostly level with one long steady climb. Pavements, tarmac paths and rough paths or tracks. One stile. 2.1km (1.3 miles) beside roads
Points of interest:	Mill Hill village, Bittacy Hill Park, former railway line, Arrandene Open Space
Signage:	Almost complete clockwise only. Logo: '10' in white circle on blue arrow on white background, with text 'Barnet Countryside Leisure Walks'
Refreshments and toilets:	Pubs at Mill Hill village and Mill Hill East. No cafés or public toilets
Public transport and break points:	LU: Mill Hill East. Buses: Mill Hill East, Pursley Road, Mill Hill village
Links:	Rural Mill Hill, Exploring Totteridge Manor
Map:	Explorer 173
LWF status:	Pending validation
Principal promoter:	LB Barnet
Further information:	Included in *Barnet Countryside Leisure Walks* pack, 50p plus + sae from LB Barnet libraries

From the official start high up in Mill Hill village, you wander along the quiet High Street and The Ridgeway, passing several notable and historic buildings, including the monumental National Medical Research Laboratory and the Adam & Eve pub. Then you drop down beside a field and wind through a residential area to pass close to Mill Hill East station. The Northern Line now terminates here, but once continued to Edgware, and you follow the disused line, now lined with trees and shrubs, on a level track among trees, passing the Copthall Sports Centre. After a roadside climb you return to Mill Hill village through Arrandene Open Space, a lovely area of woods and meadows and a haven for wildlife and flowers.

MOAT MOUNT WALK (MAP 2)

Distance:	4.7km (2.9 miles)
Location:	Barnet
Start/finish:	Totteridge Common (The Lynch House, GR 226-939)
Green factor:	52%
Blue factor:	n/a
Recommended direction:	Clockwise
Terrain and surface:	Undulating country with some gentle to steepish climbs on pavements and rough paths or tracks. 2 stiles. 1.9km (1.2 miles) beside roads
Points of interest:	Highwood Hill, Moat Mount Open Space, Totteridge Fields Nature Reserve
Signage:	Almost complete both ways. Logo: '8' in white circle on blue arrow on white background, with text 'Barnet Countryside Leisure Walks'
Refreshments and toilets:	Pub at Highwood Hill. No cafés or public toilets
Public transport and break points:	Buses: Totteridge Common, Highwood Hill
Links:	Rural Mill Hill, London Loop, Dollis Valley Greenwalk
Map:	Explorer 173
LWF status:	Pending validation
Principal promoter:	LB Barnet
Further information:	Included in *Barnet Countryside Leisure Walks* pack, 50p plus + sae from LB Barnet libraries

A fairly energetic walk in the **Barnet Leisure Countryside Walks** series. Starting near the west end of Totteridge Common (together with **Rural Mill Hill**) you follow a level path behind trees parallel to the road, then cut through grassy Holcombe Dale to Holcombe Hill, with a view of St. Mary Abbey ahead. You must take care here as you join a road at a blind corner. A steepish climb up the road takes you to the top of Highwood Hill, one of the highest points in the area, where you are greeted by an array of historic buildings: the 16th century Rising Sun pub, Highwood House and the eye-catching Hill Cottage. The quiet and supposedly haunted Nan Clark's Lane leads past two duckponds into Moat Mount Open Space, where the route is shared for a while with Section 16 of the **London Loop** and the **Dollis Valley Greenwalk**. Note that a permissive path here is closed each year on 28th February, but there are alternative paths nearby. A longish road walk leads to Totteridge Fields and back to Totteridge Common.

NASH CIRCULAR WALK (MAP 8)

Distance:	6.7km (4.2 miles). Shorter route available of 4.8km (3.0 miles)
Location:	Bromley
Start/finish:	Heathfield Road Car Park, Keston Common (GR 416-637)
Green factor:	57%
Blue factor:	n/a
Recommended direction:	Clockwise
Terrain and surface:	Undulating countryside, with some steep slopes. Mainly on rough paths, tracks and grass. Three stiles. 2.1km (1.3 miles) beside roads (shorter route 1.1km/0.7 miles)
Points of interest:	Farmland, horse stud, Nash hamlet, Well Wood, Keston village, Baston Manor, Keston Common, Keston Windmill
Signage:	Almost complete both ways. Logo: 'Nash Circular Walk' in yellow on dark green background, surrounding yellow arrow with pink flash. Some older signs still in place with stylised 'NCW' on yellow arrow with white background
Refreshments and toilets:	Pubs at Keston. No public toilets
Public transport and break points:	Buses to Heathfield Road and Keston village
Links:	London Loop, Three Commons Circular Walk
Map:	Explorer 147; also 200m on Explorer 161
LWF status:	Validated with Seal of Approval
Principal promoter:	LB Bromley
Further information:	Included in Pack One of *Bromley Circular Walks and Trails* (£2.50 plus 50p p+p) from LB Bromley Leisure & Community Services and libraries

An energetic but very pleasant route through high-lying and undulating countryside south of Hayes, in the **Bromley Circular Walks and Trails** series. The start/finish point is not at Nash but a car park off Heathfield Road on Keston Common, the highest point of the route, served by buses from Hayes and Bromley. After a short road walk you plunge (almost literally as the descent is very steep) into a valley of open fields with grazing horses near a stud farm, then climb to the pretty hamlet of Nash – just a few old houses including 18th century Nash House. From here a short cut leads with a steep climb back to Keston Common.

The longer route continues through Well Wood to Gates Green Road, then comes a final climb, up to Baston Manor, where the route is shared briefly with Section 3 of the **London Loop**. The black tower of Keston Windmill, complete with sails, looms above Keston Common, where you brush the **Three Commons Circular Walk**.

New River Path (Maps 2, 5)

Distance:	44km (28 miles) – see text
Location:	Continuing from Hertfordshire into Enfield, Haringey, Hackney and Islington
Start:	Hertford (New Gauge, GR TL 340-139)
Finish:	Islington (New River Head, Hardwick Street, GR TQ 325-875)
*Green factor:	see text
*Blue factor:	see text
Recommended direction:	North to south
Terrain and surface:	Almost completely level with some short gentle slopes. Often on grass beside the river, otherwise on pavements or tarmac paths
*Points of interest:	New River, Theobalds Park, Docwra Aqueduct, Capel Manor, Enfield Town Park, Clarendon Arch, Alexandra Park and Palace, Finsbury Park, Stoke Newington Reservoirs, Clissold Park, New River Head
Signage:	Complete both ways. Fingerposts with stylised NR and 'New River Path' in white on bright green background
*Refreshments and toilets:	Pubs and cafés at Theobalds Grove, Turkey Street, Enfield, Palmers Green, Alexandra Palace, Hornsey, Harringay, Manor House, Clissold Park and Islington. Public toilets at Capel Manor, Forty Hall, Alexandra Palace and Clissold Park
*Public transport and break points:	NR: Theobalds Grove, Turkey Street, Enfield Town, Enfield Chase, Grange Park, Winchmore Hill, Palmers Green, Bowes Park, Alexandra Palace, Hornsey, Harringay, Finsbury Park, Canonbury, Essex Road. LU: Wood Green, Manor House, Highbury & Islington, Angel. Buses at all these points
Links:	London Countryway, Lea Valley Walk, London Loop, Pymmes Brook Trail, Capital Ring, Parkland Walk, Regent's Canal Towpath
Map:	Explorer 173 (also sheet 174 for the Hertfordshire section)

*LWF status:	Pending validation
Principal promoter:	Thames Water, Groundwork Hertfordshire
Further information:	*A Walker's Guide to the New River* (£1.00 + sae) from the New River Action Group. *Exploring the New River* (Michael Essex-Lopresti, £8.95 + 90p p&p, ISBN 1-85858-075-7, Brewin Books). *An historical walk along the New River* (Stoke Newington to Islington section only, Mary Cosh, £5.00 inc. p&p, ISBN 0-9507532-7-0, Islington Archaeology and Historical Society). Free leaflet + sae: *The New River in Hertfordshire* from Thames Water. (See Appendix H for contact details for all the above)

* These details apply to the Greater London section only.

A most imaginative route following an artificial river, which since 1613 has supplied London with fresh water from Hertfordshire. Thames Water maintains the river and where possible has made its grassy banks accessible to the public. However, the riverbank is not a right of way and the distinctive bright green kissing gates, through which the riverbank is reached from roads, are locked at night. The New River Path has been created by Groundwork Hertfordshire, acting on behalf of Thames Water, and is virtually complete, though some stretches of the riverside in Greater London remain inaccessible, where the route will follow parallel roads. At time of writing it was not possible to assess the green and blue factors as the river was not fully accessible.

The New River Path may be followed in either direction, but the new guide will be written north to south. If you wish to walk the whole route, the starting point is the New Gauge beside the River Lea between Hertford and Ware, accessible in 1.6km (1.0 miles) from Hertford East station by following the **Lea Valley Walk** northeastwards. In fact the route generally runs parallel to, and within a kilometre (half a mile) or so of, the Lea Valley Walk for some 14km (8.7 miles), as they wend their way past Ware, Hoddesdon and Broxbourne, sometimes in open countryside, sometimes in more urban surroundings. You pass several pumping stations, gauges and other structures associated with the water transfer system.

East Reservoir, Stoke Newington

At Cheshunt the New River Path moves away from the Lea to pass Theobalds Park, the current home of historic Temple Bar, once the western gateway into the City of London at Fleet Street – there is a proposal to move it back to London. You can join the route here (just outside the Greater London boundary) by taking the train to Theobalds Grove and walking westwards along Theobalds Lane and across the Great Cambridge Road for just over a kilometre (half a mile). Then it is about 14km (8.8 miles) to Palmers Green, 23km (14.4 miles) to Stoke Newington or 29km (18.1 miles) to Islington.

The New River Path moves into Greater London by crossing the M25 on a broad concrete aqueduct. Soon after this you cross the Docwra Aqueduct and Section 17 of the **London Loop**, which provides a short link with Turkey Street station and reduces the distances shown above by 3km (1.9 miles). The route continues past Capel Manor, a college for land-based studies with beautiful gardens, refreshments and toilets, then describes a loop around Enfield town centre, marked by rectangular metal plates in the pavement. This ends with the pretty River View path and cottages, then in Town Park you leave the riverside for a while to follow a wooded track and residential roads through Bush Hill Park.

The New River is mostly accessible again through Winchmore Hill and Palmers Green, where you cross the **Pymmes Brook Trail**. At Wood Green it flows underground, and you walk through the open spaces that cover it to Alexandra Park. Eventually the route will follow the river through the former Hornsey Waterworks, but for the moment there is a very pleasant diversion through Alexandra Park. This includes a nature reserve and a magnificent view of titanic 'Ally Pally' – Alexandra Palace exhibition hall, partially destroyed by fire in 1980 and restored by Haringey Council in 1988.

Alexandra Palace ('Ally Pally')

At Hornsey the river is currently inaccessible again and you follow roads for a while through to Finsbury Park, within a stone's throw of Section 12 of the **Capital Ring** and the **Parkland Walk**. Soon after this you pass the Stoke Newington

Reservoirs, rich with waterbirds, then walk through Clissold Park, where you encounter the Capital Ring once more. Further south, the river is joined only briefly along New River Walk in Canonbury, but there is interesting walking through cosmopolitan Islington (where you cross the **Regent's Canal Towpath**) to the end of the route at New River Head in Hardwick Street, close to Angel station and Sadlers Wells Theatre.

NINE STILES CIRCULAR WALK (MAP 3)

Distance:	8.5km (5.3 miles) plus link with Uxbridge station 1.2km (0.8 miles)
Location:	Hillingdon, but mostly in Buckinghamshire
Start/finish:	Oxford Road canal bridge, Uxbridge (GR 051-846)
Green factor:	55%
Blue factor:	21%
Recommended direction:	Clockwise
Terrain and surface:	Almost entirely level with one moderate climb. Partly on canal towpath but mostly on rough ground. 16 stiles. 2.3km (1.4 miles) beside roads
Points of interest:	Farmland, Denham village, River Misbourne, River Colne, Denham Country Park, Colne Valley Park Visitor Centre, Grand Union Canal, Denham Lock
Signage:	Partly signed both ways with Colne Valley Park roundel: black heron and reeds on blue and white background
Refreshments and toilets:	Pubs at Uxbridge, New Denham and Denham. Cafés at Uxbridge and Denham Lock. Public toilets at Uxbridge and Colne Valley Park Centre
Public transport and break points:	LU: Uxbridge. Buses: Uxbridge, Denham
Links:	South Bucks Way, Grand Union Canal Walk, London Loop, Colne Valley Trail, Widewater Lock Circular Walk
Map:	Explorer 172
LWF status:	Pending validation
Principal promoter:	Groundwork Thames Valley
Further information:	Included in Colne Valley Circular Walks pack from Colne Valley Park Centre (see Appendix H for contact details) (enquire for price)

Considering the mainly level ground, this is a surprisingly strenuous but pleasant walk in the **Colne Valley Circular Walks** series. The title is rather confusing as in fact you cross 16 stiles in all. The nine stiles referred to were on the historic Nine Stiles Walk from Uxbridge to Rush Green, covering the first third of this circuit, and commemorated by the Nine Stiles pub, close to the route in New Denham.

The first half of the route leads mostly across farmland with lovely views, where you pass Kingcup Meadows, managed for their wildlife and landscape value, and try to ignore the noise from the M40 motorway. Just over half way you walk through the picturesque village of Denham, an ideal refreshment stop with three pubs, and much used for film locations, being close to the famous Pinewood Studios. The beguiling River Misbourne, here not much more than a stream, appears through a wall then flows beside the road and between the gardens of pretty brick cottages.

You join the **South Bucks Way** through Buckinghamshire Golf Course and Denham Country Park, passing the Colne Valley Park Visitor Centre, starting point of the **Widewater Lock Circular Walk**. A bridge over the River Colne leads on to the *Grand Union Canal*, whose towpath takes you back to Uxbridge together with Section 12 of the **London Loop** and the **Colne Valley Trail**.

NORTH DOWNS WAY NATIONAL TRAIL (MAP 7)

Distance:	246km (154 miles) – see text
Location:	Surrey and Kent, touching Bromley
Recommended direction:	West to east
Signage:	Almost complete both ways. Logo: acorn (National Trail symbol), sometimes also text 'North Downs Way' plus arrow on fingerposts or markerposts. May be black on white or white on black
Public transport	NR: Farnham, Guildford, Dorking, Boxhill & Westhumble, Betchworth, Reigate, Merstham, Oxted, Otford, Kemsing, Halling, Cuxton, Hollingbourne, Harrietsham, Lenham, Charing, Folkestone, Dover. Buses at all these points and others in between
Links:	Thames Down Link, London Countryway, Socratic Trail, Downlands Circular Walk, Vanguard Way, Berry's Green Circular Walk
Maps (London area)	Explorers 146 and 147 (route marked on these and on AZ maps and atlases). Two separate route maps (North Downs East, ISBN 1-85137-379-9; North Downs West, ISBN 1-85137-367-5, £8.95 each) published by Harvey Map Services.
LWF status:	Pending validation

Principal promoter:	Countryside Agency
Further information:	*National Trail Guide: North Downs Way* (Neil Curtis and Jim Walker, Aurum Press, ISBN 1-85410-187-0, £10.99). *A guide to the Pilgrims' Way and North Downs Way* (Christopher John Wright, Constable, ISBN 0-09-464180-3, £10.95). Free leaflet (+ sae) with general information from the Countryside Agency. web: nationaltrails.gov.uk/northdownsframeset.htm
Other details	See text – also Appendix H for all contact details

Although none of this splendid route actually lies inside Greater London, it is included for two reasons. It is a national trail easily accessible at several points from London, and it actually bounces along the boundary of the London Borough of Bromley for a while near Silverstead Lane, south of Cudham (GR 455-569), briefly sharing its route with **Berry's Green Circular Walk**. Several other routes in the London network come out to cross it (see Links above), and the **London Countryway** shares its route for a while. Both guidebooks mentioned above are written west to east, so it is better to walk in this direction if using them.

The route extends for 246km (154 miles) from Farnham in Surrey to Dover in Kent. It generally follows the ridge of the North Downs, and mostly coincides with the mystical Pilgrims' Way. The walking is often strenuous, on rough paths or tracks with steep climbs, long flights of steps and frequent stiles, but this is rewarded by splendid ridge walks, shady woodland walks, outstanding views and beautiful scenery.

Those wishing to sample this route might consider the following three sections in particular, which are easily accessible by train from London: Box Hill to Merstham (16.1km/10.1 miles), Merstham to Oxted (15.0km/9.4 miles) and Oxted to Otford (21.0km/13.1 miles). Oxted actually lies some 2km off route (included in the distances shown) but is linked with the North Downs Way via the Greensand Way.

PAINE'S & CARTER'S BROOK GREENWAY – see London Loop Section 21

PARKLAND WALK (MAP 2)

Distance:	6.3km (3.9 miles)
Location:	Haringey, Islington
Start:	Muswell Hill (GR 289-896)
Finish:	Finsbury Park (Stroud Green Road, GR 314-869)
Green factor:	87%
Blue factor:	n/a

Recommended direction:	Either way
Terrain and surface:	Mostly level but with some steep slopes. Mostly on firm track but with some rough or muddy sections. No stiles. 500m beside roads
Points of interest:	Disused railway line, Highgate Wood, Queen's Wood, Finsbury Park
Signage:	None (except where shared with Capital Ring)
Refreshments and toilets:	Pubs and cafés at Muswell Hill, Highgate, Crouch End and Finsbury Park. Cafés at Highgate Wood and Queen's Wood. Public toilets at Highgate Wood and Finsbury Park
Public transport and break points:	LU: Highgate, Finsbury Park, Manor House. NR: Crouch Hill, Finsbury Park. Buses at all these points, plus Muswell Hill and Crouch End
Links:	Capital Ring
Map:	Explorer 173
LWF status:	Pending validation
Principal promoter:	LB Haringey, LB Islington
Further information:	Free route description sheet + sae, also free leaflets + sae describing birds, trees and wild flowers along the route, from LB Haringey libraries and council offices. Route description included in book *Rails to the People's Palace*, the story of the railway line (£2.00 plus p&p, Reg Davies, Hornsey Historical Society, ISBN 0-905794-11-7). See Appendix H for all contact details.

Mostly easy and surprisingly green walking, but with some steep sections, along the former railway track that once linked Finsbury Park with Alexandra Palace, and is now London's longest nature reserve. The remaining accessible track is in two sections: Finsbury Park to Highgate and Cranley Gardens to Muswell Hill. Few road crossings are necessary as you can still use the former railway bridges and underpasses.

The free sheet describes the route in the direction Finsbury Park to Muswell Hill, but by starting at Muswell Hill (served by many bus routes) there will be more downhill than up. You can start at the road called Muswell Hill, but an interesting alternative is to walk up from Alexandra Palace station through Alexandra Park past the impressive 'Ally Pally', adding 1.7km (1.1 miles) to the distance.

From Muswell Hill you walk along an embankment above houses and gardens in the Cranley Gardens area. The railway line is inaccessible through Highgate, but this provides an opportunity to walk through Highgate Wood and hilly Queen's Wood, joining Section 11 of the **Capital Ring**, to regain the line in Holmesdale Road.

The eastern section, now with Section 12 of the Capital Ring, is sometimes in tree-lined cuttings, sometimes on embankments overlooking houses and gardens. A moment of nostalgia occurs at the former Crouch End station, still with platforms, on which you can rest with your legs dangling over the edge. A footbridge takes you across the main railway line into Finsbury Park, where the Parkland Walk Extension leads down to Stroud Green Road and Finsbury Park station.

Both sections of the disused railway line are level, but the surface is mostly very uneven and can be muddy at times. The paths through Highgate Wood are quite firm, but in Queen's Wood are very rough and steep – you can avoid these by going up Muswell Hill Road past Highgate station into Holmesdale Road.

PETTS WOOD CIRCULAR WALK (MAP 8)

Distance:	6.3km (3.9 miles). Shorter option 5.0km (3.1 miles)
Location:	Bromley
Start/finish:	Tent Peg Lane, Petts Wood (GR 441-679)
Green factor:	60%
Blue factor:	4%
Recommended direction:	Anticlockwise
Terrain and surface:	Generally fairly level with some gentle slopes. Mainly on rough paths and tracks. No stiles but three high stepped footbridges. 1.0km (0.6 miles) beside roads
Points of interest:	Jubilee Country Park, Kyd Brook, Petts Wood, Soldiering Field, Flushers Pond, Hawkwood. Bickley Manor
Signage:	Complete both ways. Logo: 'Petts Wood Circular Walk' in yellow on dark green background, surrounding yellow arrow with pale orange flash
Refreshments and toilets:	Pub and cafés at Petts Wood. No public toilets nearby
Public transport and break points:	NR/buses: Petts Wood, Chislehurst
Links:	London Loop
Map:	Explorer 162
LWF status:	Validated with Seal of Approval
Principal promoter:	LB Bromley

Further information:	Included in Pack Two of *Bromley Circular Walks and Trails* (£2.50 plus 50p p&p) from LB Bromley Leisure & Community Services and libraries. See Appendix H for contact details.

A well-wooded walk in the **Bromley Circular Walks and Trails** series. It starts and finishes at the car park serving Jubilee Country Park, easily reached in 500m from Petts Wood station on the link that serves Sections 2/3 of the **London Loop**, whose route is shared for about a third of the way.

After a short walk along the Jubilee Country Park Nature Trail you follow a long fenced footpath that leads via footbridges over three railway lines. Soon you are in Petts Wood itself, a National Trust property, briefly following Kyd Brook. Climbing steadily you pass Soldiering Field, where military volunteers were drilled in the 19th century.

Descending into a valley you pass Flushers Pond, once a popular haunt for anglers, then climb again to a fine viewpoint southwards across the valley towards Bromley. The short route now heads directly for the finish past Tongs Farm, while the long route continues through Hawkwood, another National Trust area, and skirts the suburbs of Chislehurst and Bickley. You return past Bromley High School and Bickley Manor Hotel, then make a beeline across Jubilee Country Park to the finish.

PILGRIM'S WAY – see North Downs Way National Trail

PINNER-GRIMSDYKE CIRCULAR WALK (MAP 3)

Distance:	7.7km (4.8 miles). Shorter option 4.1km (2.6 miles)
Location:	Harrow
Start/finish:	Old Reddings car park (GR 144-926) or Shaftesbury Playing Fields car park (GR 125-914)
Green factor:	61%
Blue factor:	2%
Recommended direction:	Clockwise
Terrain and surface:	Mainly level but with two long and fairly steep climbs. Mostly on rough paths, tracks and grass. 2 stiles. 2.7km (1.7 miles) beside roads
Points of interest:	Grimsdyke Open Space, Grim's Ditch, Oxhey Lane Farm Shop, farmland, Pinnerwood Farm
Signage:	Partial both ways. Yellow arrows on wooden posts, also some green fingerposts (discs due to be added at time of writing)

Refreshments and toilets:	Pub at Old Reddings. No public toilets nearby
Public transport and break points:	NR: Hatch End. Buses: Hatch End, Oxhey Lane, Brookshill (near Old Reddings)
Links:	London Loop, Bentley Priory Circular Walk
Map:	Explorer 173
LWF status:	Pending validation
Principal promoter:	LB Harrow
Further information:	Free leaflet (+ sae) from LB Harrow libraries. See Appendix H for contact details

A relatively easy walk in mostly open country, though with a couple of stiff climbs. There are two official starting points as shown above, or you can walk 500m along The Avenue from Hatch End station. From there your route soon enters open country, passing through the fields of Pinnerwood Farm, where pretty cottages, ponds, pine trees and lawns surround the farmhouse, which is also a stud farm and riding stables. From here the route is shared for a while with the *London Loop*.

A long road walk leads to Valley View Farm, where at the time of writing you had to take care as large-scale fly-tipping involves clambering over piles of builders' rubbish, then you skirt Grimsdyke Golf Course. The Old Reddings starting point is an optional diversion but well worthwhile for the remains of the Grimsdyke and the view from the car park. The *Bentley Priory Circular Walk* also comes here, providing an opportunity for a full day figure-of-eight walk. The Grimsdyke (sometimes shown as Grim's Ditch) is an ancient Saxon defensive earthwork, which leads through the woods and beside a large pond. It is one of several so named in England, Grim being the Saxon equivalent of the Norse Woden, god of war. After continuing across the golf course you return to Hatch End along pleasant residential streets and alleyways, passing another section of the Grimsdyke.

POOL RIVER – see Waterlink Way

PYMMES BROOK TRAIL (MAP 2)

Distance:	16.4km (10.3 miles)
Location:	Barnet, Enfield
Start:	Cockfosters (near Jacks Lake, Monken Hadley Common GR 271-969)
Finish:	Edmonton (Lee Valley Leisure Centre, GR 360-945, or Pickett's Lock (GR 364-937) – see text
Green factor:	31%
Blue factor:	34%

Recommended direction:	Northwest to southeast
Terrain and surface:	Almost entirely level except for some ramps or steps, and one gentle slope. Almost entirely hard surface, one short stretch on grass. No stiles. 6.6km (4.1 miles) beside roads
Points of interest:	Jacks Lake, Monken Hadley Common, Victoria Recreation Ground, Oak Hill Park, Brunswick Park, Arnos Park, Broomfield Park and House, Millfield House, Pymmes Park
Signage:	Complete both ways. Discs: white willow tree on blue background plus 'Pymmes Brook Trail'
Refreshments and toilets:	Pubs and cafés at frequent intervals. Public toilets at Cockfosters (Trent Park), Victoria Recreation Ground, Oak Hill Park, Broomfield Park, Palmers Green, Millfield House, Pymmes Park
Public transport and break points:	LU: Cockfosters, Arnos Grove. NR: Palmers Green, Silver Street, Edmonton Green. Buses at all these points plus East Barnet, Osidge Lane, Waterfall Road, North Circular Road and Lee Valley Leisure Centre
Links:	London Loop, New River Path, Lea Valley Walk
Map:	Explorer 173 (route marked)
LWF status:	Validated with Seal of Approval
Principal promoter:	LB Barnet, LB Enfield
Further information:	Free leaflet (+ sae) from LB Barnet and LB Enfield libraries, sports centres and council offices. See Appendix H for all contact details

Easy walking beside Pymmes Brook, a tributary of the River Lea. The route generally follows this stream, though it is only much in evidence in the first half of the route, being mostly inaccessible as you approach its confluence with the Lea. The second half is still quite pleasant and interesting, though mostly through built-up areas – you can avoid these by finishing at Palmers Green.

The start on Monken Hadley Common from Cockfosters station by following is signed together with Section 16 of the *London Loop* westwards for 1.2km (0.7 miles). It can also be reached along the Loop in 4km (2.5 miles) from High Barnet. Just above the start point is serene Jacks Lake, well worth the small detour. The stream that you follow at first is actually Monken Mead Brook; you first see Pymmes Brook itself briefly in Victoria Recreation Ground, then it immediately disappears from view as you follow residential roads through East Barnet.

Pymmes Brook is very much in evidence through Oak Hill, Brunswick and Arnos Parks, then a short walk up Wilmer Way takes you into Broomfield Park, where a tributary stream forms four ponds. At time of writing the remains of Broomfield House, at the centre of the park, lie forlorn beneath tarpaulins after a fire.

At Palmers Green you cross the **New River Path**, then the route is either beside roads or along brookside paths, and includes two short subways beneath the North Circular Road. Pymmes Park provides a green lung at Edmonton and also your final view of Pymmes Brook before it bends southeast and disappears to join the River Lea at Tottenham Hale. You head instead northeast past Edmonton Green Shopping Centre, then along a grassy stretch between allotments and Salmon's Brook, another Lea tributary. You can finish either at the Lee Valley Leisure Centre, (closed pending redevelopment at time of writing) or at Pickett's Lock on the **Lea Valley Walk**.

There is a hard level surface for almost the entire route, with ramped subways. The approach route from Cockfosters and the path beside Mead Brook are uneven and may be muddy, but you can omit these by starting in Baring Road or Victoria Park. The 600m grassy section beside Salmon's Brook at Edmonton Green can be avoided by continuing along Plevna Road then turning right at Town Road to rejoin the route at Montagu Road. On Pickett's Lock Lane there are ribs at the far end of the bridge over the railway and main road. There are accessible toilets at Victoria Park, and Palmers Green.

RAINHAM RIVERSIDE WALK– see Havering Riverside Walk

RAVENSBOURNE RIVER – see Waterlink Way

REGENT'S CANAL TOWPATH (MAP 6)

Distance:	12.8km (8.0 miles)
Location:	Westminster, Camden, Islington, Hackney, Tower Hamlets
Start:	Little Venice (GR 261-818)
Finish:	Limehouse Basin (GR 363-811)
Green factor:	15%
Blue factor:	91%
Recommended direction:	Can be followed either way
Terrain and surface:	Almost entirely flat but with some short slopes. Hard surface all the way. No stiles. 1.4km/0.9ml along roads
Points of interest:	Little Venice, narrowboats, canal locks, Regent's Park, London Zoo, Camden Lock Market, Pirates Castle, Camley Street Nature Park, Victoria Park, Mile End Park, Limehouse Basin
Signage:	Generally not necessary but some off-canal sections have fingerposts or pavement discs

Refreshments and toilets:	Frequent refreshment facilities, mainly pubs, some cafés. Public toilets in Victoria Park
Public transport and break points:	LU: Warwick Avenue, Camden Town, Angel. NR: Camden Road, Cambridge Heath, Limehouse. DLR: Limehouse. Buses at frequent intervals
Links:	Grand Union Canal Walk, Time Travellers, Thames Path National Trail
Map:	Explorer 173
LWF status:	Pending validation
Principal promoter:	British Waterways
Further information:	*Route included in Canal Walks Vol. 3 – South* (£7.99, Denis Needham, Cicerone Press, ISBN 1-85284-227-X). Free leaflets (+ sae): *Explore London's Canals* and *Regent's Canal – a brief history* (British Waterways); and *A walk along the Regent's Canal in Hackney* (LB Hackney libraries). Leaflets Little Venice to Camden and Camden to Kings Cross (50p each + sae) from Camden Local Studies and Archives Centre. See Appendix H for all contact details

Fascinating and easy walking along the top of Central London. The constant hard surface may be tough on the feet, but breaking the route into bite-sized chunks could not be easier with excellent public transport opportunities all the way. The route can mostly be easily followed without a guidebook along the towpath, though there are some short tunnel sections with no towpath where you have to follow parallel roads. The towpath is quite narrow where it passes under some bridges and vertigo sufferers may feel uncomfortable there. Beware too of cyclists and joggers coming up behind. Some sections are gated and closed around dusk – opening times vary between 7.30 and 9am; for details call British Waterways.

Walking west to east, you start at one of London's most colourful attractions: Little Venice, where the Regent's Canal branches off the main line of the **Grand Union Canal**. Little Venice also has a floating café and puppet theatre, and there are constant boat movements, particularly of trip boats plying between Little Venice, London Zoo and Camden Lock – you might like to walk one way and return by boat.

The towpath always follows the north bank. Soon after Little Venice you must come off it to follow Blomfield Road and Aberdeen Place, avoiding a short section of private moorings and the Maida Hill Tunnel. Rejoining the towpath, you soon come to Regent's Park, where impressive villas with stunning gardens provide an imposing backdrop to passing narrowboats. The towpath cuts through London Zoo, with the Snowdon Aviary up to your left, and ruminants such as antelopes above the far bank.

The canal turns left at Cumberland Basin, by a floating restaurant in the form of a colourful Chinese junk. Soon after this you pass the Pirates' Castle youth centre, then the famous Camden Lock market (actually beside Hampstead Road Lock), heaving with stalls and activity at weekends, but usually comparatively quiet during the week. Battlebridge Basin is a popular mooring for narrowboats, now a fashionable residential area with the London Canal Museum nearby.

The canal dives under Islington through a long tunnel with no towpath, but this provides an opportunity to walk through bustling Chapel Market and the thriving Camden Passage antiques centre. The route is marked by metal discs in the pavement, though they are not always easily spotted among the crowds – if in doubt go down Duncan Street on the far side of Upper Street to rejoin the canal.

The next few kilometres are among rather bland residential and commercial areas in Hoxton and Haggerston. However, the pupils of Laburnum School have brightened up the canalside with a series of mosaics, and some attractive residential developments have replaced the dilapidated wharves and warehouses that used to line this stretch. Several canal basins with moored boats provide some colour, and you pass the Gainsborough Studios where many famous films were made.

The final few kilometres are very interesting. Victoria Park stretches away to the east, beside the Hertford Union Canal. At the canal junction lies Bow Wharf, a cosmopolitan assembly of shops, bars and cafés. For a change from the towpath, you can divert along the parallel, recently refurbished Mile End Park, passing its small windfarm and crossing its 'green bridge' across Mile End Road. The final stretch into the colourful marina in Limehouse Basin is shared with *Time Travellers*, and a little further on is the *Thames Path National Trail*.

 The surface is level and hard all the way, but some of the access ramps are very steep. Little Venice is accessible by cobbled ramp from Westbourne Terrace Road.

Limehouse Marina

RIDDLESDOWN CIRCULAR WALK (MAP 7)

Distance:	7.4km (4.6 miles)
Location:	Croydon
Start/finish:	Riddlesdown station (GR 325-610)
Green factor:	83%
Blue factor:	n/a
Recommended direction:	Clockwise
Terrain and surface:	Generally level but some steep slopes. Mostly rough paths, tracks and grass. No stiles. 1.3km (0.8 miles) beside roads
Points of interest:	Riddlesdown, Mitchley Wood
Signage:	None
Refreshments and toilets:	Pubs off-route at Hamsey Green, Riddlesdown Quarry and Kenley. Food shops at Riddlesdown station. No public toilets nearby
Public transport and break points:	NR: Riddlesdown, Kenley. Buses at these points plus Mitchley Avenue and Hamsey Green
Links:	London Loop
Map:	Explorers 146 and 161
LWF status:	Pending validation
Principal promoter:	Corporation of London
Further information:	Included in free pack (+ sae) *Coulsdon Commons Circular Walks* from Corporation of London West Wickham and Coulsdon Commons or Downlands Project. See Appendix H for all contact details

This very green route, one of the ***Coulsdon Commons Circular Walks*** series, is mostly located on Riddlesdown, an extensive common divided into two sections owned by the Corporation of London and the London Borough of Croydon. The approach from Riddlesdown station is very steep, but this (and most of the roadwalking) can be avoided by taking the bus to Mitchley Avenue. Some of the route goes through ancient woodland including Mitchley Wood, where some rare plants grow such as toothwort. Halfway round, on a very open stretch of grassland, the route is briefly shared with Section 5 of the ***London Loop***. You pass along the top of Riddlesdown Quarry, where kestrels may be seen hovering, then drop down into more woodland above Kenley just before the finish.

Ridgeway Walk (Map 6)

Distance:	5.5km (3.4 miles)
Location:	Greenwich, Bexley
Start:	Thamesmead West (Broadwater Lock, Lower Promenade, GR 447-798)
Finish:	Thamesmead North (Crossness Pathway, GR 484-812)
Green factor:	73%
Blue factor:	18%
Recommended direction:	Either way
Terrain and surface:	Almost completely level with some short gentle slopes, on either pavements or firm paths. One stile. 300m beside roads
Points of interest:	River Thames, Broadwater, Southern Outfall Sewer Embankment, Southmere Lake, Crossness Sewage Works and Pumping Station
Signage:	Fingerpost at Thamesmead West. Entry points to embankment path marked by large blue gateways
Refreshments and toilets:	Pubs and café at Plumstead and Southmere Lake. No public toilets nearby
Public transport and break points:	NR: Plumstead, Abbey Wood. Buses: Thamesmead West, East and North
Links:	Thames Path Southeast Extension, Green Chain Walk
Map:	Explorer 162
LWF status:	Pending validation
Principal promoter:	Thames Water, LB Greenwich, LB Bexley
Further information:	No leaflet available at time of writing. Information boards at several locations along the route

A fascinating, mainly green route providing easy walking through a densely populated area. It is the southeastern equivalent of **The Greenway** north of the river, as it mostly goes along the top of the Southern Outfall Sewer Embankment. This has been planted with trees, scrub and rough grass to provide a haven for wildlife.

The route is in two sections. The shorter western part starts at Broadwater Lock beside the Lower Promenade on the **Thames Path Southeast Extension** in Thamesmead West. It mostly follows the former Arsenal Dock, now called Broadwater, to Pettman Crescent. The sections are linked by a short walk beside Plumstead Road, with Plumstead station accessible by steps to the right. Turning left, you come to the big blue gateway that marks the ramp up to the embankment that forms most of the eastern section. It is then a straight walk with a grandstand view of the surrounding warehouses, houses and gardens. At Harrow Manor Way you cross one arm of Section 1 of the *Green Chain Walk*, then a fine vista opens out across Southmere Lake. You must come off the embankment, following the other GCW arm, to pass under Eastern Way. Then you continue ahead over a stile and beside Riverside Golf Course to the end of the route, rejoining the Thames Path Southeast Extension at Crossness Sewage Works, whose grand pumping station is often open to the public.

The western section is on a hard, level surface. A flight of seven steps can be avoided either across a short stretch of grass or with a diversion along Whinchat Road. The eastern section from Plumstead to Crossness has a firm but uneven surface, with access ramps, and is quite narrow in places. Note that there is a stile to cross into the golf course approaching Crossness.

River Crane Walk (Map 3)

Distance:	8.6km (5.4 miles) via Route 1 to Old Isleworth. 7.3km (4.6 miles) via Route 2 to Richmond Lock
Location:	Hounslow, Richmond
Start:	Feltham (Pevensey Road, GR 122-730)
Finish:	Route 1: Old Isleworth (Church Street, GR 168-761). Route 2: Richmond Lock (GR 170-750)
Green factor:	Via Route 1 = 37%, Via Route 2 = 45%
Blue factor:	Via Route 1 = 71%, Via Route 2 = 51%
Recommended direction:	Southwest to northeast
Terrain and surface:	Level all the way, mostly on tarmac paths, but some rough paths and steps at the start, and steps on footbridge at Great Chertsey Road
Points of interest:	River Crane, Duke of Northumberland's River, Crane Valley Nature Reserve, Crane Park and shot tower, Kneller Gardens, Moormead Gardens, Twickenham rugby ground, Mogden Sewage Treatment Works, River Thames, Richmond Lock
Signage:	Almost complete both ways. Signed from Twickenham station. Some signs may say 'Riverside Walk'
Refreshments and toilets:	Pubs at Twickenham, Isleworth, Old Isleworth and St Margarets. Cafés at Twickenham, Mogden and Old Isleworth. Public toilets at Mogden
Public transport and break points:	NR: Whitton, Isleworth, Twickenham, St Margarets. Buses at all these points plus Hanworth Road near start

Links:	London Loop, Thames Path National Trail, Capital Ring
Map:	Explorer 161
LWF status:	Validated with Seal of Approval
Principal promoter:	LB Hounslow, LB Richmond
Further information:	Free leaflet (+ sae) from LB Hounslow and LB Richmond libraries and council offices. See Appendix H for contact details

Mostly easy walking beside one of London's less well-known rivers, where much of the riverside has been left clear of building as a flood precaution to provide pleasant open spaces. This route mainly covers the river in Richmond borough, but its higher reaches can be walked on Sections 9 and 10 of the London Loop.

The River Crane Walk starts at Pevensey Road in Feltham, and leads at first through meadows and woods in the Crane Valley Nature Reserve. The paths are rough in places, and there are some low branches to watch out for. You pass the point where the Crane disappears into a tunnel through former railway yards – a link across this area to the rest of the river is planned at time of writing.

From Hanworth Road there is a long stretch on mostly tarmac paths in Crane Park beside or near the river, shared with Section 9 of the London Loop. Looming up through the trees, an intriguing shot tower is a remnant of the gunpowder industry that once thrived in this area, while away to the north you will see planes descending to Heathrow Airport. The path dives under two main roads to reach Kneller Gardens, where you have a choice of two routes. Both lead to the River Thames, where you meet the Thames Path National Trail and Section 7 of the Capital Ring.

Route 1 follows the artificial Duke of Northumberland's River, at first on a rough path passing two famous rugby grounds – The Stoop (Harlequins) and 'Twickers', the venue for England internationals. Beyond Mogden Road (huge Tesco with café and toilets) you follow a tarmac path through Mogden Sewage Treatment Works, but this is not at all unpleasant as the water is clean and the grounds have been attractively landscaped. A short stretch of roadwalking brings you to the finish at Old Isleworth, a picturesque village by the Thames.

Route 2 stays beside the Crane along a tarmac track to Craneford Way, where the river disappears from public view. You follow residential roads through Twickenham, then cross Moormead Park to St Margarets, and finally reach the Thames beside the ornate stepped footbridge that crosses to Richmond Lock.

The first stretch through Crane Valley Nature Reserve uses some very uneven paths and has a flight of 12 steps. From Hanworth Road through Crane Park and via Route 2 there is a hard level surface all the way, but the Great Chertsey Road is crossed on a footbridge with 24 shallow steps both sides – this can be avoided by crossing carefully at traffic lights nearby. Almost half of Route 1 is on a path with an uneven surface.

RIVER PINN – see Celandine Route

RURAL MILL HILL (MAP 2)

Distance:	4.3km (2.7 miles)
Location:	Barnet
Start/finish:	Totteridge Common (The Lynch House, GR 226-939)
Green factor:	45%
Blue factor:	n/a
Recommended direction:	Clockwise
Terrain and surface:	Undulating with some fairly steep climbs. Mixture of pavements, rough paths/tracks and grass. No stiles. 1.6km (1.0 miles) beside roads
Points of interest:	Folly Brook, St Paul's Church, Mill Hill School, St Mary's Abbey, Belmont Farm
Signage:	Almost complete both ways. Logo: '9' in white circle on blue arrow on white background, with text 'Barnet Countryside Leisure Walks'
Refreshments and toilets:	Pub at Mill Hill. No cafés or public toilets
Public transport and break points:	Buses: Totteridge Common, Mill Hill
Links:	Moat Mount Walk, Mill Hill Past and Present
Map:	Explorer 173
LWF status:	Pending validation
Principal promoter:	LB Barnet
Further information:	Included in *Barnet Countryside Leisure Walks* pack, 50p + sae from LB Barnet libraries. See Appendix H for contact details

A fairly energetic walk, number 9 in the **Barnet Leisure Countryside Walks** series. From the start on Totteridge Common, shared with the **Moat Mount Walk**, a short road walk leads to a descent through fields into Totteridge Valley and across Folly Brook. Most of these fields form part of Belmont Farm, where stiles have been replaced by metal kissing gates. Racehorses are reared here and you cross a training track before climbing up to The Ridgeway at Mill Hill.

You pass the start/finish point of **Mill Hill Past and Present**, then embark on a circuit of Mill Hill village, dropping down beyond The Ridgeway past the grand buildings and playing fields of Mill Hill School. Climbing Hammers Lane you enter an intriguing area of sheltered housing called Cottage Homes, clustered around the ornate, red-brick Marshall Hall, then you are back on The Ridgeway beside St Mary's Abbey. You must take care leaving Mill Hill at a busy bend in the road, but soon you are dropping down across Belmont Farm and Folly Brook again for a final climb back to Totteridge Common.

RURAL TOTTERIDGE (MAP 2)

Distance:	5.5km (3.4 miles)
Location:	Barnet
Start/finish:	St Andrew's Church, Totteridge Village (GR 247-941)
Green factor:	78%
Blue factor:	14%
Recommended direction:	Clockwise
Terrain and surface:	Undulating country with two steady ascents and descents. Mostly on rough paths, tracks and grass. Four stiles. 0.6km (0.4 miles) beside roads
Points of interest:	St Andrew's Church, Totteridge cattle pound, farmland, Totteridge Long Pond, Dollis Brook
Signage:	Almost complete both ways. Logo: '6' in white circle on blue arrow on white background, with text 'Barnet Countryside Leisure Walks'
Refreshments and toilets:	Pub at Totteridge Village. No cafés or public toilets
Public transport and break points:	Buses: Totteridge Village, Totteridge Common
Links:	Barnet-Totteridge Loop, Exploring Totteridge Manor, London Loop, Dollis Valley Greenwalk
Map:	Explorer 173
LWF status:	Pending validation
Principal promoter:	LB Barnet
Further information:	Included in *Barnet Countryside Leisure Walks* pack, 50p + sae from LB Barnet libraries. See Appendix H for contact details

A fairly easy walk, number 6 in the **Barnet Countryside Leisure Walks** series, though with some steady climbing. The start and finish point, high up in Totteridge Village, is shared with the **Barnet-Totteridge Loop** and **Exploring Totteridge Manor** in the same series.

The route immediately descends a long, straight path beside the Darlands estate into open farmland, where the view is dominated by the green-roofed National

Medical Research Centre, then climbs again to serene Totteridge Long Pond, speckled with gliding waterbirds. Descending once more, you join the **London Loop** and **Dollis Valley Greenwalk** through grassy fields in Totteridge Park Open Space, walking close to Dollis Brook with a good view of Chipping Barnet and its church. You finish with a final climb on tarmac back to Totteridge Village.

St Mary Cray Circular Walk (Map 6)

Distance:	5.5km (3.4 miles) plus optional extension of 1.0km (0.6 miles)
Location:	Bromley
Start/finish:	St Mary Cray Recreation Ground (Rosecroft Close, GR 473-673)
Green factor:	66%
Blue factor:	11%
Recommended direction:	Anticlockwise
Terrain and surface:	Fairly level but with some gentle slopes. Mixture of tarmac and rough paths, tracks and grass. Five stiles. 1.9km (1.2 miles) beside roads
Points of interest:	Kynaston Wood, Walden Manor, Kevington Hall, St Mary Cray village, River Cray, Riverside Gardens
Signage:	Complete both ways. Logo: 'St Mary Cray Circular Walk' in yellow on dark green background, surrounding yellow arrow with pale mauve flash
Refreshments and toilets:	Pubs and public toilets at St Mary Cray
Public transport and break points:	NR: St Mary Cray. Buses: St Mary Cray, Cockmannings Road, Crockenhill Road
Links:	Cray Riverway
Map:	Explorer 162
LWF status:	Pending validation
Principal promoter:	LB Bromley
Further information:	Included in Pack Two of *Bromley Circular Walks and Trails* (£2.50 plus 50p p&p) from LB Bromley Leisure & Community Services and libraries. See Appendix H for contact details

One of the shorter and easier walks in the **Bromley Circular Walks and Trails** series, starting and finishing in St Mary Cray Recreation Ground. It describes a pleasant loop through gently undulating fields and woodlands to the east of the village and back, passing Kevington Hall. A short diversion can be made to Walden Manor, home of William Cook, who bred the Buff Orpington chicken. Care is needed on a short road section with no pavement.

Back in St Mary Cray there is a short optional extra loop through the village centre, passing some interesting new and old buildings and a red-brick viaduct dating from the early years of the railways. Finally it follows the River Cray through pretty Riverside Gardens, where the route is shared with the *Cray Riverway*.

ST PAUL'S CRAY CIRCULAR WALK (MAP 6)

Distance:	8.7km (5.4 miles). Short option 6.4km (4.0 miles)
Location:	Bromley
Start/finish:	St Paul's Wood Hill, St Paul's Cray (GR 454-693)
Green factor:	42%
Blue factor:	2%
Recommended direction:	Anticlockwise
Terrain and surface:	Generally fairly level with some gentle slopes. Mostly on tarmac paths, lanes or pavements, with some rough paths, tracks and grass. No stiles. 3.4km (2.1 miles) on or beside roads
Points of interest:	Hoblingwell Wood, St Paul's Cray village and water meadows, Paul's Cray Hill Park, Scadbury Park, Scadbury Manor, St Paul's Wood Green
Signage:	Partial both ways. Logo: 'St Paul's Cray Circular Walk' in yellow on dark green background, surrounding yellow arrow with orange flash
Refreshments and toilets:	Pubs at Sevenoaks Way and St Paul's Cray village. Public toilets at Cotmandene Crescent
Public transport and break points:	Buses: St Paul's Cray Road, Chipperfield Road, St Paul's Cray village, Sevenoaks Way, Midfield Way
Links:	Cray Riverway, London Loop
Map:	Explorer 162
LWF status:	Pending validation
Principal promoter:	LB Bromley
Further information:	Included in Pack Two of *Bromley Circular Walks and Trails* (£2.50 plus 50p p&p) from LB Bromley Leisure & Community Services and libraries. See Appendix H for contact details

A fairly easy route in the **Bromley Circular Walks and Trails** series. Though rather more urban than others in the series, it includes much of interest. The starting point is the car park on St Paul's Wood Green, with a fine view across Kent, and close to bus routes along St Paul's Cray Road from Grove Park, Petts Wood and Orpington stations. You descend into Hoblingwell Wood, then climb to cross St Paul's Cray Recreation Ground. A longish walk along residential roads and past a shopping centre follows, but after Sevenoaks Way you find yourself amongst serene water meadows in the delightful village of St Paul's Cray, complete with weatherboard inn and flint church, and where you cross the **Cray Riverway**.

The short walk turns back here, while the long route embarks on a loop of St Paul's Cray Hill Park, a former refuse tip that has been turned into a high and broad expanse of grassland with more good views. Back in the village you continue along roads leading to Scadbury Park, a nature reserve where you can visit the remains of moated Scadbury Manor, and where the route is shared with Section 2 of the **London Loop**.

SHUTTLE RIVERWAY (MAP 6)

Distance:	9.7km (6.1 miles)
Location:	Greenwich, Bexley
Start:	Avery Hill (Avery Hill Park, GR 440-741)
Finish:	Bexley (Hall Place, Bourne Road, GR 502-743)
Green factor:	65%
Blue factor:	39%
Recommended direction:	West to east
Terrain and surface:	Generally level but one steep slope (avoidable). Mostly on rough paths, tracks or grass, some tarmac paths. No stiles. 3.5km (2.2 miles) beside roads
Points of interest:	Avery Hill Park, Avery Hill House, River Shuttle, Bexley Woods, The Warren, Hall Place
Signage:	Almost complete both ways. Fingerposts or wooden marker posts with yellow and blue 'Shuttle Riverway' and logo on grey background
Refreshments and toilets:	Pubs at Eltham, Blackfen and Hall Place. Cafés and public toilets at Eltham, Avery Hill Park and Hall Place
Public transport and break points:	Buses: Eltham, Avery Hill, Blackfen, Blendon, Bexley, Hall Place
Links:	Green Chain Walk, London Loop, Cray Riverway
Map:	Explorer 162
LWF status:	Pending validation

Principal promoter:	LB Bexley
Further information:	Free leaflet from LB Bexley libraries and council offices. See Appendix H for contact details

Mainly easy walking beside the River Shuttle, a tributary of the Cray. The start is about 10 minutes' walk from Eltham town centre, following Section 6 of the **Green Chain Walk** eastwards via Footscray Road and Conduit Meadow, then the link to Avery Hill Park. You start across grass then pass the Winter Garden of Avery Hill House. There follows a stretch of tarmac paths and pavements through Blackfen, where you first pick up the Shuttle. Then you are walking on level but sometimes rough paths beside the river for most of the next 5.5km (3.4 miles) as it flows through a green corridor between houses and gardens, and through Bexley Woods.

There is some climbing to be done as you approach the Cray, because the Shuttle is inaccessible here and the route diverts across a ramped footbridge over the A2 Rochester Way. Then you climb over The Warren, a steep hill with good views, whose small woodland supports a variety of wildlife. The steepest part of the hill can be avoided by following nearby roads. Finally you descend steeply to Hall Place manor house, now a pub-restaurant, where there are also a café, toilets and buses to Bexley or Bexleyheath. It lies very close to the **Cray Riverway** and Section 1 of the **London Loop**.

SOCRATIC TRAIL (MAP 7)

Distance:	75km (47 miles) – see text
Location:	Croydon, continuing into Surrey and Sussex
Start:	Old Coulsdon (St John's Church, GR 312-582)
Finish:	Brighton Marina (Marine Drive, GR 337-034)
*Green factor:	60%
Blue factor:	n/a
Recommended direction:	North to south
Terrain and surface:	Undulating country with some steep slopes. Mainly on rough paths, tracks and grass. Five stiles (to Merstham). 4.0km (2.5 miles) beside roads*
*Points of interest:	St John's Church (Old Coulsdon), Happy Valley, farmland, Church of St Peter and St Paul (Chaldon), North Downs, Mercers Park Country Park
Signage:	Fingerpost at the start, otherwise no specific route signs
*Refreshments and toilets:	Pubs at Old Coulsdon, Merstham, Nutfield Marsh, Nutfield and Bletchingley. No cafés or public toilets nearby

*Public transport and break points:	Buses: Old Coulsdon, Chaldon, Merstham, Nutfield, Bletchingley. NR: Coulsdon South, Merstham, Nutfield
*Links:	London Loop, Downlands Circular Walk, Coulsdon Common and Happy Valley Circular Walk, Farthing Downs and Devilsden Wood Circular Walk, North Downs Way, London Countryway
*Map:	Explorer 146
*LWF status:	Pending validation
Principal promoter:	Socratic Walkers
Further information:	Route description from Socratic Walkers – £1.50 plus 33p p&p (cheques payable to M.Hencke), also available at LB Croydon Tourist Information Centre. See Appendix H for all contact details

*These details apply to Stage 1 only.

Devised by Maurice Hencke, founder of the Socratic Walkers club, this very attractive route has been adopted by LB Croydon as its Millennium Trail. It leads from Old Coulsdon across the North and South Downs to Brighton, a total distance of 75km (47 miles), with several alternatives. Stage 1, across the North Downs from Old Coulsdon to Merstham and Nutfield in Surrey (both with trains to London), provides a good walk of up to 13.0km (8.1 miles). Or you can follow one of the alternatives, via Bletchingley, adding about another 1.5km (1.0 miles).

A wooden fingerpost marks the start by St John's Church in Old Coulsdon, but there is as yet no other route specific signage. You soon cross the glorious Happy Valley into Surrey, making contact with Section 5 of the **London Loop** and several other routes in the Strategic Network (see above). Then fieldpaths lead to the 11th century Church of St Peter and St Paul at Chaldon, with its colourful 800-year-old wall painting *The Ladder of Human Salvation*. The route then skirts Chaldon village (where the alternative route branches off to Bletchingley), heading for the **North Downs Way**, which is followed across the M23 with fine views of the Surrey Hills. After crossing the M25 you can finish at Merstham station or continue through more farmland and Mercers Park Country Park to Nutfield.

SOUTH BUCKS WAY (MAP 3)

Distance:	37km (23 miles) – see text
Location:	Hillingdon, continuing into Buckinghamshire
Start:	Coombe Hill, Bucks (GR SP 849-068)
Finish:	Denham Lock (GR TQ 053-862)
Green factor:	64%
Blue factor:	5%

Recommended direction:	Northwest to southeast
Terrain and surface:	Mostly level or downhill, with one fairly short and gentle climb. Mostly on rough paths and tracks. Number of stiles not known. 5.0km (3.1 miles) beside roads
Points of interest:	Amersham Old Town, River Misbourne, Shire Lane, Denham village, River Colne, Grand Union Canal, Denham Lock
Signage:	'South Bucks Way' on waymark discs
Refreshments and toilets:	Pubs and cafés at Amersham, Chalfont St Giles, Chalfont St Peter and Denham. Tearoom at Denham Lock. Public toilets: not known
Public transport and break points:	LU: Amersham. NR: Denham. Bus: Amersham, Chalfont St Giles, Chalfont St Peter, Denham
Links:	West Ruislip to Gerrards Cross Ramble and Ride, Nine Stiles Circular Walk, Widewater Lock Circular Walk, London Loop, Grand Union Canal Walk, Colne Valley Trail
Map:	Explorer 172 (also 181 if starting at Coombe Hill) (route marked)
LWF status:	Pending validation
Principal promoter:	Buckinghamshire CC
Further information:	Free leaflet + sae (also included in pack of 19 walks in Chilterns and South Bucks £3.00 + sae) from Buckinghamshire CC. See Appendix H for contact details

A fine route starting at Coombe Hill, near Wendover in the Chilterns, and finishing just inside the Greater London boundary at Denham Lock. You can sample it by travelling to Amersham on the Metropolitan Line and walking back to Denham, a good full day's walk of 19km (12 miles). By starting there you cut out most of the climbing, but also miss some of the best scenery.

The station is actually in Amersham-on-the-Hill, and you descend to the old town to pick up the South Bucks Way. The route then follows the valley of the delightful River Misbourne for the next 8km (5 miles) past Chalfont St Giles to Chalfont St Peter. Most of the time you are in open country, on level paths and tracks through fields at the foot of the Chiltern slopes, occasionally walking beside the river but usually a little way from it.

You must climb fairly steeply out of Chalfont St Peter, but soon descend again across the M25 motorway to enjoy fine views across the Colne valley with its flooded gravel pits. Here you share the route of the Old Shire Lane Circular Walk (not covered in this book), then take care walking along a lane with no pavement to reach Denham Green, where the station is located. You follow the quaintly named Pyghtle Footpath into picturesque Denham village, where the Misbourne flows beside the road. The final stretch is shared with the **Nine Stiles Circular Walk** across the River Colne to finish at the towpath of the **Grand Union Canal**, well used by other routes in the London network (see above). For transport you can either return to Denham or turn right along the towpath for a further 2.2km (1.4 miles) into Uxbridge.

SOUTH EAST LONDON GREEN CHAIN – see Green Chain Walk

SUTTON COUNTRYSIDE WALK (MAP 7)

Distance:	7.7km (4.8 miles). Short options 5.0km (3.1 miles) or 6.0km (3.8 miles)
Location:	Sutton
Start/finish:	The Oaks Park, Carshalton (GR 275-611), or Grove Lane, Clockhouse (GR 287-602)
Green factor:	92%
Blue factor:	n/a
Recommended direction:	Anticlockwise
Terrain and surface:	Mostly level with some short gentle slopes, on rough paths, tracks and grass. 13 stiles. 600m beside roads
Points of interest:	The Oaks Park, farmland, Little Woodcote Estate
Signage:	Complete both ways. Logo: green and brown tree on white background, plus text 'Sutton Countryside Walk'
Refreshments and toilets:	Café at The Oaks Park. Pub at Clockhouse. Toilets at The Oaks Park
Public transport and break points:	NR: Carshalton Beeches. Buses: Clockhouse
Links:	London Loop
Map:	Explorer 161
LWF status:	Validated with Seal of Approval
Principal promoter:	LB Sutton, Downlands Project
Further information:	Free leaflet + sae from LB Sutton libraries and Downlands Project. See Appendix H for contact details

One of the greenest routes in the book, on a plateau in the foothills of the North Downs to the south of Carshalton, with just a few short and gentle climbs and very little roadwalking. The official start is by the cafeteria in The Oaks Park, from which the famous classic horse race at Epsom's Derby meeting is named – this was the Earl of Derby's estate. Using public transport, from Carshalton Beeches station you walk 1.2km (0.8 miles) along Beeches Avenue and Woodmansterne Road to pick up the route. Or you can take a bus from Wallington station to Clockhouse, which is on the route and has a pub for refreshment when you return.

The route is shared with Section 6 of the **London Loop** for a while, crossing preserved chalk grassland, then you walk along an ancient track with fine views across London, through the Little Woodcote Estate, an area of smallholdings with distinctive black weatherboard houses. This brings you to Clockhouse, then more fields lead to the attractive bungalow-style clubhouse of Woodcote Park Golf Club. Tree-lined Woodcote Grove leads to Little Woodcote Wood, a site of wildlife value, where the shorter option returns direct to The Oaks Park. The longer route continues along a track between more smallholdings, then you return to the starting point along The Oaks Park Nature Trail (see Other Named Self-guided Walks below).

TAMSIN TRAIL (MAP 5)

Distance:	11.7km (7.3 miles)
Location:	Richmond
Start/finish:	Any convenient point (see text)
Green factor:	100%
Blue factor:	15%
Recommended direction:	Either way
Terrain and surface:	Hard surface throughout (mostly bonded gravel). Some gentle slopes, fairly steep in places. No stiles. No roadwalking (but some park roads to cross)
Points of interest:	Richmond Park, Beverley Brook, Richmond Gate, King Henry VIII Mound, Pembroke Lodge and gardens, Hornbeam Walk, red and fallow deer
Signage:	Route marked on information boards and fingerposts at most park gates and car parks
Refreshments and toilets:	Licensed cafés near Roehampton Gate and at Pembroke Lodge, also park kiosks at some points. Pubs outside the park close to Robin Hood Gate, also at Richmond, East Sheen, Roehampton, Kingston, Ham and Petersham. Public toilets at or near most park gates and at Pembroke Lodge
Public transport and break points:	Buses at Robin Hood Gate, Roehampton, Richmond Gate, Petersham and Kingston Hill. NR: Mortlake, North Sheen, Norbiton and Richmond
Links:	Capital Ring, Beverley Brook Walk

Map:	Explorer 161
LWF status:	Pending validation
Principal promoter:	Royal Parks Agency
Further information:	Included in free leaflet + sae *Cycling in Richmond Park* from Royal Parks Agency at Richmond Park. See Appendix H for contact details

A purpose-built dual-use route for walkers and cyclists that completely encircles one of London's gems, Richmond Park. There is a hard surface throughout, but there are some fairly steep climbs in places, and park roads to cross which can be busy. You can join and leave at any convenient point, but Robin Hood Gate or Richmond Gate may be best as buses stop there. By train, you can walk up from Norbiton to Kingston Gate (1km/0.6 miles) or from Mortlake, North Sheen or Richmond (all about 1.5km/0.9 miles).

The walking is virtually all amongst greenery, though for much of the way with the brick park boundary wall or park roads close by. One stretch runs beside Beverley Brook, naturally shared with the **Beverley Brook Walk**, while Section 6 of the **Capital Ring** crosses the Trail at Robin Hood Gate and Pembroke Lodge. There are great views all the way, especially along the west side of the park from the top of an escarpment, where you overlook Petersham Park, Ham Common and the Thames valley.

 The whole route has a hard, rolled earth surface, but be prepared for some slopes and uneven stretches. All the park toilets are accessible with a Radar key.

TANDRIDGE BORDER PATH (See Appendix B)

This circular route is now open. The 80km (50 miles) starts and finishes at Tatsworth Village Green (GR413-568) and follows the boundary of Tandridge District in Surrey, mostly along footpaths and bridleways, passing near Westerham, East Grinstead, Horley and Caterham. The waymarked path comes briefly into Greater London near Selsdon (Croydon) and Biggin Hill (Bromley). As it crosses the North Downs twice, the path becomes quite steep in places. Free leaflet plus A5 sae (41p) from Per-Rambulations (see Appendix H).

THAMES DOWN LINK (MAP 7)

Distance:	24km (15 miles) – see text
Location:	Kingston, continuing into Surrey
Start:	Kingston Bridge (GR 177-694)
Finish:	Box Hill station (GR 168-519)
Green factor:	64%
Blue factor:	17%

Recommended direction:	North to south
Terrain and surface:	Almost entirely level within Greater London; with some gentle slopes, which get steeper in Surrey. Hard surface for first 3km (1.9 miles) then predominantly grass, rough paths and tracks. No stiles. 8.1km (5.0 miles) beside roads
Points of interest:	River Thames, historic Kingston, Hogsmill River, Bonesgate Stream, Castle Hill, Horton Country Park, Epsom Common, Ashtead Park, North Downs, Stane Street, Box Hill
Signage:	Complete both ways. Logo: 'Thames Down Link' encircling stylised green woodland over blue water on white background
Refreshments and toilets:	Pubs at Kingston, Villiers Road, Old Malden Lane, Chessington, Ashtead and Box Hill. Cafés at Kingston, Chessington, Ashtead and Box Hill. Toilets at Kingston and Box Hill
Public transport and break points:	NR: Kingston, Berrylands, Malden Manor, Tolworth, Chessington North, Chessington South, Ashtead, Boxhill & Westhumble. Buses at all these points plus Malden Way, Kingston Road, and Moor Lane
Links:	Thames Path National Trail, London Loop, Hogsmill Walk, Chessington Countryside Walk, North Downs Way National Trail, London Countryway
Map:	Explorer 161
LWF status:	Pending validation
Principal promoter:	Lower Mole Project
Further information:	Free leaflet + sae from Lower Mole Project. See Appendix H for contact details

The Thames Down Link, devised to link two national trails, provides a most enjoyable full day out for strong walkers, and fairly easy walking within Greater London for 12km (7.5 miles) as far as Chessington. Note that some sections of this route are shared with cyclists and horseriders.

From Kingston Bridge on the **Thames Path National Trail** you follow the Hogsmill River in company with the **Hogsmill Walk** and Section 8 of the **London Loop** (qqv for further details about this section). Through Horton Country Park you join for a while the **Chessington Countryside Walk**, which provides a link to Chessington South station. Then the route strikes out on its own across Epsom Common and through Ashtead Park before climbing into the North Downs proper. Here you rise and fall through woodland along the straight, ancient Roman road called Stane Street for several kilometres. You eventually drop down to contour along the foot of Box Hill, where you cross the A24 in a subway, also used by the **North Downs Way National Trail** and **London Countryway**, then it is a short walk up a lane to Box Hill & Westhumble station.

Thames Path National Trail (Maps 4, 5, 3)

Distance:	294km (184 miles) – see text
Location:	Greenwich, Lewisham, Tower Hamlets, City of London, Southwark, Lambeth, Westminster, Kensington & Chelsea, Wandsworth, Hammersmith & Fulham, Hounslow, Richmond and Kingston, continuing through several counties to Gloucestershire
Start:	Woolwich (Thames Flood Barrier Information Centre, GR TQ 416-793)
Finish:	Thames Head, Gloucestershire (GR ST 981-995)
Recommended direction:	Either way
Terrain and surface:	Almost completely level on hard or firm surface, but may be muddy in places. Some short slopes. No stiles
Points of interest:	See text
Signage:	Almost complete both ways. Logo: acorn (National Trail symbol) and 'Thames Path' plus arrow on fingerposts, markerposts or plates. May be black on white or white on black (blue used instead of black in some boroughs). Some links to nearby stations are signed
*Refreshments and toilets:	Pubs and cafés at frequent intervals
*Public transport and break points:	Trains, buses and riverbuses at frequent intervals
*Links:	Thames Path Southeast Extension, Green Chain Walk, Waterlink Way, Lea Valley Walk, Jubilee Walkway, Wandle Trail, Beverley Brook Walk, Grand Union Canal Walk, Brent River Park Walk, River Crane Walk, Capital Ring, London Loop, Thames Down Link, Hogsmill Walk
*Map:	Explorer 161, 162, 173
*LWF status:	Mayor of London's key route
Principal promoter:	Countryside Agency
Further information:	West to east: *The Thames Path National Trail Guide* (David Sharp, Aurum Press, ISBN 1-85410-406-3). East to west: *The Thames Path* (Leigh Hatts, Cicerone Press, ISBN 1-85284-270-9); *A guide to the Thames Path* (Miles Jebb, Constable, ISBN 0-09-466950-3). Free leaflet + sae giving general information also available from the Thames Path National Trail Office and on www.nationaltrails.gov.uk/thamespath.htm See Appendix H for contact details

*These details refer to the Greater London section only.

As a national trail, this route has to come top of the list of London's walking gems. The walking is consistently easy, though the route is subject to flooding upstream of Putney Bridge and downstream of Greenwich, at exceptionally high tides and after prolonged periods of heavy rain. You can check high tide times by calling the Port of London Authority on 020 7743 7900 or at www.tidetimes.co.uk. The Thames Path provides a link with 12 other routes in the network (see above).

The route extends westwards far beyond the Greater London boundary, right up to the river's source in the Cotswold Hills. You get two for the price of one through London, as the route follows both banks most of the way. This provides a total of 107km (67 miles) within the Greater London boundary, fairly evenly divided between the north and south banks. There are excellent public transport connections throughout this section, so you can divide the route into chunks to suit your requirements. You can easily switch from one bank to the other at any of 24 beautifully painted bridges, most of which are stunningly floodlit at night. Two ferries, a foot tunnel and several railway lines provide further bank-switching opportunities.

Approaching Richmond, by Petersham Meadows

The route is intensely interesting, as there are constantly changing and sometimes awe-inspiring views, and something is always happening on the river, whether human-initiated or otherwise. You are very likely to see all kinds of waterborne activity, including rowing in all its forms, canoeing, sailing, trip boats, tugs, barges, floating gin-palaces, narrowboats, houseboats, marinas and boatyards. Downstream of London Bridge you may spot seagoing ships carefully manoeuvring into or away from their mooring, and downstream from Greenwich the route angles around working wharves. The Thames is now the cleanest major river in Europe, and this is reflected in the range of species that inhabits both the river and its banks. There are just too many individual places of interest to mention here – the guidebooks mentioned above do them justice.

What you should not see, and must certainly not attempt, is swimming in the river, as the Thames is notoriously dangerous with strong currents and undertows. You should also be aware that much of the route is included in National Cycle Routes 1 and 4 – walkers and cyclists should treat each other with respect and consideration. On the north bank at Barnes Bridge, you will need to take care on a stretch of fairly busy road that has no pavement and blind bends.

The whole route through London is level apart from some short slopes. It is mostly on hard or firm ground, but on the south bank between Teddington Lock and Putney Bridge there are some unavoidable long stretches on rough paths that may be uneven or muddy at times. In some places alternative parallel tracks may be more suitable. Some road sections along the north bank have undropped kerbs. At Brentford the route is fiddly with several short flights of steps, and a diversion along the High Street may be necessary. At Blackfriars Bridge, a change of level linked by steps currently requires a long diversion northwards along New Bridge Street, although there are plans to provide a ramp.

On the Thames Path National Trail beside Old Deer Park

Most of the bridges are only accessible from the riverside by long flights of steps, where long diversions may be necessary. The only bridges that are ramped both sides within Greater London are at Hampton Court, Teddington Lock and Lambeth, while Hungerford Bridge and the Millennium Bridge have lifts. There are cobbled stretches around Southwark Cathedral, Wapping, Rotherhithe and Greenwich.

Limehouse Reach and Canary Wharf

THAMES PATH SOUTHEAST EXTENSION (MAPS 4, 6)

Distance:	16.5km (10.3 miles)
Location:	Bexley, Greenwich
Start:	Crayford Ness (GR 537-783)
Finish:	Woolwich (Thames Barrier, GR 415-793)
Green factor:	28%
Blue factor:	80%
Recommended direction:	Either way
Terrain and surface:	Almost completely level with some short and occasionally steep slopes. Mostly on hard surface but some stretches on rough paths. No stiles. 1.7km (1.1 miles) beside roads
Points of interest:	Erith Deep Water Jetty, Erith Pier, Riverside Gardens, working wharves, Ford ferries, Crossness Sewage Disposal Works and beam engines, Royal Arsenal, Woolwich Foot Tunnel, Woolwich Ferry, Thames Barrier
Signage:	Almost complete both ways. Logo: Thames sailing barge with 'Thames Path' in white on black background
Refreshments and toilets:	Pubs, cafés and public toilets at Erith, Thamesmead, Woolwich and Thames Flood Barrier
Public transport and break points:	NR: Erith, Belvedere, Plumstead, Woolwich Arsenal, Woolwich Dockyard, Charlton. Buses at all these points plus Thamesmead North, Central and West
Links:	Cray Riverway, London Loop, Green Chain Walk, Ridgeway Walk, Capital Ring, Thames Path National Trail
Map:	Explorer 162
LWF status:	Pending validation
Principal promoter:	LB Bexley, LB Greenwich
Further information:	No literature available at time of writing

Thames sailing barge gives way to acorn at the Thames Barrier (properly the Thames Flood Barrier), where this route becomes the *Thames Path National Trail*. The acorn symbol can only be used on national trails, so a different one had to be found for the Thames Path Southeast Extension (TPSE), which is essentially a continuation of the riverside route. The route has absorbed several separate stretches of riverside promenade including the Erith Riverside Walk, Crossness Pathway and Thamesmead Riverside Walk.

The TPSE provides mostly very easy walking and in places a feeling of isolation, especially in the working wharves at weekends when they lie idle, and in the scrubland around Thamesmead. This is a good area for birdwatching, and there are many shipping movements on the river, so binoculars would be useful. This is also part of National Cycle Route 1, so watch out for cyclists. Some parts of the route may be under water at high tide – you can check tide times by calling the Port of London Authority on 020 7743 7900 or at www.tidetimes.co.uk.

The route starts at Crayford Ness, east of Erith, on Section 1 of the *London Loop* and the *Cray Riverway*. This isolated spot can be reached in 3.0km (1.9 miles) from Slade Green station along a London Loop link. The TPSE sets off westwards along the raised flood protection bank, then a short road stretch through Erith leads to its promenade and pier. A little further on you pass the start of Section 2 of the **Green Chain Walk**, then continuing through working wharves you may need to wait while lorries rumble onto jetties.

Approaching Crossness a cluster of little ferryboats serves the Ford works opposite, then comes the massive sewage disposal works, with its prominent modern incinerator. Its historic beam engines are sometimes open to the public – check with Thames Water. There are hides here, where you can watch shorebirds feeding, and which feature interpretation panels. The **Ridgeway Walk** leads off here, to return beyond Thamesmead, and a little further on is the start of Section 1 of the **Green Chain Walk**. Fast-growing Thamesmead's present raw surroundings will surely mellow and become greener in time.

The far bank is dominated by the tall, blue and grey Barking Creek Flood Barrier. You pass a stretch of scrub, earmarked as a new park, as you round Tripcock Ness with its little red navigational beacon. A beautifully landscaped promenade through the former Royal Arsenal works leads to the Woolwich Foot Tunnel, the official starting and finishing point of the **Capital Ring**, and the Woolwich Free Ferry. Together with the Capital Ring, you pass the former Woolwich Drawing Docks, and a stylish sweptback viewing platform. Beyond that, the riverside is not yet accessible and you must divert inland, shortly joining Section 5 of the **Green Chain Walk** to reach the Thames Barrier and the east end of the **Thames Path National Trail**.

 The whole route is level and firm, but some fairly long stretches at Thamesmead are on uneven ground. There is a very steep slope on a bridge over a jetty access road near Erith.

Thamesmead Riverside Walk –
see Thames Path Southeast Extension

THREE COMMONS CIRCULAR WALK (MAP 8)

Distance:	7.5km (4.7 miles)
Location:	Bromley
Start/finish:	Warren Road, Hayes (GR 401-369)
Green factor:	80%
Blue factor:	3%
Recommended direction:	Clockwise
Terrain and surface:	After a level start becomes quite hilly, with some steep slopes which may be muddy after heavy rain. Mostly on rough paths, tracks and grass. No stiles. 400m beside roads, but many busy roads to cross
Points of interest:	Hayes, Keston and West Wickham Commons, Ravensbourne Open Space, Padmall Wood, Keston Ponds
Signage:	Almost complete both ways. Logo: 'Three Commons Circular Walk' in yellow on dark green background, surrounding yellow arrow with white flash
Refreshments and toilets:	Pubs and café at Hayes, pubs at Keston. Public toilets at Keston Ponds
Public transport and break points:	NR: Hayes. Buses: Hayes, Keston
Links:	London Loop, Farnborough Circular Walk, Nash Circular Walk
Map:	Explorers 147 and 162
LWF status:	Validated with Seal of Approval
Principal promoter:	LB Bromley
Further information:	Included in Pack 2 of *Bromley Circular Walks and Trails* (£2.50 plus 50p p&p) from LB Bromley Leisure & Community Services and libraries. See Appendix H for contact details

A very pleasant walk through woodland in popular dog-walking country, with a wide variety of flora and fauna, though there are few long views. One of the **Bromley Circular Walks and Trails** series, this route has very little roadwalking, although you do have to cross many busy roads. At two points the route is shared with Section 3 of the **London Loop**.

Starting from Warren Road, up the hill from Hayes station, it is fairly level walking at first, southwards across Hayes Common, then you start climbing as you enter Padmall Wood and the route remains hilly to the end. You reach the southernmost and highest point of the route on Keston Common, where you briefly encounter the **Farnborough** and **Nash Circular Walks**, then pass the three tranquil Keston

Ponds. A sharp turn back north takes you through Keston village and across a different part of Hayes Common on to West Wickham Common, where there are extensive views across to New Addington. You return to Hayes along the intriguingly named and very steep Polecat Alley.

THREE FORESTS WAY (MAP 4)

Distance:	96km (60 miles) – see text
Location:	Redbridge, but mostly in Essex
Start/finish:	Harlow Town station (GR TL 447-113)
Green factor:	Not known
Blue factor:	Not known
Recommended direction:	Clockwise
Terrain and surface:	Mostly undulating country with some steep climbs. Mainly on rough paths and tracks. Number of stiles and distance beside roads not known
Points of interest:	Hatfield Forest, Hainault Forest, Epping Forest, plus much open country and farmland in between
Signage:	None at time of writing
Refreshments and toilets:	Pubs and cafés at frequent intervals. Few public toilets
Public transport and break points:	Explorers 174, 175, 183 (route marked)
Links:	London Countryway, London Loop, Chigwell Country Walk, Epping Forest Centenary Walk
Map:	See text
LWF status:	Pending validation
Principal promoter:	Ramblers' Association (West Essex Group)
Further information:	Guidebook £1.00 + sae from Essex County Council (Fred Matthews and Harry Bitten, Matthews Bitten Publications, 1986, ISBN 0-9506338-7-9). See Appendix H for contact details

A delightful long-distance circular route linking three large forests in Essex, which dips briefly (for about a kilometre/half a mile) into Greater London at Hainault Forest. It was established in 1977 to commemorate the Silver Jubilee of Queen Elizabeth II. The total distance is 96km (60 miles), but you can easily sample it from London on day trips using the excellent connections by bus and/or London Underground in this area. For example, Ongar to Chigwell Row (20.0km/12.5 miles), or Abridge to Loughton (12.8km/8.0 miles) both take in the Hainault Forest section. The Three Forests Way is walked in one go in November every even year as an LDWA challenge event (see Section 3).

TIME TRAVELLERS (MAP 5)
Incorporating the Hertford Union Canal and Limehouse Cut towpaths

Distance:	10.2km (6.4 miles)
Location:	Tower Hamlets, Newham
Start/finish:	Bromley-by-Bow (Three Mills Island, GR 384-828)
Green factor:	15%
Blue factor:	92%
Recommended direction:	Anticlockwise
Terrain and surface:	Almost completely level but with some short steep slopes. Mostly on firm towpaths, some short rough sections. No stiles. 0.8km (0.5 miles) beside roads
Points of interest:	Three Mills Centre, Lee Navigation, Hertford Union Canal and locks, Victoria Park, Bow Wharf, Regent's Canal and locks, Limehouse Marina, Limehouse Cut, Bow Locks
Signage:	None (but each waterway has its own signs)
Refreshments and toilets:	Pubs and cafés at Bromley-by-Bow, Hackney Wick, Victoria Park, Bow Wharf, Limehouse. Public toilets in Victoria Park
Public transport and break points:	LU: Bromley-by-Bow, Mile End. NR: Hackney Wick, Limehouse. DLR: Pudding Mill Lane, Limehouse, Devons Road. Buses at all these points (not Pudding Mill Lane) plus Bow Wharf
Links:	Lea Valley Walk, Capital Ring, The Greenway, Regent's Canal Towpath, Thames Path National Trail, Heron and Kingfisher Walks
Map:	Explorers 162, 173
LWF status:	Pending validation
Principal promoter:	Lower Lea Project
Further information:	Free leaflet (+ sae) from Lower Lea Project. See Appendix H for contact details

Easy and interesting walking in the East End, one of the **Waterway Discovery** series, dominated by waterways where wildlife flourishes. The official starting point, shared with the **Heron and Kingfisher Walks**, is near Bromley-by-Bow station on Three Mills Island. Two of the mills still stand, one of which can be visited, and there is also a former distillery which now houses film studios. The route is almost rectangular, with Three Mills Island at one corner, but you can easily start at any of the other corners at Hackney Wick, Bow Wharf or Limehouse.

The walking is almost entirely on level and firm towpaths, however there are some steep but short slopes on access ramps or where the towpath changes level at locks. There are only two points where you have to come off the towpaths and walk beside roads: at Bow Road and Blackwall Tunnel Northern Approach. Note that the towpaths are much used by cyclists and joggers, who may come up fast from behind.

The route is in four fairly equal parts consisting of the towpaths of the Lee Navigation, Hertford Union Canal, Regent's Canal and Limehouse Cut. Along the way you pass: Victoria Park, one of London's largest open spaces; Bow Wharf, a thriving craft and entertainment centre with pubs and cafes; Mile End Park, recently refurbished; and Limehouse Marina, a colourful haven for small craft.

Parts of the route are shared with the **Lea Valley Walk**, Section 14 of the **Capital Ring** and the **Regent's Canal Towpath**. Limehouse Marina is only a short step from the **Thames Path National Trail**.

Apart from the occasional slopes mentioned above, almost the whole route is level, but there is a small flight of steps along the Limehouse Cut, which may require a diversion along nearby roads. The Hertford Union towpath has a very uneven and sometimes muddy stretch of about 200m near Hackney Wick. The bridge at Bow Locks has a steep ribbed curve.

TYLERS COMMON TO WARLEY WALK (MAP 4)

Distance:	6.0 to 12.0km (3.7 to 7.5 miles)
Location:	Havering, plus some in Essex
Start/finish:	Tylers Common car park (GR 564-908)
Green factor:	Not known
Blue factor:	n/a
Recommended direction:	Anticlockwise
Terrain and surface:	Hilly country with some quite steep slopes, mostly on rough paths, tracks and grass. Number of stiles not known. 2.3km (1.4 miles) beside roads
Points of interest:	Tylers Common, Jermains Wood, Jacksons Wood, Warley Gap, Little Warley Common, St Mary's Church, Foxburrow Wood
Signage:	No details available
Refreshments and toilets:	Pubs at Warley and Great Warley. No cafés or public toilets nearby
Public transport and break points:	Buses: Shepherds Hill, Great Warley, Warley

Links:	None
Map:	Explorer 175
LWF status:	Pending validation
Principal promoter:	LB Havering, Brentwood BC
Further information:	Free leaflet (+ sae) from LB Havering and Brentwood BC libraries and council offices. See Appendix H for contact details

This route undermines the notion that Essex is flat! The terrain is quite hilly and there are some fairly steep slopes, but the walking is rewarding as you pass through some charming countryside with good views, despite the proximity of the M25 motorway. This is more of a mini-network than a route, as alternatives provide opportunities to make short cuts or even a figure-of-eight.

The official start is at Tylers Common car park (nearest station Harold Wood), with buses passing within 500m. Alternatively you can approach from the other end at Warley or Great Warley, both served by buses. The route constantly rises and falls, with the only level stretch of any significance being at Warley Gap, altitude 115m (377ft), which boasts a dry-ski slope. The village of Great Warley is a designated conservation area, and its little church of St Mary, though of the early 20th century, is most attractive.

UPMINSTER CIRCULAR WALK (MAP 4)

Distance:	17.0km (10.6 miles)
Location:	Havering
Start/finish:	Hornchurch (Hacton Lane, either at car park GR 549-859, or near Upminster Bridge station GR 546-867)
Green factor:	57%
Blue factor:	5%
Recommended direction:	Clockwise
Terrain and surface:	Almost completely level, just a few short gentle climbs. Mixture of pavements, tarmac paths and rough paths/tracks or grass. 18 stiles. 6.3km (3.7 miles) beside roads
Points of interest:	St Andrew's Church, farmland, Ingrebourne River, Franks Wood, Cranham Hall, All Saints Church, Cranham Marsh Nature Reserve, Parklands Lake
Signage:	Partial, both ways, in rural locations only. Logo: Upminster Windmill on arrow surrounded by 'Upminster Circular Walk', green on white or yellow background

Refreshments and toilets:	Pubs at Upminster Bridge, Cranham and Hacton Lane. No cafés or public toilets nearby
Public transport and break points:	LU: Upminster Bridge. Buses: Hacton Lane, Wingletye Lane, Southend Arterial Road, Hall Lane, Moor Lane, St Mary's Lane, Corbets Tey Road
Links:	London Loop, Cranham Circular Walk
Map:	Explorer 175
LWF status:	Pending validation
Principal promoter:	LB Havering
Further information:	Free leaflet (+ sae) *Upminster Walk* available from LB Havering Countryside Service and libraries. See Appendix H for contact details

One of the **Countryside Footpaths in Havering** series, with easy walking, some fine countryside and plenty of interest. However, there are stiles aplenty and a substantial amount of roadwalking. The leaflet does not give a step-by-step route description but includes a sketch map. At the time of writing the route was well signed in rural locations but not at all on roads, and a street map or atlas may be helpful. You may catch glimpses of the well-known Upminster Mill, featured in the logo and signs, although the route does not go near it.

You can start and finish at any point: the leaflet suggests the car park at Hacton Bridge but Upminster Bridge station may be more convenient. From there turn left then left again into Highfield Crescent. At the bend keep straight ahead on the footpath into Hacton Lane.

The west side of the route lies in Hornchurch, where you pass the venerable St Andrew's Church, dating from the 12th century. After a stretch through residential roads you join Section 22 of the **London Loop** along a fieldside path, and stay with it for 3.5km (2.2 miles) through meadows and woods across the Ingrebourne River. You must take care along Bird Lane which has no pavement and a couple of blind bends. More paths through woods and meadows take you close to the M25. Extreme caution is needed when crossing a busy railway line at surface level – see Safety First in Section 1.

The highlights of the walk come towards the end. A new woodland (Great Barn Wood) is being created around Broadland Farm, the headquarters of Thames Chase Community Forest. Together with the **Cranham Circular Walk** you pass Cranham Hall, an idyllic spot at the end of a quiet lane, where All Saints Church and a few farm buildings cluster around the hall. Soon after that comes Cranham Marsh Nature Reserve and some more little woods, rich in wildlife on former marshland. Finally you walk beside tranquil Parklands Lake and through more fields to return to Hacton Lane, crossed by Section 23 of the **London Loop**.

VANGUARD WAY (MAP 7)

Distance:	107km (66 miles) – see text
Location:	Croydon, continuing into Surrey, Kent and East Sussex
Start:	East Croydon station (GR 329-658)
Finish:	Newhaven Harbour station (GR 450-009)
*Green factor:	38%
*Blue factor:	n/a
Recommended direction:	Northwest to southeast
*Terrain and surface:	Hilly in places, sometimes quite steep. Mixture of tarmac paths, pavements and rough paths, tracks and grass. No stiles. 1.5km (0.9 miles) beside roads
*Points of interest:	Lloyd Park, Coombe Wood, Littleheath Wood, Selsdon Wood Local Nature Reserve
Signage:	Almost complete both ways
*Refreshments and toilets:	Pubs and cafés at East Croydon, Coombe Wood, Selsdon and Forestdale. Public toilets at East Croydon and Coombe Wood
*Public transport and break points:	NR: East Croydon. CTL: East Croydon, Lloyd Park. Buses at all these point plus Selsdon, Forestdale and Chelsham Common
*Links:	London Loop, North Downs Way, London Countryway
*Map:	Explorer 161 (route marked)
*LWF status:	Pending validation
Principal promoter:	Vanguards Rambling Club, LB Croydon, Surrey CC, Kent CC, East Sussex CC
Further information:	*The Vanguard Way* official guidebook (Vanguards Rambling Club (See Appendix H for contact details), £2.95 plus 50p p&p, ISBN 0-9530076-0-X): includes north–south route description, comprehensive guide to accommodation, refreshments, transport and places of interest. *Wealdway & Vanguard Way* (Cicerone Press, £4.99, ISBN 0-02363-85-9): includes north–south route description, sections on transport, accommodation, equipment, useful addresses and further reading.

*These details apply to the Croydon to Chelsham Common section only

A green and scenic route linking London with the Sussex coast, created by members of the Vanguards Rambling Club. It passes through some of the best countryside in southern England, including the North and South Downs and the Ashdown Forest. Good public transport connections enable you to break the route into five or six full-day walks. An interesting introduction is provided by the Greater London section from East Croydon to Forestdale (8km/5 miles), or on into Surrey at Chelsham Common (10.5km/6.5 miles), both linked by bus with Croydon.

From East Croydon station, you soon join the historic Fairfield Path through a pleasant residential area to Lloyd Park, then wind along an ancient sunken track with a splendid view towards London. At Littleheath Wood the route is joined for a while by Section 4 of the **London Loop**. A straight path leads between residential areas into Selsdon Wood, a nature reserve, where after a stiff climb you reach the Surrey boundary at Forestdale. A steadier climb up an ancient track leads to fairly level walking beside a golf course, then you pass a delightful little church in the sleepy village of Farleigh, and walk through Great Wood to Chelsham Common.

WALK BACK IN TIME (MAP 2)

Distance:	8.0km (5.0 miles)
Location:	Waltham Forest, Hackney
Start/finish:	Lea Bridge (Lee Valley Ice Centre, GR 356-867)
Green factor:	62%
Blue factor:	18%
Recommended direction:	Clockwise
Terrain and surface:	Mostly level; some slopes including one that is quite steep. Mostly firm surface; some long stretches on rough paths which may be muddy, waterlogged or under water after heavy rain
Points of interest:	Leyton Ice Rink, Lee Navigation, Springfield Park, Coppermill Stream, Walthamstow Marsh Nature Reserve, Essex Filter Beds Nature Reserve, Friends Bridge, River Lea, Middlesex Filter Beds Nature Reserve
Signage:	None
Refreshments and toilets:	Pubs at Lea Bridge. Café at Springfield Marina. No public toilets nearby
Public transport and break points:	Buses: Lea Bridge Road, Clapton Common. NR: Clapton
Links:	Lea Valley Walk, Capital Ring
Map:	Explorer 173
LWF status:	Pending validation
Principal promoter:	Lee Valley Regional Park

Further information:	Included in free pack (+ sae) *Best Circular Walks* from Lee Valley Park Information Centre. See Appendix H for contact details

Easy walking in the Lee Valley Regional Park, in an area that is flat but full of interest. The circuit is actually a figure-of-eight, providing an opportunity to divide the walk into two halves: a southern one from Lea Bridge and a northern one from Springfield Park, near Clapton Common. Note that, after prolonged heavy rain, the marshes in places may be very muddy and knee-deep in water. Parts of Walk Back in Time are shared with Section 13 of the **Capital Ring** and the **Lea Valley Walk**.

The route goes through three nature reserves: Walthamstow Marsh, Essex Filter Beds and Middlesex Filter Beds – all more attractive and interesting than they sound! Part of the route through Walthamstow Marshes follows a boardwalk. There is a long stretch beside the Lea Navigation, including colourful Springfield Marina, and a winding path through hilly Springfield Park. By Essex Filter Beds you cross the River Lea itself (rather than the navigation) on the unusual Friends Bridge, designed to represent an opening leaf.

This is one of four routes in the **Best Circular Walks** pack, published by Lee Valley Regional Park. It is the only one in Greater London, the others lying further north in Hertfordshire and Essex, therefore not covered in this book. They include the New River Walk (Broxbourne), Walk with a View (Waltham Abbey) and Lake and Riverside Walk (Cheshunt).

Although mostly level, a substantial amount of the surface is uneven and likely to be muddy or under water. There is a short flight of steps in Springfield Park, but this can be avoided by following a different path past the bowling green, still involving a steep slope, however. A humpback bridge over the Lea Navigation has shallow steps. A short stretch of sloping grass or mud links the boardwalk to a firm track.

WANDLE TRAIL (MAPS 5, 7)

Distance:	18.1km (11.3 miles)
Location:	Croydon, Sutton, Merton, Wandsworth
Start:	Waddon Ponds (Mill Lane, GR 256-752)
Finish:	Wandsworth (The Causeway, GR 309-653)
Green factor:	46%
Blue factor:	69%
Recommended direction:	South to north
Terrain and surface:	Mostly level (one short hill at Carshalton), on tarmac paths or pavements, with some grass and rough surfaced sections. No stiles. 3.0km (1.9 miles) beside roads

Points of interest:	Waddon Ponds, Beddington Park, The Grove Park, Wilderness Island nature reserve, Ravensbury Park, Wandle Industrial Museum, Morden Hall Park, Deen City Farm, Merton Abbey Mills, Wandle Park (Colliers Wood), Wandle Meadow Nature Park, King George's Park, Bell Lane Creek, River Thames. Also remains and sites of many watermills and other historic buildings
Signage:	Partial in Wandsworth; almost complete elsewhere, both ways. Logo: white waterwheel on dark background (colours vary)
Refreshments and toilets:	Many pubs and cafés along the route. Public toilets at Beddington Park, The Grove Park (Carshalton), Morden Hall Park, Merton Abbey Mills, King George's Park (Wandsworth)
Public transport and break points:	NR: Waddon, Carshalton, Hackbridge, Mitcham Junction, Haydons Road, Earlsfield, Wandsworth Town. CTL: Wandle Park (Croydon), Mitcham, Belgrave Walk, Phipps Bridge. LU: Morden, Colliers Wood. Buses at all these points
Links:	Capital Ring, Thames Path National Trail
Map:	Explorer 161
LWF status:	Pending validation
Principal promoter:	Wandle Group, Wandle Industrial Museum, LB Croydon, LB Sutton, LB Merton, LB Wandsworth
Further information:	*Wandle Trail map and illustrated guide* (Wandle Industrial Museum, £2.00 + sae): map and description of points of interest. *The Wandle Guide* (London Borough of Sutton/Wandle Group, £4.95 plus £1.00 p&p, ISBN 0-907335-33-0): general guide to the river includes detailed route description for the Wandle Trail. All available from Wandle Industrial Museum (see appendix H for contact details), local libraries, museums and National Trust shop at Morden Hall Park. www.wandle.org

Easy walking through the southwestern suburbs, beside the River Wandle nearly all the way and with historical interest at nearly every riverbend. Most of it follows quiet riverside paths between trees, shrubs or grass, through parks and past nature reserves. You are likely to see grey herons, grey wagtails or perhaps the blue flash of a kingfisher among the abundant aquatic flora and fauna. With its fast flow, the river has over the centuries powered watermills on at least 80 sites, producing an enormous range of products. A few waterwheels survive, and at least one can sometimes still be seen in operation. There is little industry nowadays, and much of the riverside has become accessible for walking. You should take care on some stretches that are shared with cyclists.

The Wandle Trail currently starts at Waddon Ponds, source of the river's eastern branch, though a link with the Vanguard Way at East Croydon station is planned.

The route follows the river through the quiet suburb of Beddington and Beddington Park, with splendid views of historic Carew Manor. You must leave the eastern branch at London Road, Wallington, diverting along roads a short distance to The Grove Park, where you join the western branch at Carshalton Ponds.

At Wilderness Island nature reserve the two branches of the river join together. Beyond Poulter Park and the impressive Bishopsford House you divert from the river to pass the National Trust's Watermeads nature reserve. Pretty Ravensbury Park at Mitcham contains a large millpond and Ravensbury Mill, which has one of the remaining sets of waterwheels and is due to become the home of the Wandle Industrial Museum. Morden Hall Park, owned by the National Trust, has a shop, cafeteria and a collection of old buildings including the former snuff mill.

After Deen City Farm you come to Merton Abbey Mills, a popular weekend retreat. It is the former Liberty works, once a busy factory where textiles were printed for Liberty & Co's shop in Regent Street. The historic buildings house a teashop, a working waterwheel and a riverside pub, and there is a weekend craft market. The Savacentre development at Colliers Wood includes a new stretch of riverside path leading to Wandle Park, where the meandering original course of the river has been delightfully restored. You pass through Wandle Meadow Nature Park, a former sewage treatment site, and cross the Wandle's only major tributary, the River Graveney, to reach Plough Lane at Wimbledon.

The route continues along a tree-lined riverside path to Earlsfield, where the river is currently inaccessible, so you must divert along busy Garratt Lane past Earlsfield station, crossing Section 5 of the **Capital Ring**. Returning to the river, you walk through King George's Park, then Wandsworth town centre, which is rather bland, but it is worth continuing because the final stretch approaching the mouth of the Wandle is impressive. Recently constructed bridges and walkways have provided access almost to the point where the Wandle joins the Thames, and you have a fine view across to Fulham. The Wandle Trail joins the **Thames Path National Trail** here, and you can turn right along it to Wandsworth Town station (1.0km/0.6 miles), or left to Putney Bridge station (2.5km/ 1.5miles)

Manor Gardens, Wallington

♿ The route has a hard, level surface except in two places: in Beddington Park you can divert along nearby tarmac paths to avoid a grassy stretch and a stepped bridge over a lake; at Watermeads an uneven path can be avoided by diverting through Poulter Park. The surface may be rather bumpy in other places where the surface consists of crushed and rolled material, particularly in Ravensbury Park, Morden Hall Park, Wandle Meadow Nature Reserve and north of Plough Lane in Wimbledon. There are some short moderate slopes.

Morden Cottage, Morden Hall Park

WATERLINK WAY (MAP 5)

Easy walking on a firm surface throughout (mostly tarmac of various hues), linking several parks and open spaces beside the River Ravensbourne and its tributary, the Pool River. Most of the route is off-road, and it is intended that some stretches currently on roads will be improved in due course. The route has been developed by Sustrans, the agency responsible for the National Cycle Network, and is shared by cyclists and walkers, who should generally keep to their own sides of the track as marked.

The route starts from the **Thames Path National Trail** at the pleasant waterside development beside tidal Deptford Creek (where the Ravensbourne meets the Thames).

Distance:	14.3km (8.9 miles) – see text
Location:	Greenwich, Lewisham, Bromley, Croydon
Start:	Deptford Creek (GR 376-779)
Finish:	Woodside (Arena Tramstop, GR 352-676) – see text
Green factor:	43%
Blue factor:	32%
Recommended direction:	Either way
Terrain and surface:	Almost completely level, some short gentle slopes, on mostly hard surface (uneven surface in Kent House area and South Norwood Country Park). No stiles. 5.0km (3.1 miles) beside roads
Points of interest:	Deptford Creek, River Ravensbourne, Pool River, Broadway Fields, Brookmill Park, Ladywell Fields, Riverview Walk, Cator Park, South Norwood Country Park
Signage:	Almost complete both ways. Mostly fingers showing white 'London Cycle Network' on blue background, with red and white '21'. Wooden marker posts in Croydon's open spaces
Refreshments and toilets:	Pubs at Deptford Creek, Deptford, Lewisham, Ladywell, Catford, Bell Green, Clock House and Elmers End. Also cafés/kiosks at most of these places. Public toilets at Lewisham and South Norwood Country Park
Public transport and break points:	NR: Deptford, Greenwich, St Johns, Lewisham, Ladywell, Catford, Catford Bridge, Lower Sydenham, Kent House, Clock House, Elmers End. DLR: Greenwich, Deptford Bridge, Elverson Road, Lewisham. CTL: Beckenham Road, Elmers End, Arena. Buses at all these points
Links:	Thames Path National Trail, Capital Ring, Green Chain Walk
Map:	Explorer 161
LWF status:	Pending validation
Principal promoter:	Sustrans, LB Greenwich, LB Lewisham, LB Bromley, LB Croydon
Further information:	No dedicated literature available at time of writing. Route included in *Downs & Weald Cycle Map* (£5.99 + sae) from Sustrans (see Appendix H for contact details)

You follow the signs for London and National Cycle Network route 21 – look out for the zany cast-iron National Cycle Network Millennium Mileposts at several points. The route passes through several parks and open spaces, including Broadway Fields, Brookmill Park, and South Norwood Country Park. At Ladywell Fields you cross a railway line by footbridge with spiral ramps and pass the Lewisham Dutch elm – 'one of the great trees of London'. In Riverview Walk at Bell Green, the Pool River has been returned to something like its natural state – note that dogs are not permitted; they can be taken along parallel roads. In Cator Park, contact is made with Section 3 of the **Capital Ring** and Section 10 of the **Green Chain Walk**.

From Arena tramstop the Waterlink Way continues through Monks Orchard and Spring Park to New Addington, and (as Cycle Route 21) on into Surrey and Sussex, but all this is mostly on roads and lanes so not of great interest to walkers.

    The route has a hard, level surface nearly all the way. A long uneven stretch on unmade roads at Kent House can be avoided by following nearby roads.

    The track through South Norwood Country Park is uneven in places – to avoid this you would finish at Elmers End.

WATERWAY DISCOVERY SERIES

A series of four routes promoted by the Lower Lea Project (see appendix H for contact details) as part of the Millennium Festivals of Enfield and Newham boroughs. Three are included in the Strategic Network (see **Heron and Kingfisher Walks** and **Time Travellers**). The fourth (Lea Valley Enfield – see Other Named Self-guided Walks below) uses part of the **Lea Valley Walk** with a number of side trips.

WEST DRAYTON TO SLOUGH RAMBLE AND RIDE (MAP 3)

Distance:	14.2km (8.9 miles)
Location:	Hillingdon, mostly in Buckinghamshire and Berkshire
Start:	West Drayton station (GR TQ 061-801)
Finish:	Slough station (GR SU 978-801)
Green factor:	49%
Blue factor:	35%
Recommended direction:	East to west
Terrain and surface:	Mostly fairly level but with one long steady climb, and mostly on rough paths, tracks and canal towpaths. Two stiles. 3.7km (2.3 miles) beside roads
Points of interest:	Grand Union Canal and Slough Arm, River Colne, Little Britain Lake, farmland, Langley Park
Signage:	None

Refreshments and toilets:	Pubs at West Drayton, Iver, Shreding Green and Slough. Cafés at West Drayton, Iver and Slough. Public toilets: no details
Public transport and break points:	NR: West Drayton, Langley and Slough. Buses at all these points plus Cowley, Iver and Shreding Green
Links:	London Loop, Grand Union Canal Walk and Slough Arm, Beeches Way, Colne Valley Way and Iver Circular Walk
Map:	Explorer 172, plus small amount of canal towpath on 160
LWF status:	Pending validation
Principal promoter:	Groundwork Thames Valley
Further information:	Free leaflet (+ sae) from Colne Valley Park Centre (see Appendix H for contact details)

One of the **Colne Valley Ramble and Ride** series, offering fairly easy walking across the Colne Valley and along towpaths of the Grand Union Canal, but with a fairly stiff climb in between. From West Drayton station you briefly follow the **Grand Union Canal**, then the River Colne, passing Little Britain Lake. The early part of the route is shared at various stages with several others including the **London Loop** (see Links above). After crossing the M25 motorway and Colne Brook you climb up past Iver village, then a fairly long section follows consisting mostly of roadwalking, including some without pavements where care is needed. Some pleasant walking across farmland leads to the **Grand Union Canal Slough Arm**, which takes you all the way to Slough.

WEST LONDON WATERWAY WALKS

A number of Strategic Network routes following rivers and canals in West London have been promoted under this title, but the term is being phased out. You may still be able to obtain packs at £2.00 including p&p from LB Ealing Parks and Countryside Service. The six routes included in the pack are: **Beverley Brook Walk, Brent River Park Walk, Celandine Route, Dog Rose Ramble, River Crane Walk** and **Willow Tree Wander**.

WEST RUISLIP TO GERRARDS CROSS RAMBLE AND RIDE (MAP 3)

Distance:	15.5km (9.7 miles)
Location:	Hillingdon, continuing into Buckinghamshire
Start:	West Ruislip station (GR 085-868)
Finish:	Gerrards Cross station (GR 002-888)
Green factor:	81%
Blue factor:	19%

Recommended direction:	East to west
Terrain and surface:	Mostly undulating country with some steep ascents and descents, on rough paths and tracks. Long level stretch in Colne valley. Four stiles. 3.2km (2.0 miles) beside roads
Points of interest:	Farmland, Bayhurst Wood Country Park, Grand Union Canal, River Misbourne, lakes, green lanes
Signage:	None
Refreshments and toilets:	Pubs and cafés at West Ruislip, South Harefield and Gerrards Cross. Public toilets: no details
Public transport and break points:	LU: West Ruislip. NR: West Ruislip, Denham and Gerrards Cross. Buses at all these points plus South Harefield, Mount Pleasant and Denham Way
Links:	Hillingdon Trail, Celandine Route, Widewater Lock Circular Walk, Colne Valley Trail, London Loop, South Bucks Way
Map:	Explorer 172
LWF status:	Pending validation
Principal promoter:	Groundwork Thames Valley
Further information:	Free leaflet (+ sae) from Colne Valley Park Centre (see Appendix H for contact details)

A fairly energetic but very green route in the **Colne Valley Ramble and Ride** series, leading out of the northwest suburbs into Buckinghamshire. From West Ruislip you soon join green lanes and paths that climb into open countryside around New Year's Green and on past Bayhurst Wood Country Park. In this area you come into contact with the **Hillingdon Trail** and **Celandine Route**. The route descends into the Colne Valley and follows the **Grand Union Canal** towpath for a while, together with Section 13 of the **London Loop**, and passing locks and much waterborne activity. You turn off the canal to pass between lakes (flooded former gravel pits) then climb steeply into an area of mixed woodland and farmland, where you encounter the **South Bucks Way**, then cross the M25 motorway. Finally you descend steeply to cross the pretty River Misbourne into Gerrards Cross.

WIDEWATER LOCK CIRCULAR WALK (MAP 3)

A very green route in the **Colne Valley Circular Walks** series, with very little roadwalking. The official start (on a spur from the main circuit) is the car park by the Colne Valley Park Centre near Denham, but using public transport you can either take the bus to South Harefield, near Widewater Lock, or train to Denham, following the railway-side path back to join the route along the **Grand Union Canal** towpath. Here you walk between former gravel pits, now filled with water

– one is a peaceful nature reserve, another forms the colourful Harefield Marina, crowded with cabin cruisers and narrowboats. You also pass Denham Lock, the deepest on the Grand Union Canal, where several routes come together (see Links above).

Distance:	12.7km (7.9 miles) including link with Colne Valley Park Centre
Location:	Hillingdon, continuing into Buckinghamshire
Start/finish:	Colne Valley Park Centre (GR 048-865)
Green factor:	92%
Blue factor:	24%
Recommended direction:	Clockwise
Terrain and surface:	Mainly level but with some short steep slopes, on firm canal towpath and rough paths, tracks and grass. 18 stiles. 0.9km (0.6 miles) beside roads
Points of interest:	Colne Valley Park Centre, River Misbourne, Grand Union Canal and locks, Denham Country Park, Bayhurst Wood Country Park, Frays Valley Local Nature Reserve, lakes
Signage:	None
Refreshments and toilets:	Pub at Widewater Lock. Tearoom at Denham Lock. Public toilets at Colne Valley Park Centre and Bayhurst Wood
Public transport and break points:	NR: Denham. Buses: Denham, South Harefield, Harvil Road
Links:	Nine Stiles Circular Walk, South Bucks Way, London Loop, Grand Union Canal Walk, Colne Valley Trail, Hillingdon Trail, West Ruislip-Gerrards Cross Ramble and Ride
Map:	Explorer 172
LWF status:	Pending validation
Principal promoter:	Groundwork Thames Valley
Further information:	Included in *Colne Valley Circular Walks* pack from Colne Valley Park Centre (enquire for price). See Appendix H for contact details

Away from the canal, sometimes sharing the routes of **West Ruislip to Gerrards Cross Ramble and Ride** and the **Hillingdon Trail**, the route climbs, steeply in places, up to Bayhurst Wood Country Park. It then crosses farmland surrounding New Year's Green before descending back to the towpath past more water-filled gravel pits.

WILLOW TREE WANDER (MAP 3)

Distance:	8.1km (5.1 miles)
Location:	Harrow, Hillingdon
Start:	North Harrow station (GR 135-886)
Finish:	Ickenham station (GR 081-859)
Green factor:	68%
Blue factor:	51%
Recommended direction:	Northeast to southwest
Terrain and surface:	Almost entirely flat, some short gentle slopes. Mostly on rough paths, tracks and grass which may be muddy after rain. No stiles. 2.0km (1.25 miles) beside roads
Points of interest:	Yeading Brook, Roxbourne Park, RAF Northolt, Ickenham Marsh Nature Reserve
Signage:	Almost complete both ways. Logo: green willow leaves and catkins on yellow arrow on green background
Refreshments and toilets:	Pubs at North Harrow, Field End Road, Ruislip Gardens and Ickenham. Cafés at North Harrow, West Ruislip and Ickenham. Public toilets at Ickenham
Public transport and break points:	LU: North Harrow, Ruislip Gardens, Ickenham. Buses at all these points plus Village Way, Field End Road and Victoria Road
Links:	Hillingdon Trail
Map:	Explorers 172 and 173
LWF status:	Pending validation
Principal promoter:	LB Harrow, LB Hillingdon
Further information:	Free leaflet (+ sae) from LB Harrow and LB Hillingdon libraries (see Appendix H for contact details)

Easy walking in very pleasant surroundings, mostly beside Yeading Brook, and indeed several species of willow tree can be seen. The route mostly goes through parks and grassy open spaces including Yeading Brook Open Space and Roxbourne Park, leading to Ruislip Gardens. After that you skirt an area of rough pasture next to RAF Northolt and finally pass through Ickenham Marsh Nature Reserve, where birds of prey such as kestrels and buzzards may be seen, and where the route is briefly shared with the *Hillingdon Trail*.

YEADING BROOK
see Dog Rose Ramble, Hillingdon Trail and Willow Tree Wander

OTHER NAMED SELF-GUIDED WALKS

INCLUDING HERITAGE TRAILS, TOWN TRAILS, NATURE TRAILS, HEALTH WALKS

The fact that none of these routes is included in the Strategic Network does not reflect adversely on them in any way. All have the potential to provide enjoyable walking, though standards vary considerably. Most of these routes are fairly short (less than 5km/3 miles), offering easy walking, though there are some exceptions. The walking speed for these walks is likely to be slower than for those in the Strategic Network, as route descriptions usually make more of points of interest along the way – you should allow at least an hour for every 2km (1.5 miles).

The walks in this section are devised and promoted by a local authority, local society or other body, and mostly fall into one of these categories:

Town trails, usually keeping to streets, parks and urban footpaths, identifying places of interest along the route

Heritage trails, exploring one or more particular aspects of the culture or history of an area

Nature trails, woodland trails, tree trails or similar. They are usually located in less visited parts of parks, or in nature reserves, and may include muddy or steep sections

Health walks, usually easy walks designed primarily for people recovering from operations or concerned about their health, but can be used by anyone. They may include stretches on uneven ground. See also Health Walks in Section 1.

Further information

The following information is provided for each walk where possible: **borough location**, **distance** (may be author's estimate), **circular** or **linear**, **type of walk** (where not clear from the title), **promoter** and/or **source of literature** (**LB** = London Borough, **RB** = Royal Borough). Unless otherwise shown, all routes listed here offer descriptive literature, which should be available from the source indicated, though stocks may run out at times.

A list of all **contact addresses** is given in Appendix H.

sae indicates that literature for these routes is free, but if ordering by post you should enclose a large stamped addressed envelope (at least A5). Prices are shown for publications that are not free, together with **p&p** (post and packing) where known. Where p&p is not mentioned and you are ordering by post, you are advised to enclose a large stamped addressed envelope as above.

♻ Indicates routes designed specifically for, or claimed by their promoters to be suitable for, people using wheelchairs. You should obtain the relevant literature in advance and satisfy yourself that a route is suitable – if necessary check with the promoter. Many heritage or town trails are also likely to be accessible, but there may be flights of steps and stretches that are unsuitable or uneven – if not made clear in the route literature, this should be checked with the route promoter in advance.

Alphanumeric codes preceding main entries correspond with those shown on Map 9.

A1. ♿ *Accessible Thames* (Hounslow/Kingston/Richmond). 2.4 to 8.0km (1.5 to 5.0 miles). Pack of 10 circular routes beside or close to the Thames, designed for use by people using wheelchairs and pushchairs and the less able-bodied. Routes centred on Hurst Park, East Molesey, Kingston, Hampton Court, Ham, Marble Hill, Richmond, St Margarets, Old Isleworth and Kew. Some routes are linked, allowing longer walks. Promoter/packs: sae to Thames Landscape Strategy, also libraries, tourist information centres and council offices of LB Hounslow, RB Kingston, LB Richmond, and Elmbridge DC

Alps to the Thames (Newham). See Newham Walks.

A2. *Angel Trail* (Islington). 2.4km (1.5 miles). Circular town trail. Promoter/leaflet: sae: Islington Society and LB Islington some libraries and council offices.

Barbican to Guildhall (City of London). See Open Spaces in the City of London.

B1. *Barnet Gate Wood Nature Trail* (Barnet). 1.6km (1.0 miles). Circular, near Arkley. Promoter/leaflet: sae LB Barnet libraries/some council offices.

B2. *Barnet Town Trails* (Barnet). Set of four trails (distances not known) around the borough: 1) Hendon; 2) Mill Hill Village; 3) Church End Finchley; 4) Hampstead Garden Suburb. Promoter/leaflets: (20p each plus sae) LB Barnet Archives and Local Studies.

B3. *Barnsbury Walk* (Islington). 5.0km (3.1 miles). Linear town trail. Promoter: North East Thames Architectural Society. Leaflet (60p plus sae): Islington Society, LB Islington libraries.

B4. *Bay/Parkside Farm Trail* (Enfield). 1.4km (0.9 miles). Linear, near The Ridgeway. Promoter/leaflet (Rectory and Bay Farm Trails): sae LB Enfield libraries/some council offices.

B5. *Bedfords Park Nature Trails* (Havering). 1.2 to 4.8km (0.8 to 3.0 miles). Circular. Promoter/leaflet sae: LB Havering Countryside Service, also local libraries, some council offices.

B6. *Belhus Wood Country Park Butterfly Trail* (Havering). 1.5 to 3.0km (0.9 to 1.8 miles). Circular, primarily for children. Promoter/leaflet sae: Belhus Wood Country Park.

B7. *Bexley Civic Society Walks* (Bexley). 2.0 to 7.0km (1.3 to 4.4 miles). Pack of 20 town trails in various parts of LB Bexley: Barnehurst, Belvedere village, Bexleyheath, Blackfen, Blendon/Bridgen, Bostall/West Heath, East Wickham (two parts), Erith, Footscray, Lamorbey/Halfway Street, North Cray, Old Bexley, Old Crayford, Old Sidcup, Parkhurst Conservation Area, Slade Green, Upton (two parts) and Welling. Also 11 walks featuring other interesting locations in the borough. Promoter/leaflets: (60p each plus sae or full pack £8.70 plus 60p p&p): Bexley Civic Society.

B8. *Big Wood and Little Wood Nature Trail* (Barnet). 1.0km (0.6 miles). Linear, in Hampstead Garden Suburb. Promoter/leaflet sae: LB Barnet libraries/some council offices.

Blackheath Heritage Trail (Greenwich/Lewisham). See Greenwich Millennium Heritage Trails.

B9. *Brentford Walks* *(1)* (Hounslow). 2.4km (1.5 miles). Two linear routes: A) River Thames and Old Brentford, and B) Grand Junction Canal and New Brentford. Promoter: Dandelion Publications. Leaflets: (£1.00 each plus sae) from LB Hounslow Tourist Information Centre and libraries, also some other local tourist attractions.

B10. *Brentford Walk* *(2)* (Hounslow). 3.0km (1.9 miles). Circular town trail around Old Brentford, devised by Hounslow Heritage Guides and included in Boston Manor House guidebook (£4.95 plus 65p p&p – cheque payable to Hounslow Cultural & Community Services) from LB Hounslow Tourist Information Centre.

Brentham Walk, A (Ealing). 1.9km (1.2 miles). See Ealing Open House Walks.

B11. *Brixton Heritage Trails* (Lambeth). Six circular trails (distances not known) included in book (£9.99 plus £1 p&p, ISBN 1-87305-21-11) from the Brixton Society.

B12. *Bushy Park History Trail* (Richmond). 10.8km (6.7 miles). Circular, near Teddington. Promoter/leaflet sae: Royal Parks Agency, Bushy Park.

Central Park Tree Trail (Newham). See Newham Walks.

Chase Nature Trail (Barking & Dagenham). See The Chase Nature Trail.

C1. *Chelsea Walk, The* (Kensington & Chelsea). 4.6km (2.9 miles). Circular town trail. Promoter/leaflet sae: RB Kensington & Chelsea libraries and some council offices.

Chingford Millennium Trail (Waltham Forest). See Millennium Trails (Waltham Forest).

C2. *Chiswick House Grounds Tree Walk* (Hounslow). 2.2km (1.4 miles). Circular. Promoter/leaflet (includes Gunnersbury Park Tree Walk) sae: LB Hounslow libraries and some council offices.

Cleary Garden to St Bartholomew the Great (City of London). See Open Spaces in the City of London.

Church End Finchley Town Trail (Barnet). See Barnet Town Trails.

C3. *Clerkenwell Historic Trail* (Islington). 3.5km (2.2 miles). Circular. Promoter: Towards Historic Clerkenwell Association. Leaflet (£1.00 plus sae) from Clerkenwell Visitors Centre.

C4. *Coppetts Wood Nature Trail* (Barnet). 1.4km (0.9 miles). Circular, near Colney Hatch Lane, Friern Barnet. Promoter/leaflet sae: LB Barnet libraries and some council offices.

C5. *Cranham Marsh Nature Trail* (Havering). 3.1km (1.9 miles). Circular, near Stubbers Outdoor Pursuits Centre, Corbets Tey. Promoter/leaflet sae: LB Havering Countryside Service, also some libraries and council offices.

Darwin's Rural Ramble (Bromley). See English Heritage Time Trails.

Deptford Heritage Trail (Greenwich). See Greenwich Millennium Heritage Trails.

D1. Dollis Valley Health Walks (Barnet). 1.6/3.2km (1.0/2.0 miles). Linear, near Woodside Park. Promoter: LB Barnet, included in Barnet Leisure Countryside Walks pack (50p plus sae) from LB Barnet libraries and council offices.

Ealing Common Walkabout (Ealing). 2.3km (1.4 miles). See Ealing Open House Walks.

Ealing Green (Ealing). 2.8km (1.8 miles). See Ealing Open House Walks.

E1. Ealing Open House Walks (Ealing). Series of nine town trails in various parts of the borough. Numbers 1 and 7 not available at time of writing. 2) A Brentham Walk (1.9km/1.2 miles). 3) Ealing Common Walkabout (2.3km/1.4 miles). 4) Ealing Green (2.8km/1.8 miles). 5) Hanger Hill Garden Estate (1.7km/1.1 miles). 6) Hanger Hill Haymills Estate (1.7km/1.1 miles). 8) Southall Town Trail (6.2km/3.9 miles). 9) Exploring Hanwell Green Lane and Canal (3.7km/2.3 miles). 10) Exploring Hanwell Churchfields and Village Green (3.1km/1.9 miles). 11) Ealing Town Hall (indoors). Leaflets: sae from LB Ealing libraries and some council offices.

East London Views and Vistas (Tower Hamlets). See Great Days Out.

E2. Eastbrookend Country Park Walks (Barking & Dagenham). 2.2/3.1km (1.4/1.9 miles). Circular, near Dagenham East. Two routes: 'water walk' around lakes and 'country walk' into The Chase Nature Reserve. Promoter/leaflet sae: LB Barking & Dagenham libraries, some council offices, also Eastbrookend Country Park.

Eltham Heritage Trail (Greenwich). See Greenwich Millennium Heritage Trails.

E3. Engineering Discovery Trail (Westminster). 2.8km (1.8 miles). Linear heritage trail along Victoria Embankment highlighting key civil engineering projects. Promoter/leaflet sae: Institution of Civil Engineers.

Exploring Hanwell – Green Lane and Canal (Ealing). 3.7km (2.3 miles). See Ealing Open House Walks.

Exploring Hanwell – Churchfields and Village Green (Ealing).3.1km (1.9 miles). See Ealing Open House Walks.

F1. Feltham Heritage Trails (Hounslow). 1.1 to 1.8km (0.7 to 1.1 miles). Two short trails produced by Groundwork Thames Valley. Leaflet sae: LB Hounslow libraries.

Finsbury Circus to St Dunstan's in the East (City of London). See Open Spaces in the City of London.

F2. Folly Brook Circular Walk (Barnet). 4.8km (3.0 miles). Health walk near Woodside Park. Promoter: LB Barnet, included in Barnet Leisure Countryside Walks pack (50p plus sae) from LB Barnet some libraries and council offices.

F3. Forty Hall Estate Nature Trails (Enfield). 2.3 to 6.7km (1.5 to 4.2 miles). Three circular trails near Turkey Street. Promoter/leaflet sae: Forty Hall and LB Enfield some libraries and council offices. www.enfield.gov.uk/40trail.htm.

F4. Four Kings Cross Walks (Camden/Islington). 2.2 to 3.6km (1.4 to 2.2 miles). Four town trails all starting from Kings Cross or St Pancras stations to: 1) Camden Lock (3.6km/2.2 miles). 2) Angel Islington (2.2km/1.4 miles). 3) Bloomsbury

(2.2km/1.4 miles). 4) Euston (2.8km/1.8 miles). Promoter/pack sae from Kings Cross Partnership. Can also be downloaded from www.kingscrosslondon.com (click 'Visitors' then 'Four Walks').

F5. *Friary Park Circular Walk* (Barnet). 1.6km (1.0 miles). Health walk in Friern Barnet. Promoter/leaflet: included in Barnet Leisure Countryside Walks pack (50p plus sae), from LB Barnet some libraries and council offices.

F6. *Fryent Park Country Park Circular Walk* (Brent). 4.0km (2.5 miles). Very hilly nature trail near Kingsbury. Promoter/leaflet sae: LB Brent Parks Department, some libraries and council offices.

Glade Tree Trail (Bexley). See The Glade Tree Trail.

G1. *Great Days Out* (various, East London). 5.5 to 8.5km (3.4 to 5.3 miles). Six heritage or town trails in East London, north and south of the Thames, some in two or three sections linked by public transport. 1) Ships, Sculptures and the Thames (Surrey Quays to Mansion House); 2) In the Steps of Dickens (Borough to Limehouse); 3) Maritime London (Royal Victoria Dock to North Woolwich); 4) A Walk through Historic Hackney (Manor House to Liverpool Street); 5) East London's Views and Vistas (Canary Wharf to London Bridge); 6) A Lazy Day on the Lea (West Ham to Clapton Common). Promoter/booklet sae: Tour East London.

G2. *Greenwich and Deptford History Trail* (Greenwich). 2.7km (1.7 miles). Linear heritage trail from Cutty Sark to Deptford Bridge. Promoter/leaflet 50p plus sae: LB Greenwich Tourist Information Centre and Local History Library, also some other local libraries and council offices.

G3. *Greenwich Millennium Heritage Trails* (Greenwich/Lewisham). 3.6 to 6.1km (2.2 to 3.8 miles). Pack of five circular and linear heritage trails in: Blackheath, Deptford, Eltham, Greenwich and Woolwich. Promoter/packs sae: LB Greenwich Tourist Information Centre, also some LB Lewisham libraries and council offices. www.greenwich.gov.uk/council/other/trail.htm

Gunnersbury Park Tree Walk (Hounslow). See Chiswick House Grounds Tree Walk.

H1. *Hackney Walks* (**Hackney**). 1.5 to 4.0km (0.9 to 2.5 miles). Six circular and linear town trails around Hackney borough: 1) Clapton Common, Springfield Park and River Lea (3.2km/2.0 miles). 2) Victoria Park and Well Street Common (4.0km/2.5 miles). 3) Stoke Newington, Abney Park Cemetery and Clissold Park (2.0km/1.3 miles). 4) Shoreditch and Hoxton (3.7km/2.3 miles). 5) Kingsland and Dalston (3.2km/2.0 miles). 6) Heart of Hackney Past and Present (1.5km/0.9 miles) plus Market Porters' Route (2.0km/1.3 miles). Promoter/leaflets: Hackney Society. All free sae except numbers 3 and 4 (60p each + sae).

H2. *Hainault Forest Wild About Woods Trail* (Redbridge). 4.3km (2.7 miles). Circular, near Chigwell Row. One of 14 nature trails throughout Britain under the title ***Wild About Woods***, devised by the Woodland Trust (this is the only one in the London area). The leaflet states that there are also easy routes for wheelchairs, pushchairs and the less able. Promoter: Woodland Trust. Leaflet sae: Hainault Forest Country Park.

H3. *Hainault Lodge Nature Trail* (Redbridge). 0.9km (0.6 miles). Circular. Promoter/leaflet sae: Hainault Forest Country Park, also LB Redbridge some libraries and council offices.

H4. *Hammersmith Walk* (Hammersmith & Fulham). 2.3km (1.4 miles). Circular town trail. Promoter/information sheet sae: LB Hammersmith & Fulham Information Centre, also some libraries and council offices.

Hampstead Garden Suburb Town Trail (Barnet). See Barnet Town Trails.

H5. *Hampton Ferry Walks* (Richmond). 3.5 to 7.5km (2.2 to 4.7 miles). Four circular heritage walks linked to the Hampton Ferry, crossing into Surrey, including the Thames riverside, Hampton Court Park and Bushy Park. Promoter/leaflet sae: Hampton Ferry.

Hanger Hill Garden Estate (Ealing). 1.7km (1.1 miles). See Ealing Open House Walks.

Hanger Hill Haymills Estate (Ealing). 1.7km (1.1 miles). See Ealing Open House Walks.

H6. *Harrow-on-the-Hill Walk* (Harrow). 2.2km (1.4 miles). Circular town trail. Promoter/leaflet sae: LB Harrow some libraries and council offices.

   H7. *Havering Country Park Easy Access Trail* (Havering). 0.4km (0.3 miles). Circular nature trail near Havering-atte-Bower intended primarily for people using wheelchairs. Promoter/leaflet sae: LB Havering Countryside Service, also some libraries and council offices.

H8. *Havering Country Park Tree Trail* (Havering). 2.5km (1.6 miles). Circular trail near Havering-atte-Bower. Promoter/leaflet sae: LB Havering Countryside Service, also some libraries and council offices.

Heart of Hackney Past and Present (Hackney). See Hackney Walks series.

H9. *Hell Lane & Eldestrete* (Brent). 1.0km (0.6 miles). Linear heritage trail in Fryent Park Country Park near Kingsbury. Promoter/leaflet sae: Barn Hill Conservation Group.

Hendon Town Trail (Barnet). See Barnet Town Trails.

H10. *Heritage walk from Three Mills Island* (Newham/Tower Hamlets). 5.5km (3.4 miles). Circular. Promoter/leaflet sae: Lee Valley Park Information Centre.

H11. *Historic Hackney* (Hackney). 3.6km (2.3 miles). Circular town trail. Promoter/leaflet £1.20 plus sae: Friends of Hackney Archives. Also available at LB Hackney some libraries and council offices.

H12. *Hounslow Heath Nature Trail* (Hounslow). 3.6km (2.3 miles). Circular. Promoter/leaflet sae: Hounslow Heath Local Nature Reserve Information Centre.

In the footsteps of Prince Albert (Kensington & Chelsea). See Time Trails in London.

In the steps of Dickens (Tower Hamlets). See Great Days Out.

J1. *Jubilee Park Circular Walk* (Bromley). 2.2km (1.4 miles). Nature trail near Petts Wood. Promoter/leaflet, included in Pack Two of Bromley Circular Walks and Trails (£2.50 plus 50p p&p): LB Bromley some libraries and council offices.

Just Walk (Croydon). See Selsdon Wood Nature Reserve Self-guided Trails.

K1. Kensington Walk, The (Kensington & Chelsea). 4.7km (2.9 miles). Circular town trail. Promoter/leaflet sae: RB Kensington & Chelsea some libraries and council offices.

Kings Cross Walks (Camden/Islington). See Four Kings Cross Walks.

Kingsland and Dalston (Hackney). (3.2km/2.0 miles). See Hackney Walks.

K2. Kingsland Road Walk (Hackney). 2.3km (1.4 miles). Linear town trail in Shoreditch. Promoter/leaflet sae: LB Hackney some libraries and council offices, also Hackney Society.

K3 Kingston-upon-Thames Walker's Guide (Kingston). 2 x 2.5km (1.6 miles). Two circular town trails. Promoter: Kingston-upon-Thames Society. Leaflet: sae RB Kingston Tourist Information Centre.

Lazy Day on the Lea (Tower Hamlets). See Great Days Out.

L1. Lea Valley Enfield (Enfield). 8.2km (5.1 miles). Linear heritage trail beside Lee Navigation from Enfield Lock to Ponders End. One of the Waterway Discovery series (see Strategic Network). Promoter/leaflet sae: Lower Lea Project.

Lea Valley Millennium Trail (Waltham Forest). See Millennium Trails (Waltham Forest).

L2. Lee Valley Park walks and nature trails (Enfield/Hackney/Haringey/Waltham Forest). The park office can provide printed guides for accessible walks and nature trails in the park area. Details sae from Lee Valley Park Information Centre.

L3. Lesnes Abbey self-guided trails (Bexley). 2.4/3.4km (1.5/2.1 miles). Two circular nature trails near Abbey Wood. Promoter/leaflet sae: LB Bexley some libraries and council offices.

Leytonstone Millennium Trail (Waltham Forest). See Millennium Trails (Waltham Forest).

Little Ilford to Wanstead Flats (Newham). See Newham Walks.

L4. Lloyd Park Tree Trail (Waltham Forest). 1.0km (0.6 miles). Circular. Promoter/leaflet sae: LB Waltham Forest libraries.

London Ecology Unit series. See Nature Conservation Walks.

L5. London Wall Walk (City of London). 2.6km (1.6 miles). Linear heritage trail along route of London Wall (Tower Hill to Barbican) with imaginative tiled interpretation plaques. Promoter/booklet: (£1.50 plus sae, ISBN 0-904818-13-6): Museum of London.

Maritime London (Tower Hamlets). See Great Days Out.

Market Porters Route (Hackney). (2.0km/1.3 miles). See Hackney Walks.

M1. Maths for All (various). 1.0 to 2.0km (0.6 to 1.2 miles). Series of short educational trails in various parts of London aimed at schools and incorporating quizzes, initiated by the Maths Year 2000 scheme and continued in its Count On sequel. Locations include Parliament Square/Trafalgar Square, St Paul's Cathedral, Hounslow, Kingston, Kew Gardens, Lewisham and Mile End. Details from Learndirect.

M2. *Merton's Heritage Trails* (Merton). 2.5 to 5.5km (1.6 to 3.4 miles). Set of five trails: 1) Wandle Walk (linear, Merton Abbey Mills to Bennett's Hole); 2) Morden Park Heritage Trail (circular); 3) Wimbledon Common and Cannizaro Park Walk (circular); 4) Mitcham Village (circular); 5) Merton Park Circular Walk. Promoter/pack (£1.95 plus sae): LB Merton Visitors Information Service, some libraries and council offices.

  ♿ Walk 3 (5.5km/3.4 miles) in this set is stated to be accessible but includes avoidable rutted paths and a short steep section.

Merton Park Trail (Merton). See Merton's Heritage Trails.

Mill Hill Town Trail (Barnet). See Barnet Town Trails.

M3. *Millennium Heritage Trails* (Waltham Forest). Set of four trails: 1) Chingford (5.1km/3.2 miles); 2) Leytonstone (4.9km/3.1 miles); 3) Walthamstow (2.5km/1.6 miles); 4) Lea Valley (Chingford to Lea Bridge, 11.0km/6.9 miles). Promoter/leaflets: sae: LB Waltham Forest some libraries and council offices.

M4. *Millennium Mile, The* (Lambeth/Southwark). 3.0 and 4.0km (1.9 and 2.5 miles). Two linear town trails (both actually considerably longer than a mile): 1) Westminster Bridge to London Bridge (riverside); 2) Design Centre to Waterloo (riverside and inland). Promoter/leaflet sae (*Explore the Millennium Mile*): South Bank Employers Group, also Southwark Information Centre.

Millennium Trail, The (Greenwich). See Time Trails in London.

Mitcham Village Circular Walk (Merton). See Merton's Heritage Trails.

M5. *Moat Mount Tree Trail* (Barnet). 1.1km (0.7 miles). Circular, off Barnet Way. Promoter/leaflet sae: LB Barnet some libraries and council offices.

Morden Park Heritage Trail (Merton). See Merton's Heritage Trails.

M6. *Mudchute Nature Trail* (Tower Hamlets). 1.0km (0.6 miles). Circular, on the Isle of Dogs. Promoter/leaflet sae: Mudchute Park and Farm.

N1. *Nature Conservation Walks.* Series of 23 walks designed by the London Ecology Unit for five London boroughs (see below) to demonstrate their potential for nature conservation. Initially intended for school use but available to other users while leaflet stocks last. The number of walks in each borough is shown in brackets.

Nature Conservation in Barnet (3). 11.0 to 13.5km (6.9 to 8.4 miles). Booklets: £6.00 inc. p&p from LB Barnet Parks & Countryside Section.

Nature Conservation in Brent (4). 5.0 to 7.5km (3.1 to 4.7 miles). Booklets: sae from LB Brent Parks Department.

Nature Conservation in Lambeth (3). 4.5 to 6.5km (2.8 to 4.1 miles). Booklets: sae from LB Lambeth Transportation & Highways Group.

Nature Conservation in Lewisham (4). 4.0 to 7.0km (2.5 to 4.4 miles). Booklets: sae from LB Lewisham Transport Policy Group.

Nature Conservation in Merton (5). 4.3 to 9.4km (2.7 to 5.9 miles). Booklets contained in Merton Ecology Handbook: sae from LB Merton Leisure Services Division.

Nature Conservation in Tower Hamlets (4). 5.7 to 10.5km (3.6 to 6.6 miles). Included in Tower Hamlets Ecology Handbook sae from LB Tower Hamlets Planning & Policy Department.

   Two of these walks, Merton No. 5 (4.3km/2.7 miles) and Tower Hamlets No. 1 (5.7km/3.5 miles), are stated to be suitable for people using wheelchairs – details of terrain are given in the literature.

N2. *Newham Walks* (Newham). 1.6 to 5.6km (1.0 to 3.5 miles). Six town and nature trails: 1) A ramble through Beckton; 2) Three Mills and along the Greenway to St Mary's churchyard; 3) Little Ilford to Wanstead Flats; 4) The Alps to the Thames (Beckton to Woolwich ferry); 5) Central Park tree trail; 6) St Mary Magdalen and Beckton District Park. Promoter/free booklet *A Walk Through Newham* plus sae: LB Newham some libraries and council offices.

N3. *North Kensington Walk, The* (Kensington & Chelsea). 4.5km (2.8 miles). Linear town trail near Latimer Road. Promoter/leaflet sae: RB Kensington & Chelsea some libraries and council offices.

N4. *Notting Hill Walk, The* (Kensington & Chelsea). 4.1km (2.6 miles). Circular town trail. Promoter/leaflet sae: RB Kensington & Chelsea some libraries and council offices.

O1. *Oaks Park Nature Trail* (Sutton). 3.0km (1.9 miles). Circular, near Carshalton Beeches. Promoter/leaflet sae: LB Sutton some libraries and council offices.

O2. *Old Court House Tree Trail* (Barnet). 0.5km (0.3 miles). Circular, in Barnet town centre. Promoter/leaflet sae: LB Barnet some libraries and council offices.

O3. *Open Spaces in the City of London* (City of London). 2.0 to 2.1km (1.2 to 1.3 miles). Three linear town trails linking small open spaces: 1) Cleary Garden to St Bartholomew the Great; 2) Barbican to Guildhall; 3) Finsbury Circus to St Dunstan in the East. Promoter: Corporation of London, leaflet sae from City of London Information Centre.

P1. *Paxton's Heritage Trails* (Bromley). 1.6 to 3.7km (1.0 to 2.3 miles). Three circular trails from the Visitor Centre in Crystal Palace Park: 1) General heritage trail covering the whole park; 2) Geological Time Trail around the lakes; 3) Tree Trail on east side and lakes. Promoter: LB Bromley Leisure Services. Leaflets: 30p each (No. 2 15p) plus sae: LB Bromley Leisure Services, also Crystal Palace Museum. Note: all trails subject to change following park refurbishment.

P2. *Picnic walk in the Woodland Gardens of Bushy Park* (Richmond). 0.7km (0.5 miles). Linear. Promoter/leaflet sae: Royal Parks Agency, Bushy Park.

P3. *Pilgrimage and Heritage Trail* (City of London). 5.2km (3.2 miles). First of planned series telling the story of those who strove for religious freedom, with visits to 11 City churches. Promoter: City Churches Development Group. Leaflet sae City of London Information Centre, also most City churches.

P4. *Pinner Village Walk* (Harrow). 3.0km (1.9 miles). Circular town trail. Promoter/leaflet sae: LB Harrow some libraries and council offices.

P5. *Pymmes Park Tree Trail* (Enfield). 1.2km (0.8 miles). Circular, near Silver Street. Promoter/leaflet: LB Enfield some libraries and council offices.

Ramble through Beckton, A (Newham). See Newham Walks.

R1. Rectory Farm Trail (Enfield). 1.6km (1.0 miles). Linear, near Crews Hill. Promoter/leaflet sae: LB Enfield some libraries and council offices.

R2. Revealing Croydon (Croydon). 1.1/1.5km (0.7/0.9 miles). Two linear town trails in Central Croydon: 1) Two Towers Walk; 2) A Wellesley Road Walk. Promoter/leaflet (50p plus sae): LB Croydon Tourist Information Centre, also some libraries and council offices.

R3. Riverside Walk, The (Kensington & Chelsea). 3.0km (1.9 miles). Linear town trail beside the Thames, Chelsea Harbour to Chelsea Bridge. Promoter/leaflet sae: RB Kensington & Chelsea some libraries and council offices.

Romancing the Thames (Richmond). See Time Trails in London.

S1. Selsdon Wood Nature Reserve Self-guided Trails (Croydon). 1.6/3.0km (1.0/1.9 miles). Two circular health walks/nature trails in Selsdon Wood. Promoter/leaflet (*Just Walk*) sae: LB Croydon Tourist Information Centre, also some libraries and council offices.

Ships, Sculptures and the Thames (Southwark). See Great Days Out.

Shoreditch and Hoxton (Hackney). (3.7km/2.3 miles). See Hackney Walks.

Southall Town Trail (Ealing). 6.2km (3.9 miles). See Ealing Open House Walks.

S2. Streatham Millennium and Heritage Trails (Lambeth). 5.0 to 8.0km (3.8 to 5.0 miles). Eight Millennium town trails (£1.00 each) launched in 2000, being replaced by Heritage Trails (£1.50 each). For p&p add 10% (minimum 30p). Promoter/leaflet: Streatham Society.

S3. Stroll around Mildmay, A (Islington). 8.2km (5.1 miles). Circular town trail in Highbury. Promoter/leaflet sae: Pat Haynes, c/o Islington Town Hall, Upper Street, London N1 2UD.

T1. Terrace Gardens Tree Walk (Richmond). 400m. Circular. Promoter/leaflet sae: LB Richmond Parks Department. Leaflets may be available at start.

T2. The Chase Nature Trail (Barking & Dagenham). 1.5 to 4.0km (0.9 to 2.5km). Network of circular trails in The Chase Nature Reserve, adjacent to Eastbrookend Country Park near Dagenham East. Promoter/leaflet sae: London Wildlife Trust.

T3. The Glade Tree Trail (Bexley). 1.4km (0.9 miles). Circular, near Sidcup. Promoter/leaflet sae: LB Bexley some libraries and council offices.

Three Mills and along the Greenway to St Mary's Church (Newham). See Newham Walks.

T4. Three Rivers Trail (Hillingdon). 2.0km (1.2 miles). Circular nature trail in Denham Country Park from Colne Valley Park Centre, mostly in Buckinghamshire. Promoter: Bucks CC. Leaflet sae: Buckinghamshire CC and Colne Valley Park Centre.

T5. Time Trails in London 0.8 to 6.4km (0.5 to 4.0 miles). Five walks in various parts of Greater London, celebrating the Millennium. 1) Darwin's rural ramble (Downe, Bromley); 2) The Millennium Trail (Greenwich); 3) In the footsteps of Prince Albert (South Kensington); 4) Romancing the Thames (Richmond/Twickenham); 5) Tower to Tower (South Bank). Promoter: English Heritage. Leaflet out of print, details still available on www.english-heritage.org.uk (click on 'Discovery' then 'Heritage Trails').

Tower to Tower (Lambeth/Southwark). See Time Trails in London.

Two Towers Walk (Croydon). See Revealing Croydon.

  W1. *Waddon Community Trail* (Croydon). 4.0/6.0km (2.5/3.8 miles). Linear town trail from Central Croydon to Waddon. Promoter: Waddon Community Project. Leaflet sae LB Croydon Tourist Information Centre, some libraries and council offices. Leaflet states fully accessible but some steep slopes.

W2. *Walk Around... series* (Bromley). 2.2 to 7.4km (1.4 to 4.6 miles). Nine circular town trails: Bromley Town (5.8km/3.6 miles); Chislehurst (5.3km/3.3 miles); Downe (3.0km/1.9 miles); Farnborough (2.2km/1.4 miles); Hayes (6.0km/3.8 miles); Orpington (2.4km/1.5 miles); Penge (7.4km/4.6 miles); St Mary Cray (3.4km/2.1 miles); West Wickham (6.1km/3.8 miles). Promoter/leaflets: sae: LB Bromley Town Planning Department, also some libraries and council offices.

W3. Walk around Old Isleworth, A (Hounslow). 2.5km (1.6 miles). Circular town trail included in booklet *The Story of Isleworth*. Promoter/leaflet (50p plus sae): Isleworth Society.

W4. *Walk in Teddington, A* (Richmond). 5.8km (3.6 miles), circular town trail. Promoter/booklet (£1.00 plus 30p p&p): The Teddington Society.

W5. *Walk through Georgian Greenwich, A* (Greenwich). 2.5km (1.6 miles). Circular heritage trail. Promoter: Friends of Ranger's House. Leaflet sae: LB Greenwich Tourist Information Centre.

Walk through historic Hackney, A (Hackney). See Great Days Out.

W6. *Walking in Belgravia* (Westminster). 3.1km (1.9 miles). Linear town trail. Promoter/booklet sae: Grosvenor Estate Holdings.

W7. *Walking in Mayfair* (Westminster). 3.1km (1.9 miles). Linear town trail. Promoter/booklet sae: Grosvenor Estate Holdings.

Walthamstow Millennium Trail (Waltham Forest). See Millennium Heritage Trails.

W8. *Wandle Valley Nature Park Trail* (Merton). 0.8km (0.5 miles). Circular trail on former sewage works near Haydons Road, Wimbledon. Promoter/leaflet sae: LB Merton some libraries and council offices.

Wandle Walk (Merton). See Merton's Heritage Trails.

W9. *Wandsworth Town Heritage Trails* (Wandsworth). 2.2 to 2.7km (1.4 to 1.7 miles). Two circular trails: 1) The Town Centre Walk (2.2km/1.4 miles); 2) The River Walk (2.7km/1.7 miles). Promoter/leaflet sae: Wandsworth Challenge Partnership, also LB Wandsworth some libraries and council offices.

Wellesley Road Walk (Croydon). See Revealing Croydon.

Woolwich Heritage Trail (Greenwich). See Greenwich Millennium Heritage Trails.

W10. *William Morris Tapestry Tree Trail* (Waltham Forest). 1.0km (0.6 miles). Circular, in Lloyd Park, Walthamstow. Promoter/leaflet sae: LB Waltham Forest libraries.

Wimbledon Common and Cannizaro Park Walk (Merton). See Merton's Heritage Trails.

W11. Woodland walk in Harold Hill, A (Havering). 4.0km (2.5 miles). Circular town trail linking six small woods. Promoter/leaflet sae: LB Havering Countryside Service, also some libraries and council offices.

W12. Woodlands Farm Health Walks (Bexley/Greenwich). 1.7 to 2.4km (1.1 to 1.5 miles). Circular walks in farmland and meadows by Shooters Hill. Promoter/leaflet sae: Woodlands Farm Trust.

W13. Woodridge Nature Trail (Barnet). 1.0km (0.6 miles). Circular, near Woodside Park. Promoter/leaflet sae: LB Barnet some libraries and council offices.

Details of the following routes were received by the author too late to be classified in the above list, and are not shown on the map.

Around Greenwich Park (Greenwich). 4.0km (2.5 miles). Circular. Promoter/leaflet sae LB Greenwich Libraries Local History Department.

Eltham Town Trails (Greenwich). 3.8 to 10.4km (2.4 to 6.5 miles). Three interlinked circular routes. Promoter/leaflet: Eltham Society.

Great London Treasure Hunt (City of London/Southwark/Westminster). 2.7 to 4.8km (1.7 to 3.0 miles). Four town trails in Central London, each including a quiz, with a certificate for correct answers. Free pack from Athlone Travel includes book of discount vouchers.

Historical walk through Barnsbury, An (Islington). 7.2km (4.5 miles). Circular heritage trail from Angel station. Booklet: £4.50 plus 40p p&p from Islington Archaeology & History Society.

L&GR Rail Trail (Southwark/Lewisham/Greenwich). 8.0km (5.0 miles). Linear heritage trail following the route of the London & Greenwich Railway from London Bridge station to Greenwich station. Promoter/leaflet 20p plus sae from LB Southwark libraries.

Riverside Walks (Wandsworth). 10.0km/6.2ml. Linear town trail closely following the Thames in Wandsworth from Leaders Gardens to Nine Elms Lane. Promoter/leaflet sae LB Wandsworth libraries.

Walk in New Eltham, A (Greenwich). 3.0km (1.9 miles). Linear heritage trail. Promoter/leaflet from Eltham Society.

Three Wandle Walks (Merton). Three short walks beside and near the River Wandle. Promoter/booklet: (misleadingly entitled *The Wandle Trail* but not to be confused with the strategic route) (£1.50 plus £1 p&p) from Wandle Industrial Museum.

Windmill Nature Trail (Merton/Wandsworth). 1.0km (0.6 miles). Circular from Wimbledon Common windmill. Promoter/leaflet sae Wimbledon & Putney Commons Conservators.

Wimbledon Park Heritage Trail (Merton). 4.0km (2.5 miles). Circular from Wimbledon Park station. Promoter/leaflet sae Wimbledon Park Heritage Group.

WALKING IN PARKS AND OPEN SPACES

(SEE APPENDIX D FOR FULL LIST)

Approach London from the air and one of the first things that strikes you is the great number of large green spaces. These are London's famous parks, commons and heaths, and they provide some of the capital's best walking. It is estimated that an amazing 174 square kilometres (67 square miles), or 11% of the total area of Greater London, consists of public open space of one kind or another. Some are so large that a substantial walk is required just to walk around the perimeter – qvv the Tamsin Trail in Richmond Park and the Diana Princess of Wales Memorial Walk in the Central Royal Parks, both Strategic Network routes.

Appendix D has a list of the larger open spaces. There is also a multitude of smaller ones, too numerous to include. All should provide good walking, or just roaming around, and further information can usually be obtained from the organisations that own or manage them. Most are managed by the London boroughs. Several owned by the Crown are run by the Royal Parks Agency. The Corporation of London owns some very large open spaces in and around Greater London, the result of a policy to save for the people of London green areas threatened with development; the largest of these is Epping Forest, which stretches far beyond the Greater London boundary into Essex. Some of London's commons and parks (including Wimbledon Common) are owned by a trust and managed by a body of conservators. Entry to all the large parks and open spaces in Greater London is free, with the sole exception of Kew Gardens, for which there is an admission charge.

Two comparatively recent developments of interest to walkers are regional parks and community forests, which are being developed as recreational areas. Though not continuous, they offer great opportunities for walking. In and around Greater London they consist of the Lee Valley Park (northeast London and beyond), Colne Valley Park (west), Watling Chase Community Forest (north) and Thames Chase Community Forest (east).

These useful books describe many of London's parks and open spaces:

Green-spaces Guide to London (Verdant Books, 2001, ISBN 0-9535414-1-X, £5.95). Handy pocket booklet: containing brief descriptions of 140 open spaces of all sizes around Greater London.

Walking London's Parks and Gardens (Geoffrey Young, New Holland, 1998, ISBN 1-85368-469-4, £9.99). Describes walks around 24 of London's parks, gardens and squares.

The following are now out of print, but may still be found in libraries and second-hand bookshops. You could also try Waterstones Out of Print Book Search on www.waterstones.co.uk:

The Parks and Woodlands of London (Andrew Crowe, Fourth Estate, 1987, ISBN 0-947795-61-8). Contains detailed descriptions and some maps of all the larger parks.

A Walk Round London's Parks (Hunter Davies, Hamish Hamilton c/o Penguin Books, 1983, ISBN 0-241-110-408). Not actually a single walk but contains much interesting information about all 10 of London's royal parks plus several other open spaces.

OTHER PUBLICATIONS OF SELF-GUIDED WALKS

(see Appendix E for full list)

A wide range of books, magazines, audioguides and websites describes walks throughout Greater London and the surrounding countryside, which have been devised by individuals. They vary from straightforward recreational walks to walks with a theme such as theatre or ghost walks.

3: OTHER WALKING OPPORTUNITIES

If you prefer a more sociable way of walking, or are nervous about walking on your own, or finding your way, there is a huge range of guided walks on offer in and around London. Some are intended for members of clubs or groups, others are available to the general public.

GIUDED WALKS FOR CLUB MEMBERS

Joining a walking club or group is one of the easiest ways to take up walking for pleasure, and an excellent way to make new friends. Most walks are whole-day affairs and take place in the countryside around London, with members travelling by train or car to a specified meeting point. Stops are made for a pub or picnic lunch and sometimes afternoon tea as well. The distance can vary widely, depending on the leader and the club, perhaps between 13 and 35km (8 and 22 miles). Some walks, often shorter half-day or evening ones, take place within Greater London.

There is usually no charge for the walk, but there is probably a membership fee, and members may be encouraged to contribute towards the leader's expenses. In most cases these walks are intended for members, but non-members are usually welcome to come along once or twice to try them out before paying the membership fee. Do not expect the voluntary leader of a free walk to know everything about the history and wildlife of the places you pass – it takes a lot of time and effort just to reconnoitre the route, let alone research points of interest.

Most of these arrangements are offered by local groups of nationwide organisations. As secretaries of individual groups are liable to change without notice, you should contact the office of the relevant organisation for details of the current group secretary (see Appendix H).

The **Ramblers' Association** (RA) is the most active player in this field, with no fewer than 20 local groups covering various parts of Greater London, all organising regular walks with a leader. The groups are currently: Blackheath, Bromley, Croydon, Finchley & Hornsey, Hammersmith & Wandsworth, Hampstead, Havering, Hillingdon, Kensington & Westminster, Kingston, North East London, North London & South Herts, North West Kent, North West London, Redbridge, Richmond, South Bank, Sutton & Wandle Valley, West Essex and West London. Four more groups cater specifically for younger walkers: Metropolitan Walkers, Chilterns 20s & 30s Walking Group, Essex Young Ramblers and Surrey Under 35s.

The **Long Distance Walkers Association** (LDWA) has a London Group, which organises at least two walks per month for members. Most are around 32km (20 miles), but they also offer shorter evening walks in the summer. Many London-based members go on walks organised by other LDWA groups in the surrounding areas, such as Essex & Herts, Kent, Surrey and Thames Valley.

A number of other organisations offer guided walks for members, sometimes as part of their general programme of social activities. **The Youth Hostels Association** (YHA) has local groups based in Barnet, Bromley, Central London, Croydon, Ealing, Epping Forest, Harrow & Wembley, Hounslow, Kingston and South Bank. The **Countrywide Holidays Association** (CHA) has affiliated clubs in Croydon, Pinner, Sunbury and Surbiton. **HF Holidays** (formerly Holiday Fellowship) has affiliated clubs in Croydon, Epping Forest, London North, London Northeast, London Northwest, London Southeast, London Southwest and Watford. In addition, there are many independent walking clubs in London, some affiliated to the Ramblers' Association, and their details can often be obtained from local libraries. Announcements of forthcoming walks by such clubs may be included in listings magazines and the listings pages of local newspapers.

GUIDED WALKS FOR THE GENERAL PUBLIC

A list of organisations offering guided walks for the general public appears in Appendix F. They include the Inner London Area of the Ramblers' Association, which organises regular full-day, half-day and evening walks. Shorter walks, typically of 1–2 hours' duration, are led by rangers of local authorities or conservation bodies, or by volunteers from organisations such as wildlife or civic trusts; they usually take place in nature reserves and open spaces, or in historic town centres, with frequent stops for explanatory talks about local history or wildlife. Such walks may be free, or a donation towards administrative costs may be requested. Those known to the author are included in Appendix F, otherwise details may be available from tourist information centres, libraries or council offices, or simply shown on a noticeboard in your local park.

Some walks for the general public are led by **professional guides**. They are especially popular with tourists, but many local people take part and are just as welcome – provided they pay the fee! This may be in the range £2–£6, and the walks typically take 1–2 hours. Usually there is a theme, such as Shakespeare, Dickens, Jack the Ripper, the Beatles, pubs or ghosts. As well as having a prepared narrative on points of interest, the guides are usually very knowledgeable about local history in general.

WALKING EVENTS AND CHALLENGES

Many walkers are attracted by the congenial atmosphere at events where you meet old friends and make new ones. This type of walking has long been popular in continental Europe, sometimes attracting walkers in their tens of thousands, and is slowly catching on in Britain. Some walking events in Britain attract several thousand participants, but typically they have just a few hundred. Some may last for decades, others just a few years, depending on the enthusiasm and availability of the organisers. Four types of walking event are described here: annual walks, challenge walks, charity walks, and walking festivals.

Annual walks

Friends of the City Churches Walk. Takes place on the first Tuesday and Wednesday in June, exploring many of the City's churches. Details (sae) from Friends of the City Churches, St Margaret Pattens Church, Rood Lane, EC3M 1HS.

An annual walk of about 24km (15miles) takes place in early September along the Epping Forest Centenary Walk (see Section 2, Strategic Network) – for details contact the Epping Forest Information Centre. Other walks of this nature may exist but no details are available at time of writing.

Challenge walks

Some people may consider any walk a challenge, while others who regularly walk at least 30km (20 miles) every weekend need to cover at least 50km (31 miles) in one go before they feel that their capabilities have been adequately stretched.

The term 'challenge walking' is applied to a genre of events that has only really developed over the last 20–30 years. Typically, such events are self-guided with detailed route instructions, with a mass start and several checkpoints. They are not races, and the achievement is to finish, thus stamina is more important than speed. The distance can be anything from 10 to 160km (6.25 to 100 miles), and there is usually a time limit of between 3 and 48 hours, depending on the distance. Some events are called 'marathons' though they may not be the true marathon distance. Several 100km (62.5 miles) events have come on the scene, for which the time limit is typically 26 hours. The Long Distance Walkers Association holds an annual 100miles(160km) event for which there is a 48-hour time limit.

The leading lights in this field are the **British Walking Federation** (BWF, the British arm of the IVV) and the **Long Distance Walkers Association** (LDWA) (see Governing Bodies in Section 1). Their affiliated clubs and groups around the country organise events most weekends, and their publications list events in this category. By joining the LDWA you will receive their superb magazine *Strider*, which includes a detailed list of UK events. The BWF publishes a calendar with details of all IVV events in this country (a separate calendar covers IVV events in other countries). Other event organisers include the Youth Hostels Association, Scouts and Guides, schools and such bodies as local fire brigades.

At present there are no challenge events in Greater London, but several take place in the surrounding counties, and regular participants travel to events all over the country and even abroad. Events nearby include: Surrey Inns Kanter (New Year's Day), Punchbowl Marathon (Surrey, February), Ridgeway Walk (Wilts/Berks, May), Surrey Summits (May), Hertfordshire Hobble (July), Tanners Marathon (Surrey, July), Chiltern Marathon (Herts/Bucks, September), Founders Challenge (Surrey, October) and Gatliff Marathon (Surrey/Kent, November). All these have become established favourites over many years.

Three Forests Way (see Section 2: Strategic Network Walks). A biennial 100km (62 miles) walk, with a 26-hour time limit, takes place along the route on even-numbered years (2–3 November in 2002). Details (sae) from Pat Ryan, 36 Wetherford, Stansted, Essex, CM24 8JB (tel: 01279 812725).

The IVV challenge is to take part in specified events and amass distances covered, at home and abroad. On reaching certain totals you send in your record card to claim an award (generally a badge). Some long-standing British IVV participants have clocked up over 20,000km (12,500 miles). At present there are no IVV events in Greater London, the nearest being the Buffalo Stampede (Hampshire, March), Spitfire Walk (Kent, May) and Pathfinder Walk (Cambridgeshire, August).

The IVV challenge also covers walks in your own time along specified 'permanent trails', of which there are currently 12 in Greater London: Clerkenwell & City Trail (10km/6.25 miles), Hampstead & Highgate Trail (12km/7.5 miles), Hampstead Permanent Walk (12km/7.5 miles), London (Hogarth) Permanent Walk (18km/11.25 miles, Earls Court), Maritime Heritage Trail (11km/6.75 milesTower Hill to Greenwich), Oranges & Lemons City Church Trail (11km/6.75 miles), Pilgrim Trail (14km/8.5 miles, Canada Water to Victoria), Richmond Trail (12km/7.5 miles), Royal London Trail (12km/7.5miles, Hyde Park to Temple), South Bank Trail (11km/6.75 miles), Vanguard Way (107km/67 miles– included in the Strategic Network), Westminster & City of London Trail (10km/6.25 miles). Details are included in the British Walking Federation's calendar.

Charity walks

Many charity walks are held each year in London to raise funds. The largest, with several thousand participants, are the Playtex Moonwalk for Breakthrough Breast Cancer in May, organised by Walk the Walk, and the Strollerthon in July, organised by Save the Children. Many smaller ones take place on most weekends. Typically they are between 8 and 24km (5 and 15 miles). There is no co-ordinating body or listing, but you can look out for publicity material such as posters and newspaper or local radio advertisements.

Walking festivals

These are usually organised by or on behalf of a local authority, or sometimes several authorities acting together. Typically, walking festivals last 2–4 days and offer a choice of walks of varying distances with a leader. At time of writing only two take place in London – the Croydon Walking Festival in late September (details from LB Croydon Tourist Information Centre) and the Enfield Festival of the Countryside (details from LB Enfiled libraries and some council offices. There is an annual South East England Walking Festival in mid September, and the Hampshire Waling and Local Food Festival in Late September/early October (details from the South East England Tourist Board) and one on the Isle of Wight in late September (details from Isle of Wight Tourism). Details of these and of other festivals in Britain are included in www.visitbritain.com/walking.

APPENDIX A
Index of Routes by Borough and Distance

This shows the routes available in or passing through each of the London cities and boroughs, in ascending order of distance. As many routes pass through more than one borough, they may be shown more than once, and the total distance is shown for each entry (not just the distance in the named borough). Remember that most routes can be walked in shorter sections to suit your requirements. For some longer routes, the distances shown are for the suggested sections in the route descriptions. All distances are approximate, and in some cases are the author's estimates.

Key:

S   Strategic Network (see Section 2)

O   Other named self-guided routes (see Section 2)

♧   Routes which may be all or partly suitable for wheelchairs and buggies (see route descriptions)

*   Routes located just outside Greater London, touching or very close to the boundary of the borough shown

	km	ml	S/O
BARKING & DAGENHAM			
The Chase Nature Trail (short)	1.5	0.9	O
Eastbrookend Country Park Walk (short)	2.2	1.4	O
Eastbrookend Country Park Walk (long)	3.1	1.9	O
The Chase Nature Trail (long)	4.0	2.5	O
Eastbrookend Timberland Trail	5.2	3.3	S
BARNET			
Old Court House Tree Trail	0.5	0.3	O
Big Wood & Little Wood Nature Trail	1.0	0.6	O
Woodridge Nature Trail	1.0	0.6	O
Moat Mount Tree Trail	1.1	0.7	O
Coppetts Wood Nature Trail	1.4	0.9	O
Barnet Gate Wood Nature Trail	1.6	1.0	O
Dollis Valley Health Walk (short)	1.6	1.0	O
Friary Park Circular Walk	1.6	1.0	O
Dollis Valley Health Walk (long)	3.2	2.0	O
Rural Mill Hill	4.3	2.7	S
Moat Mount Walk	4.7	2.9	S
Folly Brook Circular Walk	4.8	3.0	O
Mill Hill Past and Present	5.3	3.3	S
♧ Barnet-Totteridge Loop	5.4	3.4	S
Rural Totteridge	5.5	3.4	S
Exploring Totteridge Manor	6.4	4.0	S
♧ Barnet Millennium Walk	6.5	4.1	S
♧ Capital Ring Section 11	8.5	5.3	S

Capital Ring Section 10	10.6	6.6	S
Nature Conservation in Barnet Walk 1	11.0	6.9	O
Nature Conservation in Barnet Walk 2	13.0	8.1	O
Nature Conservation in Barnet Walk 3	13.5	8.4	O
ᨉ Pymmes Brook Trail	16.4	10.3	S
ᨉ Dollis Valley Greenwalk	16.5	10.3	S
London Loop Section 16	16.8	10.5	S

BEXLEY

The Glade Tree Trail	1.4	0.9	O
Bexley Civic Society Walk 10 (Footscray)	1.5	0.9	O
Bexley Civic Society Walk 16 (Parkhurst)	1.5	0.9	O
Bexley Civic Society Walk 11 (Lamorbey/Halfway Street)	1.6	1.0	O
Bexley Civic Society Walk 14 (Old Crayford)	1.6	1.0	O
Bexley Civic Society Walk 2 (Belvedere Village)	1.7	1.1	O
Woodlands Farm Health Walk (short)	1.7	1.1	O
Bexley Civic Society Walk 3 (Bexleyheath)	2.4	1.5	O
Lesnes Abbey self-guided trails (short)	2.4	1.5	O
Woodlands Farm Health Walk (long)	2.4	1.5	O
Bexley Civic Society Walk 6 (Bostall/West Heath)	2.8	1.8	O
Bexley Civic Society Walk 13 (Old Bexley)	2.8	1.8	O
Bexley Civic Society Walks 18/19 (Upton)	3.0	1.9	O
Bexley Civic Society Walk 1 (Barnehurst)	3.2	2.0	O
Lesnes Abbey self-guided trails (long)	3.4	2.1	O
Bexley Civic Society Walk 15 (Old Sidcup)	3.5	2.2	O
ᨉ Green Chain Walk Section 1	3.5	2.2	S
Bexley Civic Society Walk 9 (Erith)	3.7	2.3	O
Bexley Civic Society Walk 12 (North Cray)	3.8	2.4	O
Bexley Civic Society Walk 20 (Welling)	3.8	2.4	O
Green Chain Walk Section 3	4.3	2.7	S
Bexley Civic Society Walk 5 (Blendon/Bridgen)	4.5	2.8	O
Bexley Civic Society Walk 4 (Blackfen)	4.8	3.0	O
Bexley Civic Society Walks 7/8 (East Wickham)	4.9	3.1	O
Green Chain Walk Section 2	5.2	3.3	S
ᨉ Ridgeway Walk	5.5	3.4	S
Bexley Civic Society Walk (Slade Green)	6.5	4.1	O
Shuttle Riverway	9.7	6.1	S
London Loop Section 2	11.5	7.2	S
London Loop Section 1	13.5	8.4	S
ᨉ Thames Path Southeast Extension	16.5	10.3	S
Cray Riverway	22.0	13.7	S

BRENT

Hell Lane & Eldestrete	1.0	0.6	O
Nature Conservation in Brent Walk 3	3.6	2.3	O
Fryent Park Country Park Circular Walk	4.0	2.5	O
Nature Conservation in Brent Walk 1	5.0	3.1	O
Nature Conservation in Brent Walk 2	5.0	3.1	O

Nature Conservation in Brent Walk 4	7.5	4.7	O
Capital Ring Section 9	8.5	5.3	S
Capital Ring Section 10	10.6	6.6	S
♿ Grand Union Canal Walk (to Rickmansworth)	42.0	26.0	S

BROMLEY

Farnborough Circular Walk (short)	1.7	1.0	S
Jubilee Park Nature Trail	2.2	1.4	O
Walk Around Farnborough	2.2	1.4	O
Dinosaur Trail	2.4	1.5	O
Walk Around Orpington	2.4	1.5	O
Paxton's Heritage Trail 1	3.0	1.9	O
Paxton's Heritage Trail 2	3.0	1.9	O
Walk Around Downe	3.0	1.9	O
Walk Around St Mary Cray	3.4	2.1	O
Paxton's Heritage Trail 3	3.7	2.3	O
Biggin Hill Circular Walk (short)	4.5	2.8	S
Nash Circular Walk (short)	4.8	3.0	S
Petts Wood Circular Walk (short)	5.0	3.1	S
Walk Around Chislehurst	5.3	3.3	O
St Mary Cray Circular Walk (short)	5.5	3.4	S
♿ Leaves Green Circular Walk (short)	5.7	3.6	S
Walk Around Bromley Town	5.8	3.6	O
Capital Ring Section 4	5.8	3.6	S
♿ Green Chain Walk Section 10	5.8	3.6	S
Walk Around Hayes	6.0	3.8	O
Walk Around West Wickham	6.1	3.8	O
Green Chain Walk Section 6	6.2	3.9	S
Petts Wood Circular Walk (long)	6.3	3.9	S
Time Trails in London 1 (Darwin's Rural Ramble)	6.4	4.0	O
St Paul's Cray Circular Walk (short)	6.4	4.0	S
Berry's Green Circular Walk (short)	6.5	4.0	S
Bromley Common Circular Walk	6.5	4.1	S
St Mary Cray Circular Walk (long)	6.5	4.0	S
Nash Circular Walk (long)	6.7	4.2	S
Farnborough Circular Walk (long)	7.2	4.5	S
Walk Around Penge	7.4	4.6	O
Green Chain Walk Section 7	7.5	4.6	S
Three Commons Circular Walk	7.5	4.7	S
Green Street Green Circular Walk (short)	7.8	4.9	S
From the Nun's Head to Screaming Alice	8.0	5.0	S
Green Chain Walk Section 8	8.4	5.2	S
St Paul's Cray Circular Walk (long)	8.7	5.4	S
Cudham Circular Walk (short)	9.1	5.7	S
Green Chain Walk Section 9	9.6	6.1	S
Chelsfield Circular Walk	11.0	6.9	S
Leaves Green Circular Walk (long)	11.0	6.9	S
London Loop Section 2	11.5	7.2	S
Biggin Hill Circular Walk (long)	11.5	7.2	S

	Green Street Green Circular Walk (long)	11.9	7.4	S
	Capital Ring Section 3	12.0	7.5	S
	Cudham Circular Walk (long)	12.9	8.1	S
	Berry's Green Circular Walk (long)	13.4	8.4	S
♿	Waterlink Way (Deptford to South Norwood)	14.3	8.9	S
	London Loop Section 4	14.5	9.1	S
*	North Downs Way (part, short)	15.0	9.4	S
	London Loop Section 3	15.5	9.7	S
♿	Cray Riverway	22.0	13.7	S
*	North Downs Way (part, long)	21.0	13.1	S

CAMDEN

	Four Kings Cross Walks 3 (Bloomsbury)	2.2	1.4	O
	Four Kings Cross Walks 4 (Euston)	2.8	1.8	O
	Four Kings Cross Walks 1 (Camden Lock)	3.6	2.2	O
♿	Jubilee Walkway (short)	14.4	9.0	S
♿	Jubilee Walkway (long)	19.4	12.1	S

CITY OF LONDON

	Maths for All	1.5	0.9	O
	Open Spaces in the City of London Trail 2	2.0	1.2	O
	Open Spaces in the City of London Trail 1	2.1	1.3	O
	Open Spaces in the City of London Trail 3	2.1	1.3	O
♿	London Wall Walk	2.6	1.6	O
	Pilgrimage and Heritage Trail	5.2	3.2	O
	Great Days Out (In the steps of Dickens)	7.5	3.3	O
♿	Jubilee Walkway (short)	14.4	9.0	S
♿	Jubilee Walkway (long)	19.4	12.1	S
♿	Thames Path National Trail (in Greater London)	107.0	67.0	S

CROYDON

♿	Revealing Croydon 1 (Two Towers Walk)	1.1	0.7	O
♿	Revealing Croydon 2 (Wellesley Road Walk)	1.5	0.9	O
	Selsdon Wood Nature Reserve Self Guided Trail (Red)	1.6	1.0	O
	Selsdon Wood Nature Reserve Self Guided Trail (Green)	3.0	1.9	O
♿	Waddon Community Trail (short)	4.0	2.5	O
	Discover New Addington	4.7	2.9	S
	Downlands Circular Walk (short)	4.8	3.0	S
	Coulsdon Common & Happy Valley Circular Walk	5.3	3.3	S
	Capital Ring Section 4	5.8	3.6	S
♿	Waddon Community Trail (long)	6.0	3.8	O
	Farthing Downs & Devilsden Wood Circular Walk	6.5	4.1	S
	Kenley Common & Dollypers Hill Circular Walk	7.2	4.5	S
	London Loop Section 6	7.2	4.5	S
	Riddlesdown Circular Walk	7.4	4.6	S
	London Loop Section 5	9.6	6.0	S
	Vanguard Way (Croydon to Chelsham Common)	10.5	6.5	S
	Downlands Circular Walk (long)	10.7	6.7	S

Socratic Trail (Coulsdon to Nutfield)	13.0	8.1	S
♿ Waterlink Way (Deptford to South Norwood)	14.3	8.9	S
London Loop Section 4	14.5	9.1	S
♿ Wandle Trail	18.1	11.3	S

EALING

Ealing Open House Walk 5 (Hanger Hill Garden)	1.7	1.1	O
Ealing Open House Walk 6 (Hanger Hill Haymills)	1.7	1.1	O
Ealing Open House Walk 2 (Brentham)	1.9	1.2	O
Ealing Open House Walk 3 (Ealing Common)	2.3	1.4	O
Ealing Open House Walk 4 (Ealing Green)	2.8	1.8	O
Ealing Open House Walk 10 (Hanwell Churchfields)	3.1	1.9	O
Ealing Open House Walk 9 (Hanwell Green Lane)	3.7	2.3	O
Ealing Open House Walk 8 (Southall)	6.2	3.9	O
Capital Ring Section 8	7.2	4.5	S
♿ Capital Ring Section 7	7.6	4.7	S
Capital Ring Section 9	8.5	5.3	S
♿ Brent River Park Walk	11.5	7.2	S
Dog Rose Ramble	12.5	7.8	S
♿ Grand Union Canal Walk (to Rickmansworth)	42.0	26.0	S

ENFIELD

Pymmes Park Tree Trail	1.2	0.8	O
Bay/Parkside Farm Trail	1.4	0.9	O
Rectory Farm Trail	1.6	1.0	O
Forty Hall Estate Nature Trail (short)	2.3	1.5	O
London Loop Section 18	6.5	4.1	S
Forty Hall Estate Nature Trail (long)	6.7	4.2	O
Lea Valley Enfield	8.2	5.1	O
Hertfordshire Chain Walk No.1	11.6	7.2	S
London Loop Section 17	14.7	9.2	S
♿ Pymmes Brook Trail	16.4	10.3	S
London Loop Section 16	16.8	10.5	S
♿ Lea Valley Walk (Waltham Abbey to Bow)	20.0	12.5	S
New River Path (Theobalds Lane to Islington)	29.0	18.1	S

GREENWICH

Woodlands Farm Health Walk (short)	1.7	1.1	O
Woodlands Farm Health Walk (long)	2.4	1.5	O
Walk through Georgian Greenwich	2.5	1.6	O
Greenwich and Deptford history trail	2.7	1.7	O
Time Trails in London 2 (Millennium Trail)	3.2	2.0	O
Greenwich Millennium Heritage Trails (Eltham)	3.6	2.3	O
Greenwich Millennium Heritage Trails (Greenwich)	4.2	2.6	O
Green Chain Walk Section 3	4.3	2.7	S
Capital Ring Section 15	4.8	3.0	S
Green Chain Walk Section 2	5.2	3.3	S
♿ Ridgeway Walk	5.5	3.4	S
Capital Ring Section 2	5.6	3.5	S

	Greenwich Millennium Heritage Trails (Blackheath)	6.1	3.8	O
	Greenwich Millennium Heritage Trails (Woolwich)	6.2	3.9	O
	Green Chain Walk Section 6	6.2	3.9	S
♿	Green Chain Walk Section 5	6.7	4.2	S
	Green Chain Walk Section 7	7.5	4.6	S
	Great Days Out (East London's views and vistas)	8.0	5.0	O
	Great Days Out (Maritime London)	8.5	5.3	O
♿	Green Chain Walk Section 4	8.8	5.6	S
	Shuttle Riverway	9.7	6.1	S
	Capital Ring Section 1	10.4	6.5	S
♿	Waterlink Way (Deptford to South Norwood)	14.3	8.9	S
♿	Thames Path Southeast Extension	16.5	10.3	S
♿	Thames Path National Trail (in Greater London)	107.0	67.0	S

HACKNEY

	Hackney Walks 3 (Stoke Newington etc.)	2.0	1.3	O
	Hackney Walks 6 (Heart of Hackney)	2.0	1.3	O
	Kingsland Road Walk	2.3	1.4	O
	Hackney Walks 1 (Clapton Common etc.)	3.2	2.0	O
	Hackney Walks 5 (Kingsland etc.)	3.2	2.0	O
	Historic Hackney	3.6	2.3	O
	Hackney Walks 4 (Shoreditch etc.)	3.7	2.3	O
	Hackney Walks 2 (Victoria Park etc.)	4.0	2.5	O
	Great Days Out (Walk through historic Hackney)	5.5	3.4	O
♿	Capital Ring Section 13	5.6	3.5	S
♿	Capital Ring Section 12	7.2	4.5	S
♿	Walk Back in Time	8.0	5.0	S
	Great Days Out (Lazy day on the Lea)	8.5	5.3	O
♿	Lea Valley Walk (Waltham Abbey to Bow)	20.0	12.5	S
	New River Path (Theobalds Lane to Islington)	29.0	18.1	S

HAMMERSMITH & FULHAM

	Hammersmith Walk	2.3	1.4	O
♿	Grand Union Canal Walk (to Rickmansworth)	42.0	26.0	S
♿	Thames Path National Trail (in Greater London)	107.0	67.0	S

HARINGEY

♿	Parkland Walk	6.3	3.9	S
♿	Capital Ring Section 12	7.2	4.5	S
♿	Capital Ring Section 11	8.5	5.3	S
♿	Lea Valley Walk (Waltham Abbey to Bow)	20.0	12.5	S
	New River Path (Theobalds Lane to Islington)	29.0	18.1	S

HARROW

	Harrow-on-the-Hill Walk	2.2	1.4	O
	Bentley Priory Circular Walk (short)	2.7	1.7	S
	Pinner Village Walk	3.0	1.9	O
	Pinner-Grimsdyke Circular Walk (short)	4.1	2.6	S
	London Loop Section 14	6.1	3.8	S

Bentley Priory Circular Walk (long)	7.2	4.5	S
Pinner-Grimsdyke Circular Walk (long)	7.7	4.8	S
Willow Tree Wander	8.1	5.1	S
Capital Ring Section 9	8.5	5.3	S
London Loop Section 15	13.3	8.3	S
Celandine Route	15.8	9.9	S

HAVERING

♿ Havering Country Park Easy Access Trail	0.4	0.3	O
Bedfords Park Nature Trail (short)	1.2	0.8	O
Belhus Wood Country Park Butterfly Trail (short)	1.5	0.9	O
♿ Havering Riverside Path	2.0	1.3	S
Havering Country Park Tree Trail	2.5	1.6	O
Havering Northern Area Circular Walk (short)	2.6	1.6	S
Belhus Wood Country Park Butterfly Trail (long)	3.0	1.8	O
Cranham Marsh Nature Trail	3.1	1.9	O
Woodland Walk in Harold Hill	4.0	2.5	O
Bedfords Park Nature Trail (long)	4.8	3.0	O
Bedfords Circular Walk	5.5	3.4	S
Tylers Common to Warley Walk (short)	6.0	3.7	S
London Loop Section 23	6.4	4.0	S
London Loop Section 21	6.9	4.3	S
London Loop Section 22	6.9	4.3	S
London Loop Section 24	7.2	4.5	S
Cranham Circular Walk	7.3	4.6	S
Havering Northern Area Circular Walk (long)	8.4	5.2	S
London Loop Section 20	9.6	6.0	S
Tylers Common to Warley Walk (long)	12.0	7.5	S
Upminster Circular Walk	17.0	10.6	S

HILLINGDON

Three Rivers Trail	2.0	1.2	O
Harefield Heights Circular Walk (short)	5.2	3.3	S
London Loop Section 10	6.1	3.8	S
London Loop Section 12	7.2	4.5	S
London Loop Section 13	7.7	4.8	S
♿ Grand Union Canal (Slough Arm)	8.0	5.0	S
Willow Tree Wander	8.1	5.1	S
Nine Stiles Circular Walk	8.5	5.3	S
Iver Circular Walk	9.0	5.6	S
Harefield Heights Circular Walk (long)	10.2	6.4	S
Colne Valley Trail	12.5	7.8	S
Dog Rose Ramble	12.5	7.8	S
London Loop Section 11	12.5	7.8	S
Widewater Lock Circular Walk	12.7	7.9	S
London Loop Section 9	13.6	8.5	S
West Drayton to Slough Ramble and Ride	14.2	8.9	S
West Ruislip to Gerrards Cross Ramble and Ride	15.5	9.7	S
Celandine Route	15.8	9.9	S

Colne Valley Way	16.5	10.3	S
South Bucks Way (Amersham to Denham)	19.0	12.0	S
Beeches Way	26.0	16.3	S
Hillingdon Trail	31.2	19.5	S
♿ Grand Union Canal Walk (to Rickmansworth)	42.0	26.0	S

HOUNSLOW

Gunnersbury Park Walks	1.0	0.6	O
Feltham Heritage Trail (short)	1.1	0.7	O
Maths for All	1.5	0.9	O
Feltham Heritage Trail (long)	1.8	1.1	O
Chiswick House Grounds Tree Walk	2.2	1.4	O
Brentford Walks (2)	2.4	1.5	O
Walk Around Old Isleworth	2.5	1.6	O
Brentford Walks (1)	3.0	1.9	O
Hounslow Heath Nature Trail	3.6	2.4	O
♿ Accessible Thames (Old Isleworth Walk)	4.0	2.5	O
London Loop Section 10	6.1	3.8	S
♿ River Crane Walk (Route 2)	7.3	4.6	S
♿ Capital Ring Section 7	7.6	4.7	S
River Crane Walk (Route 1)	8.6	5.4	S
♿ Brent River Park Walk	11.5	7.2	S
London Loop Section 9	13.6	8.5	S
♿ Grand Union Canal Walk (to Rickmansworth)	42.0	26.0	S
♿ Thames Path National Trail (in Greater London)	107.0	67.0	S

ISLINGTON

Four Kings Cross Walks 2 (Angel Islington)	2.2	1.4	O
Angel Trail	2.4	1.5	O
Clerkenwell Historic Trail	3.5	2.2	O
Barnsbury Walk	5.0	3.1	O
Stroll Around Mildmay	8.2	5.1	O
New River Path (Theobalds Lane to Islington)	29.0	18.1	S

KENSINGTON & CHELSEA

Time Trails in London 3 (In the Footsteps of Prince Albert)	0.8	0.5	O
Riverside Walk	3.0	1.9	O
Notting Hill Walk	4.1	2.6	O
North Kensington Walk	4.5	2.8	O
Chelsea Walk	4.6	2.9	O
Kensington Walk	4.7	2.9	O
♿ Diana Princess of Wales Memorial Walk	11.8	7.4	S
♿ Grand Union Canal Walk (to Rickmansworth)	42.0	26.0	S
♿ Thames Path National Trail (in Greater London)	107.0	67.0	S

KINGSTON

Maths for All	1.5	0.9	O
Kingston-upon-Thames Walker's Guide	2.5	1.6	O

♿ Accessible Thames (Kingston Walk)	3.2	2.0	O
Chessington Countryside Walk	8.0	5.0	S
Capital Ring Section 6	10.9	6.8	S
Beverley Brook Walk	11.5	7.2	S
♿ London Loop Section 8	11.7	7.3	S
♿ Hogsmill Walk	11.7	7.3	S
Thames Down Link	24.0	15.0	S
♿ Thames Path National Trail (in Greater London)	107.0	67.0	S

LAMBETH

Millennium Mile 1	3.0	1.9	O
Time Trails in London 5 (Tower to Tower)	3.0	1.9	O
Millennium Mile 2	4.0	2.5	O
Nature Conservation in Lambeth Walk 1	4.5	2.8	O
Capital Ring Section 4	5.8	3.6	S
Nature Conservation in Lambeth Walk 2	6.5	4.1	O
Nature Conservation in Lambeth Walk 3	6.5	4.1	O
♿ Capital Ring Section 5	8.5	5.3	S
♿ Jubilee Walkway (short)	14.4	9.0	S
♿ Jubilee Walkway (long)	19.4	12.1	S
♿ Thames Path National Trail (in Greater London)	107.0	67.0	S

LEWISHAM

Maths for All	1.5	0.9	O
Greenwich and Deptford history trail	2.7	1.7	O
Greenwich Millennium Heritage Trails (Deptford)	4.0	2.5	O
Nature Conservation in Lewisham Walk 3	4.0	2.5	O
Nature Conservation in Lewisham Walk 1	5.5	3.4	O
Capital Ring Section 2	5.6	3.5	S
Greenwich Millennium Heritage Trails (Blackheath)	6.1	3.8	O
Nature Conservation in Lewisham Walk 4	6.8	4.3	O
Nature Conservation in Lewisham Walk 2	7.0	4.4	O
From the Nun's Head to Screaming Alice	8.0	5.0	S
Green Chain Walk Section 8	8.4	5.2	S
Green Chain Walk Section 9	9.6	6.1	S
Capital Ring Section 3	12.0	7.5	S
♿ Waterlink Way (Deptford to South Norwood)	14.3	8.9	S
♿ Thames Path National Trail (in Greater London)	107.0	67.0	S

MERTON

Wandle Valley Nature Park Trail	0.8	0.5	O
Merton's Heritage Trails 2 (Morden Park)	2.5	1.6	O
Merton's Heritage Trails 5 (Merton Park)	3.8	2.4	O
♿ Nature Conservation in Merton Walk 5	4.3	2.7	O
Merton's Heritage Trails 1 (Wandle Walk)	4.4	2.8	O
Merton's Heritage Trails 4 (Mitcham Village)	5.0	3.1	O
♿ Merton's Heritage Trails 3 (Wimbledon Common)	5.5	6.2	O
Nature Conservation in Merton Walk 1	6.5	4.1	O
Nature Conservation in Merton Walk 3	7.1	4.4	O

♿	Capital Ring Section 5	8.5	5.3	S
	Nature Conservation in Merton Walk 4	8.5	5.3	O
	Nature Conservation in Merton Walk 2	9.4	5.9	O
♿	Capital Ring Section 6	10.9	6.8	S
	Beverley Brook Walk	11.5	7.2	S
♿	Wandle Trail	18.1	11.3	S

NEWHAM

	Newham Walk 5 (Central Park Tree Trail)	1.6	1.0	O
	Beckton Creek Trail	2.0	1.2	O
♿	Kingfisher Walk	2.4	1.5	S
♿	Capital Ring Section 15	4.8	3.0	S
	Newham Walk 1 (A ramble through Beckton)	4.8	3.0	O
	Newham Walk 4 (The Alps to the Thames)	4.8	3.0	O
♿	Heron Walk	5.1	3.2	S
	Heritage walk from Three Mills Island	5.5	3.4	O
	Newham Walk 2 (Three Mills to St Mary's)	5.6	3.5	O
	Newham Walk 3 (Little Ilford to Wanstead Flats)	6.4	4.0	O
♿	The Greenway	7.1	4.4	S
♿	Capital Ring Section 14	7.7	4.8	S
	Great Days Out (Lazy day on the Lea)	8.5	5.3	O
	Great Days Out (Maritime London)	8.5	5.3	O
	Time Travellers	10.2	6.4	S
♿	Lea Valley Walk (Waltham Abbey to Bow)	20.0	12.5	S
	Epping Forest Centenary Walk	24.7	15.4	S

REDBRIDGE

	Hainault Lodge Nature Trail	0.9	0.6	O
♿	Hainault Forest Wild About Woods Trail	4.3	2.7	O
*	Chigwell Country Walk	4.5	2.8	S
	London Loop Section 20	9.6	6.0	S
	Three Forests Way (Abridge to Loughton)	12.8	8.0	S
	Three Forests Way (Ongar to Chigwell Row)	20.0	12.5	S
	Epping Forest Centenary Walk	24.7	15.4	S

RICHMOND

	Terrace Gardens Tree Walk	0.4	0.3	O
	Picnic Walk in the Woodlands of Bushy Park	0.7	0.5	O
	Maths for All	1.5	0.9	O
♿	Accessible Thames (Marble Hill Walk)	2.4	1.5	O
♿	Accessible Thames (St Margaret's Walk)	3.2	2.0	O
	Hampton Ferry Walks (short)	3.5	2.2	O
	Time Trails in London 4 (Romancing the Thames)	4.0	2.5	O
♿	Accessible Thames (Richmond Walk)	4.4	2.7	O
♿	Accessible Thames (Ham Walk)	4.8	3.0	O
♿	Accessible Thames (Kew Walk)	4.8	3.0	O
	Walk in Teddington	5.8	3.6	O
♿	River Crane Walk (via Route 2)	7.3	4.6	S
	Hampton Ferry Walks (long)	7.5	4.7	O

♿	Capital Ring Section 7	7.6	4.7	S
♿	Accessible Thames (Hampton Court Walk)	8.0	5.0	O
	River Crane Walk (via Route 1)	8.6	5.4	S
	Bushy Park History Trail	10.8	6.7	O
	Capital Ring Section 6	10.9	6.8	S
	Beverley Brook Walk	11.5	7.2	S
♿	Tamsin Trail	11.7	7.3	S
	London Loop Section 9	13.6	8.5	S
♿	Thames Path National Trail (in Greater London)	107.0	67.0	S

SOUTHWARK

	Millennium Mile 1	3.0	1.9	O
	Time Trails in London 5 (Tower to Tower)	3.0	1.9	O
	Millennium Mile 2	4.0	2.5	O
	Great Days Out (In the steps of Dickens)	7.5	3.3	O
	From the Nun's Head to Screaming Alice	8.0	5.0	S
	Great Days Out (East London's views and vistas)	8.0	5.0	O
	Great Days Out (Ships, sculptures and the Thames)	8.5	5.3	O
♿	Jubilee Walkway (short)	14.4	9.0	S
♿	Jubilee Walkway (long)	19.4	12.1	S
♿	Thames Path National Trail (in Greater London)	107.0	67.0	S

SUTTON

	Oaks Park Nature Trail	3.0	1.9	O
	Sutton Countryside Walk (short)	5.0	3.1	S
	London Loop Section 7	6.4	4.0	S
	London Loop Section 6	7.2	4.5	S
	Sutton Countryside Walk (long)	7.7	4.8	S
♿	Wandle Trail	18.1	11.3	S

TOWER HAMLETS

	Mudchute Nature Trail	1.0	0.6	O
	Maths for All	1.5	0.9	O
	Time Trails in London 5 (Tower to Tower)	3.0	1.9	O
♿	Heron Walk	5.1	3.2	S
	Heritage walk from Three Mills Island	5.5	3.4	O
♿	Nature Conservation in Tower Hamlets Walk 1	5.7	3.6	O
♿	The Greenway	7.1	4.4	S
	Nature Conservation in Tower Hamlets Walk 3	7.2	4.5	O
	Great Days Out (In the steps of Dickens)	7.5	3.3	O
♿	Capital Ring Section 14	7.7	4.8	S
	Great Days Out (East London's views and vistas)	8.0	5.0	O
	Nature Conservation in Tower Hamlets Walk 2	8.4	5.3	O
♿	Time Travellers	10.2	6.4	S
	Nature Conservation in Tower Hamlets Walk 4	10.5	6.6	O
♿	Jubilee Walkway (short)	14.4	9.0	S

♿ Jubilee Walkway (long)	19.4	12.1	S
♿ Lea Valley Walk (Waltham Abbey to Bow)	20.0	12.5	S
♿ Thames Path National Trail (in Greater London)	107.0	67.0	S

WALTHAM FOREST

Lloyd Park Tree Trail	1.0	0.6	O
William Morris Tapestry Tree Trail	1.0	0.6	O
Millennium Heritage Trails 3 (Walthamstow)	2.5	1.6	O
Millennium Heritage Trails 2 (Leytonstone)	4.9	3.1	O
Millennium Heritage Trails 1 (Chingford)	5.1	3.2	O
♿ Capital Ring Section 13	5.6	3.5	S
London Loop Section 19	6.4	4.0	S
London Loop Section 18	6.5	4.1	S
♿ Walk Back in Time	8.0	5.0	S
Great Days Out (Lazy day on the Lea)	8.5	5.3	O
Millennium Heritage Trails 4 (Lea Valley)	11.0	6.9	O
Lea Valley Walk (Waltham Abbey to Bow)	20.0	12.5	S
Epping Forest Centenary Walk	24.7	15.4	S

WANDSWORTH

Wandsworth Town Heritage Trail 1 (Town Centre)	2.2	1.4	O
Wandsworth Town Heritage Trail 2 (River Walk)	2.7	1.7	O
♿ Capital Ring Section 5	8.5	5.3	S
♿ Capital Ring Section 6	10.9	6.8	S
Beverley Brook Walk	11.5	7.2	S
♿ Wandle Trail	18.1	11.3	S
♿ Thames Path National Trail (in Greater London)	107.0	67.0	S

WESTMINSTER

Time Trails in London 3 (In the Footsteps of Prince Albert)	0.8	0.5	O
Maths for All	1.5	0.9	O
Engineering Discovery Trail	2.8	1.8	O
Time Trails in London 5 (Tower to Tower)	3.0	1.9	O
Walking in Belgravia	3.1	1.9	O
Walking in Mayfair	3.1	1.9	O
♿ Diana Princess of Wales Memorial Walk	11.8	7.4	S
♿ Jubilee Walkway (short)	14.4	9.0	S
♿ Jubilee Walkway (long)	19.4	12.1	S
♿ Grand Union Canal Walk (to Rickmansworth)	42.0	26.0	S
♿ Thames Path National Trail (in Greater London)	107.0	67.0	S

APPENDIX B
Proposed routes

Many London boroughs and other organisations or individuals are continuously planning new self-guided routes or extensions to existing routes, subject to the availability of funding and other resources. Here is a list of those identified at time of writing. Their borough location is shown in brackets, but this does not necessarily mean that the local authority is promoting the route. Inclusion in this list does not imply that these routes will come into existence, and it is possible that names shown here may be modified or even changed completely during the gestation period. Further brief details are included where known.

Atop the Beulah Heights (Croydon/Lambeth) – Crystal Palace Park to Streatham Common via Beulah Hill. (Friends of the Great North Wood)

Beam Valley Cycleway/Footpath (Barking & Dagenham)

Bow Creek Towpath (Newham/Tower Hamlets)

Camden-Hampstead Green Link (Camden)

Ching Way (Waltham Forest)

Circle the New Heart of London (Westminster/Lambeth/Southwark)

Dagenham Corridor (Barking & Dagenham)

Dagenham Village Trail (Barking & Dagenham)

Due South (Lambeth/Southwark)

Enfield Link Walk (Enfield) – linking several parks between Pymmes Park and Trent Park

Explore Bankside (Southwark)

Frays Valley Trail (Hillingdon) – replacing the former Denham Quarry Trail

Green Links in Wandsworth (Wandsworth)

Greenwich to Eltham Palace Walk (Greenwich)

Hackney Green Links (Hackney)

Hammersmith Inner City Green Walk (Hammersmith & Fulham)

Havering & Hainault Country Parks Circular Walk (Havering/Redbridge)

Havering Country Park Historical Walk (Havering)

Havering Greenway (Havering)

Ingrebourne Valley Greenway (Havering)

Island Village Heritage Trail (Enfield)

Islington Park Walk (Islington)

Lee Valley Pathway (Enfield/Newham/Waltham Forest) – extension of existing route from Hertfordshire into Greater London

Lewisham Utility Walking Network (Lewisham)

London North City Walk (Camden/Westminster)

London Parkways (City, Westminster, Lambeth, Southwark) – linear public spaces linking public transport nodes

Mandela Way (Southwark/Westminster/Camden/Brent) – proposal by Ramblers' Association Hampstead Group linking Central London with Wendover in the Chilterns via Hertfordshire

Meridian Way (several boroughs) – 360km (230ml) route following closely the line of the Greenwich Meridian, from Lincolnshire through London to Sussex

Millennium Path (Barking & Dagenham)

Redbridge Recreational Footpaths (Redbridge)

Roding Valley Way (Redbridge/Newham/Barking & Dagenham)

Romford to Havering-atte-Bower Greenway (Havering) – has also been known as the Raphael Park Green Chain

Saffron Way (Croydon) – circular route inside the Croydon borough boundary

Southwark Green Chain Walks (Southwark)

Sundridge Circular Walk (Bromley)

Tandridge Border Path. Approximately 80km (50ml), mostly in Surrey but crosses into Croydon in places – further details from Per-Rambulations. Route now open.

Thames Chase Forest Circle (Barking & Dagenham/Havering)

Thames Path Northeast Extension (Tower Hamlets/Newham/Barking & Dagenham/Havering) – an amalgamation of several individual projects: Isle of Dogs Riverside Walk, Silvertown North Woolwich and Beckton Riverside Walk, North Thames Way, Barking Riverside Walk, Northeast Thames Path, Corniche Route and Havering Riverside Walk

Tolworth Stream Circular Walk (Kingston)

Tramlink Walks (Croydon) – walks from or between the stops of Croydon Tramlink

Walk This Way (Lambeth/Southwark/City of London/Westminster) – two routes beside or near the Thames proposed by the South Bank Employers' Group. Routes now open.

Wandle to Beverley Brook Link (Merton/Sutton)

Wandle Trail to Sutton Countryside Link (Sutton)

Whitewebbs Loop Heritage Trail (Enfield) – following a disused loop of the New River in Whitewebbs Park and Forty Hall Estate

APPENDIX C
Discontinued and dormant routes

If a walk you know of is not included elsewhere in this book, it may be because it is no longer promoted, or may be a proposal that has been dropped, at least for the time being – the latter are indicated (P) below. You may still come across out-of-print publications, signs or other references. In this list the borough location is shown for information, but this does not necessarily imply that the borough council was responsible for the route. Any of these routes or proposals may be revived in the future.

Bankside Trail, A (Southwark)

Bayhurst Wood Country Park Nature Trail (Hillingdon)

Beckenham Circular Walk (P) (Bromley)

Beddington Park Heritage Trail (Sutton)

Bermondsey Walk, A (Southwark)

Bishops Wood Country Park Nature Trail (P) (Harrow)

Bow Heritage Trail (Tower Hamlets)

Bromley Park Circular Walk (P) (Bromley)

Burgess Park Walk (Southwark)

City Church Trails (City of London)

City of London Heritage Walks (City of London)

City of London Trails (City of London)

City Walks (P) (various boroughs, also known as Metropolitan City Walks)

Coulsdon Downs Nature Trails (Croydon)

Cuckoo Wood Trail (Bromley)

Denham Quarry Trail (Hillingdon) – see Frays River Trail in Appendix B

Dragonfly Walk (Newham)

Eden Park Circular Walk (P) (Bromley)

Effra Trail (P) (Lambeth)

Elstree-Stanmore Circular Walk (P) (Barnet/Harrow)

Fryent Link (P) (Brent)

Gunnersbury Park Self-guided Tour (Hounslow)

Hayes Common Nature Trail (Bromley)

Heather Path (Bexley)

Horsenden Hill Countryside Walk (Ealing)

Isle of Dogs Heritage Trail (Tower Hamlets)

Lavender Docks Walk (Southwark)

Locksbottom Circular Walk (P) (Bromley)

Longford River Walk (P) (Richmond/Hounslow)

Oak Hill Woods Woodland Trails (Barnet)

Padmall Trail (Bromley)

Park Wood Nature Trail (Hillingdon)

Ravensbourne Nature Trail (Bromley)

Rotherhithe Walk (Southwark)

Royal Docks Links (Newham).

Ruislip Woods Nature Trail (Hillingdon)

St.Mary Magdalen and Beckton District Park (Newham)

Salmons Brook Walk (P) (Enfield)

Scadbury Park Nature Trail (Bromley)

Scratchwood Nature Trail (Barnet)

Selsdon Wood Nature Trails (Croydon)

Seven Stiles Way (Hillingdon)

Silk Stream Walk (P) (Barnet)

Southwark Trail, A (Southwark)

Surrey Docks Heritage Walks (Southwark)

Surrey Quays Walk (Southwark)

Totteridge and Mill Hill Circular Walks (Barnet)

Trail of Three Inns of Court (City of London)

Trent Park Blind Persons Trail (Enfield)

Trent Park Nature Trail (Enfield)

Turkey Brook Walk (P) (Enfield)

Walk around Central Croydon, A (Croydon)

Welsh Harp Link (P) (Barnet)

West Ham Chemistry Trail (Newham)

West Wickham Circular Walk (P) (Bromley)

Wimbledon Common Grassland Trail (Merton)

Wimbledon Common Queensmere Trail (Merton)

APPENDIX D
Larger parks and open spaces in Greater London

All these places should provide excellent opportunities for relaxed walking and roaming. For further information contact the managing organisation (see Appendix H). Those marked ♿ are mostly level with plenty of hard surface paths.

Name	Location (borough)	Managed by
Alexandra Park	Haringey	LB Haringey
Battersea Park ♿	Wandsworth	LB Wandsworth
Beddington Park ♿	Sutton	LB Sutton
Blackheath	Lewisham	LB Lewisham
Brockwell Park	Lambeth	LB Lambeth
Bushy Park	Richmond	Royal Parks Agency
Clapham Common ♿	Wandsworth/Lambeth	LB Wandsworth/Lambeth
Colne Valley RP	Havering, Berks, Bucks, Herts	Colne Valley RPA
Crystal Palace Park	Bromley	LB Bromley
Danson Park	Bexley	LB Bexley
Eltham Common/ Oxleas Wood	Greenwich	LB Greenwich
Epping Forest	Waltham Forest/ Redbridge	Corporation of London
Farthing Downs	Croydon	Corporation of London
Finsbury Park	Haringey	LB Haringey
Foots Cray Meadows	Bexley	LB Bexley
Fryent CP	Brent	LB Brent
Greenwich Park	Greenwich	Royal Parks Agency
Hackney Marsh	Hackney	LB Hackney
Hainault Forest CP	Redbridge	LB Redbridge
Hampstead Heath	Barnet/Camden	Corporation of London
Hampton Court Park ♿	Richmond	Royal Parks Agency
Hanworth Park	Hounslow	LB Hounslow
Happy Valley	Croydon	LB Croydon
Hayes Common	Bromley	LB Bromley
Hornchurch CP	Havering	LB Havering
Hounslow Heath	Hounslow	LB Hounslow
Hyde Park ♿	Westminster	Royal Parks Agency
Joydens Wood	Bexley/Dartford	LB Bexley/Dartford DC
Jubilee CP	Bromley	LB Bromley
Kenley Common	Croydon	Corporation of London
Kensington Gardens ♿	Kensington/Westminster	Royal Parks Agency

Kew Gardens ♿	Richmond	LB Richmond
Kings Wood	Croydon	LB Croydon
Lea Valley RP	Tower Hamlets/Newham /Waltham Forest/ Enfield/Herts/Essex	Lea Valley RPA
Lesnes Abbey Woods	Bexley	LB Bexley
Lloyd Park	Croydon	LB Croydon
Mitcham Common	Merton	Cons of Mitcham Common
Moat Mount OS	Barnet	LB Barnet
Monken Hadley Common	Barnet	Cons of Monken Hadley Common
Morden Park	Merton	LB Merton
Norman Park	Bromley	LB Bromley
Osterley Park	Hounslow/Ealing	National Trust
Parsloes Park	Barking & Dagenham	LB Barking & Dagenham
Pauls Cray Hill Park	Bexley	LB Bexley
Petts Wood	Bromley	LB Bromley
Putney Heath	Wandsworth	LB Wandsworth
Regent's Park ♿	Westminster/Camden	Royal Parks Agency
Richmond Park	Richmond/Kingston	Royal Parks Agency
Scadbury Park	Bromley	LB Bromley
South Norwood CP	Croydon	LB Croydon
Stockley Park CP	Hillingdon	LB Hillingdon
Syon Park ♿	Hounslow	Duke of N'berland
Thames Chase CF	Havering, Essex	Thames Chase CF
Tooting Common ♿	Wandsworth	LB Wandsworth
Trent Park CP	Enfield	LB Enfield
Valentines Park	Redbridge	LB Redbridge
Victoria Park ♿	Tower Hamlets	LB Tower Hamlets
Walthamstow Marshes	Waltham Forest	LB Waltham Forest
Wandsworth Common ♿	Wandsworth	LB Wandsworth
Wanstead Flats	Redbridge	LB Redbridge
Whitewebbs Park	Enfield	LB Enfield
Wimbledon Common	Merton	Cons of Wimbledon Common
Wimbledon Park ♿	Merton	LB Merton
Woolwich Common	Greenwich	LB Greenwich
Wormwood Scrubs	Hammersmith & Fulham	LB Hammersmith & Fulham

Key:

CF = Community Forest	DC = District Council	RB = Royal Borough
Cons = Conservators	LB = London Borough	RP = Regional Park
CP = Country Park	OS = Open Space	

APPENDIX E
Other publications of self-guided walks

This includes publications of suggested self-guided walks (books, audioguides and websites) that are not named trails listed in Section 2. They are mostly devised by individuals, and promoted through a publisher. Prices are correct at time of publication. If ordering by post from the publisher, check the p&p supplement. A list of all contact addresses is shown in Apprndix H.

BOOKS
The following books were still in print at the time of writing (all paperback unless shown otherwise):

25 Walks in and around London (Andrew McCloy, The Stationery Office, 1997, 116 pages, ISBN 0-11-495797-5, £8.99). Within and outside Greater London, distances 5.5 to 16.0km (3.4 to 10.0ml), circular and linear.

40 Walks from Ally Pally (John Twistleton, Fiennes Print, 2000, 58 pages, ISBN 1-903290-00-7, £4.50). Distances 1.5 to 32.0km (0.9 to 20.0ml) circular and linear, all starting and/or finishing at Alexandra Palace (Wood Green) in North London.

50 Walks in Greater London (Deborah King, AA Publications, 2002, 128 pages, ISBN 0-74953-340-4). Walks of between 2 and 10 miles long with details of places to visit along the way.

100 Walks in Greater London (Peter Rudd, The Crowood Press, 1996, 192 pages, ISBN 1-85223-951-4, £8.99). Within and outside Greater London, distances 4.5 to 16.0km (2.8 to 10.0ml), circular and linear.

American Walks in London (Richard Tames, Interlink Books, 1997, 198 pages, ISBN 1-56656-213-9, £14.95). Ten walks in Central London of particular interest to visitors from North America. Distances not indicated but stated to take less than two hours.

Country Walks around London (Geoff Garvey and Leigh Hatts, Mainstream Publishing, 1998, ISBN 1-85158-968-6). 25 walks spread around outer London and beyond, based on the London Transport system.

Discovering Country Walks in North London (Merry Lundow, Shire Publications, 1981, 72 pages, ISBN 0-85263-915-5. £3.95). 20 walks in various parts of North London, distances 5.5 to 14.5km (3.4 to 9.1ml), circular and linear.

Discovering Off-beat Walks in London (John Wittich and Ron Phillips, Shire Publications, ISBN 0-7478-0263-7, £4.99). A collection of walks through historic parts of London, down byways and past unsuspected treasures.

Exploring Enfield's Country Parklands (Enfield Preservation Society, 2001, ISBN 0-907318-18-5, £1.50). This booklet and its companion map contain details of country footpaths in the north of Enfield borough, together with 12 suggested short walks.

Family Walks in West London (Caroline Bacon, Scarthin Books, 1994, 80 pages, ISBN 0-907758-72-X, £5.95). 2.4 to 9.6km (1.5 to 5.9ml), all circular and graded in order of difficulty.

Green London Way (Bob Gilbert, Lawrence & Wishart, 1991, 195 pages, ISBN 0-85315-746-4, £9.99). Grand circular walk around Inner London, linking many parks and open spaces – similar to the Capital Ring, but longer at 147km (92ml).

Greenwich Riverside Path (Mary Mills, M.Wright, 2001, 32 pages, ISBN 0953-5245-3-1, £1.50). Describing the 4.0km (2.5ml) section of the Thames Path from Cutty Sark to North Greenwich.

Hampstead Heath – the walker's guide (David McDowall and Deborah Wolton, David McDowall, 1998, 176 pages, ISBN 0-9527847-1-8, £6.99). 10 walks around the heath, 2.0 to 6.2km (1.2 to 3.9ml).

In and Around London Walks (Brian Conduit, Jarrold Publishing, Pathfinder Guide, 1999, 96 pages, ISBN 0-7117-1055-4, £9.95). 28 walks from easy to challenging within and just outside Greater London, distances 4.0 to 14.0km (2.5 to 8.8ml), linear and circular.

London by Pub (Ted Bruning, Prion Books, 2001, ISBN 1-85375-4315, £10.00). 15 walks of 2.0 to 6.5km (1.2 to 4.1ml) around pubs in London.

London Theatre Walks (Jim de Young and John Miller, Applause Books, 1998, 234 pages, ISBN 1-55783-280-3, £9.99). 13 walks linking various groups of theatres in Central London, distances one hour's walking to a full day, depending on browsing time, all linear.

London Theme Walks (Frank Duerden, Cicerone Press, 2001, 144 pages, ISBN 1-85284-145-1, £5.99). 10 fascinating walks based on popular themes.

London Walks Map (Andrew Duncan, New Holland, 1999, ISBN 1-85368-991-2, £5.99). Fold-out sheet printed both sides and containing maps and main points of interest for 30 walks in and around Greater London, distances 3.0 to 9.0km (1.9 to 5.6ml), linear and circular.

Louis London walks An expanding series of pocket booklets (each about 16 pages) describing themed walks devised by their author, Paul Garner. They each cost £1.99 plus 50p p&p and can be obtained from Louis London Walks, also some bookshops, tourist information centres and bookstalls in tourist venues. Currently they include: The Beatles in London Walk (Westminster, ISBN 1-902678-03-6), A Historical Riverside London Pub Walk (City/Tower Hamlets, ISBN 1-902678-05-2), Jack the Ripper Walk (Tower Hamlets, ISBN 1-902678-02-8), A Walk Through Princess Diana's London (Westminster/Kensington & Chelsea, ISBN 1-902678-01-X), Sherlock Holmes Walk (Westminster, ISBN 1-902678-04-4), A Walk Around Charles Dickens' London (City, ISBN 1-902678-07-9).

Pub Strolls in Middlesex & West London (David Hall and Rosemary Hall, Countryside Books, 2002, 96 pages, ISBN 1-85306-728-8, £7.95). 30 circular walks of 2.4 to 8.4km (1.5 to 5.3ml).

Richmond Park – the walker's historical guide (David McDowall – also publisher, 1996, 136 pages, ISBN 0-9527847-0-X, £5.99). 11 walks around the park, concentrating on historical aspects. 2.0 to 14.0km (1.2 to 8.7km).

Rural Walks Around Richmond (various authors, Ramblers' Association Richmond Group, £2.25 including p&p – cheque payable to M Sharp). One of the most popular walk books in London, describing many linear and circular walks all in the southwest sector of Greater London, distances 4.0 to 24.0km (2.5 to 15.0ml) with optional extensions.

Short Walks in London's Epping Forest (Fred Matthews and Harry Bitten, Matthews Bitten Publications, c/o Epping Forest Information Centre, 1998, 52 pages, £2.40). 24 circular walks in various parts of Epping Forest within and outside Greater London, all around 5.0km (3.1ml) but interlinking to provide longer options.

Time Out Book of London walks (various authors, Penguin, 1998, 304 pages, ISBN 0-14-027897-4, £9.99). 31 favourite walks of 31 different celebrity authors in various parts of London, distances 2.0 to 46.0km (1.3 to 28.8ml), linear and circular.

Time Out Book of London walks – Volume 2 Similar to the above but price £11.00, published 2001.

Travelcard Walks in West London (Margaret Sharp, Mainstream Publishing, 2000, 185 pages, ISBN 1-84018-312-8, £7.99). 25 walks all over the western half of Greater London, distances 4.0 to 10.5km (2.5 to 6.6ml), linear and circular.

Village Walks in Middlesex and West London (David and Rosemary Hall, Countryside Books, 1998, 96 pages, ISBN 1-85306-528-5, £6.95). 20 walks visiting old villages on the north and west sides of Greater London, distances 3.0 to 11.5km (1.9 to 7.2ml), all circular.

Walking Haunted London (Richard Jones, New Holland, 1999, 160 pages, ISBN 1-85368-992-0, £9.99). 25 walks visiting places in various parts of London and nearby that are said to be haunted, distances 1.5 to 24.0km (0.9 to 15.0ml), linear and circular.

Walking Literary London (Roger Tagholm, New Holland, 2001, 192 pages, ISBN 1-85974-555-5, £9.99). 25 circular and linear walks in the range 1.6 to 9.6km (1 to 6 miles).

Walking London (Andrew Duncan, New Holland, 1991, 184 pages hardbound, ISBN 1-85368-073-7, £9.99). 30 walks in various parts of and just outside Greater London, distances 3.0 to 9.5km (1.9 to 5.9ml), linear and circular.

Walking London's Parks and Gardens (Geoffrey Young, New Holland, 1998, 176 pages, ISBN 1-85368-469-4, £9.99). 24 walks around a selection of London's open spaces, distances not shown but suggested timings range from 30 minutes to 4 hours, linear and circular.

Walking Notorious London (Andrew Duncan, New Holland, 2001, 160 pages, ISBN 1-85974-464-8, £9.99). Nine walks in Central London (all circular except two), distances 2.8 to 6.0km (1.8 to 3.8ml), highlighting the scandals and lowlife of yesteryear.

Walking Village London (Andrew Duncan, New Holland, 1997, 160 pages, ISBN 1-85974-271-8, £9.99). 25 walks visiting villages all over Greater London, distances 3.0 to 7.0km (1.9 to 4.4ml), all circular except one.

OUT OF PRINT BOOKS

The following books are no longer in print but might be found in libraries or secondhand bookshops. You could also try Waterstones Out of Print Book Search on www.waterstones.co.uk.

Best Pub Walks in and around Central London (Ruth Herman, Sigma Leisure, 1995).

Discovering Country Walks in South London (Susan Owen and Angela Haine, Shire Publications, 1982, ISBN-0-85263-610-5).

Dogs' London (Mary Scott, Sigma Leisure, 1997, ISBN 1-85058-558-X).

Face the Dawn (Eddie Critchley, Ramblers' Association, 1984, ISBN 0-900613-556). Long distance walk of 275km (172ml) from Bristol to London.

London and Beyond (Denise Sylvester-Carr and Gerald Colton, Jarrold Ordnance Survey Landranger Guidebook, 1988, ISBN 0-319-00084-2).

London Walks (Guy Williams, Constable, 1981, ISBN 0-09-462740-1).

London Walks (Anton Powell, Robson Books, 1988, ISBN 0-86051-274-6).

London Walks (Tiffany Daneff, Michael Joseph, 1989, ISBN 0-7181-3116-9).

Mystery Readers' Walking Guide to London (Alzina Stone Dale and Barbara Sloan Hendershott, Sphere Books, 1988, ISBN 0-7474-0315-5).

Outer London Step by Step (Christopher Turner, Faber & Faber, 1986, ISBN 0-571-138987-6).

The Perfect London walk (Roger Ebert and Daniel Curley, Catto Press, 1988, ISBN 1-871111-00-5).

Strolling through London (Frank Cook, Frank Cook Publications, 1981, ISBN 0-9506503-1-5).

Walk London (Andrew Davies and Fran Hazelton, Bartholomew, 1987, ISBN 0-7028-0771-0).

Walking London's Royal Parks (Roger Jones and Thomas Lowry, Footmarks, 1995, ISBN 0-9524618-0-3). One circular walk of 22.5km (14ml) connecting all six royal parks in Central London. Copies available from royal park offices at time of writing.

MAGAZINES

Country Walking. Monthly, published by EMAP Active. The insert 'Down Your Way' includes walks in the London area (as well as other parts of the country) on a regular basis. Refer to Governing Bodies in Section 1 for information on subscription magazines published by walking associations.

AUDIOGUIDES

These are aimed particularly at tourists, but if you prefer not to keep referring to a book, it can be relaxing to wander round interesting areas with an audioguide, listening to route instructions and descriptions of points of interest. Those identified at time of writing include:

Londonwalks Audio Guide. Four walks covering: Adelphi and Covent Garden, the Inns of Court, St James's and Chelsea.

Richmond Town Centre Audioguide. LB Richmond . Tourist Information Centre.

Talking Tour Company. Walks of about two hours' duration around Whitechapel (Jack the Ripper), Dickens's London and London during the Blitz.

WEBSITES

Walking World. www.walkingworld.com contains self-guided walks in various parts of Britain, which can be downloaded with a charge against a debit or credit card. At time of writing walks offered seem to be mostly outside London, but some are within easy reach.

It is likely that websites of this kind will become more common in the near future. You may like to search for sites by typing, for example, 'London, walking, self-guided', but be prepared for literally hundreds of irrelevant ones!

APPENDIX F
Guided walks for the general public

The author has tried to identify as many organisers as possible. There may be others, consequently the lists that follow should be considered an unbiased selection. Some operators have been omitted as no suitable contact details were available at the time of writing. Inclusion in this list does not constitute a recommendation, and you are advised to satisfy yourself by obtaining literature or contacting the organiser that any walk is suitable. Travelling costs to the meeting point and refreshments are not normally included. For further information, contact as indicated (see Appendix H).

♿ People with disabilities welcome

* A charge is made for the walk – details on application to the organiser. Most fee-paying walks (generally about £2 to £6) are led by professional guides and based on themes such as historical events or personalities. Walks for which no charge is made may be led by volunteers who are not expert on matters of interest along the route.

*Angel Walks Half day (mostly morning) themed walks in Islington.

Belhus Woods Country Park Occasional themed walks with a park ranger.

Brixton Society Short walks with volunteer leaders in Brixton area mid-June to October.

*City of London Walks Half day themed walks in the City.

*Crystal Palace Foundation Morning and afternoon walks on the second Sunday of each month around the site of the Crystal Palace and Crystal Palace Park.

*Deptford Tour Guides Association Weekly Saturday and Sunday afternoon walks in historic Deptford and New Cross.

Environment Bromley (EnBro) organises a regular programme of guided walks in the borough. At time of writing they are oversubscribed and new participants are not being accepted for the time being.

Friends of West Norwood Cemetery Monthly Sunday afternoon tours of the cemetery (mornings in winter). Donation requested.

Greenwich Tour Guides Association c/o LB Greenwich Tourist Information Centre. Morning and afternoon walks around historic Greenwich from the tourist information centre.

Historical Walks of London Half day and evening themed walks in central London.

Hounslow Heritage Guides Sunday afternoon walks May to October around Brentford, Chiswick or Isleworth.

Into the Great Green Yonder LB Croydon Cultural Services. Half day wildlife walks led by rangers and wardens in parks, commons and other open spaces in and around Croydon borough.

Kingston Tour Guides Sunday afternoon walks around historic Kingston from the Market Place.

Mystery Walks Sunday and Wednesday evening Jack the Ripper walks from Aldgate station.

Original London Walks, The Half day and evening themed walks in Central and Inner London.

Ramblers' Association (Inner London Area) Regular free walks with volunteer leaders in three programmes. *Ramble excursions:* whole day walks on Sundays throughout the year in surrounding counties using trains from Central London and suburbs. *Saturday strolls:* afternoon walks throughout the year within or just outside Greater London. *Canal and riverside walks:* Wednesday evening strolls in summer within Greater London. Details published in *London Rambler*, three issues per year for £2 (payable Ramblers' Association).

Richmond Society of Voluntary Guides. Half day themed walks in Richmond, Twickenham and Kew.

Ripping Yarns Ltd Evening Jack the Ripper walks from Tower Hill station.

Stepping Out Half day themed walks in various parts of Greater London.

Streatham Society Sunday afternoon walks in Streatham area June to September with volunteer leader.

Wackydo Walks Half day themed walks in Westminster, Whitehall, Soho and Covent Garden, all starting from Green Park station.

♿ ***Ye Olde Walks of London*** Half day themed walks in the City of London.

APPENDIX G
Equipment and map/book retailers

See Equipment and Maps in Section 1. Inclusion in these lists in no way constitutes a recommendation. You are advised to phone first to check that what you need is in stock. In the online and mail order sections, only retailers trading in the London area are included – there are many more in other areas, which you should be able to identify by an online search or looking in Yellow Pages or Thomson Local under 'Camping and Outdoor Equipment'.

OUTDOOR AND WALKING EQUIPMENT

For a wide choice of competing retailers, or just window-shopping, Covent Garden and Croydon are hard to beat, each having half a dozen outdoor shops within strolling distance, while in Kensington High Street four lie almost adjacent.

Millets the Outdoor Store and Milletts Camping & Countrywear, formerly two separate chains with a common origin and intentionally different spelling, have been acquired by Blacks Leisure Group, supplementing its existing retail chain, Blacks Outdoor Leisure, and resulting in the group having two branches in some locations. The retail arm of Scout Shops (formerly Camping & Outdoor Centre) now trades as Outdoors.

Barnet.
John Pollock Adventurer's Shop, 67 High Street, EN5 5UR.Tel: 020 8440 3994
Nomad Travel Store, 4 Potters Road, EN5 5HW. Tel: 020 8441 7208

Bayswater. Blacks Outdoor Leisure, Whiteleys (1st floor), Queensway, W2 4YH. Tel: 020 7727 1313

Bexleyheath. Millets the Outdoor Store, 119 The Broadway. Tel: 020 8303 5089

Bloomsbury. Nomad Travel Store, 40 Bernard Street, WC1N 1LJ. Tel: 020 7833 4114

Brent Cross. Blacks Outdoor Leisure, Mall 4, Brent Cross Shopping Centre, NW4 3FP. Tel: 020 8203 9895

Brentford. I & M Steiner, Reynard Mills Trading Estate, Windmill Road, TW8 9LY. Tel: 020 8847 4422

Bromley.
Field & Trek, 66 High Street, BR1 1EG. Tel: 020 8460 2270
Millets the Outdoor Store, 65 High Street, BR1 1JX. Tel: 020 8460 0418

Burnt Oak. SAS, 107 Burnt Oak Broadway, HA8 5EN. Tel: 020 8951 1892

Camden Town.
Ben Nevis Clothing, 237 Royal College Street, NW1 9LT. Tel: 020 7485 9989
The Outdoor Emporium, 67 Camden Road, NW1 9EU. Tel: 020 7428 9533

Chiswick.
Blacks Outdoor Leisure, 378 Chiswick High Rd, W4 5TF. Tel: 020 8747 4735
Millets the Outdoor Store, 167 Chiswick High Rd, W4 2DR. Tel: 020 8994 5807

City.
Outdoors, 41 Ludgate Hill, EC4M 7JU. Tel: 020 7329 8757
YHA Adventure Shops, 16 Ludgate Hill, EC4M 7DR. Tel: 020 7329 4578

Clapham. Blacks Outdoor Leisure, 61 St John's Road, SW11 1QX.
Tel: 020 7223 7004

Covent Garden.
Backpacker, 136 Charing Cross Road, WC2H 0LA. Tel: 020 7836 1160
Ellis Brigham, 30 Southampton Street, WC2E 7HE. Tel: 020 7240 9577
Field & Trek, 64 Long Acre, WC2E 9JD. Tel: 020 7379 8167
Field & Trek, 42 Maiden Lane, WC2E 7LJ. Tel: 020 7379 3793
London Trading Post , 405 Strand, WC2R 0NE. Tel: 020 7240 1788
Snow & Rock, 4 Mercer Street, WC2H 9QJ. Tel: 020 7420 1444
Trekmate, 3 Earlham Street, WC2H 9LL. Tel: 020 7836 8818

Croydon.
Blacks Outdoor Leisure, 145 North End, CR0 1TN. Tel: 020 8688 7830
Field & Trek, 32 Church Street, CR0 1RB. Tel: 020 8680 8798
Hewitts of Croydon, 45 Church Street, CR9 1QQ. Tel: 020 8688 1830
Millets the Outdoor Store, 52 High Street, CR0 1YB. Tel: 020 8688 6066
Outdoors, 40 St George's Walk, CR0 1YJ. Tel: 020 8688 1730
YHA Adventure Shops, 37 St George's Walk, CR0 1YL. Tel: 020 8686 7225

Crystal Palace. Crystal Palace Camping, 15 Central Hill, SE19 1BG. Tel: 020
8766 6060

Ealing.
Blacks Outdoor Leisure, 8 The Arcadia Centre, The Broadway, W5 5JY.
Tel: 020 8840 1514
Ealing Sports, 7 The Mall, W5 2PJ. Tel: 020 8840 6865

Earls Court. Trekmate, 137 Earls Court Road, SW5 9RH. Tel: 020 7373 2364

Eltham. Millets the Outdoor Store, 122 Eltham High Street, SE9 1BJ.
Tel: 020 8850 2822

Enfield. Millets the Outdoor Store, 10 The Town, EN2 6LQ. Tel: 020 8363 1682

Fulham. Expedition Kit, 6d Farm Lane Trading Centre, SW6 1QJ.
Tel: 020 7381 8398

Harringay. Urban Rock, Castle Climbing Centre, Green Lanes, N4 2HA.
Tel: 020 8211 0475

Harrow.
Outdoors, 324a Station Road, HA1 2DX. Tel: 020 8427 3809
Blacks Outdoor Leisure, 316 Station Road, HA1 2DX. Tel: 020 8861 6482

Higham Hill. Army & Navy Stores, 6 Lockwood Way, Blackhorse Lane, E17 5RB.
Tel: 020 8527 3735

Holborn.
Snow & Rock, 150 Holborn, WC1X 8HG. Tel: 020 7831 6900
Blacks Outdoor Leisure, 10 Holborn, EC1N 2LE. Tel: 020 7404 5681

Hornsey. Nomad Travel Store, 3 Wellington Terrace, Turnpike Lane, N8 0PX.
Tel: 020 8889 7014

Hounslow. Millets the Outdoor Store, 156 High Street, TW3 1LR.
Tel: 020 8570 4309

Ilford. Millets the Outdoor Store, 169 High Road, IG1 1LL. Tel: 020 8478 7341

Kensington.
Blacks Outdoor Leisure, 190 Kensington High Street, W8 7RG.
Tel: 020 7361 0060
Ellis Brigham, 178 Kensington High Street, W8 7RG. Tel: 020 7937 6889
Snow & Rock, 188 Kensington High Street, W8 7RG. Tel: 020 7937 0872
YHA Adventure Shops, 174 Kensington High Street, W8 7RG. Tel: 020 7938 2948

Kentish Town. Urban Country, 302 Kentish Town Road, NW5 2TG.
Tel: 020 7482 5959

Kilburn. The Camping Centre, 44 Birchington Road, NW6 4LJ. Tel: 020 7328 2166

Kingston.
Blacks Outdoor Leisure, 107 Clarence Street, KT1 1QY. Tel: 020 8549 9944
Cotswold Outdoor, 72 Clarence Street, KT1 1NW. Tel: 020 8549 9500
Head for the Hills, 40 High Street, KT1 1HL. Tel: 020 8974 8882
Millets the Outdoor Store, 3 Thames Street, KT1 1PH. Tel: 020 8546 5042

Lewisham. Millets the Outdoor Store, 205 Lewisham High Street, SE13 6LY.
Tel: 020 8852 1909

Limehouse. Cover, 789 Commercial Road, E14 7HG. Tel: 020 7987 4246

Orpington. Millets the Outdoor Store, 178 High Street, BR6 0JW.
Tel: 01689 826794

Putney. Millets the Outdoor Store, 98 Putney High Street, SW15 1RB.
Tel: 020 8788 2300

Richmond. Millets the Outdoor Store, 36 The Quadrant, TW9 1BP.
Tel: 020 8940 2805

Romford. Millets the Outdoor Store, 42 South Street, RM1 1RB.
Tel: 01708 743751

Shepherds Bush. Cotswold Outdoor, 42 Uxbridge Road, W12 8ND.
Tel: 020 8743 2976

Soho. YHA Adventure Shop, 152 Wardour Street, W1F 8YA.
Tel: 020 7025 1900.

Sutton. Millets the Outdoor Store, 86 High Street, SM1 1JG. Tel: 020 8643 4251

Tottenham. Kelly's International Trading, 110 Markfield Road, N15 4QF.
Tel: 020 8808 1728

Victoria.
Outdoors, 27 Buckingham Palace Road, SW1W 0PP. Tel: 020 7834 6007
Victoria Camping and Government Surplus, 39 Wilton Road, SW1V 1LJ.
Tel: 020 7834 3371
YHA Adventure Shops, 120 Victoria Street, SW1E 5LA. Tel: 020 7233 6500

West End.
Aigle, 172 Regent Street, W1R 7DF. Tel: 020 7439 3565
Blacks Outdoor Leisure, 53 Rathbone Place, W1P 1AB. Tel: 020 7636 6645
Field & Trek, 105 Baker Street, W1M 1FE. Tel: 020 7224 0049

Wimbledon.
Blacks Outdoor Leisure, 1 The Crescent, SW19 8AW. Tel: 020 8947 6882
Millets the Outdoor Store, 34 The Broadway, SW19 0BB. Tel: 020 8946 6644

Worcester Park. Emjay's Camping and Leisure World,
1 Central Road, KT4 8DN. Tel: 020 8330 5152

Online and mail order

Blacks Outdoor Leisure. www.blacks.co.uk Tel: 0800 214890

Cotswold Outdoor. www.cotswold-outdoor.com Tel: 01285 643434

Ellis Brigham. www.ellis-brigham.com Tel: 0161 834 5555

Field & Trek. www.fieldandtrek.co.uk Tel: 01268 494444

Outdoors (Scout Shops). www.oudoors.ltd.uk Tel: 01903 755352

YHA Adventure Shops. www.yhaadventure.com Tel: 01784 458625

MAPS AND GUIDEBOOKS

Some shops selling outdoor equipment also sell a limited range of maps and
guidebooks. For a wider choice you could try one of the specialist map shops
listed below. Guidebooks with an ISBN number should be obtainable from any
good bookseller.

Covent Garden. Stanfords, 12 Long Acre, WC2E 9LP Tel: 020 7836 1321

Holborn. Stationery Office (for Ordnance Survey maps), 123 Kingsway,
WC2 6PQ Tel: 020 7242 6393

Victoria. National Map Centre, 22 Caxton Street, SW1H 0QU
Tel: 020 7222 2466

West End. Stanfords at the Britain Visitor Centre, 1 Regent Street, SW1Y 4XT
Tel: 020 7808 3891

Online and mail order

Maps by Mail. www.mapsbymail.co.uk Tel: 020 8399 4970

National Map Centre. www.mapsnmc.co.uk Tel: 020 7222 2466

Stanfords. www.stanfords.co.uk Tel: 020 7836 1321

APPENDIX H
Contact details

The details in this list are correct at time of publication but are subject to alteration. For borough councils, where text in this book refers to a department as the contact, call the main switchboard number shown in this list and ask for that department. Much of the literature is available from tourist information centres or libraries which are also shown.

When writing, please remember to send a stamped addressed envelope for the reply.

* Premium rate telephone number

Contact	Address	Phone/Fax	Email/web
AA Publications	Fanum House Basing View, Basingstoke, RG21 4EA	Tel: 01256 491524 Fax: 01256 322575	customer/services@theaa.com www.theaa.com
Angel Walks	26b Canonbury Square, London N1 2AL	Tel: 020 7226 8333	
Applause Books	c/o Combined Book Services, Units I/K, Paddock Wood Distribution Centre, Paddock Wood, Tonbridge, TN12 6UU	Tel: 01892 837171 Fax: 01892 837272	orders@combook.co.uk
Athlone Travel UK Ltd	PO Box 32786, London SE1 8BX	Tel: 07960 023060 Fax: 0870 1374408	info@walkingtoursinlondon.com www.walkingtoursinlondon.com
Aurum Press	25 Bedford Avenue, Bloomsbury, London WC1B 3AT	Tel: 020 7637 3225 Fax: 020 7580 2469	sales@aurumpress.co.uk www.aurumpress.co.uk
Barn Hill Conservation Group	Roe Green Walled Garden, Roe Green Park, Kingsbury, London NW9 9HA		
Belhus Wood Country Park	Romford Road, Aveley, RM15 4XJ	Tel: 01708 865628 Fax: 01708 865628	www.essexcc.gov.uk/countryparks
Bexley Civic Society	65 Longlands Road, Sidcup, DA15 7LQ	Tel: 020 8300 3136	eynswood@btinternet.com

Brentwood Borough Council	Town Hall, Ingrave Road, Brentwood, CM15 8AY	Tel: 01277 261111 Fax: 01277 260836	genoff@brentwood-council.gov.uk www.brentwood-council.gov.uk
Brewin Books	56 Alcester Road, Studley, B80 7UG	Tel: 01527 854228 Fax: 01527 852746	
British Walking Federation	112 Crescent Road, Reading, RG1 5SW		info@bwf-ivv.org.uk www.bwf-ivv.org.uk
British Waterways *London Region*	The Toll House, Delamere Terrace Little Venice, London W2 6ND	Tel: 020 7286 6101 Fax: 020 7286 7306	enquiries.london@britishwaterways.co.uk www.britishwaterways.co.uk
Brixton Society	82 Mayall Road, Herne Hill, London SE24 0PJ	Tel: 020 7207 0347	
Buckinghamshire County Council	County Hall, Walton Street, Aylesbury, HP20 1UY	Tel: 01296 395000 Fax: 01296 382611	enquiries@buckscc.gov.uk www.buckscc.gov.uk
Camden Local Studies and Archives Centre	Holborn Library, 32 Theobalds Road, London WC1X 8PA	Tel: 020 7974 6342 Fax: 020 7974 6284	localstudies@camden .gov.uk
Castlemead Publications	12 Little Mundells, Welwyn Garden City, AL7 1EW	Tel: 01920 465525	
Chesterton, Keith	Firle, Chestnut Avenue, Guildford, GU2 9HD		
Cicerone Press	2 Police Square, Milnthorpe, LA7 7PY	Tel: 01539 562069 Fax: 01539 563417	info@cicerone.demon.co.uk www.cicerone.co.uk
City of London	See Corporation of London		
City of London Information Centre	St Paul's Churchyard, London EC4M 8BX	Tel: 020 7332 1456 Fax: 020 7332 1457	stpaul.informationcentre@corpoflondon.gov.uk
City of London Walks		Tel: 020 7813 3874	www.cityoflondonwalks.co.uk
Clerkenwell Visitors Centre	53 Clerkenwell Road, London EC1R 0EA	Tel: 020 7251 6311	visitorsat53@aol.com

Organization	Address	Telephone / Fax	Email / Website
		Fax: 020 7689 3661	www.clerkenwell.org
Colne Valley Park Centre	Denham Court Drive, Denham, Uxbridge, UB9 5PG	Tel: 01895 833375 Fax: 01895 833552	tv@groundwork.org.uk
Constable & Co	3 Lanchesters, 162 Fulham Palace Road, London W6 9ER	Tel: 020 8741 3663 Fax: 020 8748 7562	enquiries@constablerobinson.com www.constablerobinson.com
Corporation of London	Guildhall, PO Box 270, London EC2P 2EJ	Tel: 020 7606 3030 Fax: 020 7332 1119	pro@corpoflondon.gov.uk www.corpoflondon.gov.uk
Corporation of London *West Wickham & Coulsdon Commons*	Merlewood Estate Office, Ninehams Road, Caterham-on-the-Hill, CR3 5LN	Tel: 020 8660 8533 Fax: 020 8763 8598	
Countryside Agency *Headquarters*	John Dower House, Crescent Place, Cheltenham, GL50 3RA	Tel: 01242 521381 Fax: 01242 584270	info@countryside.gov.uk www.countryside.gov.uk
Countryside Agency *London Region*	Dacre House, 19 Dacre Street, London SW1H 0DH	Tel: 020 7340 2900 Fax: 020 7340 2911	
Countryside Books	Highfield House, 2 Highfield Avenue, Newbury, RG14 5DS	Tel: 01635 43816 Fax: 01635 551004	info@countrysidebooks.co.uk www.shop.countrysidebooks.co.uk
Countrywide Holidays Association	Miry Lane, Wigan, WN3 4AG	Tel: 01942 823487 Fax: 01942 242518	assoc@countrywide-walking.org www.countrywide-walking.org
Crowood Press, The	The Stable Block, Crowood Lane, Ramsbury, Marlborough, SN8 2HR	Tel: 01672 520320 Fax: 01672 520280	enquiries@crowood.com www.crowood.com
Crystal Palace Museum and Foundation	84 Anerley Road, Crystal Palace, London SE19 2AH	Tel: 020 8676 0700 Fax: 0870 133 7920	www.crystalpalacefoundation.org.uk
Deptford Tour Guides Association		Tel: 020 8692 6919	

Downlands Project	Omnibus Building, Lesbourne Road, Reigate, RH2 7JA	Tel: 0737 737700	alex.baxterbrown@surreycc.gov.uk www.countryside-management.org.uk
Eastbrookend Country Park	The Millennium Centre, The Chase, Dagenham Road, Romford, RM7 0SS	Tel: 020 8595 4155 Fax: 020 8984 9400	
Elmbridge District Council *Civic Centre*	High Street, Esher, KT10 9SD	Tel: 01372 474474	(email via website) www.elmbridge.gov.uk
Eltham Society, The	1 Clare Corner, New Eltham, London SE9 2AE		
EMAP Active *Country Walking subscriptions*	c/o Tower Publishing Services, Tower House, Sovereign Park, Market Harborough, LE16 9EE	Tel: 0845 601 1356 Fax: 01858 434958	emap@subscription.co.uk www.countrywalking.com
Enfield Preservation Society	Jubilee Hall, 2 Parsonage Lane, Enfield, EN2 0AJ	Tel: 020 8363 9495	
English Heritage *Customer Services Dept*	PO Box 569, Swindon, SN2 2YP	Tel: 0870 333 1181 Fax: 01793 414926	customers@english-heritage.org.uk www.english-heritage.org.uk
Epping Forest District Council *Civic Offices*	High Street, Epping, CM16 4BZ	Tel: 01992 564000 Fax: 01992 578018	information@eppingforestdc.gov.uk www.eppingforestdc.gov.uk
Epping Forest Information Centre	High Beach, Loughton, IG10 4AF	Tel: 020 8508 0028 Fax: 020 8532 0188	eppingforest@corpoflondon.gov.uk
Essex County Council	Freepost CL3636, Chelmsford, CM1 1XZ	Tel: 01245 492211 Fax: 01245 456693	corp.comms@essexcc.gov.uk www.essexcc.gov.uk
Fiennes Print	268 Alexandra Park Road, Wood Green, London N22 7BG	Tel: 020 8366 3411 Fax: 020 8367 9098	johntwisleton@easynet.co.uk www.twisleton.co.uk/fiennesprint
Forty Hall Estate	Forty Hill, Enfield, EN2 9HA		

Organisation	Address	Tel/Fax	Email/Web
Friends of Hackney Archives	43 De Beauvoir Road, London N1 5SQ	Tel: 020 7241 2886 Fax: 020 7241 6688	archives@hackney.gov.uk
Friends of the Great North Wood	16 Knoll Court, Farquhar Road, Norwood, London SE19 1SP		doug.brooks@cwcom.net
Friends of West Norwood Cemetery	c/o 119 Broxholm Road, West Norwood London SE27 0BJ	Tel: 020 8670 5456 or 020 8653 2741	
Greater London Authority	City Hall, The Queen's Walk Southwark, London SE1 2AA	Tel: 020 7983 4000 Fax: 020 7983 4057	mayor@london.gov.uk www.london.gov.uk
Green Chain Walk Project	Peggy Middleton House, 50 Woolwich New Road, London SE18 6HQ	Tel: 020 8921 5876 Fax: 020 8921 5442	greenchain@cwcom.net www.greenchain.com
Grosvenor Estate Holdings	70 Grosvenor Street, Mayfair, London W1X 9DB	Tel: 020 7408 0988 Fax: 020 7629 9115	ros.langford@geh.com www.geh.com
Groundwork Thames Valley	Colne Valley Park Centre, Denham Court Drive, Denham, Uxbridge, UB9 5PG	Tel: 01895 832662 Fax: 01895 833552	tv@groundwork.org.uk
Groundwork Hertfordshire	Mill Green, Hatfield, AL9 5PE	Tel: 01707 260129 Fax: 01707 270867	
Hackney Society, The	Studio B12, 3 Bradbury Street, Dalston, London N16 8JN	Tel: 020 7254 0212 Fax: 020 7275 8971	hackneysociety@poptel.org
Hainault Forest Country Park	Visitor Centre, Romford Road, Chigwell, IG7 4QN	Tel: 020 8500 7353 Fax: 020 8501 2258	
Hampton Ferry	The Boathouse, Thames Street, Hampton, TW12 2EA	Tel: 020 8979 7471	
Harvey Map Services	12 Main Street, Doune, Perthshire, FK16 6BJ	Tel: 01786 841202 Fax: 01786 841098	sales@harveymaps.co.uk www.harveymaps.co.uk

Organisation	Address	Telephone/Fax	Email/Web
HF Holidays	Imperial House, Edgware Road, Colindale, London NW9 5AL	Tel: 020 8905 9556 Fax: 020 8205 0506	info@hfholidays.co.uk www.hfholidays.co.uk
Historical Walks of London	3 Florence Road, South Croydon, CR2 0PQ	Tel: 020 8668 4019	johnmuffty@dial.pipex.com
Hornsey Historical Society	The Old Schoolhouse, 136 Tottenham Lane, Hornsey, London N8 7EL	Tel: 020 8348 8429	sales@hornseyhistorical.fsnet.co.uk www.hornseyhistorical.org.uk
Hounslow Heath Local Nature Reserve Information Centre	450 Staines Road, Hounslow, TW4 5AB	Tel: 020 8577 3664 Fax: 020 8577 3664	hounslow-heath@cip.org.uk
Hounslow Heritage Guides		Tel: 020 8230 8583	
Institution of Civil Engineers, The	1 Great George Street, Westminster, London SW1P 3AA	Tel: 020 7222 7722 Fax: 020 7222 7500	www.ice.org.uk
Interlink Books (USA)	Interlink Publishing, 46 Crosby Street, Northampton, MA 01060-1804, USA		info@interlinkbooks.com www.interlinkbooks.com
Isle of Wight Tourism	Westridge Centre, Brading Road, Ryde, PO33 1QS	Tel: 01983 813813 Fax: 01983 823033	info@islandbreaks.co.uk www.islandbreaks.co.uk
Isleworth Society, The	c/o 31 Brantwood Avenue, Isleworth, TW7 7EX		
Islington Archaeology & History Society	8 Wynyatt Street, London EC1V 7HU	Tel: 020 7833 1541	
Islington Society, The	35 Britannia Row, Islington, London N1 8QH	Tel: 020 7226 2207	www.islingtonsociety.co.uk
Jarrold Publishing	Whitefriars, Norwich, NR3 1TR	Tel: 01603 660211 Fax: 01603 662748	publishing@jarrold.com www.jarrold-publishing.co.uk
Kings Cross Partnership, The	Wicklow Mill, 31a Wicklow Street, St Pancras, London WC1X 9XJ	Tel: 020 7713 1177 Fax: 020 7713 7117	enquiries@kingscrosslondon.com www.kingscrosslondon.com

Kingston Tour Guides		Tel: 020 8942 7015 or 020 8546 8048	
Lawrence & Wishart Ltd	99a Wallis Road, Hackney Wick, London E9 5LN	Tel: 020 8533 2506 Fax: 020 8533 7369	l-w@l-w-bks.demon.co.uk www.l-w-books.co.uk
Learndirect *(Maths Year 2000)*	c/o Dept. for Education & Employment, Sanctuary Buildings, Great Smith Street, Westminster, London SW1P 3BT	info@dfee.gov.uk Tel: 0800 100 900 Fax: 020 7925 6001	www.mathsyear2000.org also www.counton.org
Lee Valley Park *Information Centre*	Abbey Gardens, Waltham Abbey, EN9 1QX	Tel: 01992 702200 Fax: 01922 702 330	info@leevalleypark.org.uk www.leevalleypark.org.uk
London Borough of Barking & Dagenham *Civic Centre*	Wood Lane, Dagenham, RM10 7BN	Tel: 020 8592 4500 Fax: 020 8227 2806	enquiries@barking-dagenham.gov.uk www.barking-dagenham.gov.uk
Central Reference Library	Shopping Centre, Barking, IG11 7NB	Tel: 020 8227 3613 Fax: 020 8227 3625	reference@barking-dagenham.gov.uk
London Borough of Barnet *Town Hall*	The Burroughs, Hendon, London NW4 4BG	Tel: 020 8359 4000 Fax: 020 8359 2197	info.centre@barnet.gov.uk www.barnet.gov.uk
Main Reference Library	The Burroughs, Hendon, London NW4 4BG	Tel: 020 8359 2883 Fax: 020 8359 2885	hendon.ref@barnet.gov.uk
London Borough of Bexley *Civic Offices*	Broadway, Bexleyheath, DA6 7LB	Tel: 020 8303 7777 Fax: 020 8308 4917	customer.services@bexley.gov.uk www.bexley.gov.uk
Central Reference Library	Townley Road, Bexleyheath, DA6 7HJ	Tel: 020 8301 1066 Fax: 020 8303 7872	central.library@librarian.co.uk
London Borough of Brent *Town Hall*	Forty Lane, Wembley, HA9 9HD	Tel: 020 8937 1234 Fax: 020 8937 1202	customer.services@brent.gov.uk www.brent.gov.uk
Town Hall Reference Library	Forty Lane, Wembley, HA9 9HV	Tel: 020 8937 3500 Fax: 020 8937 3504	townhalllibrary@brent.gov.uk

London Borough of Bromley *Civic Centre*	Stockwell Close, Bromley, BR1 3UH	Tel: 020 8464 3333	signpost@bromley.gov.uk www.bromley.gov.uk
Central Reference Library	High Street, Bromley, BR1 1EX	Tel: 020 8460 9955 Fax: 020 8466 7860	reference.library@bromley.gov.uk
London Borough of Camden *Town Hall*	Judd Street, London WC1H 9JE	Tel: 020 7278 4444 Fax: 020 7974 1484	info@camden.gov.uk www.camden.gov.uk
Central Reference Library	88 Avenue Road, Swiss Cottage, London NW3 3HA	Tel: 020 7974 6522 Fax: 020 7974 6532	swisscottagelibrary@camden.gov.uk
London – City of London	See Corporation of London		
London Borough of Croydon *Council Offices*	Taberner House, Park Lane, Croydon, CR9 3JS	Tel: 020 8686 4433 Fax: 020 8760 0871	corp_info@croydon.gov.uk www.croydon.gov.uk
Tourist Information Centre	Croydon Clocktower, Katharine Street, Croydon, CR9 1ET	Tel: 020 8253 1009 Fax: 020 8253 1008	tic@croydononline.org
London Borough of Ealing *Council Offices*	Perceval House, 14 Uxbridge Road, Ealing, London W5 2HL	Tel: 020 8579 2424	customers@ealing.gov.uk www.ealing.gov.uk
Central Reference Library	103 Ealing Broadway Centre, Ealing, London W5 5JY	Tel: 020 8567 3656 Fax: 020 8840 2351	infonet@ealing.gov.uk
London Borough of Enfield *Civic Centre*	Silver Street, Enfield, EN1 3XY	Tel: 020 8366 6565 Fax: 020 8379 4453	customerservices@enfield.gov.uk www.enfield.gov.uk
Central Reference Library	Cecil Road, Enfield, EN2 6TW	Tel: 020 8379 8391 Fax: 020 8379 8401	enfield.library@dial.pipex.com
London Borough of Greenwich *Town Hall*	Wellington Street, Woolwich, London SE18 6PM	Tel: 020 8854 8888	(email via website) www.greenwich.gov.uk
Tourist Information Centre	Pepys House, 2 Cutty Sark Gardens, Greenwich, London SE10 9LW	Tel: 0870 608 2000 Fax: 020 8853 4607	tic@greenwich.gov.uk

Local History Library	Woodlands, 90 Mycenae Road, Westcombe Park, London SE3 7SE	Tel: 020 8858 4631 Fax: 020 8293 4721	local.history@greenwich.gov.uk
London Borough of Hackney *Town Hall*	Mare Street, Hackney, London E8 1EA	Tel: 020 8356 3000	fss@hackney.gov.uk www.hackney.gov.uk
Central Reference Library	Shoreditch Library, 80 Hoxton Street, London N1 6LP	Tel: 020 8356 4358 Fax: 020 7739 7180	hackref@hotmail.com
London Borough of Hammersmith & Fulham *Town Hall*	King Street, Hammersmith, London W6 9JU	Tel: 020 8748 3020	information@lbhf.gov.uk www.lbhf.gov.uk
Information Centre	20 Broadway Shopping Centre, Hammersmith, London W6 9YD	Tel: 020 8748 3928 (Visitor Development)	
London Borough of Haringey *Civic Centre*	High Road, Wood Green, London N22 8LE	Tel: 020 8489 0000	webcoordinator@haringey.gov.uk www.haringey.gov.uk
Central Reference Library	Wood Green Central Library, High Road, Wood Green, London N22 6XD	Fax: 020 8489 2555	Tel: 020 8489 2700
London Borough of Harrow *Civic Centre*	Station Road, Harrow, HA1 2UU	Tel: 020 8863 5611 Fax: 020 8424 1134	info@harrow.gov.uk www.harrow.gov.uk
Central Reference Library	Civic Centre, Station Road, Harrow, HA1 2UU	Tel: 020 8424 1055 Fax: 020 8424 1971	civiccentre.library@harrow.gov.uk
London Borough of Havering *Town Hall*	Main Road, Romford, RM1 3BD	Tel: 01708 434343	info@havering.gov.uk www.havering.gov.uk
Central Reference Library	Central Library, St.Edward's Way, Romford, RM1 3AR	Tel: 01708 432394 Fax: 01708 432391	romfordlib2@rmplc.co.uk
London Borough of Hillingdon *Civic Centre*	High Street, Uxbridge, UB8 1UW	Tel: 01895 250111 Fax: 01895 273636	internet@hillingdon.gov.uk www.hillingdon.gov.uk

Information Service	Central Library, 14 High Street, Uxbridge, UB8 1HD	Tel: 01895 250600 Fax: 01895 239794	clibrary@hillingdon.gov.uk
London Borough of Hounslow Civic Centre	Lampton Road, Hounslow, TW3 4DN	Tel: 020 8583 2000 Fax: 020 8583 2598	information.services@dial.pipex.com www.hounslow.gov.uk
Tourist Information Centre	Treaty Centre, High Street, Hounslow, TW3 1ES	Tel: 020 8583 2929 Fax: 020 8583 4714	
London Borough of Islington Town Hall	Upper Street, Islington, London N1 2UD	Tel: 020 7527 2000	www.islington.gov.uk
Central Reference Library	2 Fieldway Crescent, Holloway, London N5 1PF	Tel: 020 7527 6931 Fax: 020 7527 6937	library.information@islington.gov.uk

London

Kensington & Chelsea Kingston-upon-Thames	See Royal Borough of Kensington & Chelsea See Royal Borough of Kingston-upon-Thames		
London Borough of Lambeth Town Hall	Brixton Hill, Brixton, London SW2 1RW	Tel: 020 7926 1000	infodesk@lambeth.gov.uk www.lambeth.gov.uk
Brixton Reference Library	Brixton Oval, Brixton, London SW2 1JQ	Tel: 020 7926 1067 Fax: 020 7926 1070	
London Borough of Lewisham Town Hall	Catford Road, Catford, London SE6 4RU	Tel: 020 8314 6000	www.lewisham.gov.uk
Central Reference Library	199 Lewisham High Street, London SE13 6LG	Tel: 020 8297 9430 Fax: 020 8297 1169	reference.library@lewisham.gov.uk
London Borough of Merton Civic Centre	London Road, Morden, SM4 5DX	Tel: 020 8543 2222	postroom@merton.gov.uk www.merton.gov.uk
Visitors Information Centre	Wimbledon Library, 35 Wimbledon Hill Road, London SW19 7NB	Tel: 020 8946 9192 Fax: 020 8944 6804	visitor.info@merton.gov.uk

London Borough of Newham *Town Hall*	Barking Road, East Ham, London E6 2RP	Tel: 020 8430 2000	customer.services@newham.gov.uk www.newham.gov.uk
Central Reference Library	East Ham Library, High Street South, East Ham, London E6 6EL	Tel: 020 8430 3648 Fax: 020 8503 5383	
London Borough of Redbridge *Town Hall*	128 High Road, Ilford, IG1 1DD	Tel: 020 8478 3020	firststopshop@redbridge.gov.uk www.redbridge.gov.uk
Central Reference Library	Clements Road, Ilford, IG1 1EA	Tel: 020 8708 2420 Fax: 020 8553 3299	
London Borough of Richmond-upon-Thames *Civic Centre*	44 York Street, Twickenham, TW1 3BZ	Tel: 020 8891 1411	www.richmond.gov.uk
Tourist Information Centre	Old Town Hall, Whittaker Avenue, Richmond, TW9 1TP	Tel: 020 8940 9125 Fax: 020 8940 6899	information.services@richmond.gov.uk
London Borough of Southwark *Town Hall*	Peckham Road, Camberwell, London SE5 8UB	Tel: 020 7525 5000 Fax: 020 7525 7295	www.southwark.gov.uk
Central Reference Library See also Southwark Information Centre	Newington Reference Library, 155 Walworth Road, London SE17 1RS	Tel: 020 7708 0516 Fax: 020 7252 6115	newingtonreference.library @southwark.gov.uk
London Borough of Sutton *Civic Offices*	St Nicholas Way, Sutton, SM1 1EA	Tel: 020 8770 5000 Fax: 020 8770 5404	postmaster@sutton.gov.uk www.sutton.gov.uk
Central Library	St Nicholas Way, Sutton, SM1 1EA	Tel: 020 8770 4700 Fax: 020 8770 4777	sutton.information@sutton.gov.uk
London Borough of Tower Hamlets *Town Hall*	Mulberry Place, 5 Clove Crescent, Blackwall, London E14 2BG	Tel: 020 7364 5000 Fax: 020 7364 3063	www.towerhamlets.gov.uk

Reference and Information Service	Bethnal Green Library, Cambridge Heath Road, London E2 0HL	Tel: 020 8980 3902 Fax: 020 8981 6129	100633.624@compuserve.com
London Borough of Waltham Forest *Town Hall*	Forest Road, Walthamstow, London E17 4JF	Tel: 020 8527 5544 Fax: 020 8527 8313	wfdirect@lbwf.gov.uk www.lbwf.gov.uk
Information Service	Central Library, High Street, Walthamstow, London E17 7JN	Tel: 020 8520 3017 Fax: 020 8520 9654	info@al.lbwf.gov.uk
London Borough of Wandsworth *Town Hall*	Wandsworth High Street, London SW18 2PU	Tel: 020 8871 6000	www.wandsworth.gov.uk
Central Reference Library	Battersea Library, Altenburg Gardens Battersea, London SW11 1JQ	Tel: 020 8871 7467 Fax: 020 7978 4376	
London – Westminster	See Westminster City Council		
London, City of	See Corporation of London		
London Tourist Board and Convention Bureau	Glen House, Stag Place, Victoria, London SW1E 5LT	Tel: 020 7932 2000 Fax: 020 7932 0222	enquiries@londontouristboard.co.uk www.londontouristboard.co.uk
London Transport Information		Tel: 020 7222 1234	travinfo@tfl.gov.uk www.tfl.gov.uk
London Walking Forum	c/o Corporation of London, Guildhall, PO Box 270, London EC2P 2EJ	Tel: 020 7606 3030 Fax: 020 7332 1119	info@londonwalking.com www.londonwalking.com
London Wildlife Trust	Harling House, 47 Great Suffolk Street, London SE1 0BS	Tel: 020 7261 0447 Fax: 020 7261 0538	enquiries@wildlondon.org.uk www.wildlondon.org.uk
Long Distance Walkers Association *National Membership*	c/o 63 Yockley Close, Camberley, GU15 1QQ	Tel: 01276 65169 Fax: 01276 65169	membership@ldwa.org.uk www.ldwa.org.uk

London Group	c/o 37 Holmdale Road, West Hampstead, London NW6 1BJ		paulmlawrence@aol.com www.ldwa.org.uk/london
Lower Lea Project	The Miller's House, Three Mills Island, Three Mills Lane, Bromley-by-Bow, London E3 3DU	Tel: 020 8981 0040 Fax: 020 8983 1689	lowerlea@netscapeonline.co.uk
Lower Mole Project	2 West Park Farmhouse, Horton Country Park, Horton Lane, Epsom, KT19 8PL	Tel: 01372 743783 Fax: 01372 742291	nick.owen@surreycc.gov.uk www.countryside-management
Louis London Walks	54 Braeside Avenue, Wimbledon, London SW19 3PT		llw@blueyonder.co.uk www.llwalks.co.uk
McDowall, David	31 Cambrian Road, Richmond, TW10 6JQ		
Mainstream Publishing	7 Albany Street, Edinburgh, EH1 3UG	Tel: 0131 557 2959 Fax: 0131 556 8720	enquiries@mainstreampublishing.com www.mainstreampublishing.com
Mudchute Park and Farm	Pier Street, Millwall, London E14 9HP	Tel: 020 7515 0749	
Museum of London	150 London Wall, London EC2Y 5HN	Tel: 020 7600 3699 Fax: 020 7600 1058	www.museumoflondon.org.uk
Mystery Walks		Tel: 020 8558 9446	mystery.walks@virgin.net www.mysterywalks.com
National Rail Enquiries		Tel: 08457 484950	www.railtrack.co.uk
New Holland Publications	Garfield House, 86 Edgware Road, London W2 2EA	Tel: 020 7724 7773 Fax: 020 7724 6184	postmaster@nhpub.co.uk www.newhollandpublications.com
New River Action Group	c/o 27 Elm Park Road, Winchmore Hill, London N21 2HP	Tel: 020 8292 5987	
Open Spaces Society	25a Bell Street, Henley-on-Thames, RG9 2BA	Tel: 01491 573535 Fax: 01491 573051	hq@oss.org.uk www.oss.org.uk

Ordnance Survey	Romsey Road, Southampton, SO16 4GU	Tel: 08456 050505 Fax: 023 8079 2615	enquiries@ordsvy.gov.uk www.ordsvy.gov.uk
Original London Walks, The	PO Box 1708, London NW6 4LW	Tel: 020 7624 3978 Fax: 020 7625 1932	london@walks.com www.walks.com
Pedestrians Association (now Living Streets)	31 Bondway, Vauxhall, London SW8 1SJ	Tel: 020 7820 1010 Fax: 020 7820 8208	info@pedestrians.org.uk www.pedestrians.org.uk
Penguin Books	80 Strand, London WC2R 0RL	Tel: 020 7010 3000 Fax: 020 7010 6060	customer.service@penguin.co.uk www.penguin.co.uk
Per-Rambulations	Larkshill, Cranston Road, East Grinstead, RH19 3HL	Tel: 01342 315786 Fax: 01342 315786	larkshill@btinternet.com
Prion Books	Imperial Works, Perren Street, Kentish Town, London NW5 3ED	Tel: 020 7482 4248 Fax: 020 7482 4203	books@prion.co.uk www.prionbooks.com
Race Walking Association	c/o Hufflers, Heards Lane, Shenfield, Brentwood, Essex CM15 0SF	Tel: 01277 220687 Fax: 01277 212380	race.walking.association@snyde.com
RADAR (Royal Association for Disability & Rehabilitation)	12 City Forum, 250 City Road, London EC1V 8AF	Tel: 020 7250 3222 Fax: 020 7250 0212	radar@radar.org.uk www.radar.org.uk
Ramblers' Association *London Office*	Camelford House, 87 Albert Embankment, Vauxhall, London SE1 7TW	Tel: 020 7339 8500 Fax: 020 7339 8501	ramblers@london.ramblers.org.uk www.ramblers.org.uk
Inner London Area	c/o 64 Catherine Drive, Sunbury-on-Thames, TW16 7TG	Tel: 020 7370 6180 *(info.hotline)*	
Richmond Group	59 Gerard Road, Barnes, London SW13 9QH	Tel: 020 8748 0049	
Richmond Society of Voluntary Guides		Tel: 020 8977 2806	

Ripping Yarns Ltd	3 Maytrees, St.Ives, Cambs, PE17 4WS	Tel: 020 7488 2414	ripyarns@aol.com www.rippingyarns.8m.com
Royal Borough of Kensington & Chelsea *Town Hall*	Hornton Street, Kensington, London W8 7NX	Tel: 020 7937 5464 Fax: 020 7938 1445	information.services@rbkc.gov.uk www.rbkc.gov.uk
Central Reference Library	Phillimore Walk, Kensington, London W8 7RX	Tel: 020 7361 2828	information.services@rbkc.gov.uk
Royal Borough of Kingston-upon-Thames *Guildhall*	High Street, Kingston, KT1 1EU	Tel: 020 8546 2121	www.kingston.gov.uk
Tourist Information Centre	Market House, Market Place, Kingston, KT1 1JS	Tel: 020 8547 5592 Fax: 020 8547 5594	
Royal Parks Agency *Headquarters*	The Old Police House, Hyde Park, London W2 2UH	Tel: 020 7298 2000	www.royalparks.gov.uk
Bushy Park	The Stockyard, Bushy Park, Hampton Court Rd, Hampton, TW12 2EJ	Tel: 020 8979 1586 Fax: 020 8941 8196	
Richmond Park	Holly Lodge, Richmond Park, Richmond, TW10 5HS	Tel: 020 8948 3209 Fax: 020 8332 2730	
Save the Children *Strollerthon Hotline* *020 7252 4141*	17 Grove Lane, Camberwell, London SE5 8RD	Tel: 020 7703 5400 Fax: 020 7703 2278	email (via website) www.scfuk.org.uk
Scarthin Books	The Promenade, Scarthin, Cromford, Derbyshire DE4 3QF	Tel: 01629 823272 Fax: 01629 825094	clare@scarthinbooks.demon.co.uk www.scarthinbooks.demon.co.uk
Shire Publications	Cromwell House, Church Street, Princes Risborough, HP27 9AA	Tel: 01844 344301 Fax: 01844 347080	shire@shirebooks.co.uk www.shirebooks.co.uk

Organisation	Address	Telephone/Fax	Email/Website
Socratic Walkers	c/o 25 Placehouse Lane, Old Coulsdon, CR5 1LA		
South Bank Employers Group	99 Upper Ground, London SE1 9PP	Tel: 020 7928 6193 Fax: 020 7620 1608	info@sbeg.demon.co.uk www.southbanklondon.com
South East England Tourist Board	The Old Brewhouse, Warwick Park, Tunbridge Wells, TN2 5TU	Tel: 01892 540766 Fax: 01892 511008	enquiries@seetb.org.uk www.southeastwalks.com
Southwark Information Centre	6 Tooley Street, London SE1 2SY	Tel: 020 7403 8299 Fax: 020 7357 6321	info@southwark-online.co.uk www.southwark-online.co.uk
Stationery Office, The	123 Kingsway, London WC2B 6PQ	Tel: 0870 600 5522 Fax: 0870 600 5533	esupport@clicktso.com www.clicktso.com
Stepping Out		Tel: 020 8881 2933	step.out@tesco.net www.walklon.ndirect.co.uk
Streatham Society	c/o 220 Woodmansterne Road, Streatham, London SW16 5UA	Tel: 020 8764 8314	admin@streathamsociety.org.uk www.streathamsociety.org.uk
Sustrans *London Office*	14 Cowcross Street, Farringdon, London EC1M 6DG	Tel: 020 7336 8203 Fax: 020 7336 8204	info@sustrans.org.uk www.sustrans.org.uk
Talking Tour Company	2 Rigault Road, Fulham, London SW6 4JL	Tel: 020 7610 9940	nigelbremner@hotmail.com www.talkingtour.co.uk
Teddington Society	c/o 1 Avenue Road, Teddington, TW11 0BT		
Thames Chase Community Forest	The Forest Centre, Broadfields Farm, Pike Lane, Cranham, Upminster, RM14 3NS	Tel: 01708 641880 Fax: 01708 640581	enquiries@thameschase.org.uk www.thameschase.org.uk

Organisation	Address	Contact
Thames Landscape Strategy	Holly Lodge, Richmond Park, Richmond, TW10 5HS	Tel: 020 8940 0654 Fax: 020 8332 2730 tls@richmond.gov.uk www.richmond.gov.uk/thameslandscape
Thames Path National Trail Office	c/o Cultural Services, Holton, Oxford, OX33 1QQ	Tel: 01865 810224 Fax: 01865 810207 mail@rway-tpath.demon.co.uk www.nationaltrails.gov.uk
Thames Water Utilities	PO Box 436, Swindon, SN38 1TU	Tel: 0845 9200 800 email (via website) www.thames-water.com
Tour East London	c/o Docklands Railway Management Ltd, Castor Lane, London E14 0DS	Tel: 020 7531 1996 Fax: 020 7531 1997 toureast@dircon.co.uk www.eastlondon.org.uk
Transport for London	See London Transport Information	
Vanguards Rambling Club	c/o 109 Selsdon Park Road, South Croydon, CR2 8JJ	
Verdant Books	PO Box 83, Hexham, NE48 3YY	Tel: 01434 230489 Fax: 01434 230725 gsguides@green-spaces.co.uk www.green-spaces.co.uk
Wackydo Walks		Tel: 07946 090086 enquiries@walkslondon.com www.wackydo.com
Walk the Walk	Britannia Wharf, Monument Road, Woking, GU21 5LW	Tel: 01483 291472 Fax: 01483 291013 www.walkthewalk.org
Walking the Way to Health Initiative *London Office*	c/o Countryside Agency, 19 Dacre Street, London SW1H 0DH	Tel: 020 7340 2959 Fax: 020 7340 2999 www.whi.org.uk
Wandle Industrial Museum	The Vestry Hall, London Road, Mitcham, CR4 3UD	Tel: 020 8648 0127 Fax: 020 8685 0249 curator@wandle.org www.wandle.org
Wandsworth Challenge Partnership	17 Arndale Walk, Wandsworth Shopping Centre, Wandsworth, London SE18 2PU	Tel: 020 8871 8277

Waterstones			(online enquiry form on website)
Out of Print Book Search	Hawarden Terrace, Larkhall, Bath, BA1 6RE	Tel: 01225 820320 Fax: 01225 444732	www.waterstones.co.uk
Watling Chase Community Forest	Gardener's Cottage, Shenley Park, Radlett Lane, Shenley, WD7 9DW	Tel: 01923 852641 Fax: 01923 854216	chase.watling@hertscc.gov.uk www.watlingchase.org.uk
Westminster City Council *City Hall*	64 Victoria Street, London SW1E 6QP	Tel: 020 7641 6000 Fax: 020 7641 8000	email (via website) www.westminster.gov.uk
Main Reference Library	109 Marylebone Road, London NW1 5PS	Tel: 020 7641 1039 Fax: 020 7641 1028	
Wimbledon & Putney Commons Conservators	Manor Cottage, Wimbledon Common, London SW19 5NR	Tel: 020 8788 7655 Fax: 020 8780 2975	jimreader@globalnet.co.uk www.wpcc.org.uk
Wimbledon Park Heritage Group	127 Arthur Road, Wimbledon Park, London SW19 7DR	Tel: 020 8944 8747 Fax: 020 8944 8717	sim@simcomfort.demon.co.uk www.wphg.demon.co.uk
Woodland Trust, The	Autumn Park, Dysart Road, Grantham, NG31 6LL	Tel: 01476 581111 Fax: 01476 590808	enquiries@woodland-trust.org.uk www.woodland-trust.org.uk
Woodlands Farm Trust	331 Shooters Hill, Welling, DA16 3RP	Tel: 020 8319 8900 Fax: 020 8319 8900	wfarmtrust@gn.apc.org www.thewoodlandsfarmtrust.org
M.Wright Ye Olde Walks of London	24 Humber road, London SE3 7LT	Tel: 020 8672 5894	cityguide39.london@virgin.net
Youth Hostels Association	Trevelyan House, Dimple Road, Matlock, DE4 3YH	Tel: 01629 592600	www.yha.org.uk

NOTES

NOTES

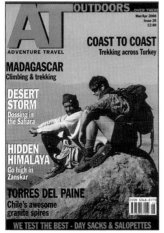

LISTING OF CICERONE GUIDES

Cicerone's mission is to inform and inspire by providing the best guides to exploring the world

Since its foundation over 30 years ago, Cicerone has specialised in publishing guidebooks and has built a reputation for quality and reliability. It now publishes nearly 300 guides to the major destinations for outdoor enthusiasts, including Europe, UK and the rest of the world.

Written by leading and committed specialists, Cicerone guides are recognised as the most authoritative. They are full of information, maps and illustrations so that the user can plan and complete a successful and safe trip or expedition – be it a long face climb, a walk over Lakeland fells, an alpine traverse, a Himalayan trek or a ramble in the countryside.

With a thorough introduction to assist planning, clear diagrams, maps and colour photographs to illustrate the terrain and route, and accurate and detailed text, Cicerone guides are designed for ease of use and access to the information.

If the facts on the ground change, or there is any aspect of a guide that you think we can improve, we are always delighted to hear from you.

Cicerone Press
2 Police Square Milnthorpe Cumbria LA7 7PY
Tel:01539 562 069   Fax:01539 563 417
e-mail:info@cicerone.co.uk   web:www.cicerone.co.uk